Bible Prayer
Study Course

Kenneth E. Hagin

Unless otherwise indicated, all Scripture quotations in this volume are from the *King James Version* of the Bible.

Second Edition
Eleventh Printing 2002

ISBN 0-89276-084-2

In the U.S. write:
Kenneth Hagin Ministries
P.O. Box 50126
Tulsa, OK 74150-0126

In Canada write:
Kenneth Hagin Ministries
P.O. Box 335, Station D,
Etobicoke, Ontario
Canada, M9A 4X3

Contents

Chapter 1

Seven Steps to Answered Prayer — Part 1

Learning how to pray effectively is one of the most important things a believer can ever do in his Christian walk. Really, a believer cannot be a success in fulfilling God's purpose in his life if he does not know how to pray according to biblical principles.

A believer's prayer life should be based and built upon the Word of God. In this study course, we're going to discuss the many principles of prayer that are found in the Word of God.

As you study these principles of prayer, determine to get them into your heart so you can practice them in your own private prayer life. This is what I began doing more than fifty-five years ago, and I have been receiving the answers to my prayers ever since!

In this chapter, we will look at seven steps that any believer can take in order to receive the answer to his prayer. If a person will faithfully practice the following seven steps in prayer, he can be sure of an answer every time.

Step Number One:
Be Specific and Stand on God's Promises

Step number one to receiving answered prayer is *decide what you want from God and find the scripture or scriptures that definitely promise you these things.*

So many times we are indefinite in our praying. I would rather folks pray two or three minutes and know what they're praying about than to pray for two or three hours and not know what they're praying about.

Sometimes when I ask people what they are praying about, they answer that they don't know. I asked one person once what he was praying about, and he said he was praying just to be praying!

I realize there is one kind of prayer whereby we pray to have fellowship with God. But I am talking about praying to God specifically in order to receive an *answer* to prayer. If we are not careful, the first kind of praying I talked about — praying to have fellowship with God — will spill over into the realm of praying specifically in order to receive an answer.

One time a certain minister asked me to pray for him. I asked him what he wanted me to pray for, and he said he didn't know. Now if you went to a grocery store and pushed your cart up and down the aisles, but didn't buy anything, people would think something was wrong with you!

But on the other hand, if someone went to the store to buy a few things, and he bought just those things, you wouldn't think anything was wrong. In fact, you could say he was being definite in what he was doing. In the same way, decide what you want from God and be definite about it. Then find scriptures from the Word that promise you whatever it is you want. Be specific in your praying.

Pray According to the Word

Too few Christians realize the importance of the Word of God in prayer. We know that faith begins where the will of God is known. And we know that God's Word is His will. So find scriptures that definitely promise the things you are asking for.

If the Scriptures don't promise you the things you are desiring, you don't have any business praying for those things. And you shouldn't want anything that the Word of God says you shouldn't have. Many believers are trying to pray beyond their faith. But it's the Word that gives you faith.

The reason many people are not praying with confidence and faith is that they are not finding Scripture that proves that God wants them to have those things they are desiring. They don't know for sure if it's God's will or not. They may *hope* it is, but they can't know for sure, because faith begins where the will, or the Word, of God is known.

Once you find the scriptures that promise you what you desire from God, get those scriptures firmly fixed in your heart, not just in your mind. To do that, you'll have to meditate on the Word of God.

JOSHUA 1:8
8 This book of the law shall not depart out of thy mouth; but thou shalt MEDITATE therein day and night, that thou mayest observe to do according to all that is written therein: for THEN thou shalt make thy way prosperous, and THEN thou shalt have good success.

Another translation says, ". . . that thou mayest be able to deal wisely in the affairs of life." Success in life comes by meditating on God's Word. That's the way you'll build God's Word into your inner consciousness, into your spirit. And as you feed upon the Word by meditating, you will be ready to use these scriptures against demons who will try to make you doubt God and who will try to rob you of what you want. It is the devil who tries to make you doubt God.

So many times people who have not known the Word have prayed, and if they did not get the answer when they thought they should, they said, "Well, it must not be the will of God." But all the time the promises of God were there for them to appropriate. If whatever you're praying about is in the Word, then it is the will of God.

One time a woman had many others pray with her for her son who was afflicted with a certain sickness. But when he didn't get better, she concluded that it just wasn't God's will for her son to be healed. She didn't have any scriptures ready to use against the devil because she wasn't standing on the Word. She didn't have the Word hidden in her heart (Ps. 119:11).

To tell the truth about it, the devil told her that it wasn't the will of God for her son to be healed, and she believed him. Unconsciously, she made the Bible out to be a lie and Jesus to be unjust because the Bible clearly tells us healing is part of our redemption (Isa. 53:4,5; Matt. 8:17; 1 Peter 2:24).

Use the Sword of the Spirit Against the Devil

When you get the Word firmly fixed in your heart and mind, you can use it against the devil. When Jesus was tempted by the devil to turn the stones into bread, Jesus just answered with the Word. He said, ". . . *It is written, Man shall not live by bread alone, but by every word that proceedeth out of the mouth of God"* (Matt. 4:4).

Then the Bible says Satan took Jesus upon a pinnacle of the temple and tempted Jesus again.

MATTHEW 4:7-11
7   Jesus said unto him, It is written again, Thou shalt not tempt the Lord thy God.
8   Again, the devil taketh him up into an exceeding high mountain, and sheweth him all the kingdoms of the world, and the glory of them;
9   And saith unto him, All these things will I give thee, if thou wilt fall down and worship me.
10   Then saith Jesus unto him, Get thee hence, Satan: for it is written, Thou shalt worship the Lord thy God, and him only shalt thou serve.
11   Then the devil leaveth him, and, behold, angels came and ministered unto him.

Jesus did not use a single weapon to defeat the devil on this occasion that the saints of God do not have available to them today. When you are being tempted by the enemy, all you have to do is say, "It is written" and use the Word of God against Satan.

But in order to be able to say that and to resist the devil effectively, you have to be armed with the sword of the Spirit, the Word of God. In other words, you have to hide God's Word in your heart by meditating on it continually in order for it to work for you. Then you will be able to withstand the attacks of the enemy.

I was preaching in Houston once when a preacher friend of mine came over and asked me to agree with him for healing of his high blood pressure. So we joined hands and agreed. Some time later I was in his church and was using the scripture in Matthew 18:19, which says, ". . . *That if two of you shall agree on earth as touching any thing that they shall ask, it shall be done for them of my Father which is in heaven."*

This preacher friend of mine testified how he had agreed with me and had gone home feeling terrible because his blood pressure was even higher than usual. The devil told him that he wasn't going to get his healing. But every time the devil bothered him, he would say, "It is written," and he would quote the Word.

He kept confessing that if two shall agree on earth as touching anything that they shall ask, it shall be done for them by the Father (Matt. 18:19). He said after he stood his ground like that for three nights, all the symptoms left and he won the victory!

Fight the Good Fight of Faith

It takes a little time sometimes to build the Word into your spirit so you can stand in faith for an answer to prayer. The Bible says, *"Fight the good fight of faith . . ."* (1 Tim. 6:12). If there weren't any hindrances to faith, there wouldn't be a fight. When it comes to the natural things, people will fight tooth and toenail for what belongs to them. But when it comes to spiritual things, many times they just roll over and play dead!

For instance, if someone came to your house and claimed your children and your home, you'd fight him for your family — for what belongs to you. Or what if your husband came home and said he had found another woman and he wanted to bring her into your house and move you out? You would sure put up a fight, wouldn't you?

Well, if God's Word says something belongs to you, *then it belongs to you!* So put up a fight by standing your ground on God's Word. If God didn't intend for you to have what He promised you, then He wouldn't have promised it to you. It's up to you to fight the good fight of faith with the Word and receive your promised blessing and all that God has promised you.

When it comes to *natural* things, people will stand up for what belongs to them. But when it comes to *spiritual* things and receiving healing or the blessings and benefits of God that belong to us, many believers don't stand their ground with the Word of God. Some think they are being humble by saying, "Well, the will of God be done," when really it is the will of Satan that is being done. You see, there is a good fight of faith that the believer must fight in order to appropriate and receive his promised blessing, his rightful inheritance in Christ.

In order to fight the good fight of faith, you must learn how to use the sword of the Spirit, which is the Word of God. Fighting the good fight of faith is speaking the Word out of your mouth that you believe in your heart or your spirit.

That's why it's important to hide the Word of God in your heart and be ready to use scriptures against demons when they try to attack you and try to make you doubt God's Word. Be ready to say to Satan, "It is written" and to quote God's Word, which is God's will, about the situation.

There will be many who will side in with the devil and believe his lies over God's Word. And there are also folks who, in the natural, will unconsciously side in with the devil to try to discourage you in spiritual things, in your faith. But stand your ground on God's Word if the enemy attacks you in spirit, soul, or body.

I was holding some services in Texas once when there was an outbreak of influenza. So many people were ill that the schools had to close down. Later I read in the paper that more people in Dallas county had died from this epidemic in 1960 than in the dangerous influenza epidemic that broke out in the year following World War I. This influenza epidemic in Texas affected our meetings terribly. Some people became ill and never did get back into the meetings. The symptoms of this particular type of influenza were extremely severe.

Every one of those symptoms came upon my body in the nighttime, but I never told a single person. I just kept saying, "It is written," and I stood my ground in faith on the Word. I refused to accept influenza because it wasn't God's will. I was in a revival meeting and sinners were being saved. It wasn't God's will to close that meeting down. People sometimes have the silliest ideas about these things. They say, for example, that it is the will of God for people to be sick. But that contradicts God's Word!

If it were true that sickness is the will of God, why have many churches built hospitals to try to get people well! That would get people out of the will of God! Doctors are fighting sickness and disease, too, but they're fighting with different weapons. If it were God's will for people to be sick, then it would not be God's will for people to go to doctors because doctors are fighting sickness and disease too. Also, if it is the will of God for people to be sick, then why not pray for others to become sick so they can enjoy the same "blessing" of sickness and disease and be in God's will!

After I prayed and said, "It is written" and stood on God's Word against these influenza symptoms that tried to attack my body, I got better and continued on with my services. And I never did get influenza. When you have the foundation of God's Word under you, you can stand your ground against Satan's attacks.

Step Number Two:
You Must Ask God for What You Want

We talked about the first step to receiving answered prayer. Step one is to decide what you want from God and find scriptures that promise you the things you desire.

Step number two to receiving answered prayer is *ask God for the things you want and believe that you receive them.*

Certainly, the Lord knows what we need even before we ask, but He still said for us to ask Him. The Bible says, "*. . . your heavenly Father knoweth that ye have need of all these things*" (Matt. 6:32). But He also tells you *to ask* for what you need: "*. . . ask, and ye shall receive, that your joy may be full*" (John 16:24). To say that you're leaving it up to God and that you know He will automatically do whatever is best is unscriptural. Jesus Himself said we are to ask God for what we need.

JOHN 16:23,24
23 And in that day ye shall ASK me nothing. Verily, verily, I say unto you, Whatsoever ye shall ask the Father in my name, he will give it you.
24 Hitherto have ye asked nothing in my name: ask, and ye shall receive, that your joy may be full.

MATTHEW 7:7,8
7 ASK, and it shall be given you; seek, and ye shall find; knock, and it shall be opened unto you:
8 For every one that asketh receiveth; and he that seeketh findeth; and to him that knocketh it shall be opened.

MARK 11:23,24
23 For verily I say unto you, That whosoever shall say unto this mountain, Be thou removed, and be thou cast into the sea; and shall not doubt in his heart, but shall believe that those things which he saith shall come to pass; he shall have whatsoever he saith.
24 Therefore I say unto you, What things soever ye desire, when ye pray, believe that ye receive them, and ye shall have them.

So ask God for the things you want and need, and then believe that you have them. In other words, when you pray, believe you receive what you asked for.

I love a challenge, and Mark 11:24 challenges me. It says in effect, "Believe you receive right then when you pray." *The Amplified Bible* says, ". . . whatever you ask for in prayer, believe — trust and be confident — that it is granted to you, and you will [get it]." You've got to believe you've got your answer before you get it!

Sense Knowledge Truth vs. Revelation Truth

In one of my prayer lines once, one woman said that she wasn't going to believe she had something her physical senses told her she didn't have. I told her just to go sit down then because according to the Scriptures, she would never get anything from God believing the way she did.

Believe God and not Satan. Satan will tell you that you don't have the answer to your prayer. Satan operates in the sense realm. Satan is operating as the god of this world (2 Cor. 4:4). You'll never get anywhere spiritually until you realize that there are two kinds of truth, sense-knowledge truth and revelation truth, which is the truth of God's Word.

Some people think truth pertains to things they can see with their physical eye, but you can't see the things of the spirit. Spiritual things are not natural and they are not material. Everything we need is provided for us in the spiritual realm by God's Word.

EPHESIANS 1:3
3   Blessed be the God and Father of our Lord Jesus Christ, who hath blessed us with ALL SPIRITUAL BLESSINGS in heavenly places in Christ.

This scripture means that everything we need has been provided for us *in Christ Jesus.* You can't see those things, but they are there because God's Word says they are there.

There is sense-knowledge truth and there is revelation truth. When sense-knowledge truth contradicts revelation truth — the truth of God's Word — then I start walking by revelation truth. I walk by what *God* has said in His Word. That which is in the spiritual realm is made real in the natural realm through my faith in the Word of God. My faith grasps it and creates the reality of it in my life (Rom. 4:17).

So when you pray, believe that you receive whatever it is you are praying for, and you shall have it. That's beyond natural thinking. In fact, the natural mind can't grasp it. The majority of the leaders of our churches today are sense-knowledge people. Sense knowledge has taken the church captive. We are to walk by faith and not by sight (2 Cor. 5:7). Believe the truth and not a lie.

Once I was preaching at a certain church which met in a small building. The weather outside was cold, so they were using stoves to heat the building. Sometimes the inside of the building grew very hot and I would get too warm when I preached. One night I was perspiring as I stepped out of that small building to get some air. When I stepped outside, the cold air hit me in the face and my throat started hurting. By the time I got to the parking lot I could hardly talk. The next day, all day long, I couldn't talk above a whisper. Then my chest started hurting.

I started reading scriptures on healing. With my Bible opened before me, I prayed silently. I said, "Lord, Your Word tells me that I am healed. If I asked my flesh or other people around me if I was healed, the answer would be no. If I asked my feelings if I was healed, they would say I wasn't healed. But Your Word says, '. . . *let God be true, but every man a liar . . .*' [Rom. 3:4]. So if I say I'm not healed, I am a liar because Your Word says that *You* cannot lie."

ROMANS 3:4
4   God forbid: yea, let God be true, but every man a liar; as it is written, That thou mightest be justified in thy sayings, and mightest overcome when thou art judged.

I told the Lord that I was going to get up and go over to the church and preach. So I went next door where the church was and went into the service. When I got up to preach, I went up to the microphone and said, "I want to thank God that I am healed." The congregation looked at me like I was crazy because I was just barely whispering.

I began to tell them what the Word of God says about healing, and I proved to them from the Word that I was healed. I told them what God says is true, and that if I said I wasn't healed, I would be lying. I told them I wanted them all to stand and praise God with me because I was healed. Some stood and we began praising God.

I hadn't said, "Hallelujah!" three times when my voice came back. I started preaching, and I preached up a storm! That crowd saw what God did. They saw faith in God's Word work right in front of their eyes. All you have to do is ask God for the things you need and want that His Word has promised and believe you receive them when you ask for them. Then you will have whatever it is you need from God.

Some people continually ask me why God won't heal them after they have had many people pray for them and have had no results. Very often I ask them if they have ever acted as though the Word is so.

People must *act* like the Scriptures are true. If they don't act like the Word is true, they are walking by what their senses are telling them and not by what the Bible says. That's what is throwing them off. They're missing the faith realm entirely, which is based on what the *Word* says, not on what they *see* or *feel*.

Step Number Three:
Be Positive in Your Thinking

Step number three to receiving answered prayer is *let every thought and desire affirm that you have what you asked for.*

After you pray in faith according to God's Word, never permit a mental picture of failure to remain in your mind. Now I'm talking about receiving answers to prayer. Once you've prayed and asked God for something, never doubt for one minute that you have the answer. If doubts persist, rebuke them. Get your mind on the answer. To get your mind on the answer, you will have to get your mind on the Word. The Bible says to "... *Resist the devil, and he will flee from you*" (James 4:7).

1 PETER 5:8
8   Be sober, be vigilant; because your adversary the devil, as a roaring lion, walketh about, seeking whom he may devour.

Resist Doubt

Doubt is from the devil. You have to resist doubts and rebuke them. You have to get your mind on the answer — on God's Word.

In order to receive answers to your prayers, you must eradicate every image, suggestion, vision, dream, impression, feeling, and all thoughts that do not contribute to your faith and that do not affirm that you have what you have asked God for.

The word "eradicate" means *to uproot* or *remove.* Remember, Satan moves in the sense realm, in the natural realm, and he uses the tool of suggestion. Some people think that every kind of vision, dream, impression, or feeling they have is from God. But that is not true.

Reject Anything That Contradicts the Word

Satan can move in the supernatural realm, too, because he is a spirit being, as is God. You've got to be able to know whether a vision, dream, impression, or suggestion is from God or Satan. Those suggestions that do not line up with the Word are of the devil.

A minister friend of mine had a good church that he had built and had pastored for twenty-five years. He had built up a notable work. He was in his fifties, but he was going to have to quit his work because of a physical deficiency. This physical condition hindered him and kept him from doing his best. He was a Full Gospel minister but still didn't know how to believe for his healing.

As this minister awoke one morning, he saw someone standing in his room in shining apparel, and he thought it was Jesus. This "someone" said, "It is not my will to heal you." But this being could not have been Jesus because what the spirit being said contradicted the Word.

MATTHEW 8:17
17   That it might be fulfilled which was spoken by Esaias the prophet, saying, Himself took our infirmities, and bare our sicknesses.

HEBREWS 1:1,2
1   God, who at sundry times and in divers manners spake in time past unto the fathers by the prophets,
2   Hath in these last days SPOKEN UNTO US BY HIS SON, whom he hath appointed heir of all things, by whom also he made the worlds.

Jesus is God speaking to us. Jesus is the Word of God. He is the Word made flesh (John 1:1-5,14). If you want to see God at work, look at Jesus. Jesus was the will of God in action while Jesus was on the earth. The Bible says Jesus "... *went about doing good, and healing all that were oppressed of the devil ...*" (Acts 10:38).

In other words, if Jesus appeared to you in a vision and said that it wasn't His will to heal you, He would be making Himself out to be a liar. Could it be His will for you to have what He bore for you? No, of course not. Jesus bore your sicknesses and diseases so you wouldn't have to bear them.

It was the devil who brought that vision to that minister, and that minister accepted it. God doesn't propagate doubt and unbelief. Every image, suggestion, vision, dream, impression, feeling, and all thoughts that do not contribute to your believing that you have what you have asked for, should be completely cast down and eradicated. They should be replaced with God's Word (2 Cor. 10:3-5).

God's Word says that you have your answer if you based your petition on the Word and believed you received it when you prayed. When you believe you receive your answer before you *see* it manifested, you are appropriating God's Word by faith. It's that kind of faith that moves God!

So many times people say that they *feel* like God heard them when they prayed. I know those people are in for a fall the minute they say that. When I pray, I say I *know* God heard me. I say I believe I have my answer because *the Word* says I do, not because I feel anything (Mark 11:24). God's Word is so whether I feel like it is or not.

Faith's confession creates reality. So stand your ground and refuse to be defeated.

My Own Fight of Faith

In the earliest days of my life, I nearly lost out. I was sickly most of my life and bedfast for sixteen months with organic heart trouble and was almost completely paralyzed. The doctor told me that every tube in my chest was open and undeveloped. There was no operation that could help me.

I learned to pray the prayer of faith by reading the Scriptures, especially Mark 11:24 which says, *"Therefore I say unto you, What things soever ye desire, when ye pray, believe that ye receive them, and ye shall have them."* I believed that I had received healing for my heart before I actually saw my healing manifested. I began to say with my mouth that I believed I was healed according to God's Word.

People keep on struggling when it comes to prayer and faith because they don't actually believe what the *Word* says. But after I prayed and believed I received, without one single manifestation of my healing, I sat up in my bed, determined to get up and walk! No one was around to pick me up if I fell because my other relatives weren't there, and my mother was too weak to pick me up.

I took ahold of the bedpost and pulled myself up. I became dizzy, but I continued to pull myself up out of bed. I was still hanging on to the bedpost when everything stopped spinning. I wasn't dizzy anymore. I began to have feeling in my legs, and it felt like a million pins were sticking me. It felt good even though it

hurt! I soon felt normal and had complete feeling in my body! I started walking around the room for a while, and I got up and walked again the next day.

I didn't tell my family what I was doing because they would have cautioned me against it. In fact, when I finally did say something to my mother, it took me some time to talk her into getting my clothes for me. But the next morning I put on my clothes and walked to the breakfast table. My grandfather looked at me and asked, "Has the dead been raised?" I told him, "Yes, God has raised me up."

After breakfast I went in and lay down and fell asleep for about ten minutes. When I awoke, I heard an audible voice (it was coming from outside, not from within my spirit). The Voice that had told me to get up out of bed and walk had come from the inside — in my spirit. It was the Voice of God speaking to my spirit.

But this voice coming from the outside said, *". . . For what is your life? It is even a vapour, that appeareth for a little time, and then vanisheth away"* (James 4:14). "And today thou shalt surely die" (Isa. 38:1). I knew that both of those statements were from the Bible. James had said the first one and Isaiah had said to Hezekiah, *". . . Set thine house in order: for thou shalt die, and not live"* (Isa. 38:1).

Then the thought came to me again that I was going to die. I got up then and sat in a chair in the room until 2:00 that afternoon, just waiting to die. I thought that voice was God talking to me.

But that afternoon while I was sitting there, from on the inside of me came the words, *"With long life will I satisfy him, and shew him my salvation"* (Ps. 91:16).

I didn't pay any attention to those words, since I was preparing to die! But those words just kept coming to me. It was like they were floating through me over and over on the inside; I didn't realize it then, but they were coming from my spirit. The Holy Spirit was trying to guide me.

In Proverbs it says, *"The spirit of man is the candle of the Lord . . ."* (Prov. 20:27). God guides you through your spirit if you are born again. My spirit was trying to pass that truth from Psalm 91 on to my conscious mind. The third time those words came floating up, I picked them up and toyed with them in my mind.

The fourth time I asked, "Who said that?" Something on the inside of me spoke up and said, "It's the Ninety-First Psalm." I looked it up and found where it was written. Then I jumped up and, holding my Bible, I kicked my foot in the air and told the devil to get out of there! I told him that I wasn't going to die. I told him that God had promised me long life.

Acting on God's Word brings results. My battle was won by eradicating every image, imagination, vision, or thought that didn't contribute to my believing for the thing which I had asked for.

Step Number Four: Guard Your Mind

Step number four to receiving answered prayer is *guard against every evil thought that comes into your mind to try to make you doubt God's Word.*

Thoughts are governed by observation, association, and teaching. So this step is closely associated with step number three. The Bible says we are to cast down every imagination that exalts itself against the knowledge of God (2 Cor. 10:5). That's why you should stay away from all places and things that do not support your affirmation that God has answered your prayer. Your thoughts are governed and affected by observations, associations, and teaching.

That means that sometimes you will have to stay away from the kind of churches that can put more unbelief in you than anything else. Also, be sure to enjoy fellowship with those who contribute to your faith.

2 CORINTHIANS 10:5
5 Casting down imaginations, and every high thing that exalteth itself against the knowledge of God, and bringing into captivity every thought to the obedience of Christ.

PHILIPPIANS 4:8
8 Finally, brethren, whatsoever things are TRUE, whatsoever things are HONEST, whatsoever things are JUST, whatsoever things are PURE, whatsoever things are LOVELY, whatsoever things are OF GOOD REPORT; if there be ANY VIRTUE, and if there be ANY PRAISE, think on these things.

The Bible tells us in Philippians exactly what to think on. Many people are thinking on the wrong things, and they're defeated in life as a result. But if you will guard against every evil thought and think only on those things which affirm that God has heard and answered your prayers, you will be cooperating with God in faith. You will have to guard your mind in order to develop in faith. And as you stand your ground firm in faith, your faith will see you through to victory.

Questions for Study

1. Why is it important to be specific about what you want from God when praying?

   _____

   _____

2. What role should Scripture play in your prayer life?

   _____

   _____

3. What does it mean if you can't find scriptures that promise you what you want from God?

   _____

   _____

4. How do you fight the good fight of faith?

   _____

   _____

5. What is the difference between sense-knowledge truth and revelation truth?

   _____

   _____

6. How can you resist doubt when you keep having mental pictures of failure?

   _____

   _____

7. What should you do when circumstances contradict the Word of God?

   _____

   _____

8. How can you be sure that God has heard your prayer when you don't feel as though He did?

   _____

   _____

9. Why do so many people struggle when it comes to prayer and faith?

   _____

   _____

10. What does guarding your mind have to do with cooperating with God?

   _____

   _____

Chapter 2

Seven Steps to Answered Prayer — Part 2

In Chapter One, I discussed four of the seven steps to answered prayer. The four steps already covered are as follows:

1. Decide what you want from God and find the scripture or scriptures that definitely promise you these things.
2. Ask God for the things you want and believe that you receive them.
3. Let every thought and desire affirm that you have what you asked for.
4. Guard against every evil thought that comes into your mind to try to make you doubt God's Word.

Step Number Five:
Meditate on God's Promises

Step number five to receiving answered prayer is *meditate constantly on the promises upon which you based the answer to your prayer.*

In other words, you must see yourself in possession of what you've asked for and make plans accordingly as if it were already a reality.

PROVERBS 4:20-22
20 My son, ATTEND TO MY WORDS; incline thine ear unto my sayings.
21 Let them not depart from thine eyes; keep them in the midst of thine heart.
22 For they are life unto those that find them, and health to all their flesh.

God said, *"My son, attend to my words . . ."* (Prov. 4:20). God will make His Word good in your life if you'll act on it. If it's healing you need, for instance, God's Word says, *". . . Himself took our infirmities, and bare our sicknesses"* (Matt. 8:17), and *". . . with his stripes we are healed"* (Isa. 53:5). If you don't see yourself healed, then the Word of God has departed from your eyes.

See Yourself With Your Answer

When I was on the bed of sickness, before I even started walking again, I began to see myself well. I was in faith, so I began to make plans accordingly — according to my faith. Up until then I had seen myself dead. For a long time, I had even pictured my funeral and everything that went with it. I had envisioned the open grave and the cemetery. But as the light of God's Word came, I began to see myself alive and well and serving God.

I began to make plans according to my faith because I believed I had received my healing. I had Momma get me a pencil and a tablet and I began to write down sermons because I wanted to preach. I was acting in faith. I never did preach but one of those sermons, and I still have that one sermon today.

One day the doctor came in while I had all my notes and my Bible out on the bed. He told me I shouldn't read only the Bible all the time. When he asked me if I ever read comics, a newspaper, or anything like that, I told him that I never had time. He asked me if I ever read books, and I told him that I never had time.

I know that doctor thought I was a nut because I read the Bible all the time. He thought I was going to lose my mind by constantly reading the Bible. But no one loses his mind by reading the Bible! Reading the Bible will restore your mind and will uplift and refresh your spirit.

Years ago on the flyleaf of my Bible I wrote in red ink, "The Bible says it, I believe it, and that settles it." I'm not interested in what this or that church believes. I'm interested in what the Bible says. I'm not interested in church creeds or church doctrines. I'm interested in what the Bible says.

If God's Word says He hears and answers prayer, and if that Word doesn't depart from before your eyes, then you're bound to see yourself with the things you asked for. If you don't see yourself with the things you desire, then God's Word has departed from before your eyes.

If you don't stand by the Word, although God wants to stand by you, He can't, because the only way God works is through His Word. Remember, God only works and moves in line with His Word. He has bound Himself by His Word. He has magnified His Word above His Name (Ps. 138:2). If you stand by the Word, God will stand by you and will make His Word good in your life. But if you don't stand on God's Word, then He has nothing to make good in your life.

Many folks pray and pray and pray, but they don't pray according to the Word. But John 15:7 says, *"If ye abide in me, and my words abide in you, ye shall ask what ye will, and it shall be done unto you."*

Jesus didn't just say, "If you abide in Me, you shall ask what you will." He also said, *"If ye abide in me, AND MY WORDS ABIDE IN YOU,* [then] *ye shall ask what ye will, and it shall be done unto you"* (John 15:7). With God's Word abiding in us, we have a good foundation to stand upon.

Once I was holding a meeting in Fort Worth, Texas, in a Full Gospel church. I was staying in the parsonage and one day the pastor asked me to go with him to see an elderly lady evangelist under whose ministry he had been saved.

This woman was eighty-two years old. She had been operated on and the doctors had found seven cancers in her. But the doctors just sewed her back up and didn't touch them, and they told her that she would probably die soon. Months had come and gone but she was still alive, although bedfast.

When we got there, she insisted that she was old enough to die, but we told her to let God heal her first. The minister told her that if she lived she could still win many souls to God because so many had been saved and filled with the Holy Spirit under her ministry. We read Proverbs 4:20-22 to her and told her to begin to see herself well and up preaching.

That was in September and the next May when I was back for a meeting in this minister's church again, he told me this woman had received her healing. He told me that the night I would be beginning my revival in his church, this lady evangelist was closing a two-week revival meeting. She had phoned and said she would be in my meeting on Tuesday night. When she came on Tuesday evening, I didn't recognize her. She came up to me and just threw her arms around me and hugged me.

It startled me, and then she said, "You probably don't recognize me."

I told her I didn't (she looked so different because she had gained weight, and she looked younger than her age). Then she explained who she was and that she was so glad we hadn't let her die. She had done just what we had told her to. She began to see herself well and she received her healing. She said she had the entire summer booked up with meetings. I later heard that she lived to be ninety-one. So, you see, she lived several years and didn't die from cancer.

In 1943 when I was pastoring a church in Texas, one of the older women in the church had cancer of the stomach. The doctors had sent her home to die. She was eighty-three years old and felt it was time for her to die. I told her not to die sick and diseased. I told her to let God heal her and then die if she wanted to. So I prayed with her that she wouldn't die sick. I asked the Lord to help her get back her confidence in divine healing. I went back to visit her again, but she was still wanting to die.

This woman finally decided she would attend the healing services we were having. She came for about a week or two, but nothing happened because she was talking doubt and unbelief. She had a big growth that had eaten out her stomach and was eating out her back.

One night I perceived that she was going to be healed. So I spoke to her and told her that I'd had a mini-vision that she was going to be healed. I told her that within ten minutes she would be out of her chair and dancing. When I anointed her with oil and prayed for her, she came out of that chair and began dancing. She was completely healed.

She later testified in church about her complete healing. She said she had ridden the bus to church the evening she received her healing, and on the way home, she had testified to others on the bus. Nine years later, when she was ninety-two, we stopped by to see her but she was out visiting.

We asked about her and were told that she had been to her doctor for a checkup, and the doctor said that she was still in perfect health. He couldn't find a single thing wrong with her! I was so glad I didn't let her die.

Now these two women had similar stories. They had begun to see themselves dead. We had to get them to see themselves with what God had provided for them. You have to see yourself with what you've asked for.

Step Number Six:
Continually Thank God for the Answer

Step number six to receiving answered prayer is *in your every waking moment, think on the greatness of God and His goodness, and count your blessings.* This will increase your faith.

Lift your heart to God continually in increasing praise and gratitude for what He has done and for what He is doing for you now.

PHILIPPIANS 4:6
6 Be careful for nothing; but in every thing by prayer and supplication with thanksgiving let your requests be made known unto God.

That phrase, "Be careful for nothing" means *in nothing be anxious.* It also means, "Do not fret or have any anxiety about anything . . ." (Phil. 4:6 *Amp.*). As long as you fret and have anxiety, all the praying and fasting in the world isn't going to do any good.

The rest of Philippians 4:6 says, "with *thanksgiving*." When you pray and make your requests known to God, then you must thank Him for the answer. We are to pray *with thanksgiving*.

We were preaching in Overton, Texas, some years ago, and we were invited for dinner at the home of one of the families in the church. The woman told us that she'd had asthma and had been sent to a specialist. The specialist told her that it was the worst case of asthma he had ever seen. She had found some relief but not much. She'd had just about everyone who had a healing ministry pray for her but nothing had happened.

One time she went to Raymond T. Richey's revival which was being held in that area. She was in the healing line, and he told her to start praising God from that moment on that she was healed. She told him that she wasn't healed. Richey told her to thank God for the Word and to say, "The Word says I *am* healed."

So she began to do that, and soon she got so taken up with praising God that she didn't even know when all the asthma attacks left her. When she related this, it had been more than fourteen years since she'd had any symptoms.

The Scripture says, "Do not fret or have any anxiety about anything . . ." (Phil. 4:6 *Amp.*). (Anything means *anything*!) Therefore, you can let your request be known with *thanksgiving* because you know God is going to hear you.

When I come across situations which seem impossible, I just say that all things are possible to him that believes (Mark 9:23), and that I'm a believer. Sometimes the devil will tempt me with thoughts that try to hinder my belief, but I have the Word to stand on. And because God's Word is true, I thank God for my answer before I ever see it come to pass!

Step Number Seven:
Make Every Prayer a Statement of Faith

Step number seven to receiving answered prayer is *make every prayer relative to what you've asked a statement of faith instead of unbelief.*

You can think and say words of faith just as easily as you can think and say words of doubt and unbelief. *It is thinking faith thoughts and speaking faith words that leads the heart out of defeat and into victory.*

Speaking about the prayer of faith, Smith Wigglesworth once said, "If you pray seven times for any one thing, you prayed six times in unbelief."

Andrew Murray said, "It's not good taste to ask God for the same thing over and over again."

Andrew Murray also said that if what you've prayed for hasn't materialized, and you do pray again, don't pray for it again in the same way because that would be unbelief. He said to remind God that you asked for it and remind Him of what His Word says; put Him in remembrance of His promises (Isa. 43:26). Tell Him that you're expecting it, and thank Him for it.

Let me give you an example of saying and thinking words of faith and receiving a bountiful benefit and blessing. I was holding a meeting once in west Texas. A man and his wife who were both singers were traveling with me. The man had promised me he would stay with me for a certain period of time because I had taken a good deal of time to train him. He said he wouldn't start preaching on his own just when I had him trained sufficiently so he could really be of help to me.

We were holding a meeting in a motel conference room, and this man and his wife were staying with the pastor. One day during the meetings the man and his wife drove up to the motel. Just as they drove up, I had a revelation that God was calling this man to preach, but the man was afraid to tell me.

The man and his wife talked to me about several things. Finally, the man told me he had to tell me something. I told him that I knew what it was because the Lord had already shown me. I assured him that it was all right and that I wouldn't try to stand in the way of the Lord.

Later he tried out for the pastorate of a little church in an area where I had pastored, and they voted him in. He told them that all he knew was what he had heard me say. Later he asked me to come and hold a meeting for him.

This man had told the people in that church that in sixty days they would be running sixty people in attendance in Sunday school. When I finally did go there to hold a meeting, the Sunday school superintendent told me that they'd had good pastors at the church before, but they'd never had more than seventy in Sunday school. The Sunday school superintendent said that on the day that this new pastor said they would have sixty in Sunday school, they had sixty. (This pastor had learned the principles of faith!)

Then the pastor said that in ninety days, they would be running ninety in Sunday school, and they did! He then said that in another sixty days, they would be running 120, and they did that too.

In that nine months' time they had grown from 18 to 120 in Sunday school. The pastor then told the congregation that they were going to build a new brick church building there. The Sunday school superintendent told me that by that time he was ready to believe anything, and he said he would give the first $1,000 for it himself. He said that his father, who was mayor of the town, would also give $1,000. When I went to hold my meeting in that church, we had a full house.

Don't Undo Your Prayers

This new pastor who had traveled with me knew how to believe God. He knew how to receive from God through prayer, and he knew how to hold on to the answer by standing his ground in faith.

Many times people undo their prayers. They get into unbelief and just stay there, and it is as if they are spinning their wheels in prayer. They need to get into faith and stay *there*. They may have to stand their ground for a period of time. But if they stay in the arena of faith, the answer *will* come.

An example of people undoing their prayers occurred in one of my meetings that I held in this pastor's church. One night a woman came in to that church just before the service was turned over to me. When the minister turned it over to me, she jumped up and said that she had a special prayer request. She said she had just come from Sister Gray's house and that Sister Gray wasn't supposed to live past midnight.

My minister friend said he had been to see Sister Gray that day, and he confirmed that what this woman had said was true. So he told everyone to stand and pray for her. I thought we were standing to pray for her healing. So we all stood and prayed. Then we thanked God for the answer.

The next night this same woman came back again, and during the service she said she thought we ought to pray for Sister Gray again. She said the doctor had examined Sister Gray and that he couldn't understand why she hadn't died. In fact, he said she was going to live after all. They had gotten the woman up out of bed and she had been sitting in a chair, although she was still very weak. It is only natural that her body would be weak after being bedfast.

This sister said that it was evident God had *touched* Sister Gray, but that now we should pray that God would *heal* her! But that wouldn't be right because if we did that, we would not be making every prayer relative to what we've asked for — a statement of faith. Instead of making a statement of faith, we would be making a statement of unbelief.

We hadn't prayed the first time that God would *touch* her; we had prayed that He would heal her! And He had answered our prayers! Therefore, for us to pray again that God would heal her would have been praying in unbelief.

While all of this was going on, I had a feeling I should get up and say something, but I hesitated. I knew that because Sister Gray had been healed by mass faith, that is, by the corporate faith of the congregation, that if the congregation kept praying that Sister Gray would be healed, their unbelief would be taking her out of God's hands and she would probably die. You see, by that time, Sister Gray was beyond using her own faith to receive her healing.

But I was reluctant to say anything. I knew on the inside of me that within three days she would be dead. Sure enough, three days later, she died.

Many times we're cheated out of the blessings God wants us to have in this life because we're not cooperating with Him. Instead of praying again for Sister Gray's healing, the congregation should have raised their hands and thanked God that she had been healed.

In a district convention in Texas many years ago, a call came that one of the pastors in that city was in the hospital, dying. The district superintendent called us to pray, so we all prayed for this dying man. After we prayed, we thanked God that He had heard us.

Brother Raymond T. Richey, who was the minister who had led us in prayer, started to walk away, but then he turned around and came back to the microphone.

He asked, "How many of you are still going to keep praying for this brother in the hospital?"

I didn't lift my hand, but nearly everyone else did.

Then he asked the crowd, "What do you want to do that for?"

Then Richey went on to explain to the congregation that they had already prayed in faith and that they were just to keep on praising God because God had heard our prayer and had healed that man. Praying any other way would be praying in unbelief.

We continued on with the service, and afterwards, a man came in and announced that the man who had been dying had suddenly revived and was going to be all right. The sick man had seen Jesus walk into his room, and Jesus had said to him, "I am the Lord that healeth thee." The man had been unconscious, but he had revived and had seen Jesus. This happened while we were praying. The man immediately revived and was well.

Use the Faith You Have

ROMANS 12:3
3 For I say, through the grace given unto me, to every man that is among you, not to think of himself more highly than he ought to think; but to think soberly, according as GOD HATH DEALT TO EVERY MAN THE MEASURE OF FAITH.

God has dealt to every man the measure of faith. Therefore, every believer can receive answers to his prayers. If you say you don't have faith, then you are making God out to be a liar. You do have faith. Every man has faith if he is saved. But it's *thinking faith thoughts* and *speaking faith words* that lead the heart out of defeat into victory.

In other words, you need to use the faith you have in order for your faith to be effectual.

Follow these seven steps to answered prayer, and expect to receive answers to your prayers. Do not accept no for an answer and do not be denied! It's your family right in Christ, your redemptive right, your gospel right, and your right as a recreated blood-bought, child of God to have what God has promised you. By faith appropriate what belongs to you and it will come. It's yours now by faith. So accept God's Word and believe it and it will become a reality in your life!

Questions for Study

1. Why should you meditate on the promises upon which you based the answer to your prayer?

   _____

   _____

2. What steps do you have to take in order for God to make His Word good in your life?

   _____

   _____

3. How can you increase your faith?

   _____

   _____

4. What effect does worry have on your prayers?

   _____

   _____

5. Why is it important to make every prayer relative to what we've asked for a statement of faith?

   _____

   _____

6. What are some things you can do to lead your heart out of defeat and into victory?

   _____

   _____

7. If what you're praying for hasn't materialized, what should you do?

   _____

   _____

8. What happens when we don't cooperate with God?

   _____

   _____

9. What must we do in order for our faith to be effectual?

   _____

   _____

10. What are the seven steps to answered prayer?

   _____

   _____

Chapter 3

Praying in Jesus' Name — Part 1

Jesus is our Mediator, Intercessor, Advocate, and our Lord. He stands between us and the Father.

No place in the Bible is it recorded that Jesus told His disciples to pray *to* Him. They were always to pray to the Father *in Jesus' Name*.

If we wish to be sure of reaching the throne of God with our prayers, we must come to God according to the rules laid down in His Word.

JOHN 16:23,24
23 And in that day ye shall ask me nothing. Verily, verily, I say unto you, Whatsoever ye shall ask the Father in my name, he will give it you.
24 Hitherto have ye asked nothing in my name: ask, and ye shall receive, that your joy may be full.

Notice Jesus said, *". . . in that day ye shall ask me nothing . . ."* (v. 23). Jesus said this just before He died and rose again to sit at the right hand of the Father on our behalf. Jesus also said, *". . . Whatsoever ye shall ask the Father IN MY NAME, he will give it you"* (John 16:23).

Jesus was talking about His mediatorial position at the right hand of the Father where He would soon ascend and be seated (Heb. 1:3). Another translation of John 16:23 reads, "In that day you shall not pray to Me." Jesus said we are to ask the Father *in His Name*. There isn't any other way to approach God.

Certainly, we can worship Jesus, and worship is a type of prayer. We can tell Jesus how much we love and appreciate Him, but when it comes to praying and asking, we must ask the Father in the Name of the Lord Jesus Christ.

Ephesians 3:14 and 15 also tells us that: *"For this cause I bow my knees UNTO THE FATHER of our Lord Jesus Christ, Of whom the whole family in heaven and earth is named."*

We are to bow our knees to our Heavenly Father in prayer, using the Name of Jesus. It's not as important which church you belong to, as it is which *family* you belong to. Praise God, believers are in the family of God. And we can approach the Father God in prayer in the Name of Jesus!

Many people know about praying to God, but they don't know anything about praying to *the Father*. In other words, when they're praying they don't sound as if they really know God as *Father*. He's God to the world, but He's Father to me. There is real joy in knowing that the Father will answer our prayers.

Ask, That Your Joy May Be Full

Smith Wigglesworth told of an incident which happened when he first started preaching. (His wife was really the preacher, and he was a plumber. In fact, Wigglesworth put plumbing in many of the houses in England which in that day had never had plumbing.)

Wigglesworth said that one day he was working, installing plumbing in a certain home for people of some nobility. He noticed the lady of the house would come time after time to the door where he was working, and stand looking at him. She would look, then go away and come back and look again at him. He couldn't figure out what was wrong with her.

After a while he needed more material, so he sent his apprentice back to the shop to get it. When the helper left, the woman came into the room where Wigglesworth was working and shut the door. He couldn't figure out what in the world was going on. She finally asked Wigglesworth what that wonderful light was on his face.

At this time Wigglesworth was a plumber; it wasn't until later that he became a preacher. Wigglesworth was full of light because he was full of joy. You don't have to be a preacher to be full of joy. The Word will work for you, whoever you are.

Wigglesworth proceeded to tell that woman an incident that had occurred at breakfast time that morning. He said that when he had come down for breakfast that morning, he sat down at the table and his wife told him that two of their children were sick, not even able to get out of bed. The illness had come upon them during the night.

Before Wigglesworth even gave thanks for his food, he got up from the table, went upstairs with his wife, and they laid hands on the two children and prayed. The children were both instantly healed. They had contracted a children's sickness that usually lasted for several days. But it left them instantly when Wigglesworth and his wife prayed.

We make a mistake by accepting sickness and adverse circumstances in our lives (John 10:10). I've done it before because I didn't know any better, but I've since learned better — I learned what the *Word* said! For example, our son, Ken, had the mumps for about forty-five minutes one time. But when we prayed, they left him and never returned. We make a mistake by accepting such things which are not from God.

So Wigglesworth's joy was full! And that joy was evident to those around him. God had healed his children and had answered his prayer! The children had gotten out of bed and had come to breakfast *healed*! That was the reason for this wonderful light on Wigglesworth's face.

There is a joy that comes when you get answers to prayer. But if you're not getting answers to prayer, if you're not getting results, then there can be a look of perplexity and trouble on your countenance. There is an air of doubt, perplexity, fear, and confusion about you. You have the attitude, "I'm uncertain; I don't know."

But you can *know* God hears you when you pray according to His Word. And your joy can be full even before you see the answer because you are resting on the integrity of God's Word.

There is no joy in all the world like seeing God moving in your family and in your home, answering your prayers. In John 16:23 Jesus is talking about *individual* prayer, not corporate prayer. He said, "*. . . Whatsoever YE shall ask. . . .*" Jesus is talking about something that concerns *you*. Jesus said, "*. . . ask, and YE shall receive, that your joy may be full*" (John 16:24).

This woman asked Wigglesworth if she could have that joy too. He told her that she could, but she would have to first get saved. She wanted to get saved and to know Jesus. She said they had a prayer book in the house, but that they'd never known anything about the new birth or about the wonderful joy that comes from having your prayers answered. Right there in that room, Wigglesworth led this woman to the Lord, and light broke through to her spirit; she was born again. She became happy and full of joy because the burden of sin had rolled away.

She asked Wigglesworth if she would be able to keep this new joy and have it every day. He assured her that she could, but that the best way to keep it is to give it away. He told her to tell everyone she came in contact with about her salvation.

Wigglesworth had been working there long enough to know that she had many lady friends in social clubs. She was a woman of wealth. He told her that at the club meeting she was to have that afternoon, she should tell all the women present about what had happened to her.

The reason many a Christian life becomes stagnant is there is no "giving away." Many Christians do not share what they have received from the Word with others. Christians can increase their joy by witnessing about the Lord's goodness in their own lives.

There is no joy in all the world like leading a poor lost soul to Christ. So if you're not doing that, remember, the way to keep your joy is to give it away.

Jesus wants our joy to be full or complete. We know that one way to ensure continual joy is to give our joy away. And Jesus also told us in John chapter 16 that we could have fullness of joy by *asking* the Father in Jesus' Name and by receiving whatsoever we ask for in prayer.

Have Joy *Before* the Answer Comes

On another occasion I was reading about Wigglesworth. Wigglesworth was telling about a time in his life when he was facing dire financial needs. He was visiting in London in the home of a very wealthy man. As the story goes, if Wigglesworth had even hinted of his financial needs, that wealthy man would have given him all the money he needed. But Wigglesworth didn't tell anyone but the Lord about his need.

As Wigglesworth and the wealthy man were walking in the park, Wigglesworth was happy and singing because he had cast all the care and the burden of his need upon the Lord (1 Peter 5:7). Therefore, Wigglesworth didn't have a care.

The wealthy man wasn't in the same happy mood. He told Wigglesworth that he would give all he owned just to have the spirit of joy Wigglesworth had. Wigglesworth told him that joy wouldn't cost him anything. All he had to do was cast all of his cares on Jesus.

Wigglesworth told the man that he himself didn't have a care in the world, although at that very moment, Wigglesworth was in great financial need. But Wigglesworth didn't tell the man he had needs because Wigglesworth had cast his cares upon the Lord. Now the Lord had Wigglesworth's burden and Wigglesworth was free and happy. If Wigglesworth would have even hinted to his friend that he had some kind of a need, the man would have helped him. But Wigglesworth didn't mention it.

Many times I've been around folks when I've had great financial needs, but I didn't reveal it in any way. I just smiled because I was happy and free. I had cast all of my cares over on the Lord. God's Word is true.

I remember many years ago I was preaching in a little church close to home. I had gone there to preach Monday through Sunday. The first night the building was nearly full. God really began moving by His Spirit in the services and soon the building was completely full.

The pastor said that they couldn't just close the meeting down and so he asked me if I would stay and teach for a while. He asked me what the minimum amount of money was that I needed in order to get by.

I hesitated to tell the pastor what I needed because I was sure he would think it was too much. But I did come up with a figure for him. I finally got it down to a very bare minimum — just barely enough to make my budget. I wanted to stay on to try to help that church.

I quoted him a certain figure. He said it was more than they ever paid anyone before. He said he didn't know if they could pay it or not. I told him that if he would agree with me, the money would come in. He said he would, so we announced that the meeting was going to continue.

We went to the service on the following Sunday night. I had just found out that afternoon that some emergencies had arisen at home, and I needed several hundred dollars more than what I had quoted the pastor.

I knew when I got back that evening and told the pastor the additional amount I needed, he would probably nearly faint (I'd already obligated myself to stay on with him a couple of weeks). I needed about twice as much as I had quoted him previously. Actually, I had told him I needed $150 a week, but since there were emergencies, I needed $300 a week. The most that church had ever paid anyone was $90 a week.

I preached on Sunday night. They took the offering, and after church I went to the parsonage. We had a bite to eat, and the pastor said he was reluctant to give me the offering. He said they didn't meet the budget. He said there was only about $123, and he knew I couldn't get by on that. I took it and just smiled.

Then I told him about the emergencies that had arisen and that I needed $300 a week, instead of the $150 I had previously quoted him. I told him to just stay in agreement with me, and that I would do the believing and he could do the agreeing. He extended his hand to shake mine and said all right, so we went on and had a time of fellowship together. Later on, his wife said she noticed that I didn't seem to get upset when they told me the offering was so small. She said she noticed how happy I was about it.

By the time the meeting was over, I had the money I needed without making any great pulls on the congregation for money. The pastor told me it beat anything he had ever seen in his life. But the need was there, and God meets needs (Phil. 4:19). Actually, I needed $900 for those three weeks, and I had more than $1,000 when the meetings were over. I'm glad God knows how to meet our needs!

Here's the point I want to make: I acted with just as much joy *before* I had the money as I did *after* I had the money. That's what the pastor's wife had said. She said that she watched me closely, and I had just as much joy when it looked like the money wasn't coming in as I did when the money came in. She told her husband about it and said I actually seemed to be more joyous before he actually handed me the money. I told her it was because I walk by faith and not by sight (2 Cor. 5:7).

Worry Blocks God's Answer to Your Prayers

Our text says, *". . . ask, and ye shall receive, that your joy may be full"* (John 16:24)! God wants us to receive answers to our prayers and be full of joy. How can we be full of joy and victory when the circumstances look dark and we have needs in our lives? We are full of joy because we walk by faith, not by sight. We know that whatever we ask of the Father according to the Word, He will give it to us — that our joy may be full (John 16:23,24)!

Could your joy be full if you had great financial burdens pressing upon you? If you had bills to be paid and couldn't pay them? No, your joy couldn't be full then.

However, once you've asked the Father to meet your need in Jesus' Name, sometimes you need to have joy before you ever see the money you asked for. You have to be just as joyous before you see the answer as you are once the answer materializes. You'll block or hinder God from helping you if you're worrying and trying to figure out how the answer is going to come. If you are trying to figure things out, then you have the care or burden of the problem, and that means God *doesn't* have it. You're still carrying that load and God can't help you.

We need to realize this fact. It does very little good, if any, to pray if you're going to continue to worry and fret and wrestle with the problem yourself. You might as well say amen because it's so!

My mother told me that when she knew I was traveling, she would pray that the Lord would be with me. I would finish a meeting in California and then travel straight through until I got home. She would just stay awake worrying, waiting for the telephone to ring, announcing bad news. I told her that she was wasting her time, that she might as well not pray if she was going to keep on worrying. She would pray that God would protect me, and then she would stay awake worrying.

That's the way many people act when they pray. But worry can hinder you from receiving answers to prayers. Worry can stop God from being able to move on your behalf.

Thank God, prayer means more than that. John 16:24 says, *". . . ask, and ye SHALL RECEIVE, that your joy may be full."* When you pray in faith, according to God's Word, you are full of joy and rejoicing even before the answer materializes because you know God heard you. You have His Word for it.

1 JOHN 5:14,15
14 And this is the confidence that we have in him, that, if we ask any thing according to his will, he heareth us:
15 And if we know that he hear us, whatsoever we ask, we know that we have the petitions that we desired of him.

Follow Biblical Teaching on Prayer

EPHESIANS 5:20
20 Giving thanks always for all things unto God and the Father in the name of our Lord Jesus Christ.

Notice here that Paul tells us that we are to give thanks always for all things to God the Father in the Name of our Lord Jesus Christ. He tells us our thanks are to be given to the Father. In all of our real praise and thanksgiving, the Name of Jesus is our access to the heart of the Father. When you wish to get an answer to prayer, follow the teachings of the Word.

Someone said that it doesn't make much difference how you pray. But if it doesn't, then why did Jesus ever teach us about prayer? Why did the Holy Ghost inspire Paul to write the epistles just as they are? It *is* important how you pray.

To say that these verses about the scriptural way to pray aren't important would make just as much sense as it would to say that John 3:16 is not important. John 3:16 *is* important. So when you wish to get an answer to prayer, follow the teachings of the Word and pray to the Father in the Name of Jesus, giving thanks always to God — in Jesus' Name (Eph. 5:20)!

'In Jesus' Name' — Not 'For Jesus' Sake'

Many people conclude their prayers by saying, "For Jesus' sake." But we are not to pray that way. There is a difference between praying in *the Name* of Jesus and praying for *the sake* of Jesus. We are to pray in the *Name* of Jesus.

What's the difference between praying for Jesus' sake and in His Name? There is quite a difference.

When you go to God, and you ask Him to do something for Jesus' sake, you're asking that it be done to help Jesus — on your credit. Can't you see how foolish that sounds? In the first place, Jesus doesn't need the help. And in the second place, you don't have any credit to guarantee the answer to your prayer if He did! No, it's the other way around. *We* need the help and Jesus has the credit.

I don't mean to imply that people do this consciously when they add, "For Jesus' sake" to their prayers. But that is the way it sounds in heaven.

Even if Jesus *did* need our help, you and I don't have any standing in heaven that would guarantee help for Him. We are the ones who need the help. It's for *our* sake that we are praying. And Jesus has the standing or the credit in heaven that enables us to come to God in His Name and receive those things we need.

For example, if you go to the bank with a friend's check and ask the cashier to cash that check, the cashier will ask if you have the money on deposit in your own account to guarantee the amount of the check. If you don't, he'll refuse to cash it. When you pray, "For Jesus' sake," it's like trying to cash a check when there is no money in your account because you don't have the credit in heaven — Jesus does.

But if you go to the bank with a check endorsed by a wealthy man who has an account at that bank, then there will be no questions asked. The cashier will hand over the money.

Jesus is our "credit" in heaven, so to speak: He has all the credit we could ever need to get "our check cashed" — our prayers answered. And when God hears His children pray in faith in the Name of Jesus, He responds to their prayers based on Jesus' credit or Jesus' standing in heaven. In that mighty Name, God gives us the answer to our prayers.

If I have a stomachache, for example, and I am praying for healing, I wouldn't ask God to heal me for Jesus' sake — to help Jesus. I don't want to be healed *for* Him. It's *my* stomach that needs help, not His! I'm the one who is hurting. It's for *my* sake, on Jesus' credit.

Similarly, if I need $100, and I ask the Father to help me get this money for Jesus' sake, I would be praying foolishly because Jesus does not need the $100. The money is for *my* sake, not His. Jesus doesn't need $100; I do. I need the $100 to help *me*, so it's for my sake, on Jesus' credit.

Many an honest prayer fails because of folks ending their prayers, "For Jesus' sake." If you have been doing that, stop it. It makes a lot of difference whether or not our prayers are scripturally based.

That's the reason we fail many times in our praying. Our approach is all wrong. Peter and John said when they were at the Gate Beautiful, "... *why look ye so earnestly on us, as though by our own power or holiness we had made this man to walk?*" (Acts 3:12). In other words, it isn't by the believer's own power or holiness that he gets an answer to prayer.

You don't get your prayers answered because you're good either. You get an answer to prayer because of Jesus — and because of your standing *in* Jesus. Thank God. Jesus has a standing in Heaven. He is the only way to approach the Father. You can't get there any other way.

Thank God, in Jesus' Name we can come boldly to the throne of God (Heb. 4:16). Let's use a little sense and go as wise children, using the mighty Name of Jesus which He has given us. Jesus gave us the right and the authority to use His Name.

Jesus' Name Is the Key

Notice John 16:23: "*And in that day ye shall ask me nothing. Verily, verily, I say unto you, Whatsoever ye shall ask the Father in my name, he will give it you.*" Jesus gave us the right and the authority to use His Name in prayer. He gave us the authority to use His Name. He gave it to us. We now have that right. He said, "*... In my name shall they cast out devils ...*" (Mark 16:17). We have a right to use that Name against the devil. Thank God, that Name has authority. We have the right to use that Name to call out demons that bind men's souls with darkness and disease.

I was holding a meeting in east Texas the first week in September in 1952. I was studying along this line, and there were two things I began to see about the authority in Jesus' Name. Those two things changed my life. They helped me immeasurably.

Even as a Baptist boy preacher I had believed in divine healing, and I had ministered to the sick. But there were certain cases, particularly mental cases which were evidently caused by demonic obsession or possession, which almost frightened me when I came up against them.

But as I began to study about the Name of Jesus, I realized something, which I will try to illustrate with this example.

When you go to your automobile, you have a key that unlocks the door. You say that you unlock the door, but really *you* don't unlock the door: the *key* does it. You also have a key that fits the ignition. Ordinarily, you couldn't start the car if you didn't have a key. Again, *you* don't actually start the car; the *key* does it. The key is the important factor to the entire process of unlocking and starting your car.

I began to look at the authority in the Name of Jesus from this standpoint. In other words, *I'm* not the one who is going to cast out any devils. *I* don't have any authority in myself, in the natural. But Jesus gave me the key to all the authority I would ever need — and it's in His Name.

Jesus' Name is the key! His Name has the authority! All I have to do is use the key, and the key does the work. This alleviated the fear I had. I was able to use the Name because the Name is the key, and the Name works!

Meditation on the Word Brings Light

Also, I began to see some other things from the Scriptures as I began to study about the Name of Jesus.

Let me encourage you to meditate on the Word after you have studied it. Your spirit can be educated and trained. But just because you read the Word of God doesn't mean your spirit is educated. You can read the Bible and not understand what you're reading, and it won't mean a thing to you. The Word has to get down on the inside of you, in your heart or spirit. You get the revelation of the Word in your heart by meditating on it.

When I was nineteen or twenty years old, I heard talk about Einstein's theory of relativity. I decided I would read it, since I'd heard so much about it. Before I read it, I didn't know a thing in the world about it. When I finished reading it, I knew less than I had before I read it!

I think sometimes that's the way it is with people who read the Word of God. They know less when they finish reading it than they did when they began. They're trying to grasp the truth of God's Word with their minds. But you have to get the revelation of God's Word in your heart.

After studying the Word, I would then shut my eyes and begin to meditate on the Word and just think about the scriptures I had been reading and studying. I've had a number of visions and revelations, but this revelation I had concerning the Name of Jesus was a revelation of the Word that any believer might have. The Holy Ghost will teach us the Word. As I meditated on the Word, on the inside of me I began to see something that I had never seen before.

The Authority in the Name of Jesus To Bind the Work of the Devil

In the first place, I began to see that the devil is the author of all that's evil and wrong, for he is the god of this world. The New Testament says that Satan is the god of this world and that Satan has blinded men from seeing the glorious light of the gospel (2 Cor. 4:4). Several scriptures talk about this. And the devil tries to bind men's souls.

I began to see that folks in my own family who were unsaved and who were bound by the devil didn't understand where they were heading. They were spiritually blinded by the god of this world. For example, no man would go out on the highway driving his automobile one hundred miles an hour and pass red lights and signs that read, "Danger Ahead" if he were in his right mind. But a man who is doped and drunk will do this because he doesn't know what he's doing.

No intelligent person in his right mind will go through life wheeling and dealing in sin and just purposely plunge off into eternity and go to hell. If he doesn't want to accept Jesus, he is not in his right mind. He is spiritually blind. For example, the Bible said about the prodigal son, "when he came to himself" he returned home (Luke 15:17). So there was a time when the prodigal son wasn't in his right mind. But when he came to himself, he decided to go back home.

In the second place, I began to see the authority that the believer possesses in the Name of Jesus. All the power of heaven is at our disposal, in that Name. But if believers don't exercise their rightful authority in the Name of Jesus, then nothing will be done about their situation.

That day as I was studying the Word, I had such a revelation of this, that I was challenged. I know it was the Holy Ghost talking to me. When the light comes, you're obligated to walk in the light. The devil will see if you believe what you claim you believe. If you've learned your lesson well, you'll stand your ground. You'll triumph over the temptation to doubt God's Word.

It just seemed as if something on the inside was challenging me to act on God's Word. You see, at that time, my oldest brother, whose nickname was Dub, was the black sheep of the family. Anything bad you might want to mention, he had probably done it. I was really challenged about putting this revelation of the Word of God to work on behalf of Dub.

You see, over a fifteen-year period, I had prayed and prayed for Dub and had fasted as much as three days at a time. But as I was lying across my bed that day, I realized that all my fasting and praying had been done in unbelief.

Why do I say that? Because if you are expecting just prayer to do it, it won't work. It's exercising faith in God's Word that makes prayer work. To expect prayer itself to do the job is the same as expecting your physical hand to unlock a car door; it can't do it by itself. You have to have the key to unlock the door. And in prayer you have to have faith in the Name of Jesus and in the Word of God in order to get the job done. The Name of Jesus is our key.

I think sometimes we think we can move God with our tears and our prayers and our fasting. But God doesn't ever change. He's always the same (Mal. 3:6; Heb. 13:8). God moves when you come to Him according to His Word and use the Word and the Name of Jesus as the key. Then prayer will work for you, and you'll have your answer.

All those years I had been praying for Dub, he had gotten worse instead of better. But that day something challenged me that the authority in the Name of Jesus would work for him. I knew it would! I didn't know where Dub was, but I rose up with my Bible in my hand, and I lifted my Bible and said, "In the Name of the Lord Jesus Christ, you foul demon that binds my brother's soul, I bind you in the Name of Jesus. I claim Dub's deliverance and salvation in the Name of the Lord Jesus Christ."

I knew in my spirit it was as good as done, and I was full of joy! I laid my Bible down and went out of the room whistling and singing, and I went on about my business.

After that meeting in east Texas, I went home for a few days before starting another meeting. I was there about ten days, and it had been a couple of weeks or more since I'd claimed Dub's salvation. As I started across my living room into the bedroom, I had a peculiar experience. I'd never had one quite like it. As I walked across the floor, I seemed to hear a voice telling me, "Oh, come on now, you don't really think old Dub will ever be saved do you?" I stopped dead still in my tracks and shut my mind off to those thoughts.

Don't ever touch those kinds of thoughts in your thought life because it's doubt and unbelief. If you're tempted to think thoughts of doubt, repent of it. I just shut my mind off, and I wouldn't even think about it.

Then from down on the inside of me, I started laughing. The laughter sort of bubbled up and came out of my mouth, and I laughed out loud. I said, "No, devil, I don't *think* he'll be saved; I *know* he'll be saved! I took the Name of Jesus and broke your power over his life and claimed his deliverance. To me that settles it." Then I went on rejoicing.

Two days later I heard that same voice again. It said the same thing again. I shut my mind off to it, and again I started laughing from way down on the inside. The laughter just started bubbling up on the inside of me. I told the devil again that I knew my brother would be saved because I had taken the Name of Jesus and had broken his power over Dub's life. I had claimed Dub's deliverance and salvation. That happened on Tuesday and again on Thursday.

The next week, I got a letter from my wife saying that Dub had been saved. I wrote her back and told her that I had known it for two or three weeks. It wasn't news to me.

Stay in the Arena of Faith!

The Name of Jesus belongs to you too. That Name has authority on earth. You have a right to use that Name just as much as I do or anyone else does. However, if the devil can hold you in the thought arena, the arena of reasoning, he'll whip you. But if you can hold him in the arena of faith, then he's defeated. *"Fight the good fight of faith . . ."* (1 Tim. 6:12).

1 PETER 5:8,9
8 Be sober, be vigilant; because your adversary the devil, as a roaring lion, walketh about, seeking whom he may devour:
9 Whom resist stedfast IN THE FAITH....

Another translation says, "Whom resist stedfast in your faith." *You* are to resist the adversary in *your* faith. You have to believe in your own heart — with your own spirit — that what the Word says about Jesus is true and that what the Word says about the devil is true. You have authority over him in the Name of Jesus.

The devil will try to fight you though. When I broke his power over Dub's life, using the Name of Jesus, the devil tried my faith. He tried to get me into the thought realm. Satan tried to pull me into the arena of thought and reasoning. He tried to get me to think that Dub wouldn't ever be saved. That's how many people try to solve their problems — with their minds. Then they get all confused. They're worried practically to death, and they continually fret and are anxious.

Your heart is your spirit. You should believe God's Word with your spirit, from inside you, and then shut your mind off to doubt and unbelief and thoughts that are contrary to the Word of God, and believe with your heart. Act from the inside of you, from your heart. Jesus said, *". . . whosoever shall say . . . and shall not doubt in his heart . . ."* (Mark 11:23). This is the principle that is involved in believing God and receiving answers to prayer.

The same year that Dub got saved, I was preaching in Port Arthur, Texas, in a Full Gospel church. We had people coming to the meetings from nearly all the churches in the area. Many exciting things were happening by the Spirit of God. For instance, eighty people were filled with the Holy Ghost, and more than one hundred responded to the altar call, and there were also many healings.

The Authority in the Name of Jesus
To Bring Healing and Deliverance

In one of the meetings, a Methodist woman came forward to thank me for teaching the Word of God. She had been sick for twenty years and hadn't been able to do her own housework. She hadn't been able to get up in the mornings and cook breakfast. She was forty-seven years of age. The doctors hadn't been able to help her.

She had been to many healing meetings but had failed to receive healing. In my meetings, she said she finally understood how to receive her healing.

I went my way, and sometime later I received a letter from this woman. She sent me an offering, saying she wanted to be a part in helping others as she had been helped. She reminded me of what she had told me before and said she was grateful for what she had learned about the Word. She had not known the importance of studying and meditating on the Word. But now she knew the importance of the Name of Jesus and that she, too, could use that Name.

In the privacy of her own home, she did just what I had taught and looked up the scriptures and took notes on them. Then lifting her Bible to heaven she said, "Satan, you who have bound my body for all these years, I break your power over my life, and I claim my deliverance and my healing."

She said she was forty-seven years old and for the first time in twenty years or more, she was doing all of her own housework. She could get up and cook breakfast for her husband, and she said she never felt better!

After six or seven months, she was still well and healed. She said she had the vigor and vitality of a teenager and had not felt that good since she was sixteen. She felt full of life.

Then she said in her letter that her husband had never been saved. Although he was a wonderful husband, he would never go to church with her. In the privacy of her own home, she said, "In the Name of the Lord Jesus Christ, I break the power of the devil over my husband and claim his deliverance and salvation." She said it was amazing how it worked! Her husband was saved and they were happier than they had ever been.

This couple had two daughters who were about twenty years of age. Since her husband had never gone to church, their daughters hadn't gone either. They were grown, single girls still living at home. She said she knew they were doing things they shouldn't do; both of them smoked and danced. She said that in the privacy of her own home, she again meditated on the authority in the Name of Jesus, and then in Jesus' Name broke the power of the devil over the lives of her two daughters. She claimed their salvation and deliverance.

Within ten days' time, that woman's daughters became new creatures in Christ. They were born again. She said they were delivered and set free from every habit that bound them. Their eternal home had now become heaven.

The Spirit of God said to me once, "The mighty Name, the Name of the Mighty One belongs unto the Church and unto the child of God. Now use your lips to speak forth that Name, for that Name carries authority in heaven and on earth and under the earth, among men, angels, and demons. And they shall obey your voice in that Name."

So pray to the Father in the Name of Jesus as you make petitions for yourself and for others. And in the power of the mighty Name of Jesus, bind the works of the enemy and set free those who have been held captive in spiritual darkness. Remember, the Name of Jesus is the key, and God has given that key to *you!*

Questions For Study

1. How can we ensure that our prayers reach the Throne of God?

   _____

   _____

2. What is the only way we should approach God in prayer?

   _____

   _____

3. How can your joy be full _before_ you see the answer to your prayer?

   _____

   _____

4. What is one way to guarantee that you will experience continual joy?

   _____

   _____

5. Why is it so important to follow biblical teaching on prayer?

   _____

   _____

6. What is the difference between praying for Jesus' sake and in His Name?

   _____

   _____

7. How can you get the revelation of God's Word in your heart?

   _____

   _____

8. Name two things believers can do through their authority in the Name of Jesus.

   _____

   _____

9. What is the principle involved in believing God and receiving answers to prayer?

   _____

   _____

10. Who does the mighty Name of Jesus belong to?

   _____

   _____

Chapter 4

Praying in Jesus' Name — Part 2

And IN THAT DAY ye shall ask me nothing. Verily, verily, I say unto you, Whatsoever ye shall ask the Father IN MY NAME, he will give it you.

Hitherto have ye asked nothing in my name: ask, and ye shall receive, that your joy may be full.
— John 16:23,24

I'm talking about prayer secrets or keys that unlock answers to our prayers. Notice that Jesus said, *"And in that day ye shall ask me nothing . . ."* (John 16:23). Jesus said this just before He went to the Cross. He was speaking of the day in which we now live under the New Covenant. Jesus is now our Mediator, our Intercessor, and our Lord (Heb. 8:6; 9:15; 12:24; 7:25; Phil. 2:9-11). He stands between the Father and us.

Jesus said, *". . . in that day. . . ,"* referring to the day of the New Covenant when He would ratify a new and better covenant with His own blood. You see, the New Covenant or Testament was not yet in force when Jesus spoke these words because the blood of Jesus had not yet been shed for the remission of sins. The New Testament couldn't be put into effect until Jesus entered into the Holy of Holies with His own blood. He had to obtain an eternal redemption for us (Heb. 9:12).

When Jesus was here on earth, He personally told his disciples these things we read in John chapter 16 about using His Name. When Jesus was on the earth, the disciples could ask Him questions and talk to Him personally. But in John 16:23 Jesus was talking about another day. Another translation reads, "In that day you shall not pray to Me. But whatsoever you shall ask the Father *in My Name*, he will give it you."

JOHN 16:23,24 (*Amplified*)

23 And when that time comes, you will ask nothing of Me — you will need to ask Me no questions. I assure you, most solemnly I tell you, that My Father will grant you whatever you ask in My name [presenting all I AM].

24 Up to this time, you have not asked a [single] thing in My name [that is, presenting all I AM] but now ask and keep on asking and you will receive, so that your joy (gladness, delight) may be full and complete.

We are to pray to the Father in the Name of the Lord Jesus.

Discovering Hindrances to Prayer

When we are praying and believing God, and we don't get answers to our prayers, we need to find out what is hindering our prayers and correct the problem.

Now, personally, for more than fifty-five years I have never asked God for anything for myself that I didn't receive the answer. I usually receive my answer immediately except for such things as finances, for instance, which might take a few days to come in.

However, if someone else asks me to pray for his needs, then that means his will also comes into the picture. The Bible says we have to be able to agree *together* (Matt. 18:19). That person's will can override my will and block my faith for him. You see, we have authority over demons and evil spirits in our own lives, but we don't have authority over human spirits. If we had authority over human spirits, then we could make everyone get saved.

So there's no such thing as my pushing something over on another person in prayer without that person's cooperation. The Lord hears me, but that person's unbelief can nullify my faith when it comes to praying about something in *his* life.

Many times when I pray for people, particularly when it comes to healing, I know by the Holy Spirit what is standing between them and the answer to their prayers. If the Holy Spirit tells me to, I speak to the people I am praying for and tell them what is hindering them in their prayers.

In one of John G. Lake's books, Lake relates a story that is an example of how prayer can be hindered. Lake tells of a man he prayed for who had sugar diabetes.

The man had come to Dr. Lake's office and had asked for prayer. They got down to pray, but soon Lake got up off his knees and told the man to get up.

Lake asked the man about the $5,000 that kept coming up before Lake in his spirit. The man told Lake how he and his brother had been in business together years ago. When his brother died, his brother's wife wanted him to liquidate the business. He did, but since he felt he had put a lot of time into the business, he kept back $5,000 of her money.

Lake asked the man if he had $5,000 in the bank, and the man said he had much more than that. Lake told him to write a check out to his sister-in-law for $5,000 and then he would pray for him. The man wrote out the check and went down the street and mailed it. When he came back, he was healed.

Now, it won't happen exactly that way with everyone. But in this case, Lake could not pray for that man and get him healed because something this man had done was nullifying the effects of his own prayer.

One Hindrance to Prayer: Praying to Jesus Instead of to the Father *in Jesus' Name*

I have a friend who at one time had a real struggle in the area of prayer. He had been in the ministry for years, but he wasn't receiving answers to any of his prayers.

This minister friend of mine was older than I was and had also been in the ministry longer. But he talked to me about his problem of not receiving answers to his prayers, because he knew I always received what I asked for in prayer. He was confused about what he was doing wrong.

I had observed in being with this minister and hearing him pray that he always prayed *to* Jesus, instead of to the Father in Jesus' Name. So I told him that praying to *Jesus* was not how the Bible instructs us to pray. I told him that I always pray to the *Father* in the Name of Jesus, for that was how Jesus said we are to pray: *". . . in that day ye shall ask me nothing. Verily, verily, I say unto you, Whatsoever ye shall ASK THE FATHER in my name, he will give it you"* (John 16:23).

Someone might say, "I believe that verse, but. . . ." There is not a "but" in that verse, so don't put one in. There's not an "if" in that verse either, so don't put one in. Remember, *Jesus* said those words, so just take Him at His Word!

When we don't pray according to how the Bible teaches us to pray, we can block God's answer to our prayers. This minister had been praying to Jesus instead of to the Father in Jesus' Name, and it had hindered his prayers from being answered.

Ask and You *Shall* Receive

JOHN 16:24
24 Hitherto have ye asked nothing in my name: ASK, AND YE SHALL RECEIVE, that your joy may be full.

The word "hitherto" means *up till now — until this time*. People did not pray in Jesus' Name while Jesus was still here on the earth. It wouldn't have done any good: *"Hitherto* [up till this time] *have ye asked nothing in my name: ask, and ye shall receive, that your joy may be full"* (John 16:24). Your joy couldn't be full with needs unmet. Your joy couldn't be full if you couldn't pay your rent. Your joy couldn't be full if your children were sick.

Of course, after your children grow up, they're on their own as far as developing their own faith is concerned. They will have to use their own faith; you can't carry them then on your faith. But as long as they're small, you can pray the prayer of faith for them, and they'll receive their healing. My children were always healed when I prayed for them. My son had the mumps once for forty-five minutes. But the Lord healed him.

This happened years ago. We were holding a meeting in Port Arthur, Texas. One evening the telephone rang just after 6:00 in the evening. My wife was with me, and her mother was at home with our children. My mother-in-law called and asked me what she should do with our son, Ken; he had the mumps. She said his jaws were swollen, and he was running a fever.

I told my mother-in-law that God would heal him. She said he had been crying all afternoon (he was about eleven or twelve years old). I told her to call Ken to the phone. She did, and he told me that he had told his grandmother that if she would call me, I would pray for him and God would heal him. I assured him that God would heal him. I told him that the minute we hung up, I would kneel down and pray for him and God would heal him.

Then I told his grandma what we were going to do. She told us later that he lay on her bed and went to sleep immediately. She let him sleep awhile, and after forty-five minutes, she woke him and told him to put his pajamas on and get in his own bed. When he awakened, he noticed that his jaws weren't swollen anymore and his fever was gone. From that minute on he was all right and never did have the mumps again.

God hears and answers prayers. You might as well settle that. The Word works. Too much of the time people just make a little stab in the dark at praying. They call it praying, and then they let it go. In other words, they just *hope* something will work out some way or somehow. But we need to firmly take our stand on God's Word and let heaven, hell, and the earth know that God's Word is true and that we believe it.

It Makes a Difference How We Pray

Some people say that how one ends his prayers doesn't make a lot of difference, but it does because you can't plead your case scripturally before the

Father based on the words, "for Jesus' *sake*." But you can plead your case based on the words, "in Jesus' Name." And if it makes no difference, Jesus wouldn't have told us to pray that way.

But Jesus told us that we are to pray to the Father in His Name (John 16:23). If we say that this scripture isn't important, we might as well say that other scriptures in the Bible aren't important. But *all* of God's Word is important. In fact, God's Word says, *"Heaven and earth shall pass away, but my words shall not pass away"* (Matt. 24:35).

For example, Jesus spoke the words in John 3:16 too. Since John 3:16 is true, these words in John 16:23 are just as true. I know God has helped us many times when we didn't know any better, but we ought to be able to grow in the areas of faith and prayer. Many times God condescends to meet us where we are spiritually, but it is better when we can grow up spiritually and meet God on His level, which is praying in faith according to His Word.

Growing Up Spiritually Includes Growing in Prayer

Some Christians never think about growing spiritually. But the Bible teaches us that there is a similarity between physical growth and spiritual growth. The Word of God says that as newborn spiritual babies, we are to desire the sincere milk of the Word (1 Peter 2:2).

In the natural, no one is born a full-grown human being. People are born as babies and then they grow up. In much the same way, no one is born a full-grown Christian. The Bible says Christians are born as newborn babes and then they are to grow up (Eph. 4:13).

Therefore, we ought to be able to improve on our praying. You've improved in many things physically since you were a baby, haven't you? For example, you're not still on the bottle. You've matured since babyhood, both physically and mentally. Some might mature more mentally than others; but at least we can say we've matured physically.

When I was a child, I used to pray, "Now I lay me down to sleep . . ." But I don't pray that way anymore. I've grown beyond that. When we were spiritual babes we might have prayed certain ways, but God wants us to grow spiritually. So God may have met us and helped us, but it makes a lot of difference when we can meet God on His level — according to His Word.

Actually, God will require more of the Body of Christ in these present days than He did even a few years ago. When light comes and teaching is given, God requires us to walk in the light of what we know. Then we become responsible for what we know.

The Right To Use Jesus' Name

We found out that Jesus gave us the power of attorney, or the right to use His Name. We have a right to use that Name, not only in prayer but in every area of our lives.

We need to witness to people in that Name. The Word of God teaches witnessing. But sometimes in dealing with one's own family, it is most difficult.

Sometimes family members don't want to listen to us because then they'll have to admit that we know more than they do. Sometimes there's a little family pride involved also. So sometimes it is better to let someone else witness to your own family than for you to try to do it, although, you understand, I certainly believe in witnessing.

I was saved on the bed of sickness and I became a Baptist boy preacher and then I received the Holy Ghost and spoke in tongues. My folks felt I had disgraced the whole family because I was fellowshipping with those "tongue-talkers."

In 1937 there was more reproach connected with speaking in tongues than there is today, although in some quarters even today religious prejudices still exist. People become proud of their name, and my family felt that I had disgraced our name.

When I was filled with the Holy Spirit I didn't say one word to my family; I didn't even invite them to go to church with me. I felt in my spirit that if I would just live right and not try to push anything off on them, the reality of the baptism in the Holy Spirit would become obvious to them and they would follow me in this New Testament experience.

And in the course of time, every one of my family members did receive the baptism in the Holy Spirit, including both of my brothers and my sister, and even my nephews and nieces.

Later the folks beyond my immediate family followed me in that experience, too, because they could see the difference in my life. My aunt, my mother's youngest sister, held out the longest. She felt that I had really disgraced her. She was a great church worker, but there is a difference between being a church worker and being a Christian.

In 1950 my aunt came to visit us. I wasn't there, but my mother and my wife were. My aunt said to my mother, "You know, there's just a difference in this home. I get blessed spiritually every time I'm here, and I feel comforted and blessed. There's a peace and a tranquility in this home. I felt that Kenneth had disgraced us, but, you know, I believe he made the right move. I'm going to begin attending his church." And she did.

She also said, "Not only that, but I've watched him over the years. His children are never sick. Other children in the family are ill, but Kenneth's children never have any illness — very seldom even a cold — but nothing more serious than that. Other children in the family have serious illnesses. There's just a difference in this family."

When she said that, I thought of the scripture in First Timothy 4:8: *"For bodily exercise profiteth little: but GODLINESS IS PROFITABLE UNTO ALL THINGS, having promise of the life that now is, and of that which is to come."* If something is profitable, it pays off, doesn't it? Godliness pays off. It is profitable unto all things, paying off in this life and in the life which is to come.

1 TIMOTHY 4:15
15 Meditate upon these things; give thyself wholly to them; that thy profiting may appear to all.

You see, the thing that influenced my aunt and made her begin attending a Full Gospel church (which she had vowed she would never do) was the profiting that she saw in my life.

Dealing With the Devil in Jesus' Name

We discussed the right we have in Jesus' Name to be a witness. We also have a right to use Jesus' Name to exercise authority over the devil and all his works. In Mark 16:17, Jesus said, *". . . In my name shall they cast out devils. . . ."* Thank God, we have power and authority over the devil in the Name of Jesus.

Jesus did not say in this passage of Scripture that this sign would only follow preachers. It is not just ministers, but *all* believers, who have authority over demons in the Name of Jesus. Jesus has given *every* believer *". . . power to tread on serpents and scorpions, and over ALL the power of the enemy . . ."* (Luke 10:19).

Evil spirits *have* to bow to the Name of Jesus, for it is the Name above every other name.

PHILIPPIANS 2:9,10
9 Wherefore God also hath highly exalted him [Jesus], **and given him a name which is above every name:**
10 That at the name of Jesus EVERY KNEE SHOULD BOW, of things [beings] **in heaven, and things** [beings] **in earth, and things** [beings] **under the earth.**

Demons have to go at the mention of that Name. It is the Name that does it. What a treasure we have in the Name of Jesus — and yet how we have failed to utilize what belongs to us. No work of the enemy need ever have dominion in our lives, if we will only exercise the authority we have in the Name of Jesus!

Speaking With Tongues in Jesus' Name

That passage in Mark chapter 16 continues, *". . . In my name . . . they shall speak with new tongues"* (Mark 16:17).

All believers have a right to be filled with the Holy Spirit and to speak with tongues. The Bible says the promise of the baptism in the Holy Spirit is for all those who believe (Acts 2:38,39); therefore speaking in tongues, which is the initial evidence of the Spirit's infilling (Acts 2:4), is also for all those who are born again.

Speaking with tongues does not occur as just one initial experience of being filled with the Holy Ghost, and then it ceases. Speaking with tongues is to be a continual experience for the rest of one's life, an integral part of the believer's devotional prayer life.

Speaking with tongues is also the door into all the other spiritual gifts. I have found in my own life over a period of more than fifty-five years that the more I pray and worship God in tongues, the more manifestation of the other gifts of the Spirit I have in my life too.

God has given us a supernatural means of communication with Him. We should be taking advantage of this precious gift of speaking with tongues. We can do it in Jesus' Name!

Exercising Power and Authority Over Serpents in Jesus' Name

Jesus said, *". . . In my name . . . They shall take up serpents . . ."* (Mark 16:17,18). That doesn't mean that a believer is going to take up serpents and handle them to try to prove something. It means if a believer is accidentally bitten, he can just shake off the serpent and claim immunity in the Name of Jesus. This is not extreme teaching. It's Bible teaching, and it's the truth.

These things are in the Word. As you know, when Paul was shipwrecked on the Island of Melita and was picking up sticks to build a fire, a viper came out and fastened itself on his hand. The people of the island looked at Paul and thought he had done something terrible and was being cursed. They said, "... *No doubt this man is a murderer, whom, though he hath escaped the sea, yet vengeance suffereth not to live*" (Acts 28:4).

They thought the judgment of God had come upon Paul, and they expected him to fall dead. They watched him, and when he didn't get sick and fall dead, they finally decided he must be a god (Acts 28:1-6).

I remember reading in a Pentecostal periodical years ago about a woman who was an Assemblies of God missionary. She was ministering in a foreign country. There was a particular kind of scorpion in that country whose sting was fatal. They had no antidote for the sting in those days and when it stung a person, he or she died; no one had ever been known to live.

One of these deadly scorpions stung this woman missionary. Actually, she was right out on the street when the thing stung her. People watched her and expected her to swell up and die because that's what always happened. But she just shook the scorpion off in the Name of the Lord Jesus Christ. As the people watched her, they saw that she didn't even get sick to her stomach! It made a marvelous impression on those people in that country, and many were saved as a result.

Many years ago a minister friend of mine in east Texas was the pastor of a country church. He and some men, who were sinners, went out fishing. (Their wives were members of the pastor's church and had been praying for their husbands' salvation.)

The pastor and these men were fishing in one of the lakes in east Texas, and as they were grappling for fish, a cotton-mouth moccasin fastened itself onto the pastor's hand. The pastor shook the snake off of his hand, and in the Name of Jesus declared he would suffer no ill effects.

They were way out in the country in the middle of the lake, and it greatly frightened those men who were sinners; they wanted to get him to a doctor in a hurry.

The pastor told the men, "You'd never get me to a doctor in time, anyway." The pastor was not concerned because he knew the authority he had in the Name of Jesus, and he went right on fishing. The men watched him, but that snakebite never did have any effect on him. Friends, this is not extreme. This is the Word of God (Mark 16:18). Every single one of those men got saved as a result of that incident.

Immunity From Poison in Jesus' Name

Mark 16 further says, "... *if they drink any deadly thing, it shall not hurt them* ..." (v. 18). That doesn't mean believers can drink poison just to try to prove something. But it does mean if you *accidentally* drink something that is harmful to you, you have a right to claim immunity in the Name of the Lord Jesus Christ.

A number of years ago, I heard the superintendent of a certain denomination relate an incident that took place at one of their conventions in Corpus Christi, Texas. After the people of this particular denomination began to gather at the convention grounds, some of them began to feel ill. Soon about twenty or thirty of them were very ill, and they began praying for one another.

As they prayed, God revealed to them that the water in one of the hotels was poisoned. In those days, they didn't have running water; they only had a pitcher and bowl in each room on a wash stand. They told the rest of the people not to drink any more of the water. God healed every single person and no one needed to have his stomach pumped.

They took the remaining water to a local lab to have it tested. The doctors in the laboratory told them there was enough poison in the water to kill a regiment of men! It was known that this group of people believed in miracles and healings, and someone was trying to play a deadly trick on them and have a laugh on them. But the laugh was on the trickster because although those believers got sick, none of them died.

God's Word works. These people didn't drink poison to try to prove something; they *accidentally* drank poison. The devil was behind it to try to harm them, but the people innocently drank the water, not knowing what they were drinking.

Under those circumstances, believers have a right to claim immunity in Jesus' Name, according to Mark 16:18. As I said before, this is not extreme teaching. It is in the Word! In fact, Jesus spoke these words!

Laying Hands On the Sick in Jesus' Name

Jesus also said, "... *they shall lay hands on the sick, and they shall recover*" (Mark 16:18).

I want to call your attention to this fact, friends. Everything we have discussed in Mark 16:15-18 is done *in the Name of Jesus*. It is the Name of Jesus that gives us the authority to cast out devils; it is the Name of Jesus that gives us the authority to speak with tongues; it is the Name of Jesus that gives us immunity against poison; it is the Name of Jesus that gives us the authority to lay hands on the sick and have them recover.

There is a little side thought here that is important for you to understand. Notice, Jesus said, *". . . In my name . . . they shall speak with new tongues"* (Mark 16:17). Verse 18 says, *". . . they shall lay hands on the sick, and they shall recover." You* are the one who is to do the laying on of hands, not Jesus, and not the Holy Ghost. You are the one who lays hands on the sick in Jesus' Name.

By the same token, *you* are the one who is to do the talking in tongues. Someone said, "I'm afraid that was just me," referring to receiving the Holy Ghost with the evidence of speaking in tongues. Of course, that is you; you are the one who does the talking in tongues in Jesus' Name! You do the talking in tongues just as you do the laying on of hands for the sick. You do the talking, but the Holy Ghost gives the utterance in tongues. You have a right to speak with other tongues in the Name of Jesus.

The baptism in the Holy Spirit with the evidence of speaking in tongues belongs to every believer, not just to someone especially called to the fivefold ministry. Any child of God has just as much right to use the Name of Jesus against the devil as anyone else, and he can also use the Name in any of these ways I have mentioned.

Don't Struggle for Faith — Use the Authority That Is Yours in Jesus' Name

I want to call your attention to something else. Believers do not need to struggle for faith in using the authority in Jesus' Name. I heard someone say, "If I had enough faith, I could do such and such." Did you notice Jesus never said a word about faith in connection with using His Name? He said, *"And these signs shall follow them that believe; IN MY NAME . . ."* (Mark 16:17).

Jesus didn't say we could use His Name if we had enough faith because believers do have faith! You do believe in the Name of Jesus, don't you? Then just use His Name. Jesus said believers would do those exploits listed in Mark 16:17, because of *His Name —* not if they had enough faith.

You don't have to struggle for faith to use the Name of Jesus. Just exercise the authority that rightfully belongs to you in that Name. Simply take your rights in Christ and boldly use what you know already belongs to you. For instance, according to the laws of our government, you have a right to what legally belongs to you. You don't question, *Do I have enough faith to possess what is already mine?* No, that thought would never enter your mind!

Many of us own automobiles. At the close of a church service, you would not stand up and say, "I have a prayer request. I want you to pray that I'll have enough faith to get in my car and go home." We would laugh about that, but, you know, that wouldn't be any funnier than if someone lifted his hand in church and said he had a terrible headache and wanted folks to pray that he would have enough faith to get his healing.

It would be just as silly to say that as it would be for you to say you wanted faith to get in your car and go home. Or some people say, "I know if I had enough faith I'd get my healing; but I didn't get my healing, so I must not have enough faith."

Acting on What Belongs to You

It's only when one acts on what belongs to him that he gets results. You know your car belongs to you; and you have the title and the keys to prove it. All you have to do is drive the car. It's yours. You don't need faith to drive your own car.

In much the same way, when someone needs healing and he acts on what he knows belongs to him, he is healed!

Not receiving what already belongs to you spiritually would be just about as strange (and it really would be funny if it weren't so pathetic) as it would be for you to want to go to the post office, for example, but then not get in your car and go. And then wonder why you couldn't get to the post office!

But if you didn't act on your ability to go to the post office, you would just be mentally assenting to the fact that you *could* go to the post office. But you wouldn't be *acting* on that knowledge. However, when you act on what you know belongs to you, *then* you will have results. In this case, you will get to the post office!

You see, you can mentally agree that the Bible is so, and you can mentally agree that the Name of Jesus is wonderful, but until you act on and use the Name of Jesus the way the Word of God says to do, you'll not get the desired result or benefits of the authority in that Name.

When we act on the Word, it works. That is the reason James said, *"But be ye doers of the word, and not hearers only, deceiving your own selves"* (James 1:22). In the margin of my Bible it says, "he deludes himself."

We have many self-deluded people who are blaming the devil or someone else for their failures. The truth is they've deluded themselves because they haven't acted on the Word. Actually, it is just a matter of knowing what belongs to you as a believer and then acting on it. It's not struggling to have faith in the Name of Jesus; it's taking your legal right and boldly acting on the authority in that Name. *That* is what brings results. After all, what is yours, is yours to possess and to use, and if you are a believer the Name of Jesus belongs to you.

The Name of Jesus belongs to me just as much as my hands and feet belong to me. In the morning I don't pray for God to give me faith to get up and walk. I just get up and walk because I know my feet are there and that they are mine to use.

Of course, Satan will surely try to withstand you. Certainly, he will because that's his business (John 10:10). Satan will try to withstand you and all of hell will seek to oppose and confuse you. If you think these blessings are just going to fall on you like ripe cherries off a tree, and that you will float through life on flowery beds of ease, you have another thought coming.

Yet, thank God, Jesus' Name is yours! It is yours, so take the blessing God has promised you in His Word and act on it. Many people pray, but the results do not prove that their prayers were of any value. If you do not get results from your praying, then you are failing in your prayer life. If we are not praying for results and expecting results, then there is no need to pray.

Praying for Results

Pray to profit! Great businesses do business in order to profit; they seek to do business in order to make a profit. Industry demands the best technical education and demands that men and women train to do their jobs. We must make a business of prayer. Actually, it is the greatest business there is. It's *God's* business.

Regardless of what some people say, the foundation of this great country *is* Christianity. From a practical side, the essence of Christianity is a living relationship with a living God who hears and answers prayers.

Prayer is of the utmost importance. Just simply talking into the air is not prayer. Taking up twenty minutes on Sunday morning, giving God a homily on what His duties are toward the Church and the local congregation, is not prayer. Or giving the congregation a lecture about the do's and don'ts of the Bible is not prayer. I believe we should pray for *results*. If we pray, and results have not followed, we should immediately seek to find out why we have not received our answer.

Christianity is a supernatural relationship with a supernatural God. If the supernatural is not wrought in our midst and if adverse circumstances aren't changed by the power of God through our prayers, it shows that we simply have the form of godliness without the power (2 Tim. 3:5). All the things that God has and which He has provided for us are offered to us through His Word and through our union with Him. And if we do not have the things in our lives He has freely offered, it may be that we have not made our prayer connection and that we have not appropriated God's promises by faith.

We know that God does hear prayer that is based on the Name of Jesus. You know it and I know it. We have seen many souls saved in answer to prayer. We have seen people's finances helped in answer to prayer. Demons have been cast out by using the mighty Name of Jesus. We have seen the miraculous power of God manifested again and again in our behalf because of that wonderful Name. Thank God, God is still in the same business of saving, healing, and setting people free.

And yet, through the years, I've gone to some churches where not a soul had been saved there for many years. And I'm not necessarily talking about denominational churches; I am talking about Full Gospel churches.

Many times these same people are praying and seeking God, but they go right on praying with no results. But why not just go to the principles of God's Word and find out where the prayer failure is? Is God untrue? No, He is not untrue! Is the day of praying or the day of miracles over? No!

Have we been depending upon the promises of a God who has gone bankrupt? No! Then if we're not receiving answers to prayer, there is something wrong somewhere, isn't there? Is it that we are not known in the bank of heaven? We need to find out where the hindrance in our prayer life is because Jesus stands back of the Word to make it good in our lives. He has become the surety of a new and better covenant than the Old Covenant because it is established upon better promises (Heb. 7:22; 8:6).

The Book of Hebrews tells us, *"By so much was Jesus made a surety of a better testament"* (Heb. 7:22). What does that phrase mean, "a surety of a better testament"? That means that the very throne on which Jesus sits is the authority to back up His Word. From the Book of Matthew through Revelation, Jesus is the surety of a better covenant. Jesus must keep His Word; He cannot go back on it. Yes, He hears and answers prayer!

Miraculous Results Through Prayer
In Jesus' Name

I once read a testimony by I. J. Jamison who was formerly a Presbyterian minister. He had been giving some lectures in a western state when a forest fire broke out in the area. The fire was raging, and valuable timber and animals and some homes were being destroyed. The fire was simply burning out of control.

Rev. Jamison was in the barber shop one morning getting a shave. The barber had put a towel on his face, and as Rev. Jamison was lying there in the chair, a man came in with a telegram. The man with the telegram said he didn't know what to do with the telegram. Someone had sent it around the city. It said, "Pray for rain." The fire had gotten so out of hand that there was no telling what would happen if it didn't rain.

Someone said, "Well, there is a preacher in that chair. Maybe you could give the telegram to him." About that time, the barber raised the chair and took the towel off the preacher's face and asked him if he would pray for rain. Rev. Jamison said, "We don't believe in that sort of thing."

So someone in the barber shop spoke up and said, "Well, there is a little tent meeting going on at the edge of town, and they believe in praying for anything."

Someone asked, "Who are they?"

The answer was, "I don't know. Some of them are 'Holy Rollers.'"

No one would volunteer to take the telegram out to the tent, as they were all afraid of those "Holy Rollers." Rev. Jamison said if no one else would do it, he would. Someone said, "They have a prayer meeting about 10:00 every morning."

So the next morning, Jamison took that telegram out to the tent meeting. He said there were about twenty people there. Three or four of them were kneeling on the platform praying. He didn't know which one was the preacher, but he picked out the one he thought might be and tapped him on the shoulder.

The man looked up and Rev. Jamison said to him, "Here is a prayer request that someone asked me to bring to you." The man took it and read it. Meanwhile, Rev. Jamison backed away from the group just to see what they would do.

Rev. Jamison said the man got up and began to holler for everyone to stop praying. (All the people had been praying all at once, out loud.) He hollered until he got everyone to listen and then he read the prayer request. He asked how many believed God would hear, and they all lifted their hands. So he said, "All right, let's go to prayer about it."

Rev. Jamison said that all twenty of them began to pray and they just prayed up a storm. One by one they ceased, and finally the man said to them, "How many of you believe God heard you?" They all raised their hands.

He said, "Then let's lift both hands and praise God for the answer." They raised their hands and praised God for rain.

Rev. Jamison said later, "That man shocked me." The preacher turned and handed the telegram back to Rev. Jamison and said, "Here, send a telegram back and tell them it will be raining by 10:00 tonight."

Rev. Jamison said, "I went back to town to the barber shop and told them what the man had said."

All the men in the barber shop slapped one another on the back and laughed about it because they had all read the weather report and no rain was in sight for days.

Jamison and his wife were in bed by 9:00 that evening. He said he happened to see the moon shining bright and clear outside. His wife had washed some laundry and had left it hanging on the line. When he saw the clothes on the line, he remembered what that preacher had said about the rain. He began laughing and told his wife what had happened that day. They both lay there and laughed.

He said to her, "You had better get your laundry in because it's going to rain." They both laughed and she said, "I read the evening paper and it's not going to rain." He said they must have talked and laughed about it until about 9:30 or so and then they fell off to sleep.

After a while, Rev. Jamison was awakened by what sounded like thunder. He thought he was hearing things, but then he saw lightning flash, and before he could get out of bed, it began to rain in torrents. He said he got up and turned on the light and it was exactly 10:00 p.m.

Jamison said, "Then I couldn't go to sleep. I thought, *Did God hear those people? Is there something to that? Do they know something I don't know? What about that?*" He began to slip into those Pentecostal meetings after his own services were dismissed, sitting in the very back.

After Jamison finished his lectures in this town he was visiting, he went back to his home state. He would slip over to the little Pentecostal church there at first, and he began sitting on the back row. But he kept sitting closer and closer to the front, until he finally sat on the front row.

He said he took notes on the scriptures and messages and would go home to read in the privacy of his study, and there he discovered the truth of God's Word. He thought, *Why didn't I see the truth before, particularly scriptures on the Holy Ghost?* He continued to go to Pentecostal services, just watching and observing.

There was a woman in this Pentecostal church whose daughter was in a mental institution. Jamison heard the mother talking to several folks about meeting her at a certain time in the morning outside the mental institution.

Jamison said, "I just intruded on their private conversation because I didn't want to miss out on anything. I found out that they were going to meet outside the institution, and that this woman was going to cast the devil out of her daughter. She had about a dozen spiritual women who were going along with her to back her up in prayer.

"I just blurted out, 'Can I come along?' And they replied, 'All right, meet us out there at 10:00 in the morning.'"

Jamison met them there. He said he wondered how all of them were going to get inside the institution. But he said he had been around them long enough to believe that because of their faith in God, they could do just about anything.

The woman told the attendant that she wanted to see her daughter. Jamison related, "We all went parading down the halls." Then the woman said to the guard, "I want you to open the door and let me in that cell because I'm going to pray for my daughter."

The attendant said, "Why, you can't do that! She'll kill you! She's violently insane."

Jamison said they stopped before a padded cell where there was a woman who looked more like an animal than a human. Her hair had grown long, her nails were long and claw-like, and she hissed and spit at them like an animal. The attendant told the woman he couldn't let her into the cell because he would lose his job if he did, but all the time he was unlocking the door! The woman stepped in and he locked the door again.

Rev. Jamison said he and the attendant were the only men there, and they stepped back to watch. The twelve women who had come with them fell on their knees and prayed quietly. They didn't look at what was happening in the cell; they just knelt down and all prayed quietly.

As Jamison and the attendant watched, the daughter backed away and climbed about halfway up that padded wall, then made a leap at her mother like an animal. Her mother sidestepped her and the daughter fell (the daughter was a woman in her early thirties). When her daughter rolled over to get up, the mother jumped on her and held her down and said, "Come out of her, devil, in the Name of Jesus."

Jamison said, "That mother got her nose down within an inch of her daughter's nose, and she said for about ten minutes over and over, 'Come out of her, devil, in the Name of Jesus.'" Suddenly the daughter relaxed, looked up, and said, "Mama! Is that you, Mama?" The daughter threw her arms around her mother's neck and hugged her and kissed her.

Jamison said, "I am a witness to the fact that the authorities dismissed that woman that day as being totally well." Then he said, "Bless God, I want the Holy Ghost. If people can pray like that, I'm a candidate." And, thank God, he was gloriously filled with the Holy Ghost, speaking with other tongues.

Friends, we ought to pray for results! Jesus Christ is the same today, yesterday, and forever (Heb. 13:8). And God our Father never changes (Malachi 3:6). We have access to the Father in the Name of Jesus just as those people did! Our prayers to the Father in the Name of Jesus can be just as effective as those believers' prayers were. So pray for results!

Questions for Study

1. When Jesus taught His disciples about prayer in John 16:23, He used the phrase *". . . in that day . . . ."* What time period was He referring to?

   _____

   _____

2. What is the one hindrance to prayer discussed in this chapter?

   _____

   _____

3. Why shouldn't a mature Christian pray the same way he did as a baby Christian?

   _____

   _____

4. Who has power and authority over the devil in the Name of Jesus?

   _____

   _____

5. Name the five specific areas examined in this chapter in which we have a right to use the Name of Jesus.

   _____

   _____

6. According to Mark 16:17 and 18, under what circumstances do believers have a right to claim immunity from snake bites and poisons in Jesus' Name?

   _____

   _____

7. As important as faith is to the believer, Jesus didn't say we needed faith to use His Name. Why is that?

   _____

   _____

8. When will you reap the benefits of the authority in the Name of Jesus?

   _____

   _____

9. If you pray, and results have not followed, what should you do?

   _____

   _____

10. In Hebrews 7:22, what does the phrase "a surety of a better testament" mean?

    _____

    _____

Chapter 5

Praying for Results

And in that day ye shall ask me nothing. Verily, verily, I say unto you, Whatsoever ye shall ask the Father in my name, he will give it you.

Hitherto have ye asked nothing in my name: ask, and ye shall receive, that your joy may be full.

— John 16:23,24

As I discussed in previous chapters, prayer should be addressed to the Father in the Name of the Lord Jesus Christ. We are to pray to the Father *in the Name of Jesus.*

Also, we're not to pray for Jesus' sake. We found that out. And we know we are not to pray just to be praying. We are to pray for *results.* If results do not follow our prayers, then our prayer life is a failure, and we need to find out why our prayers are not being answered.

Examples of Praying for Results

I remember reading an account by Dr. Charles Price. He said someone had phoned him and asked him if he would come to the hospital. He ordinarily didn't do that because he usually didn't have the time. But this person who was in the hospital had been a friend of his in days gone by; this was a woman who had been converted under his ministry.

He went to the hospital to visit her and found that she was dying of cancer. Dr. Price was there when the physician came, and Dr. Price told the woman he was going to go home and pray for her. The woman's physician heard Dr. Price say that. Outside the hospital room, Dr. Price and the physician talked, and the physician told Dr. Price he'd better pray because it would be just a few hours before the woman would be gone. The physician then said that he believed in prayer and that he knew it would soothe the woman's mind and calm her down and prepare her for what was ahead.

Dr. Price told the doctor he wasn't going to pray just to prepare her for death! She already had peace because she was a believer. He said he was going to pray that she would be healed. The doctor looked at him as if he had been slapped with a wet dish rag. Dr. Price then went back into the room and laid hands on the woman and prayed, and she was healed and raised up! Dr. Price was praying for *results.* We should pray for results too.

I remember reading from the pen of P. C. Nelson, who was a Baptist minister for a great number of years. Actually, thirty of his fifty-two years of ministry were spent as a Baptist.

Nelson had a wonderful testimony of healing. In 1921 he was run over by an automobile in Detroit, Michigan. The doctor said Rev. Nelson would lose his leg or else it would be stiff for the rest of his life. But Nelson was healed. Then he held healing meetings across the nation for different denominational churches.

P. C. Nelson was once holding a meeting in Arkansas for the Baptists and was praying for the sick. A pastor of another Baptist church in the state who had gone to seminary with Dad Nelson heard that he was in the area, so he decided to go and hear this new "doctrine" of healing Rev. Nelson was teaching. The Baptist pastor went to the meeting and was very much opposed to what Nelson was teaching. The Baptist pastor talked about it at home and aroused the curiosity of his family. They had never heard anything like it, so he took the family to Nelson's meeting, including his mother who was living with them.

The next morning at the breakfast table, this Baptist family was again discussing what Dad Nelson was teaching about healing. This pastor thought it was all right to pray for someone, but he thought it shouldn't be done publicly. He didn't think they should have a healing line; and if they did pray, they should just pray that the will of the Lord be done. His wife and some of the older children agreed with him. But his mother said that she wouldn't criticize what Rev. Nelson was teaching.

Finally the five-year-old son, who was the baby of the family, spoke up and said, "Well, Dad, the only difference I can see is that we pray in our church on Sunday morning, 'Lord, bless the sick,' and don't expect anything, but that man prays for them in front of everyone and expects God to heal them right then."

That got this pastor to thinking, so he went over and began to attend the meetings. He began to really listen to the teachings, and he began to understand that believers ought to pray for results. That's true, isn't it? What's the use of praying, if we're not praying for results! Thank God, God does hear and answer prayer. He *wants* to hear and answer your prayers.

Remind God of His Promises

God didn't put all of the promises and all of the statements relative to prayer in the Bible just to fill up space! They are there for our benefit. They are for us to use. They are for us to act on. One of the best ways in the world to pray is to just follow the admonition and instruction of God's Word.

ISAIAH 43:25,26
25 I, even I, am he that blotteth out thy transgressions for mine own sake, and will not remember thy sins.
26 PUT ME IN REMEMBRANCE. . . .

In other words, remind God of what He said in His Word. Those who have been mighty in prayer have always been those who have come before God and have reminded Him of His promises and of His Word.

I suppose Charles G. Finney was one of the most outstanding exponents of prayer who ever lived. He is known as the man who prayed down revivals. As far as church history is concerned, he had the greatest success concerning converts of any other minister since the days of the Early Church. Supposedly, more people remained saved under his ministry after conversion than in any point in history since the days of the evangelistic journeys of the Apostle Paul. Whole cities were stirred because of Charles Finney's prayers.

For instance, I read in his autobiography that in 1829, Finney went to Rochester, New York, and conducted a meeting, and practically everyone in town got saved. All of the honky-tonks and beer joints were closed down. There wasn't a place in town left where one could buy anything alcoholic to drink. Nearly everyone in town had to have gotten saved in order for that to happen.

The only theater in town closed up. Vaudeville was popular then, but there was no need to put on a show if no one went to the theater! There was such a move of God that when the circus came to town, there was only one performance and only two people showed up! The circus had to close down and leave town. Everyone was interested in God. The revival was on. The people just weren't interested in anything else. You can learn something from a fellow like Finney.

I also read from Finney's autobiography that he was a Presbyterian minister and then a Congregationalist. When Finney was a Presbyterian, he was holding a meeting sponsored by the Presbyterian church. He told about going to another place in New York to preach in a Presbyterian church on a Sunday afternoon.

Finney had been talking for about fifteen minutes when suddenly the power of God fell on him, and four hundred people fell off their seats onto the floor (there were more than four hundred people present). They fell to the floor under the power of God. Finney hadn't seen that happen before. He found out that all four hundred people had gotten saved; they had all been sinners.

I also read about George Whitefield. He came over from England to preach and held street meetings. He was preaching on the square in Boston, Massachusetts, and because the crowds were large, some would climb up in trees to be able to see. Whitefield would tell them to come down out of the trees when he preached, because if the power of God did come down, they might fall out of the trees. He was Methodist, and many were saved in his meetings. This was old-time Methodist preaching.

These were men who knew how to pray for results! They made prayer their business for the glory of God. For example, when you read about Finney, you find that he was a real man of prayer. I read in his autobiography years ago, and he said that he'd had some experiences in prayer that alarmed him. (I wish we could say in the same way Finney meant it that we had experiences in prayer that alarmed us!)

What Finney meant was that many times in prayer, he found himself saying to the Lord, "Lord, You don't think that we're not going to have revival here do you! You don't think that Thou couldst withhold Thy blessings. You said in Your Word to ask and it would be given us."

Finney said he found himself telling the Lord what the Lord had said in His Word. He found himself telling the Lord that He was obligated to perform His Word because He had said it. The following is an excerpt from something Finney said, and it shows us that Finney prayed for results, basing his petitions firmly on the promises in God's Word.

> I was constrained to pray without ceasing. [I could not rest in the house and was obliged to retire to the barn frequently through the day, where I would unburden my soul and pour out my heart to God in prayer. I had wonderful faith given to me at that time, and had some experiences that alarmed me. When alone I would wrestle and struggle, and my faith would rise till I would say to God] that He had made a promise to answer prayer, and I could not, and would not, be denied.

[I could be so burdened as to use such strong language to God in prayer.] I felt so certain that He would hear me, and that faithfulness to His promises, and to himself, rendered it impossible that He should not hear and answer, that frequently I found myself saying to Him, "I hope Thou dost not think that I can be denied. I come with Thy faithful promises in my hand, and I cannot be denied."[1]

You can see how necessary it is to find scriptures that cover your case. If you don't know what God's Word has to say about a situation, you can't put Him in remembrance of His promises. If God wants us to put Him in remembrance, then put Him in remembrance! He's asked us to do so, so let's do it.

ISAIAH 43:26
26 PUT ME IN REMEMBRANCE: let us plead together: declare thou, that thou mayest be justified.

We are certainly facing great need everywhere. People are dying because of their lack of knowledge about Jesus. The sick are needing healing. The weak are needing strength. What is our part in this mighty prayer life?

Are you doing what He wants you to do? Is your life right with God? Does your heart condemn you? If so, get right with Him now. Thank God, it doesn't take very long. He said that *"If we confess our sins, he is faithful and just to forgive us . . . and to cleanse us from all unrighteousness"* (1 John 1:9). Then whatever it is you're praying about, pray through to victory by faith in God's Word.

Praying for Finances in the Name of Jesus

If you're praying for money, let me say it again, bind Satan over your finances and command the money to be loosed in the Name of Jesus. You are to command money to be loosed because the money you want or need is here on this earth. God is not a counterfeiter; He's not going to make money and send it down from heaven. All the money is here in this realm.

God put all the silver and the gold (Haggai 2:8), and the cattle upon a thousand hills (Ps. 50:10), and the world and the fullness thereof (Ps. 24:1; 89:11; 50:12) on this earth for you and me. He didn't put it here for the devil and his crowd.

God put it here and then gave Adam dominion over all of it. Then Adam committed high treason and sold out to the devil, and the devil became the god of this world (2 Cor. 4:4). Actually, Adam had dominion (Gen. 1:26-30), but he sold out to Satan and now Satan is the god of this world. The devil is the one who is controlling the finances on the earth.

But, thank God, Jesus came and defeated the devil. Jesus gave us the right to use His Name. If you want deliverance, the Bible tells you how to obtain it. The Lord taught me this.

I was poverty-stricken and my nose was to the grindstone. I began to see this truth, and the Lord told me never to pray for money anymore. In other words, I was not to ask God to give me money. He said that He would *not* send it from heaven; it is already down here on earth. He said that in the Name of Jesus, I should command the money I need to come to me, because it is already here in this earth.

Jesus said that whatever amount of money I needed or wanted, I should claim. It's Satan, the god of this world, who is trying to withhold money from us. But God has said that He wanted His children to have the best. He said His Word declares *"If ye be willing and obedient, ye shall eat the good of the land"* (Isa. 1:19). God says in His Word that He would give good gifts (Matt. 7:11; James 1:17).

We need to realize the principles by which God works. He has given us the Name of Jesus to use. The Lord told me He was not the one who was withholding finances from me. He said He wasn't the one who wanted me to be poverty-stricken and to go through life without anything. He said He wouldn't be the right kind of Father if He wanted this for His children. He said that even any sinner who has a heart is concerned about his children. Even an animal is concerned about his offspring.

The Lord said He would be out of step with His whole creation if He wanted less than the best for His children. He said there never was an earthly parent who desired to do more for his children than He did for His children. But He said most of His children wouldn't cooperate with Him.

God told me to command the devil to take his hands off my finances. You see, God can't do anything for believers if we don't cooperate with Him. And we can't pray for God to do something when we are not doing our part by standing in our place of authority in the earth — in the Name of Jesus.

You see, if we just pray for the Lord to do everything, when God is actually waiting on us to stand in our place of authority with the Name of Jesus, then we are putting all the responsibility on God. That is not where the responsibility is. *We* have a part to play because through Jesus Christ deliverance has already been obtained for us. Now we are to stand in our authority against the devil and against circumstances which do not line up with God's Word. God will do *His* part, but we must do *our* part.

I immediately began to do what the Lord said to do, and from that day to this, I never prayed anymore about money. I just always tell Satan to take his hands off of my money, and I claim whatever amount of money I need in the Name of Jesus. You see, when I am standing in my place of authority in that Name, then I am doing my part. (For further study, *see* Rev. Kenneth E. Hagin's minibook *How God Taught Me About Prosperity*).

Angels Are Ministering Spirits
For Believers

HEBREWS 1:14
14 Are they not all ministering spirits, sent forth to minister for them who shall be heirs of salvation?

Angels are ministering spirits that are sent to minister for those who are heirs of salvation. The word "to minister" means *to wait on* or *to serve*. I used to think that Hebrews 1:14 said that the angels would minister *to* those who were heirs of salvation. But, actually, it says angels minister *for* the heirs of salvation. That means that angels — ministering spirits — wait on or serve those who are heirs of salvation. If you go into a restaurant, a waitress waits on you and serves you. This is an illustration the Lord once gave me while I was praying in the Spirit.

Actually, I had a vision and saw an angel. I asked the Lord who it was. He said it was my angel. He related what His Word says about the time He was on the earth and some families brought their children to Him to be blessed.

The disciples thought Jesus was tired, so they rebuked the parents. *"But Jesus said, Suffer little children, and forbid them not, to come unto me: for of such is the kingdom of heaven"* (Matt. 19:14; Mark 10:14; Luke 18:16). Then Jesus said that the children's angels were ever before His Father's face (Matt. 18:10). He told me that just because you grow up, you don't lose your angel.

Jesus also said if Christians, those who are heirs of salvation, would learn to read and study the Bible, they could put their angels to work for them according to God's Word.

Jesus said the angel of the Lord told Philip to go to Gaza (Acts 8:26). And the angel of the Lord appeared to Paul when he was on board a ship (Acts

27:23). The Lord had been talking to me about prosperity when He told me this.

So, the Lord told me to say, "Ministering spirits, go and cause the money to come in Jesus' Name." I've been doing this ever since and it has been working because there is authority in the Name of Jesus — authority that the Church has yet to fully utilize!

Pray Specifically
When Praying for People

Once you get the revelation of prayer, life will be so different for you. If you're praying for souls, stand on God's Word until you see the answer. Prayer is the life of the Church. I challenge you as a Christian to give yourself to prayer. I believe we are only in the beginning of the prayer conquest — (the great prayer fight of faith) that is to end this dispensation. I believe that.

Learn the secret of intercessory prayer — praying for the lost and backslidden. Pray for men and women by name. Don't just lump them together and put them into a group. Don't just pray that God will save souls; actually, praying like that is not scriptural because God has already done that through Jesus' redemption at the Cross. Claim people's salvation and pray for the Lord of the harvest to send laborers to them (Matt. 9:38; Luke 10:2). Claim a harvest of souls in specific countries. Pray for people by name if you can. Call out their names to God and claim their souls in the Name of Jesus.

In the last church I pastored, we had a unique prayer meeting. I told my congregation that when they came to church the following Thursday night, I wanted them to write on a piece of paper the name of the person they most wanted to get saved.

If it was a couple, they were to write down both names. If the person had never been saved, they were to put a small letter "s" beside the name. If the person was a backslider, they were supposed to leave the space beside the name blank. They were to bring this piece of paper with them on Thursday night.

We didn't have very many severe winters in east Texas, but a "norther" (a strong north wind or storm) blew in that week and it rained and then the rain turned into snow and sleet. By Thursday there were four or five inches of snow and sleet on the ground.

The highway department was encouraging people to stay off the streets unless it was an emergency, so I didn't expect anyone to come. It was hazardous to get out on the roads, and there was no equipment to remove the sleet. Nonetheless nineteen people came to church that night. A couple of families lived close enough they could walk to church.

We took all the names and put them in the offering plate, mixed the names up, and then passed the plate around so each one could take out a name. I drew one and spoke out the name, then asked everyone to stand. Then I quoted God's Word: *". . . if two of you shall agree on earth as touching any thing that they shall ask, it shall be done for them of my Father which is in heaven"* (Matt. 18:19).

As I drew out each name, I told the people I was going to pray for that particular person to be saved during the meeting. (I had asked people not to put in the names of those who lived far away. I was wanting people to be saved during the meeting, although we were concerned about and would pray for other folks later.)

I asked everyone to listen intently to what I was about to pray and then to agree with it. I asked that no one pray out loud except me so people could hear me well enough to agree with me. When I finished my prayer, the people agreed with it out loud. I told them to lift their hands and thank God that the person we had just prayed for was saved.

Then I told the people not to pray for that person anymore; but if they thought about it, they should say that the matter was already settled and the prayer was answered, and they should thank God for the answer. We went right down through the list of names, praying for each one by name. Sometimes just one person would pray out loud, and other times we would all join in and pray together.

All but two of the people for whom we prayed that night got saved during that meeting! I never had that much success in praying for souls in my life. I began to see the power in the prayer of agreement, and I began to get ahold of a few prayer secrets.

This happened in 1948. In 1954 at a camp meeting where I was preaching, I saw a woman who had been in my church. Her husband had not been saved but was one for whom we had prayed that night at church. (All the others for whom we had prayed, had gotten saved within a month's time except for the two I mentioned. Those two were saved before a year was out. We had a one-hundred-percent batting average on that prayer meeting!)

After the camp meeting service, the woman and her husband came up to talk to me. The husband said he wanted to hug my neck because he was my brother now. I told him I had heard he had gotten saved.

He had gotten saved the next year after that prayer meeting in 1949. Then his wife spoke up and said she had told her pastor at the church where they were now attending about that prayer meeting, and that pastor said he had never heard of anything like it! I was glad to see those folks and to know that our prayers worked because they were based securely on God's Word.

So pray for men and women by name. Don't just group them together. Also, pray for ministers; don't criticize them. God knows that it's hard for ministers in this day to stand before their congregations without suffering persecution.

It's sometimes hard to face the criticism that those in the ministry face. The same spirit that's in the world will try to creep into the local church, and come against Christian folks.

So pray; don't criticize. Criticism won't get the job done. Praying will. Pray for Christian workers as well. And as you pray for others, the dew of heaven will fall upon your own soul. Praise God, that's the truth!

God's Word Does Not Fail

When we come to God according to God's Word, God's Word does not fail. Jesus said if two of us would agree on earth as touching anything we ask, it would be done (Matt. 18:19). Did Jesus say it, or did He *not* say it?

MATTHEW 18:19
19 Again I say unto you, That if two of you shall agree on earth as touching any thing that they shall ask, IT SHALL BE DONE FOR THEM of my Father which is in heaven.

Jesus didn't say it *might* be done. He didn't say there was *a possibility* that it could be done. He didn't say if it was the will of God, it would be done. He said it *would* be done. Of course, you won't get any results unless you're praying according to His will.

Years ago when I first went out into field ministry, I was preaching in west Texas. The meeting ran for six weeks, right up until Christmastime. The pastor had said to me, "Brother Hagin, how are you scheduled?" I told him I was supposed to start another meeting right before Christmas. He asked me to stay longer.

The pastor said the church made a big payment every year in December on their property. They did it then because most of the people in the church were farmers and they always had more income at harvest time.

Every Sunday night in December, they took up an offering for the property and he said if I did stay, they would have to take up an offering on the mortgage first, and then they would take up my offering. The pastor said he knew I would be needing extra money for Christmas, but he couldn't give me any more than I had been getting. He also said it was doubtful the meeting would run as good as it had been running.

But he finally said that if I did stay, he would at least guarantee me as much as I had been getting. So I told him I would stay on those conditions. I told him to go ahead and take the special offering first, and then they could take my offering separately. I told him I would do the believing, and he could do the acting in faith by taking up the offering, and we would receive the needed money.

Then I wrote to my wife, and I told her I was going to stay longer. I told her that on the next Sunday afternoon I wanted her to open her Bible to Matthew 18:19, and I would do the same thing where I was. I told her to lay her hands on the Bible and say, "Lord, my husband and I claim so much money," and I would do the same where I was. We claimed fifty percent more than I had been getting previously because we needed extra money for Christmas and for the time following the Christmas holidays.

The Sunday night the pastor received the offering, I got three dollars more than we had agreed on. The next week, I wrote to my wife and asked her to pray again on the following Sunday afternoon as she had before. We claimed the same amount that week and received $1.49 above what we had asked for.

Then on the last Sunday night before Christmas, the church sponsored a Christmas program, and afterwards I preached my message. They took up an offering for me, and later at the parsonage the pastor asked me how much I had received that week. I told him I didn't know. He said the ushers probably forgot to count it.

We found the offering plates and the money hadn't been counted, so we took it over to the parsonage and started counting it. The pastor had half of it and I had the other half. We totaled it up, and he said that I didn't get as much that week — the offering was about $20 short.

But my wife and I had already claimed the entire amount, so I told him it had to be there. I told him that my wife and I had agreed on Matthew 18:19 for a certain amount, and that if our prayer based on God's Word didn't work, then I would have to go to every church where I had preached on the subject and tell them that Jesus is a liar and the Bible isn't so. I'm just that honest.

I don't mean to imply that you're to expect the blessings of God to just fall on you like ripe cherries off a tree, because there are some times when you're going to have to stand your ground in faith on God's Word. You have to stand your ground against the devil.

Anyway, the pastor said that we must have missed it. But I told him I didn't miss it because God's Word never fails! So we counted the offering again.

If a bank is out of balance, they're going to have to find out where the shortage is. Even if they're just a little bit off, they'll spend time and money trying to figure out where the shortage is because that kind of accuracy is important.

Then I happened to remember that this preacher's wife had bought a Bible from me and had paid me for it before church. She had given me an envelope which I had put in my pocket, and I had forgotten about it. She had included $7.50 for the Bible (which was the wholesale price), plus a personal offering for me. She didn't want to record it through the church treasurer as it was a personal offering.

In the envelope was a $25 offering. So I told the pastor I had a $25 offering someone had handed me. After counting that offering, I had about $5 above what my wife and I had claimed. I knew the money had to be there because God's Word works!

Stand your ground on God's Word and declare that it has to be according to the Word. Look the storm in the face like Paul did when he was on that ship. As Paul stood his ground, an angel of the Lord appeared to him and told him their lives would be spared (Acts 27:1-25). Jesus' Word is more sure than the word of an angel. God's written Word is even more sure than the word of an angel.

Look the storm in the face in the Name of Jesus! Look contradictory circumstances in the face and say as Paul did, ". . . *I believe God, that it shall be even as it was told me*" (Acts 27:25). You'll find out that the devils and demons will limp away in defeat in their attempt to oppose you, and the answer will come. Stand your ground because God hears and answers prayer!

[1] Charles G. Finney, *Answers to Prayer*, ed. Louis Gifford Parkhurst, Jr. (Minneapolis, Minnesota: Bethany House Publishers, 1983), p. 60.

Questions for Study

1. Why did God put all of the promises and statements concerning prayer in the Bible?

   _____

   _____

2. What is one of the best ways to pray?

   _____

   _____

3. What did those who have been mighty in prayer do when they went before God in prayer?

   _____

   _____

4. What did Charles Finney mean when he said that he had some experiences in prayer that alarmed him?

   _____

   _____

5. How should you pray about your finances?

   _____

   _____

6. Who controls the finances on the earth?

   _____

   _____

7. According to Hebrews 1:14, who are angels?

   _____

   _____

8. How do Christians put their angels to work?

   _____

   _____

9. What is described as "the life of the Church"?

   _____

   _____

10. When does God's Word not fail?

    _____

    _____

Chapter 6

The Prayer of Faith

Praying always with all prayer and supplication in the Spirit, and watching thereunto with all perseverance and supplication for all saints.
— Ephesians 6:18

In the next several chapters, we will discuss the different kinds of prayer which are found in the Word of God.

Moffatt's translation of Ephesians 6:18 says, ". . . praying at all times in the Spirit, with all manner of prayer. . . ." Another translation says, "Praying with all *kinds* of prayer."

In this study course, we are examining the kinds of prayer that are illustrated in the New Testament. We are primarily interested in the New Testament because that is the Covenant under which we are living. We're not living under the Old Covenant. Those under the Old Covenant were living under a shadow of what was to come. But why live under the shadow, when you can live under the light!

New Covenant Kinds of Prayer

Much damage has been done by taking some examples of prayer from that dispensation, the Old Covenant, and using them in this dispensation. We are living under a better covenant, in a better day. Those living under the Old Covenant didn't have the Name of Jesus to use because Jesus had not yet come. Therefore, they had more of a struggle with evil spirits and demons than we do. But Jesus came, and Colossians 2:15 says, *"And having spoiled principalities and powers, he [Jesus] made a shew of them openly, triumphing over them in it."*

Therefore, prayer is an entirely different matter with us living under the New Covenant because Satan has been defeated. And Jesus has given believers the authority to use His Name in prayer.

MATTHEW 21:21,22
21 Jesus answered and said unto them, Verily I say unto you, If ye have faith, and doubt not, ye shall not only do this which is done to the fig tree, but also if ye shall say unto this mountain, Be thou removed, and be thou cast into the sea; it shall be done.
22 And all things, whatsoever ye shall ask in prayer, believing, ye shall receive.

Jesus is talking about prayer here. He is talking about believing prayer. He is talking about the prayer of faith.

Jesus said almost the same thing in the Gospel of Mark.

MARK 11:24
24 Therefore I say unto you, What things soever ye desire, when ye pray, believe that ye receive them, and ye shall have them.

This is the prayer of faith. And it applies primarily to a person's own life — to his own situations and circumstances. In other words, it applies to *your* desires. Mark 11:24 is talking about *your* praying. It is not talking about someone else praying with you. That would be the prayer of agreement (Matt. 18:19).

Mark 11:24 is not talking about someone agreeing with you. It says, *". . . when YE pray, [ye] believe that ye receive . . . and ye shall have them [what things soever ye desire]"* (Mark 11:24). Jesus is saying you can have what you desire if you pray according to His Word and believe you receive your petition.

We make the mistake sometimes of taking these different kinds of prayer and lumping them all together. When we do that, we miss out on some of the blessings of God. We need to realize that there are certain principles or rules or spiritual laws that govern certain kinds of praying. And each of those principles do not apply to every kind of praying.

For example, there are certain rules that govern certain games, which, generally speaking, would all come under the category of *sports*. Similarly, when we talk about prayer, all kinds of prayer, generally speaking, would come under the category of *prayer*. But there has to be more than one kind of prayer because Ephesians 6:18 says, *"Praying always with ALL PRAYER [or all kinds of prayer] and supplication in the Spirit. . . ."* All praying is prayer, but there are different *kinds* of prayer.

For example, there are many different games and they each have their own set of rules. There are some rules which apply to baseball that do not apply to football. If you used the same rules for different games, you would get terribly confused.

I heard a news story about someone who came over from Europe, and for entertainment, he was taken to a baseball game in New York City. This person really didn't know very much about baseball because it was not played in his country. He asked many questions and couldn't understand some of the expressions used.

I think we are this way sometimes spiritually. Thus, people become confused if they don't understand the rules which govern the different kinds of prayer. You see, although there are all kinds of prayer, the same rules don't apply in each case. If you try to apply the same rules to all the different kinds of prayer, it will become confusing.

The Prayer of Consecration vs. The Prayer of Faith

For example, some people think you ought to end every prayer with the phrase, "If it be Thy will." When you question them about it, they'll say that Jesus prayed that way. But He didn't pray this way *every time* He prayed. He just prayed that way on one occasion and for one kind of prayer (Luke 22:42).

For example, when Jesus raised Lazarus from the dead, Jesus didn't stand at Lazarus' tomb and say, "Lord, if it be Thy will, raise up Lazarus." No, Jesus said, "*. . . Father, I thank thee that thou hast heard me. And I knew that thou hearest me always . . .*" (John 11:41,42).

Then Jesus told Lazarus to come forth, and Lazarus came forth out of the grave. The prayer Jesus prayed was a prayer to change something. Anytime you are praying a prayer to get something or to change something, never put an "if" in it. "If" is the badge of doubt. Should you pray that way, you're using the wrong rule, and your prayer won't work. It's that simple.

What kind of prayer did Jesus pray, using the phrase, "*If* it be Thy will"? It was *the prayer of consecration and dedication.* Then there are other kinds of praying that will require the use of the word "if" when we don't *know* exactly what the will of God is in that situation.

In the Garden of Gethsemane, Jesus knew the will of God. However, Jesus prayed a prayer of consecration to God's will, "*Saying, Father, if thou be willing, remove this cup from me: nevertheless not my will, but thine, be done*" (Luke 22:42).

Jesus wasn't praying a prayer to change something. He was praying a prayer of consecration and dedication. We use the phrase, "If it be Thy will" in our prayers because we want to be available to do what Jesus wants us to do. We should be willing to go anywhere and do anything God has called us to do, whether it is to pastor, to be a missionary, or to be anything else He wants us to be. Therefore, in a prayer of dedication and consecration, we are to pray, "Lord, if it be Thy will" or "Lord, Thy will be done."

However, when it comes to changing things and receiving something from God according to His Word, we do not pray, "If it be Thy will." We already know God's will because we have God's Word for it. It is God's will that our needs be met. God wants to give us what we need. And we receive our needs met by faith.

Receiving the Desires of Your Heart

MARK 11:24
24 Therefore I say unto you, What things soever ye desire, when ye pray, believe that ye receive them, and ye shall have them.

Mark 11:24 has to do with receiving the desires of your heart. It has to do with receiving "things": "*. . . What THINGS soever ye desire. . . .*" It has to do with things in the natural, like the fig tree that just dried up when Jesus cursed it (Mark 11:14,20,21).

Mark 11:24 also pertains to healing. The devil tried to tell me on the bed of sickness that Mark 11:24 wasn't talking about physical things. The devil said that scripture only meant whatever I desired *spiritually.* Many people listen to the devil and are robbed of blessings that God intended for them to have in life.

The Bible says, "*. . . What things SOEVER ye desire . . .*" (Mark 11:24). We have God's Word, His promise, that these desires can be met — that we can have those things we desire.

Someone might ask, "What if my desires are wrong?"

Well, if your desires are wrong, then why don't you get saved? Or if you're out of fellowship with God, then you will need to repent.

Those who are out of fellowship with God and those who are unsaved aren't going to be able to make Mark 11:24 work for them anyway. But a man who is saved and walking in fellowship with God has the right desires in his heart.

You can't tell me a believer's desires will be wrong if he is walking with God and keeping his flesh under subjection to his recreated, human spirit! The Christian is supposed to crucify the flesh. But in Mark 11:24, God is talking about the desires of the *heart.* We must realize that it is God's will that all of our needs be met — spiritual, physical, and financial or material.

We do not live under the Old Covenant, but you can understand something further about the nature of God by studying the Old Testament. You'll see from the Old Testament that God promised His people more than just spiritual things. He promised them that if they would obey Him, they would prosper financially and materially (Deut. 28:1-14).

God also told the Israelites that He would take sickness away from them and the number of their days they would fulfill (Exod. 23:26). The Bible says in the Book of Psalms, in talking about delivering the Israelites from Egypt, that there were no feeble people among them (Ps. 105:37). That's quite a statement when you realize that there were approximately two million Israelites whom God led out of Egypt!

God is interested in everything that touches our lives. He has made full provision for us for every area of our lives. He told His people in the Old Covenant that if they would keep His commandments, they would eat the good of the land (Deut. 28:1-14; Isa. 1:19). The phrase, "the good of the land" carries the implication that God's people are to prosper materially.

Then over in the New Testament the Lord says almost the same thing, except in different words. The Holy Spirit says through John in Third John 2, *"Beloved, I wish above all things that thou mayest prosper and be in health, even as thy soul prospereth."*

The Lord said that He would give good gifts to His children (Matt. 7:11). He is concerned about us (1 Peter 5:7). And in Mark 11:24, Jesus is talking about granting us the desires of our heart, and He tells us how to get them.

Your Prayer of Faith Won't Always Work for Others

Let's operate according to the rules set down in God's Word. In other words, using Mark 11:24, I can make my faith work for myself, but I can't always make it work for others. The other person's will and the other person's faith enter the picture too.

In the prayer of agreement, the unbelief of one person can nullify the effects of the other person's faith. As long as people are baby Christians, we can very often carry them on our prayers and on our faith. But it is also true that after a certain period of time, God expects people to develop their own prayer life and their own faith. That's why your faith won't always work for others. But your faith will *always* work for you if your faith is based on God's Word.

I noticed as a pastor that there were people who would get healed primarily on my faith. Usually these were people who would come in from denominational churches or who had just recently been saved. They were spiritual babies on the subject of divine healing. It was the easiest thing in the world to get them healed.

The older Christians were the hardest ones to get healed. I don't mean older in physical age. I mean those who had been Christians the longest. You see, God expects more out of the person who has been taught the truth of God's Word and who has had the opportunity to grow in his own faith.

After World War II, there was a revival of divine healing in America. It began in about 1947 and lasted through about 1957 or 1958. I talked to many healing evangelists and every one of them said the same thing. (I was having the same experiences along this line that they were having.) Primarily those ministers who held meetings in the churches were the ones who would run up against this problem.

All these healing evangelists said that they could never really get people healed until they got past all the Full Gospel Christians. The healing evangelists would just sigh in relief when they got past them. Why? Because most Full Gospel folks were expecting to be healed by the minister's faith.

They had done very little themselves in the way of studying the Word and getting it down on the inside of their hearts or spirits. They had not developed their own faith as they should have. Therefore, God couldn't heal them any longer based on the minister's faith because He expected them to have developed their own faith. And since they hadn't, they were having a hard time receiving their healing.

In 1953 in a large church where I was preaching, I was talking about this problem of Full Gospel Christians not getting healed. The executive presbyter of a Full Gospel organization told me he had experienced the same problem in their organization. In fact, he related a story that showed how big the problem was.

He told me that during the previous year, Brother Oral Roberts had held a meeting in their state. (This was prior to 1953.) Brother Roberts' meeting was sponsored by the Full Gospel churches, most of which were prominent churches. Six weeks after the meeting was over, they sent out several thousand cards on which two questions had been printed. All the people had to do was to answer the questions by checking the card and sending it back. They didn't even have to sign it.

They asked every person if he received his healing when Brother Roberts laid hands on him and prayed for him. The other question was whether or not the person was still healed. They sent out several thousand cards just in their own state. They received six thousand cards back. And out of the six thousand people questioned, only three percent of the Full Gospel people said they were healed. That means only three out of one hundred Full Gospel folks received their healing.

But out of the denominational people, seventy percent of them received their healing. And after six weeks, seventy percent of them still had their healing! That's seventy out of one hundred denominational folks who not only received their healing, but *kept* their healing. That's good!

What made the difference? God expected more of those Full Gospel people who knew more. But many of them had not developed their faith sufficiently on their own to be able to receive their healing. God expected their faith to be developed to the point that they could receive on their own faith, so He could not heal them based on Brother Roberts' faith.

These Full Gospel people had been taught the Word of God concerning faith and healing. They had been attending Full Gospel churches. However, these other folks, the denominational people who came to the meeting, had never been taught about faith and healing, so it was easier for them to receive healing based on Brother Roberts' faith.

Usually in a circumstance like this when a person is a baby Christian and is unschooled in the Word of God, the prayer of faith will work for him — I can get him healed on my faith in the Word. Most of the time, the very fact that baby Christians or denominational Christians come forward to receive prayer proves that they want their healing and they aren't opposed to divine healing. So if they will just remain neutral, I can get results for them based on my faith in the Word.

However, sometimes even more mature believers still want to be babies and let someone else carry them and do their believing for them. But that won't work. God expects folks who know how to use their own faith to use it and to believe God for themselves.

As a pastor of a church, I saw people who would get their healing when I prayed for them, but then after a year or so, I could never get those same people healed again. I know that I prayed for them with just as much faith as I had before. In fact, I know I had more faith when I prayed for them the second time because my faith had developed since I prayed for them two or three years before when they readily received their healings. You see, my faith was growing too. Yet I couldn't get them healed the second time. That disturbed me as a pastor because a pastor is concerned about his people.

In one church we pastored, we began to have a healing service every Saturday night. There was one woman in a wheelchair who attended the meetings. She had arthritis, and her body was just stiff. She could roll herself around in the wheelchair and was able to cook her own meals and do her own housework. If she happened to get the flu, for example, I could pray for her and she would always get healed. She would always get healed of any minor ailment.

Finally a group of us went down to her house to pray for her healing from arthritis. I knew what God was going to do, and so I just asked the prayer group to stand away from her. I said to her, "In the Name of Jesus, rise and walk." All the others in that room with me were witnesses to the fact that the power of God lifted that woman right out of the chair! It was as if someone were holding her up in midair!

There she was suspended above that chair! Then the power of God started pulling her upward, but she reached back down, grabbed ahold of that wheelchair, and when she did, she just fell back down into it!

I said to her, "Sister, you don't have a bit of faith, do you?"

She blurted out, "No, I don't. I'll go to my grave from this chair." And she did.

We weren't to blame that this woman didn't receive her healing because when we prayed for her, the healing power of God came down upon her. If she had believed God and had cooperated with His healing power, her body would have been loosed, and every joint in her body would have been healed.

That's the reason we have meetings and seminars — in order to teach people so they can grow in faith. Some people have had the opportunity to grow in their faith but they just haven't done it. Now they're on their own, but they still don't give the proper attention to the Word, so their faith doesn't grow. That's a sad situation.

Years ago when I learned that my sister had cancer, I went to the Lord in prayer on her behalf. (I stood my ground on the Word for her life, and the Lord told me that she would live and not die.) Well, she was healed, and there were no symptoms of cancer left in her body whatsoever. Five years went by, and then she had cancer in another part of her body. There was no relation to the other kind of cancer that she had. This time it was in the bone. She gradually lost so much weight, she was down to seventy-nine pounds.

The Lord kept telling me that she was going to die. I kept asking the Lord why I couldn't change it. He told me that she'd had five years in which she could have studied the Word and built up her own faith, but she hadn't done it. She was saved, but the Lord told me that she was going to die. He had expected her to do something about developing her own faith. She hadn't done it, and she died.

This is a sad example, yet it is true. God wants us to develop our own faith and grow as Christians and not just stay babies, expecting others to carry us with their faith.

We're willing to help others, and we do so, but believers cannot continue to remain spiritual babies. If you had ten children and all of them remained babies, they wouldn't be able to help one another, and you would be in a mess! Children should grow up in the natural, and then the older ones can help the younger ones. It should be the same way spiritually. God wants all of His children to grow up in Christ.

If the Church is growing, there will continue to be babies born, as is proper and natural. But if everyone in the Church remained in a babyhood state of spiritual growth, who would take care of the babies? We would have a real problem on our hands spiritually speaking!

God has set different ministries in the Church (Eph. 4:11,12). For example, an evangelist is primarily interested in winning the lost. But if everyone were an evangelist, all we would ever do is get people saved, and those new converts would always be babies because there would be no one to teach them or shepherd them. But spiritual babies need to grow up, and it will take other ministry gifts in the Body of Christ to help them do that.

God saw that spiritual babies need a shepherd, so He set pastors in the Church (Eph. 4:11). He wanted His sheep to be matured further, so he put teachers in the Church too. Sometimes a pastor can be a teacher and a preacher. But the point is, God wants all of His children to grow spiritually. That is one reason He has put us in a local body of believers. Committing ourselves to a local church and sitting under the pastoral ministry is one way to grow spiritually.

If we let our flesh dominate us, we will still want to be babies and let someone else carry us spiritually. But as a Christian you can pray the prayer of faith for yourself. Stop saying you can't. Say that the ability to pray in faith belongs to you.

Continually say what the Word says about you. Put your name in Mark 11:24 where Jesus says "you." Take Mark 11:24 as a personal promise to *you*. Say, "Jesus says unto *me*, what things soever *I* desire, when I pray, I am to believe that I receive them, and I *will* have them!" Learn to pray the prayer of faith for yourself and receive answers to your prayers.

Questions for Study

1. How is prayer different for those living under the New Covenant than it was for those living under the Old Covenant?

   _____

   _____

2. To whose situations and circumstances does the prayer of faith primarily apply?

   _____

   _____

3. What happens when you try to apply the same rules to all kinds of prayer?

   _____

   _____

4. When it comes to the prayer of faith, what is "the badge of doubt"?

   _____

   _____

5. For whom will Mark 11:24 work?

   _____

   _____

6. Which of our needs does God want to meet: spiritual, physical, and financial or material?

   _____

   _____

7. Why won't _your_ prayer of faith always work for others?

   _____

   _____

8. When will your faith work for you?

   _____

   _____

9. What can you do to make your faith grow?

   _____

   _____

10. Why did God set the different ministries in the Church?

    _____

    _____

Chapter 7

The Prayer of Praise and Worship

Now there were in the church that was at Antioch certain prophets and teachers; as Barnabas, and Simeon that was called Niger, and Lucius of Cyrene, and Manaen, which had been brought up with Herod the tetrarch, and Saul.

As they MINISTERED TO THE LORD, and FASTED, the Holy Ghost said, Separate me Barnabas and Saul for the work whereunto I have called them.

And when they had fasted and prayed, and laid their hands on them, they sent them away.

So they, being sent forth by the Holy Ghost, departed unto Seleucia; and from thence they sailed to Cyprus.

— Acts 13:1-4

I want you to notice the expression in verse 2 that we emphasized as we read, *"As they ministered to the Lord, and fasted . . ."* (Acts 13:2).

We are talking about different kinds of prayer. Oftentimes the only kind of prayer we are familiar with is the prayer of petition, or the prayer to change things. We also call that the prayer of faith. We are almost always petitioning God to do something for us and, of course, it is scriptural to pray the prayer of petition and to receive our needs met.

But in our text in Acts 13:1-4, the people were not *petitioning* God to do anything. It says they *ministered* to the Lord and *fasted*. Ministering to the Lord is *the prayer of praise and worship.*

When we come together as a local church, we usually minister to one another, as most of our services are designed that way. We sing, but many times very few of the songs we sing actually minister to the Lord; they usually minister to *us.* We have "special" singing, but many times we're still not ministering to the Lord, we're ministering to one another.

When we pray in church, our praying is primarily petitioning God. We are petitioning the Lord to move in our midst and to manifest Himself among us. Then when the song service is over and the minister speaks, he is not ministering to the Lord, he is ministering to the congregation.

The Lord ministers to us as a congregation through the speaker, manifesting Himself in our midst. Then when the service is being concluded, if we do have a time of waiting on God in prayer, it is still usually petitioning prayer. We come to church, not necessarily to minister to the Lord, but to pray and to seek God on our own behalf, praying that certain needs will be met, and then we minister to certain needs of each other.

And often in the church setting, people come forward for prayer. They want *something* from God, but they are not always sure exactly *what* it is that they need. We should ask folks who come to the altar just what they came for.

Many times, I've seen folks respond to an altar call and others gather around to pray with them and just start praying. As we say from a natural standpoint, they just start bombarding heaven on their behalf. I have come along and asked some of these people what they came to the altar for, and they have said, "Well, I don't know."

How would others know what to pray for if the people themselves didn't know what they had come forward for? I can't understand that, can you? Those praying with people who respond to an altar call should find out whether the people came for salvation, to be filled with the Holy Spirit, or to receive some other particular blessing or benefit. Then they will know how to direct them in line with the Word of God, and they can pray with them in faith.

Coming to church to seek God on our own behalf and to minister to needs of others isn't wrong. But most of that kind of praying is the prayer of petition — *not* the prayer of worship or ministering to the Lord. My personal observation is that by far the majority of our praying is more the petitioning kind of prayer than any other. It seems we have gotten away from (if we were ever really there to begin with) the prayer of worship.

Ministering to the Lord

But in Acts 13, we see the Early Church ministering to the Lord with the prayer of worship. And notice there is more than just a one-way conversation involved in this account in Acts 13, for it says, *"As they ministered to the Lord, and fasted, the Holy Ghost SAID . . ."* (Acts 13:2).

This is the prayer of worship. You see, God made man so He would have someone to have fellowship with. It is true that God is concerned about us and is interested in us and wants to meet our needs, for He tells us in His Word to *ask* for the things we need

(John 16:23,24). Jesus also said our heavenly Father knows what things we have need of. But He said for us to *ask* (Matt. 6:5-8; John 16:23,24).

However, too much of the time we are praying much like the little boy I heard about who said, "Lord, my name is Jimmie, and I'll take all You'll gimme." When it comes to praying, this seems to be the only kind of praying we know anything about. I wonder sometimes if maybe the Lord doesn't get a bit tired of that. If that is all we're doing, just asking God, "Give me. . . ," we need to examine our hearts and begin to take time, both corporately and in our individual prayer lives, to wait upon God and to minister to the Lord.

When we wait upon God and minister to Him, we are not asking Him for anything, nor are we petitioning Him for anything; we are *ministering* to Him. As I said, this kind of praying should not only be the practice of individuals, but we need to do this kind of praying as a group, as a local church body. Worship can involve more than one person. Our text says, *"As THEY ministered to the Lord . . ."* (Acts 13:2).

I also want to call your attention to the fact that it is in this kind of atmosphere of praise and worship to God that God can do more for people. He can move more readily and mightily in our midst. Notice in Acts 13 as they ministered to the Lord and fasted, the Holy Ghost said something to them. The Holy Ghost manifested Himself.

As I said, God made man for His own pleasure, so He would have someone with whom to have fellowship. He is our Father, for we are born of God (1 Peter 1:23). I am sure of this, that no earthly parent ever enjoyed the fellowship of his children more than God enjoys the fellowship of His sons and daughters. And I am sure God would speak to Christians more, as He did to Saul and Barnabas in Acts 13, if Christians would take more time to minister to the Lord.

I remember one particular meeting we held. The meeting had been running about six weeks, when I said to the people, "Let's have some different kinds of services. Three nights a week for these last two weeks of the meeting, I want us to come to the services just to minister to the Lord. I may read just a little bit from the Word and make a few comments, but I'm not going to do a lot of teaching or preaching. We're not going to come to petition God to do anything, but as a group we are going to wait upon the Lord and minister to Him."

I also told the people, "I don't want us to come and wait before the Lord in worship for just ten minutes or so. I want us to come with the thought in mind that when we get down to pray, we're going to wait at least an hour, perhaps longer, ministering to the Lord. We're just going to tell Him how much we love Him and praise Him and thank Him for His goodness and mercy. That's what ministering to the Lord is.

"If you don't want to do that," I told the congregation, "please don't come to these services. Just stay home, because if you come, you'd just hinder the rest of us. You wouldn't be a blessing to the rest of us unless you are prepared just to wait on the Lord and worship Him."

I can report to you that the crowd didn't fall off during these meetings. They came and praised the Lord, and I found that they *wanted* to wait upon God. And in that kind of an atmosphere, God did minister to us in very unusual ways. Although that was years ago, there are still things that are happening today in my ministry as a result of some of what the Lord shared with me during those times of waiting upon Him and ministering to Him.

That convinces me of this one thing: We miss out on many things in life because we don't take time to get into the right attitude of worship and to the right place of worship in order to minister to the Lord.

I heard one of the assistant general superintendents of a Pentecostal church say that something happened along this line in his own life as a young minister. I believe he began to preach when he was about fourteen years old. Later, he was holding a revival meeting in a certain church where the pastor had been called out of town.

Relating the story, this superintendent said that someone in the church called the parsonage in the nighttime, asking for help. When they found that the pastor was gone, they asked the pastor's wife to come to help them. A little baby was having convulsions.

So this pastor's wife awakened this young man — this teenage evangelist — who was staying in the parsonage with the family, so he could go with them to pray for this baby.

The superintendent said, "Of course, I was very young in spiritual things, but I went along. When we arrived, we rebuked the devil, we prayed at the top of our voices, and we went through all the motions that Pentecostal, Full Gospel folks do. We carried on like this for about thirty to forty minutes, but that little child just continued to have convulsions."

He continued, "I had done about all I knew to do, and I'd done everything I'd seen anyone *else* do, but nothing happened. Then as I got quiet, it seemed that the group that was there to pray (several people had come to pray too) also got quiet.

"I'll never forget what this pastor's wife did," the superintendent said. "She was quiet for a while, then she began to say, 'Praise the Lord. Praise the Lord. Thank You, Jesus. Hallelujah. Glory to God.' Praise and worship was just rolling out from the inside of her, so to speak. She must have praised God that way for about ten minutes.

"Finally, one by one, all of us picked it up, until all of us were praising God. In the midst of that atmosphere, the convulsions ceased and the child fell asleep.

"After awhile, we stopped praising God and began just conversing with one another. Then while we were talking, the child awakened and the convulsions began again. We all got alarmed and started to pray again, rebuking the devil. We anointed the child with oil and laid hands on him. We went through all the usual maneuvers, but nothing seemed to happen.

"Again after we settled down, the pastor's wife began to praise the Lord, just ministering to the Lord and telling Him how much she loved Him. We all joined in, and shortly after that, the child's convulsions stopped, and he went to sleep — perfectly healed." The child never did have any more convulsions. The prayer of praise and worship worked on behalf of another when nothing else worked.

The Lord has not left us helpless in any situation! God has given us His Word and the means through prayer whereby every need can be met.

Notice in our text, "*As they ministered to the Lord, and fasted, the Holy Ghost said . . .*" (Acts 13:2). In other words, we could put it this way: "As they ministered to the Lord, the Holy Spirit manifested Himself." That is what happened in the case of the little child with convulsions. As they ministered to the Lord, the manifestation of healing they needed and desired for the child occurred. Praise the Lord!

Ministering to the Lord Brings Deliverance

I believe there is a close relationship between ministering to the Lord and receiving deliverance from tests and trials. We have scripture to support this.

ACTS 16:22-24
22 And the multitude rose up together against them: and the magistrates rent off their clothes, and commanded to beat them [Paul and Silas].

23 And when they had laid many stripes upon them, they cast them into prison, charging the jailor to keep them safely:
24 Who, having received such a charge, thrust them into the inner prison, and made their feet fast in the stocks.

In Acts chapter 16, we have the account of Paul and Silas in jail in Philippi.

We read here about how Paul and Silas were arrested, beaten with many stripes, and cast into prison. The jailer was charged to keep them safely. Verse 24 says, "*Who, having received such a charge, thrust them into the inner prison, and made their feet fast in the stocks.*" But notice what Paul and Silas did in the midst of their suffering.

ACTS 16:25
25 And at midnight Paul and Silas PRAYED, and SANG PRAISES unto GOD. . . .

Now notice that Paul and Silas didn't sing praises to one another; they sang praises unto *God*.

Notice also that in the account of the Antioch prophets and teachers in Acts 13, as well as in this account of Paul and Silas in Acts 16, we see that believers *joined together* in united prayer to minister to the Lord. In Acts 13:2 the Bible says, "*As THEY ministered to the Lord. . . .*" That means all of them together were ministering to the Lord.

In Acts chapter 16 only two people were involved. Verse 25 says, ". . . *PAUL AND SILAS prayed, and sang praises unto God. . . .*" Paul and Silas' prayer and praise to God was also an example of united prayer. We'll discuss in the next chapter how God's power is manifested in united prayer.

Paul and Silas couldn't have been singing some of the praise songs that are used in some church services today, because some of the songs Christians sing today don't praise or magnify God. Too many times the songs we sing are more of a complaint than they are a praise. Many of them indicate a "poor-old-me" attitude. Some of them talk about us as wandering through life destitute and downtrodden, walking through the dark valley of life.

Notice those kinds of songs are almost always about us — what *we* are doing and how tough it is down here on earth for us. Even when we do sing about heaven, we sing about how good it's going to be when *we* all get there. That still doesn't give God any praise for His goodness to us here and now. But Acts 16:25 says Paul and Silas sang praises *unto God*. Hallelujah!

Verse 25 says that *at midnight* Paul and Silas prayed and praised God. I believe that verse was actually, literally speaking of midnight — the midnight hour. But I believe there is something else here that is significant.

The midnight hour can also refer to the midnight hour in our lives. "Midnight" could also be symbolic of times of seeming darkness, or of tests and trials in our lives. But, thank God, we have a resource of power that's available to us to withstand the onslaught of the enemy. We have God's Word and we can pray. Many times just to pray is not enough. Notice that after Paul and Silas *prayed*, they sang *praises* to God (Acts 16:25).

Anyone can pray when he finds himself in trouble. But it takes a person of faith to sing praises, too, in the midnight hour of life. Paul and Silas' backs were bleeding and their feet were in stocks. It was literally midnight, but it was also the midnight hour of tests and trials. It was a dark and seemingly hopeless situation.

When Paul and Silas sang praises to God, their backs were still in the same condition as before — bleeding and hurting. Their feet were still in stocks. They were still in the inner prison. It was still midnight. The situation was bad and it hadn't changed. They had no manifestation of help or deliverance at all when they began singing praises to God.

I am convinced that if most Christians would quit continuing to pray over and over about the same things and would begin praising God, it wouldn't be long until their answers would come. It wouldn't be long before the praises of God would dispel their "midnight hour" — the tests and trials they are facing.

At midnight Paul and Silas prayed and sang praises. Praise and worship get the job done. Notice Paul and Silas didn't pray and then gripe and fuss and bellyache about their circumstances.

If you're going to complain about your circumstances, you are not going to receive anything from God or get any results in prayer. You are just wasting your time! You might just as well mark that down right now! It is praying and believing God and His Word that gets the job done, not griping and complaining. Griping and complaining is a result of doubt and unbelief. God answers *believing* prayer.

HEBREWS 4:3
3   FOR WE WHICH HAVE BELIEVED DO ENTER INTO REST, as he said, As I have sworn in my wrath, if they shall enter into my rest: although the works were finished from the foundation of the world.

When you pray and really believe, you enter into rest. Then you can sing praises to God. It doesn't say that when you pray and believe you enter into a state of fretting. It doesn't say when you pray and believe, you enter into a state of worry, agitation, confusion, perplexity, and anxiety. It says when you are believing God, you enter into *rest*. The believing prayer is the prayer that God hears and answers.

MATTHEW 21:22
22   And all things, whatsoever ye shall ask in prayer, BELIEVING, ye shall receive.

In Acts 16:25, we know that Paul and Silas were believing God — they were in faith. I know they believed because the Bible says those who believe enter into rest. Paul and Silas were singing praises to God because they were in faith.

Isn't it strange how people pray about things, but instead of believing, they will go into a tirade of worry and doubt. Also, many people want to blame their problems on someone else when things don't work out as they planned. They insist on continuing to talk doubt and unbelief and to keep on griping and complaining. But if they do that, their prayer is not going to work. Paul and Silas prayed and *sang praises* unto God. That was their faith in action.

Now notice something else. Acts 16:25 says, ". . . [they] *prayed, and sang praises unto God: and THE PRISONERS HEARD THEM.*" Paul and Silas weren't quiet about praising God, were they? If they hadn't sung out their praises, then the prisoners wouldn't have heard them. In other words, Paul and Silas didn't pray quietly.

Some people say that they want to pray quietly because the Lord knows they have a song in their heart. But if there is really a song in your heart, it is going to come out of your mouth. The Bible says that out of the abundance of the heart, the mouth speaks (Matt. 12:34). So if a song is in your heart, it is going to come out!

Paul and Silas were peculiar folks — faith folks — because who in the world would praise and worship God like they did in the midnight hour? Someone might say, "I would."

Well, I don't know whether you would or not. If you're not doing much praising God right where you are, you probably wouldn't do very much praising in the midnight hour when the circumstances look bad. If you can't praise God where you are right now, how do you think you could praise God in prison with your back bleeding!

In Acts 16:25, it doesn't say what Paul and Silas prayed about. I do not know whether they prayed for deliverance or not. But I hardly think so. I believe they were just praying and thanking God for the privilege to suffer for His Name.

I say that because there is a significance between prayer and praise in this verse. It says Paul and Silas ". . . *prayed, AND sang praises unto God . . .*" (Acts 16:25). "And" is a conjunction; it hooks together praying and praising.

Let's read this verse in *The Amplified Bible*.

ACTS 16:25 (*Amplified*)
25 But about midnight, as Paul and Silas were praying AND singing hymns of praise to God. . . .

I like that, don't you? Paul and Silas were singing hymns of praise! That is the kind of hymns they were singing — hymns or songs of praise unto God. I believe what the Bible says — that in their prayer, Paul and Silas were praising and thanking God. And as they did, not only did the prisoners hear them, but *God* heard them, and they were delivered!

ACTS 16:26
26 And suddenly there was a great earthquake, so that the foundations of the prison were shaken: and immediately all the doors were opened, and every one's bands were loosed.

As I said, I do not know if Paul and Silas were praying for deliverance. But one thing I do know, according to this scripture, the deliverance didn't come while they were *praying*. The deliverance came while they were *praising*! For it says, ". . . *Paul and Silas prayed, AND sang praises unto God. . . . And suddenly there was a great earthquake . . .*" (Acts 16:25,26).

No wonder some people's prayers never shake anything. Their prayers don't even move *them* into faith — to believe God. But something happened when Paul and Silas prayed and praised God.

If Paul and Silas would have been like most people in similar circumstances, they would have been griping and complaining, and these verses probably would have read like this:

At midnight Paul and Silas griped and complained.

Silas said to Paul, "Paul."

Paul said, "Yeah, Silas?"

Silas asked, "Are you still there?"

Paul responded, "Where else *could* I be?"

Silas said, "I tell you, my poor back is hurting me so bad. I don't understand, Paul, why God ever put this on us. I can't understand why God let this happen to us. He knows we've tried to serve Him and do our best!"

But that kind of praying would have just gotten them further into the problem, instead of getting them out of it. If they'd been like many Christians, Silas would have said, "I tell you, Paul, I never did get put in jail when I was serving the devil!"

I know what I'm talking about! I pastored for nearly twelve years, and I've had church members say to me when they were in a test or a trial, "I never had it this rough when I was serving the devil!"

How do you help folks like that? Well, you just smile and say, "God will forgive you for saying that, if you'll repent." But I believe we can learn something from Paul and Silas in Acts chapter 16 if we'll pay attention.

After all, Paul and Silas were in trouble, weren't they? Their backs were bleeding, and I'm sure they were hurting. They were in jail and their feet were in stocks. They had been cast into the inner prison. It was a dark picture. But, as someone once said, Paul and Silas were in *jail*, but they didn't let the jail get in *them*!

I believe that is the reason many people are defeated; they let the circumstance overcome *them*, instead of overcoming the *circumstance*. After all, the tests and trials of life come to everyone. There are some trials that are peculiar to us as individual human beings living in this world.

Basically, the tests and trials we face are all the same. But it's the *attitude* we have during times of tests and trials that makes all the difference. How we look at a situation makes all the difference in the world as to how we come out of the test or trial, or whether we come out of it at all.

I believe there is real truth in this passage in Acts chapter 16, as well as light and instruction to help us in our midnight hour — in our hour of tests and trials. We can do as Paul and Silas did in the "midnight hour" of our lives, when the storms of life come, and we don't understand why things have happened as they have when we've been trying to do our best.

Being in the Will of God Doesn't Guarantee Easy Circumstances

Remember, Paul and Silas weren't in Philippi on a vacation. They were there to do the Lord's work. They weren't out of the will of God. Sometimes when things don't go right, people think, *Well, I must be out of the will of God.*

I've had people say to me, "What awful sin have I committed to cause God to put this on me?" I tell them that *God* didn't send the test or trial they are facing; the *devil* sent it: *"The thief cometh not, but for to steal, and to kill, and to destroy . . ."* (John 10:10). It wasn't God who whipped Paul and Silas. It was ungodly men who did it. God didn't stir up these ungodly fellows. It was the devil who stirred them up. Some say, "Well, God permitted it. What awful sin have I committed to cause God *to permit* this to happen to me?"

But if you think you're going to determine whether you are in the will of God by whether or not everything runs smoothly in your life, then you are mistaken. A life of ease, with no rough or difficult places to endure and no sacrifices to make, does not indicate whether or not a person is in God's will. If it did, then Paul never did get in the will of God in his entire ministry! He missed it from beginning to end. No, you can't judge being in the will of God by whether or not you have tests and trials in life and obstacles to overcome.

I was on the field as an evangelist for many years, and I would sometimes get amused at pastors. I have had them tell me, "I tell you one thing! If I can just get my Sunday school attendance back up where it was at its highest point, I am leaving!" Some pastors were upset because the Sunday school was down and things weren't going right. Well, you don't judge whether or not you're in the will of God just because the Sunday school isn't what you think it should be. That kind of thinking would be funny if it weren't so sad.

I have also had pastors say to me, "If I can just get the finances of this church to the place they were when I came here, then I'm going to resign and leave." They felt that because the finances had fallen off it indicated they weren't in the will of God.

But a church is made up of individual people, and just as individual people go through phases in their lives, so do churches. A pastor can't determine that he is out of the will of God just because his church is experiencing some difficult circumstances.

When I pastored, I never did try to ascertain whether I was in the will of God by whether or not things ran smoothly. I would determine the will of God by listening to my own spirit, and by doing just what they did in Acts 13:2. I would wait upon the Lord and minister to Him until I knew in my spirit what God wanted me to do.

I only missed it one time, as far as pastoring the right church was concerned. I missed God concerning this particular church because I put out a fleece. You see, I hadn't been in Pentecostal circles very long. It had only been about three years since I'd received the baptism of the Holy Ghost and had become Pentecostal.

I never had heard anything about fleeces before then. I had never heard anyone in my former church say anything about putting out a fleece. But I began to hear certain preachers and others talk about putting out a fleece, so I decided to put out a fleece too. I decided maybe I'd like to change churches and pastor another church. So I put out a fleece about whether or not I should take another church.

A certain church opened up, and I was invited to preach, so I went. Before I left, I put out a fleece. I told the Lord if a certain "sign" occurred, I would accept it as His confirmation that I should accept this new pastorate. And according to my fleece or "sign" I had asked for, I was to change churches. I did, and I got fleeced!

When I was finally able to leave that church, I was never so glad to get away from a place in all my life as I was that place! I should have left that church a long time before I did, but sometimes when you miss it, it's hard to get back on the right track again.

And yet, I went back there afterwards to hold a revival meeting and had one of the greatest meetings they had ever had in the history of the church. But I went that time in the will of God, when God said, "Go." I missed it previously even when I followed the fleece instead of following God, waiting on God, and ministering to Him, until I *knew* what to do.

However, as I said, just because I was in the will of God pastoring those other churches doesn't mean everything always ran smoothly. It doesn't mean we broke the Sunday school record every Sunday. And it doesn't mean the finances topped out every Sunday above anything that we had ever received before.

Yet in pastoring those churches, I knew in my spirit, in my heart, that it was the right thing to do because I had taken time to minister to the Lord and to wait upon Him. I *knew* that was where He wanted me to be. At different times I'd say to the Lord, "Lord, things are not running just right, but I'm not going to worry about it. I'm going to trust You to work it out."

The devil will just try to aggravate you to death with circumstances, if you'll listen to him. But if you'll learn how to deal with the devil, you'll be all right. And if you don't, then the circumstances of life will overwhelm you. Because if Satan can get the least edge on you, he'll just hound you and try to worry you to death. But believers don't need to be easy prey for the devil. Rather, we need to spend our time ministering to the Lord.

Acts 13:2 says they ministered to the Lord and fasted. I believe in fasting, and I take some time to fast. But we have to fast in the right way. One can't fast under some conditions. If you did, it would be a confession of defeat and unbelief. Sometimes Christians will fast instead of just believing the Word — instead of just taking God at His Word. That kind of fasting won't profit you if it's done from a position of doubt and unbelief in the Word.

When I have faced dark circumstances in my life, I'd just say to the devil, "I want you to know that I'm not going to miss a meal or lose any sleep, because I'm in faith. I'm standing on God's Word."

You see, I had already done something about the problem. I had committed it into the hands of the Lord, and I was not going to take the problem back and worry about it.

I would say to the Lord, "Lord, I know I have a certain responsibility because I'm pastor here. I'm going to preach the Word, and I'm going to treat everyone right and visit the sick and do the best I can. But as for the rest of it, I'm going to leave it to You, Lord."

When I did that, we had almost a constant revival in that church. People were saved, healed, and filled with the Spirit every single weekend. Now I could have become disturbed and could have been defeated because of conditions that existed. One can do that very easily.

I believe there is something in praise and worship and ministering unto the Lord that would benefit us if we would just begin to practice this in our lives. We don't have to be disturbed, disquieted, or defeated because of tests and trials, or difficult circumstances.

Ministering to the Lord In the Early Church

Let's notice a few expressions concerning praise and worship in the Word. I want you to notice a particular characteristic of the disciples and the Early Church: They were always praising and worshipping God.

LUKE 24:50-53
50 And he [Jesus] led them out as far as to Bethany, and he lifted up his hands, and blessed them.
51 And it came to pass, while he blessed them, he was parted from them, and carried up into heaven.
52 And they WORSHIPPED HIM, and returned to Jerusalem with great joy:
53 And were CONTINUALLY in the temple, PRAISING AND BLESSING GOD. Amen.

ACTS 2:46,47
46 And they, CONTINUING DAILY with one accord in the temple, and breaking bread from house to house, did eat their meat with GLADNESS and SINGLENESS OF HEART,
47 PRAISING GOD, and having favour with all the people. And the Lord added to the church daily such as should be saved.

Notice the expression here, ". . . they, continuing DAILY with one accord . . . did eat their meat with gladness. . . . PRAISING God . . ." (Acts 2:46,47). This is what I want you to see. With these Christians, praising God wasn't something they did once in a great while, or just from time to time. No, praise and worship was a way of life. I believe verse 47 records the results of the believers' continual praise and worship: ". . . And the Lord added to the church DAILY such as should be saved."

Too many times, what happens with us is about once every six months some believers get "prayed through," and they have a high time praising and blessing God. If you were writing about people like that in Luke chapter 24 and Acts chapter 2, you'd have to say, "Occasionally they praised God." And for some believers, you'd even have to say, "Semiannually they praised the Lord"! For others, you'd have to say, "Annually they praised the Lord"!

But here in Luke chapter 24 and Acts chapter 2, they praised God continually. The prayer of praise and worship should be a continual thing with us today too. Then we'd see some of the same results the Early Church experienced!

There's something admirable about Smith Wigglesworth that I have noticed in reading about him. He said this: "First thing every morning, when I get out of bed, I jump out of bed — I don't just drag myself out — but I jump out. And when my feet hit the floor, I say, 'Praise the Lord.' And I praise God that way every morning." That's a good way to start the day, isn't it?

Someone who knew Wigglesworth told me that he used to get out of bed and dance a jig every morning, praising God out loud. That would be a good way for all of us to start the day! Too many times we just drag out of bed. But we need to be so excited about God, that we daily jump out of bed praising Him!

Again in Acts 2:46, we read, *"And they, continuing daily with one accord in the temple. . . ."* Notice the phrase "continuing daily." They *daily* gathered together in the temple to praise God. *Daily!* Also notice the phrase, *". . . with gladness and singleness of heart. Praising God . . ."* (vv. 46,47).

I believe one reason the disciples had such gladness of heart was that they daily praised the Lord! Read the Book of Acts and you'll see how effective the disciples were in everything they did for the Lord. The reason the disciples were effective was that they had this continual gladness of heart because they were continually praising God.

ACTS 5:42
42 And daily in the temple, and in every house, they ceased not to teach and preach Jesus Christ.

In Acts 5:42, the word "they" is specifically referring to the apostles. Yet in the Early Church being effective in the Body of Christ and the work of the ministry was not limited to the apostles.

For example, in Acts 2:46 and 47 which we just looked at, "they" is not talking about the apostles; it is talking about everyone who was a believer in that locality. It included the laity or the lay members — the whole church. *Everyone* in the church was continuing daily to meet in the temple and minister to the Lord.

Developing a Habit of Praise and Worship

If we would just walk in the light of the Word and continually be in an attitude of praise and thanksgiving, we would be a witness to other people for the Lord. People would see our continual gladness of heart and would desire to experience that joy and gladness for themselves.

This is just one area in which the baptism of the Holy Spirit is a help to us. Although a person can have joy and a thankful heart as a result of the new birth (Luke 24:49), the baptism of the Holy Spirit can help us in our praise and worship of God and enable us to be a powerful witness for the Lord.

P. C. Nelson was an example of how a person who makes a habit of praise and worship can be a witness to others. I heard Dad Nelson tell the story of how he had received the baptism of the Holy Ghost as a denominational pastor back in the early 1920s.

After Rev. Nelson had received the baptism of the Holy Ghost with the evidence of speaking in other tongues, a friend of his (actually they were roommates in seminary together) wrote to him saying he had heard that Rev. Nelson had received the baptism of the Holy Ghost and had spoken in other tongues. He wanted to know if there was any truth to it. Brother Nelson wrote back and told him that he had indeed received this Pentecostal experience.

P. C. Nelson's friend wrote him again and invited him to come over and tell him about it and to preach in his church on a certain Sunday. This was years ago when folks traveled by train. Somehow Rev. Nelson and his traveling companions were delayed, and Rev. Nelson didn't arrive early for the service. He didn't get a chance to renew acquaintances with his school chum and roommate before meeting at church.

Actually, when Rev. Nelson finally arrived at the church, the service had already begun. As Nelson stepped onto the platform, this pastor shook hands with him and they renewed their acquaintance. They sat down and about this time someone was to sing a special song. Rev. Nelson didn't think anything about it, but before he knew what he was doing, he said out loud, "Praise the Lord!" When he did that, his pastor friend sort of jumped and then just looked at him. Rev. Nelson became a little self-conscious, but he soon forgot it.

After a little while the woman began singing the second verse. Rev. Nelson heard something that he liked and without thinking he said out loud, spontaneously from his heart, "Well, Hallelujah!" That pastor jumped again and just looked at Rev. Nelson. Only then did Rev. Nelson become conscious of what he was doing because praise was such a habit with him. Nelson began to listen to the song again and without thinking, he said, "Glory to God." And the pastor sort of jumped again.

Then the pastor introduced Rev. Nelson to the congregation and explained that they had been roommates together in seminary. He said he appreciated Rev. Nelson and his ministry and without thinking, Brother Nelson said, "Glory to God." That poor pastor jumped and nearly lost his introduction!

But Rev. Nelson didn't think anything about it; those praises to God were automatic with him! He had simply gotten to thinking about the goodness of God and what He had done for him and was glad about it. He had this same gladness of heart that the disciples in the Book of Acts had!

When Rev. Nelson and his pastor friend got into the night service, once in a while as he was just sitting on the platform, Rev. Nelson would say, "Praise the Lord." Every time he did this, that pastor would sort of jump and look at him. Rev. Nelson just had gladness of heart and it got the attention of this pastor.

Finally, this pastor said to him, "Nelson, I believe this is just a habit with you."

Rev. Nelson said, "What do you mean?" He didn't even know what his friend was talking about.

"Well," his friend said, "every now and then you'll just say, 'Praise the Lord' right out loud, or you'll say, 'Hallelujah' or 'Glory to God' or 'Thank You, Jesus.' I believe that has just gotten to be a habit with you."

Rev. Nelson answered, "Well, it's a habit I never had before I was filled with the Holy Spirit!" Praise is a good habit to have!

Incidentally, as a result of Rev. Nelson's witness of continual joy and praise, this pastor was also filled with the Holy Ghost! Brother Nelson had made an impression on him because of the spirit of gladness and the praise and worship that flowed out of his heart. This pastor also wanted that same gladness and spirit of praise. Pastoring a church without it would be very discouraging. But thank God for this spirit of gladness! The Holy Ghost will help you to be a witness, too, as you minister to the Lord in praise and worship.

The Early Church also had that habit of continually praising and worshipping God. The Bible says in Luke 24:53 that the disciples were continually in the temple praising and blessing God. They continued to praise God daily, with gladness of heart (Acts 2:46,47). And Acts 5:42 says they also continued daily to preach the gospel: *And daily in the temple, and in every house, they ceased not to teach and preach Jesus Christ.*

And Acts 16:25 says, "*. . . at midnight Paul and Silas prayed, and sang praises unto God: and the prisoners heard them.*"

God's Power Is Manifested When His People Praise Him

There is a counterpart passage of Scripture to these verses, which is found in the Old Testament. In Second Chronicles chapter 20, King Jehoshaphat and Judah went out against the enemy, the armies of the Ammonites, Moabites, and the people of Mount Seir. These enemies of Judah had banded together against Judah. From the natural standpoint, Jehoshaphat didn't have enough men or an army big or strong enough to withstand these enemy forces.

Jehoshaphat called a prayer meeting. The children of Israel fasted and prayed. Usually in the Old

Testament the Spirit of God would move upon certain ones, the prophets, for example, to bring a message to His people. The Spirit of God moved upon a young man in the congregation, Jahaziel, and he stood up and prophesied.

2 CHRONICLES 20:15,17
15 And he [Jahaziel] **said, Hearken ye, all Judah, and ye inhabitants of Jerusalem, and thou king Jehoshaphat, Thus saith the Lord unto you, Be not afraid nor dismayed by reason of this great multitude; for the battle is not yours, but God's. . . .**
17 Ye shall not need to fight in this battle: set yourselves, stand ye still, and see the salvation of the Lord with you, O Judah and Jerusalem: fear not, nor be dismayed; tomorrow go out against them: for the Lord will be with you.

The Lord told the people not to have any fear, but to go out against the enemy, for the battle was the Lord's. So the following morning the Israelites went out against the enemy and the Bible says they put the praisers up front (2 Chron. 20:21).

Just picture this: The children of Israel went out against three enemy armies that had banded together against the people of God. The enemies' armies consisted of trained soldiers with swords, javelins, and spears. Yet Jehoshaphat sent the praisers out to meet them! The praisers were right up front, leading the parade, so to speak. Jehoshaphat didn't have a man leading his army with a sword or shield or spear. He only had those who were singing and praising the Lord.

2 CHRONICLES 20:21
21 And when he had consulted with the people, he appointed singers unto the Lord, and that should praise the beauty of holiness, as they went out before the army, and to say, Praise the Lord; for his mercy endureth for ever.

Notice what the Israelites did. They sang and praised God. They ministered to the Lord and sang praises to God, just as Paul and Silas did. I want you to notice something here. The children of Israel said, "*. . . Praise the Lord; for his mercy endureth for ever*" (2 Chron. 20:21). Evidently, they just marched along singing, "Praise the Lord; for His mercy endures forever."

What happened as a result of the Israelites' singing praises to God? This is what happened as a result of the prayer of praise and worship.

2 CHRONICLES 20:22-25
22 And when they began to sing and to praise, the Lord set ambushments against the children of Ammon, Moab,

and mount Seir, which were come against Judah; and they were smitten.

23 For the children of Ammon and Moab stood up against the inhabitants of mount Seir, utterly to slay and destroy them: and when they had made an end of the inhabitants of Seir, every one helped to destroy another.

24 And when Judah came toward the watch tower in the wilderness, they looked unto the multitude, and, behold, they were dead bodies fallen to the earth, and none escaped.

25 And when Jehoshaphat and his people came to take away the spoil of them, they found among them in abundance both riches with the dead bodies, and precious jewels, which they stripped off for themselves, more than they could carry away: and they were three days in gathering of the spoil, it was so much.

When the children of Israel began to sing and to praise God, God did something! That's when God's power was manifested and the enemy was defeated!

I believe we need to have more praise services where we just take time to minister to the Lord. Folks need to come to church to praise God and to wait upon Him. We need to have services where we minister to the Lord — not just to one another. We don't need to come together to talk about one another. No, we need to minister to the Lord and brag on Him! We need to sing praises to the Lord.

I believe we'd have some mighty manifestations of God's Presence if we would do that. Christians need to learn the importance of different kinds of scriptural praying. And one very vital kind of scriptural prayer is the prayer of ministering unto the Lord — waiting upon the Lord in praise and worship.

Questions for Study

1. What is the prayer of praise and worship?

   _____

   _____

2. The majority of our prayers are what type of prayer?

   _____

   _____

3. In what kind of atmosphere can God move more readily?

   _____

   _____

4. What is ministering to the Lord?

   _____

   _____

5. What is the relationship between ministering to the Lord and receiving deliverance from tests and trials?

   _____

   _____

6. Griping and complaining are the result of what?

   _____

   _____

7. When we face trials, what determines how or if we will come out of them?

   _____

   _____

8. How can you determine whether or not you're in the will of God?

   _____

   _____

9. Why were the disciples so effective in everything they did for the Lord?

   _____

   _____

10. What happens when God's people praise Him?

   _____

   _____

Chapter 8

United Prayer

. . . they lifted up their voice to God WITH ONE ACCORD. . . .

— Acts 4:24

Another important kind of prayer the Bible teaches about is *united prayer*. In this chapter we'll look at some examples in the Bible of the results of united prayer. I'm convinced that believers have not realized the potential of power there is in united prayer.

United, Vocal Prayer Is Biblical

There is so much in the realm of prayer that every one of us could learn if we would keep an open heart to the Word and the Spirit of God. Often in ignorance we can hold beliefs about prayer that are not in line with the Word at all, but are really just traditions of men.

For example, when I first entered into Full Gospel circles, everyone prayed out loud all together in meetings and it bothered me. I wasn't used to hearing any noise when I was praying, so it was almost too much for me. I would try to pray with these Full Gospel folks, but it was hard to concentrate on what I was saying to the Lord.

I was raised in a Southern Baptist church. In my early days I never remember people praying corporately in united prayer as these Christians did in the Book of Acts. Usually someone led in prayer, but we never lifted our voices. I was saved and healed, yet I knew nothing about united prayer, such as the Early Church practiced in the Book of Acts.

Healing was what caused me to begin associating with Full Gospel folks. I'd never heard the name "Full Gospel" before. I didn't know of anyone who believed in divine healing except me. But some people came to my town about a year after I got my healing and put up a tent. They were Full Gospel folks. I didn't go to the meetings at that time because I was busy with church work.

My grandmother was saved in an old-fashioned Methodist camp meeting. An altar call was given and my grandmother went forward and knelt at a makeshift altar where everyone came to pray all together out loud.

Back then in those old-fashioned camp meetings, the Methodists would all pray together out loud. The believers would kneel down to pray in the hay that was scattered all around the benches that were used as altars.

My grandmother attended the Full Gospel tent meeting they were having in my town and she wanted me to go with her to the meetings. I asked her why I should attend. She said that the minister preached like I believed. She said he sounded very much like me. I stopped by one night and stood outside the tent, and I enjoyed his message. The next week I went in and sat down under the tent and decided to attend the entire week of services.

After the minister preached, he came back through the crowd doing personal work. He walked around the tent, shaking hands with people, asking if they were Christians. After he shook hands with folks, practically everyone gathered around the altar to pray.

The Full Gospel minister came up to me and asked me if I was a Christian. I told him that I was a minister. He told me it wouldn't hurt me to go to the altar and pray with the others. Then he just went on shaking other people's hands.

We didn't do things this way in our church, and for a moment, I felt a little bit insulted. But the more I thought about it, the more I felt he was right. After all, I'd never heard of prayer hurting anyone. So I went down there and prayed. But it bothered me because the people all prayed out loud, and I was used to praying quietly.

Later these same Full Gospel folks built a church, and I attended their services because the services helped and blessed me. The services seemed to stimulate my faith. I would go down to the altar and pray after the services, but I would get as far away from the others as I could because they prayed out loud and all that noise bothered me.

One time I ventured to say something to them. I said, "God is not hard of hearing."

They responded, "He's not nervous either!" Praise the Lord, He isn't!

But at that time, I didn't know any better. I was sure they were wrong about this kind of united praying. But then I got to thinking about it. I remembered that these folks knew about divine healing when my church didn't. And they were right about divine healing. I thought that possibly they might know some other things, too, that I didn't know.

They could be right about praying out loud together, and I could be wrong.

I decided that I was going to read through the Book of Acts and underline with a red pencil everywhere the believers prayed in a group with two or more praying. I was going to see how they prayed corporately back in the Early Church. After all, I claimed to be preaching the same new birth they preached in the Book of Acts, and so I thought I might as well be following the Early Church in prayer too.

I began to really study the Word about it. One by one the Lord answered all the arguments I had against praying out loud. As I went through the Book of Acts and underlined those passages that talked about prayer, I couldn't find one single place where they would call on one person in a group to lead them in prayer. They never called on just one person to lead them in prayer.

But I found in several places where it said they lifted their *voices*. (Acts 1:14; 2:1; 4:24; 16:25) They all prayed at once and they all prayed out loud. This is what is known as united or corporate prayer.

After I read this, the next time I went to the Full Gospel service, I got right in the middle of them as they were praying around the altar. I finally realized that I was not praying just to hear myself anyhow; I was praying to God.

Someone might ask, and I have thought the same thing, "How can God hear all those people praying at once?" Then I began to think, *Well, how many people all over the world are praying at once?* Of course, there would be many praying at one time. And yet God hears them all, doesn't He?

After my mind had been renewed with the Word, I got blessed in a way that I hadn't been blessed when I had been praying quietly alone. Certainly, there are times in our own private devotions when we should pray alone. But there are also times when we need to pray together.

I was already convinced that praying out loud was right, but the account of Paul and Silas in Acts chapter 16 was the clincher for me.

We have already looked at this account in relation to the prayer of praise and worship. But this passage of Scripture also illustrates that united, vocal prayer — or believers praying out loud together — is biblical.

ACTS 16:20-25
20 And brought them [Paul and Silas] **to the magistrates, saying, These men, being Jews, do exceedingly trouble our city,**

21 And teach customs, which are not lawful for us to receive, neither to observe, being Romans.
22 And the multitude rose up together against them: and the magistrates rent off their clothes, and commanded to beat them.
23 And when they had laid many stripes upon them, they cast them into prison, charging the jailor to keep them safely:
24 Who, having received such a charge, thrust them into the inner prison, and made their feet fast in the stocks.
25 And at midnight Paul and Silas PRAYED, and SANG PRAISES UNTO GOD: and THE PRISONERS HEARD THEM.

Here Paul and Silas were in jail at midnight. They had been whipped, and their backs were bleeding. Their feet were in stocks. They were in the inmost prison (v. 24). But it says that at midnight Paul and Silas prayed.

That is a good time to pray! It was actually midnight when this happened, but I believe this word "midnight" is also significant in another way. Midnight can be symbolic of times of tests and trials in our life.

It can be "midnight" in your life even when it is daytime. That is a good time to pray — at midnight — when you are faced with tests and trials. At midnight, Paul and Silas prayed and sang praises to God in one accord, and the prisoners heard them.

Before I read this passage of Scripture, I would sometimes say to myself, *I believe in praying and praising God, all right, but I believe in being quiet about it! I have praises in my heart.* But when I read verse 25, I saw that it says the prisoners *heard* Paul and Silas praying and praising God. So Paul and Silas weren't quiet in their prayers.

You couldn't very well hear a praise in someone's heart! It would have to be on his lips for you to hear it. If I understand it correctly, the Bible not only says that the prisoners heard Paul and Silas praising God, but they heard Paul and Silas praying *and* praising. I'm sure it had an effect on those prisoners.

We don't see enough of this kind of praying and praising God out loud in the Church today. After I received the baptism of the Holy Ghost and left my denominational church, I accepted the pastorate of a Full Gospel church where people knew how to pray like this. Actually, the folks in this Full Gospel church did *many* things differently than we did in my former denomination, but I soon learned!

Someone in this church told me about a revival they'd had at the church some time before I came to pastor. People had come to this revival, not because they believed in revival, but rather as one would go to a show or circus just to observe. Actually, these people had come to make fun. But God had entered in and the same people who had mocked what was going on got saved. They had become members of this church that I had just begun to pastor.

The person who was telling me about this revival said that some of the folks would meet in the church in the daytime and pray for the evening revival services. These people had a heart to pray and didn't mind *who* heard them.

One couple in the church had a son who was grown and married. The son had come to visit his parents and was attending church during his visit. During the day this son was driving his car past the church, and he heard people praying in the church.

Later he said to his father, "We ought to go tonight because they are going to have a *big* one!"

His father asked, "Why do you say that?"

And the son answered, "Because they are already at the church practicing up. They have already started to practice in the middle of the afternoon!"

I believe sometimes that is the reason we don't have a "big one." We haven't practiced for it through prayer and praise!

The Power in United Prayer: Paul and Silas

The account of Paul and Silas in Acts chapter 16 which we've been looking at is an illustration of the power in united prayer.

Remember, Paul and Silas had been beaten and thrust into the inner prison with their feet put in stocks, all for preaching the gospel. But instead of griping and complaining about their difficult circumstances, Paul and Silas lifted their voices together in united prayer and praise to God.

ACTS 16:25
25 And at midnight PAUL AND SILAS prayed, and sang praises unto God: and the prisoners heard them.

Would you be praying and praising God out loud if you had been beaten and you were in jail with your feet in stocks and it looked like your life might be over? Paul and Silas did. And notice as Paul and Silas were praying and singing praises to God in one accord, something happened. As both Paul and Silas lifted their voices to God in united prayer and praise, God wrought a mighty deliverance.

ACTS 16:26
26 And suddenly there was a great earthquake, so that THE FOUNDATIONS OF THE PRISON WERE SHAKEN:

and immediately all the doors were opened, and every one's bands were loosed.

Isn't it interesting that the Bible doesn't record that the earthquake shook anything else but that prison? That is, there is no report in the Bible about any other house or building in that town being shaken. I wouldn't be surprised if that earthquake only shook that jail where two believers were praying and praising God in one accord.

But, bless God, that jail was shaken and every door in that jail was opened! The Bible says the very foundations of the prison were shaken. The stocks came off Paul and Silas' feet and Paul and Silas were loosed from their bonds. This is what united prayer will do!

When the prisoners were loosed, the jailer was going to kill himself because he was responsible for guarding them, and he thought they had escaped. But Paul ". . . *cried with a loud voice, saying, Do thyself no harm: for we are all here*" (Acts 16:28).

The jailer knew he had witnessed the supernatural that night and that Paul and Silas were no ordinary men, serving an ordinary God. The Bible says the jailer came trembling to Paul and Silas, falling down before them and asking what he could do to be saved (Acts 16:29-33). And as a result of the power of God that was wrought by the united prayer of Paul and Silas that night, the jailer and his entire family were saved and baptized in water.

A lot of folks today are just sitting around doing nothing, waiting for God to do something for them.

They say, "If God sees fit, He will move on my behalf."

But if that is true, then why didn't Paul and Silas just suffer in silence and not pray and sing praises to God? Why didn't they just wait and see if God would see fit to do something in their lives?

If that is true why didn't Paul and Silas say, "Let's just leave everything to the Lord"?

No, they prayed in one accord and sang praises to God! And notice their situation did not change *until* they prayed and praised in one accord. As a result, God heard them and they were delivered!

We need that kind of praying today too. How desperately we need that kind of praying! And when things begin to be shaken, some *people* are going to be shaken too.

You see, the shaking will cause some people to come into the church and others who aren't sincere to leave the church. Folks who don't want to change won't stay around long if things are being shaken, because some things believers should get rid of, such as sin, will be shaken too!

And in some churches there are even some *people* who need to be shaken, because they will never commit themselves to a local body and to walk uprightly. Those people will go when the shaking begins, but others will come into the church and stay.

The Power in United Prayer:
The Early Church

In Acts chapter 4, we read an account of a company of believers in the Early Church who lifted their voices to God in united prayer.

ACTS 4:23-31
23 And being let go, they went to their own company, and reported all that the chief priests and elders had said unto them.
24 And when they heard that, THEY LIFTED UP THEIR VOICE TO GOD WITH ONE ACCORD, and said, Lord, thou art God, which hast made heaven, and earth, and the sea, and all that in them is:
25 Who by the mouth of thy servant David hast said, Why did the heathen rage, and the people imagine vain things?
26 The kings of the earth stood up, and the rulers were gathered together against the Lord, and against his Christ.
27 For of a truth against thy holy child Jesus, whom thou hast anointed, both Herod, and Pontius Pilate, with the Gentiles, and the people of Israel, were gathered together,
28 For to do whatsoever thy hand and thy counsel determined before to be done.
29 And now, Lord, behold their threatenings: and grant unto thy servants, that with all boldness they may speak thy word,
30 By stretching forth thine hand to heal; and that signs and wonders may be done by the name of thy holy child Jesus.
31 And WHEN THEY HAD PRAYED, THE PLACE WAS SHAKEN where they were assembled together; and they were all filled with the Holy Ghost, and they spake the word of God with boldness.

This incident occurred after God had used Peter and John in the healing of the crippled man at the Gate called Beautiful. As Peter and John entered into the temple through the Gate called Beautiful, they met a man sitting at the gate who sat there daily to beg alms (Acts 3:1-3). Peter said to the man, ". . . *Look on us*" (v. 4). The man looked at them, expecting to receive something from them.

ACTS 3:6-8
6 Then Peter said, Silver and gold have I none; but such as I have give I thee: In the name of Jesus Christ of Nazareth rise up and walk.

7 And he took him by the right hand, and lifted him up: and immediately his feet and ankle bones received strength.
8 And he leaping up stood, and walked, and entered with them into the temple, walking, and leaping, and praising God.

When the crippled man was healed, the Bible says Peter and John were taken into question by the authorities. They were threatened by the priests and the Sadducees and were commanded not to preach and teach any more in the Name of Jesus (Acts 4:18). Then we read in verse 23 how Peter and John went to their own company to report what had happened.

It's good to be with your own company when you're in trouble. It's good to be with those of like-precious faith who know how to pray.

I have thought many times that if this company of believers had been like some folks in churches nowadays, they would have suggested that they nominate a committee to go and talk to these leaders to make some kind of a deal whereby everyone could get along together.

These leaders were religious people — they just didn't accept Jesus as being the Messiah. They believed in the same God, and they believed in prayer. They believed in going to church or to the temple to meet.

But if this group of believers who were of Peter and John's company were like some folks today, they would have wanted to work out some kind of a deal to compromise with these religious leaders who opposed them.

But it doesn't say those believers did that. In Acts 4:29 it says that this company of believers prayed for *boldness*.

ACTS 4:29
29 And now, Lord, behold their threatenings: and grant unto thy servants, that WITH ALL BOLDNESS THEY MAY SPEAK THY WORD.

These believers did not ask the Lord to remove the persecution or to strike down their enemies. They didn't pray, "Lord, make our way easy." Instead, they prayed one very specific prayer: "In the midst of this persecution, give us boldness to speak Thy Word!" (v. 29).

And in verse 31 we see that the Lord answered these believers' prayers. As a result of their united prayer, a building was shaken by the power of God!

ACTS 4:31

31 And WHEN they had prayed, THE PLACE WAS SHAKEN where they were assembled together; and they were all filled with the Holy Ghost, and they spake the word of God with boldness.

This passage of Scripture gives us an instance of how the power of God is made available when believers pray together corporately. The Bible says when this company of believers prayed, "the place was shaken" (Acts 4:31). Do you know of many groups of people praying and shaking anything nowadays for God's glory?

As a result of the prayers of these believers in Acts 4:31, the entire building was shaken! There is something about the power of united prayer that brings the power of God on the scene to meet every need. These Christians in the Book of Acts weren't praying just to hear themselves pray. They were praying about the problem they were facing at the moment, and all of them were praying out loud all at once.

The Bible says that when these believers lifted their voices and joined together in united prayer, ". . . THE PLACE WAS SHAKEN where they were assembled together . . ." (v. 31). The same thing happened in Acts 4:31 as a result of the united prayer of these believers that happened to Paul and Silas in Acts 16 when they prayed and praised God together in jail.

In Acts 4:31 it says the place was shaken where the believers were all assembled together. And in Acts 16 it says that the foundations of the prison were shaken and every door was opened in that old jail (v. 26). It was a strange thing, though, that the buildings weren't shaken *until* the believers prayed.

I believe that Christians ought to be shaking things today for God too! If believers today would get together and pray "with one accord," they would shake the world for Jesus. There is supernatural *power* in united prayer!

Ushering in the Glory of God
Through United Prayer

Believers can usher in the glory of God as they join together in united prayer and praise. In the Old Testament times it says that the glory of the Lord filled the temple where people were gathered to pray.

2 CHRONICLES 5:6,7,11-14

6 Also king Solomon, and ALL THE CONGREGATION OF ISRAEL that were assembled unto him before the ark, sacrificed sheep and oxen, which could not be told nor numbered for multitude.

7 And the priests brought in the ark of the covenant of the Lord unto his place, to the oracle of the house, into the most holy place, even under the wings of the cherubims. . . .

11 And it came to pass, when the priests were come out of the holy place: (for all the priests that were present were sanctified, and did not then wait by course:

12 Also the Levites which were the singers, all of them of Asaph, of Heman, of Jeduthun, with their sons and their brethren, being arrayed in white linen, having cymbals and psalteries and harps, stood at the east end of the altar and with them an hundred and twenty priests sounding with trumpets:)

13 It came even to pass, AS THE TRUMPETERS AND SINGERS WERE AS ONE, TO MAKE ONE SOUND TO BE HEARD IN PRAISING AND THANKING THE LORD; and WHEN THEY LIFTED UP THEIR VOICE with the trumpets and cymbals and instruments of musick, and praised the Lord, saying, For he is good; for his mercy endureth for ever: that then the house was filled with a cloud, even the house of the Lord;

14 So that the priests could not stand to minister by reason of the cloud: FOR THE GLORY OF THE LORD HAD FILLED THE HOUSE OF GOD.

2 CHRONICLES 7:1-3

1 Now when Solomon had made an end of praying, the fire came down from heaven, and consumed the burnt offering and the sacrifices; and THE GLORY OF THE LORD FILLED THE HOUSE.

2 And the priests could not enter into the house of the Lord, because THE GLORY OF THE LORD HAD FILLED THE LORD'S HOUSE.

3 And when ALL THE CHILDREN OF ISRAEL saw how the fire came down, and the glory of the Lord upon the house, THEY BOWED THEMSELVES with their faces to the ground upon the pavement, and WORSHIPPED, and PRAISED THE LORD, saying, For he is good; for his mercy endureth for ever.

Did you ever stop to think about *when* the glory of the Lord filled the temple? It was when all the people were praying and singing praises to God out loud in one accord. The glory cloud of the Lord filled the temple so that the priests were not even able to stand and minister. A white cloud came in and filled the temple. That's what united prayer can do!

I have seen instances when people have prayed until it looked like the whole building was going to shake. I have seen some of the most amazing things happen in the realm of the Spirit when people lifted their voices to God in prayer in one accord — in united prayer.

Sometimes it seemed that the power of God would come in waves. In some of my services every single unsaved and backslidden person in the building responded to be saved. I didn't have to beg or plead. They would come to the altar and pray and every one of them would be gloriously saved.

I remember one service in which everyone present who was sick was healed. I've ministered in a number of services in which every believer there received the baptism of the Holy Ghost. We don't see that much today. But I have felt the Spirit of God pass through services just like a strong wind.

We need more united praying. We need vocal praying, or praying out loud in one accord, in the church too. Let us avail ourselves of the power that is in united prayer, so that we do not miss out on any good thing the Lord has made available for us today. Let's pray the kind of united prayer that will shake things for the Kingdom of God!

Questions for Study

1. How can we learn more about the realm of prayer?

    _____

    _____

2. How many times in the Book of Acts do we find one person being called upon to lead in prayer?

    _____

    _____

3. What is united or corporate prayer?

    _____

    _____

4. Which Bible passages illustrate that united, vocal prayer is scriptural?

    _____

    _____

5. In Acts 16:25, what is the symbolism of the word "midnight"?

    _____

    _____

6. How will others know that someone has praises in his heart?

    _____

    _____

7. What happened when Paul and Silas lifted their voices in united prayer while in prison?

    _____

    _____

8. What effect did Paul and Silas' prayer have on the jailer?

    _____

    _____

9. Why is it good to be with those of your own company when you're in trouble?

    _____

    _____

10. How can believers usher in the glory of God?

    _____

    _____

Chapter 9

The Prayer of Commitment

Praying always with all prayer and supplication in the Spirit, and watching thereunto with all perseverance and supplication for all saints.

— Ephesians 6:18

Be careful for nothing; but in every thing by prayer and supplication with thanksgiving let your requests be made known unto God.

— Philippians 4:6

Casting all your care upon him; for he careth for you.

— 1 Peter 5:7

Let's look at another kind of praying which the Bible talks about — *the prayer of commitment.* Paul touched on it in Philippians 4:6. Then Peter talks more about it in First Peter 5:7, where he said, *"Casting all your care upon him; for he careth for you."*

I believe the *Amplified* translation is the most illuminating and enlightening translation of First Peter 5:7.

1 PETER 5:7 (*Amplified*)
7 Casting the whole of your care — all your anxieties, all your worries, all your concerns, once and for all — on Him; for He cares for you affectionately, and cares about you watchfully.

Peter said, "*Casting* all of your cares upon the Lord." This is done in prayer, through the *prayer of commitment.* As we cast our cares upon the Lord, we definitely commit our problems to Him. This is what it means to pray the prayer of commitment.

Certainly, there are different kinds of prayer; all prayer is not the same. For instance, we already discussed the prayer of faith, the prayer of praise and worship, and united prayer.

But if Christians would do more *casting* their cares upon the Lord, or praying the prayer of commitment, there would be many things about which they would not have to pray using other kinds of prayer. Sometimes simply casting their cares upon the Lord would eliminate some of the problems and situations people are praying about because then the Lord would begin to work the problem out.

Worry Hinders Your Prayers

Some folks are praying about certain situations and are getting no results. They don't get an answer because they are not praying in line with the Word of God. They are not doing what God said to do about cares, anxieties, worries, and concerns. It is not going to do any good to pray concerning your cares, anxieties, worries, and your concerns unless you are going to do what God tells you to do about them.

In other words, there are some things about which we do not need to pray — about which we *should not* pray.

This surprises some people. They say, "Brother Hagin, I thought you were supposed to pray about everything." Well, you aren't. There are many things you don't have to pray about and shouldn't pray about.

You don't have to pray about the Bible, for example. You need to just accept God's Word and believe it. The Bible is true, and it will read the same way when you get through praying as it did when you started praying. Therefore, if you would just believe what the Bible says and do what the Bible says, you would not have to do some of the praying you've been doing.

Some way or another some people seem to get helped temporarily by just thinking of or acknowledging the fact that God knows and understands what they're going through. But they still hold on to their cares and, thus, they don't receive *deliverance* from their problems or situations. God wants to deliver you out of all your afflictions (Ps. 34:19).

But in order for God to help you, you're going to have to cooperate with Him. You're going to have to do what the Word says. You're going to have to cast all of your cares on Him, for the Lord cares for you (1 Peter 5:7).

If you want to receive total victory and deliverance, it is not enough just to know that God knows and understands and cares. We must go on from there and do what God said in His Word to do. God wants us to cast all of our cares, all of our anxieties, all of our worries, and all of our concerns upon Him, for He cares for us!

This is the prayer of commitment, the prayer of casting or rolling our burdens — our cares, our anxieties, and our worries — upon the Lord. A verse in

Psalm 37 may help us see a little more clearly what Peter was talking about in First Peter 5:7.

PSALM 37:5
5 Commit thy way unto the Lord; trust also in him; and he shall bring it to pass.

The margin in my *King James* translation says, "Roll thy way upon the Lord." The words "cast," "commit," and "roll" are all words that convey the same thought. We are to simply *cast* or *roll* our cares upon the Lord. We are to *commit* our way and our cares to Him. Isn't that what the Bible is saying in these verses? We are to cast or roll our cares over onto the Lord.

Notice God is not going to *take* your cares away from you. You are going to have to do something about your cares by casting or rolling them over onto the Lord yourself.

Some people request, "Pray that the Lord will lighten my load." But the Lord is not going to do that. No, the Lord tells *you* what to do about your cares. And if *you* don't do something about them, nothing will be done.

I say as humbly as I know how, that if you hold onto your cares, your praying will be in vain. It's as simple as that. So *cast* your cares upon the Lord. *You* cast your cares upon the Lord (1 Peter 5:7).

"You" is the understood subject in First Peter 5:7. *You* cast all of your cares or burdens upon the Lord. In Psalm 37:5 it says, *"Commit thy way unto the Lord. . . ."* "You" is the understood subject of this verse too. In other words, *you* commit your way unto the Lord.

PSALM 37:5 (*Amplified*)
5 Commit your way to the Lord — roll and repose [each care of] your load on Him; trust (lean on, rely on and be confident) also in Him, and He will bring it to pass.

You roll your cares upon the Lord. *You* commit your way to Him. If anything is plain in God's Word, it is this: God does not want His children to be full of worry and anxiety, burdened down with the cares of life or bowed down with worry, anxiety, and concerns.

MATTHEW 6:25-27
25 Therefore I say unto you, Take no thought for your life, what ye shall eat, or what ye shall drink; nor yet for your body, what ye shall put on. Is not the life more than meat, and the body than raiment?
26 Behold the fowls of the air: for they sow not, neither do they reap, nor gather into barns; yet your heavenly Father feedeth them. Are ye not much better than they?

27 Which of you by taking thought can add one cubit unto his stature?

What Jesus is simply saying is, which of you by worrying and being overly anxious is going to change anything? *You* can't do it; *you* can't change anything simply by worrying. The same thought is recorded in Luke chapter 12.

LUKE 12:22
22 And he said unto his disciples, Therefore I say unto you, TAKE NO THOUGHT FOR YOUR LIFE, what ye shall eat; neither for the body, what ye shall put on.

Another translation reads, "Be not anxious about tomorrow."

We know we have to think about some things and make some plans concerning our future. But the main thought in these scriptures is, God doesn't want us to be filled with worry and anxiety about tomorrow. He doesn't want us to be burdened down with care about tomorrow. Even though we have to think about the future sometimes so we can make some plans and provisions, we can do so in a care-free, anxiety-free, worry-free manner.

LUKE 12:25
25 And which of you with taking thought can add to his stature one cubit?

No one can "add to his stature one cubit" or change the circumstances of his life simply by thinking about those things and worrying about them.

Notice again what Paul said in Philippians 4:6: *"Be careful for nothing. . . ."* We've been a little blind to that truth and have not readily grasped what this scripture is saying. Again, I believe the *Amplified* translation will help us.

PHILIPPIANS 4:6 (*Amplified*)
6 Do not fret or have any anxiety about anything. . . .

I want you to notice something, friends. This is something *you* do. I want to reiterate it. Too many times people want to pray and get *God* to take away their worries and their anxieties. But it is not scriptural to pray that way and it won't work. God will do something about your worries and anxieties — about the problems you face — but not until you give them to Him.

Again, here in Philippians 4:6, *"you"* is the understood subject. So when God says, *"Be careful for nothing. . . ,"* He is actually saying "*You* be careful for nothing." He is saying, "*You* don't fret or have any anxiety about anything" (Phil. 4:6 *Amp.*).

The *American Standard Version* says, "In nothing be anxious. . . ." The rest of that verse says, ". . . but in everything by prayer and supplication with thanksgiving let your requests be made known unto God."

It is also important to realize that as long as you are going to fret or have anxiety about whatever it is you are praying about, you are nullifying the effects of your praying.

In other words, if you are worrying about something, you haven't cast the care of your problem on the Lord; *you* still have it, and you're not trusting God with it. And if *you* have it, the Lord doesn't have it. But if the *Lord* has it, you don't have it!

Cast Your Cares on the Lord Once and for All

After you've prayed and have definitely committed your particular situation to the Lord, if you are still trying to figure out the answer, then you have taken back the problem, and the Lord doesn't have it. If you are still perhaps lying awake at night trying to figure out the problem, and you are tossing from one side of the bed to the other, unable to sleep, then the Lord doesn't have the problem anymore. You have it. You have taken it back.

If you go to the table and try to eat, but you can't because of your worry, anxiety, and concern, then the Lord doesn't have the problem; you do. If you do eat, and your food won't digest properly, and your stomach is constantly upset, then really, all of your praying about the situation is in vain and will not work. Your prayer won't work because you still have the problem. You haven't cast it over onto the Lord. (Some of you are in this predicament right now!)

But if that's where you're at — if you haven't cast all of your cares upon the Lord — you can do something to change your situation. I want you to notice something, particularly in the *Amplified* translation of First Peter 5:7.

1 PETER 5:7 (*Amplified*)
7 **Casting the whole of your care — all your anxieties, all your worries, all your concerns, ONCE AND FOR ALL — on Him. . . .**

This isn't something you do every day. This is a once-and-for-all proposition. In other words, when you obey this scripture and cast all your cares upon the Lord *once and for all*, that gets rid of them right then and puts them over into His hands. Then once you make that commitment and purpose not to carry your own burdens, any time anxieties try to come to mind, you refuse to take them upon yourself because you have made the commitment to cast them on the Lord.

There is much the Lord would have already done for us as believers, but we wouldn't let Him. We may have been honest and sincere, but we still didn't let Him because we did not come to Him according to His rules — according to His laws that govern the operation of prayer. We did not do what He told us to do.

You see, we have not prayed scripturally if we haven't cast our cares upon Him. We fail many times to cast our cares upon the Lord, and then we wonder why God doesn't work certain things out for us.

I am well satisfied that there are some who do not really want to get rid of their cares. They claim they do, but they don't really, for if they got rid of their cares, they would have nothing with which to gain someone else's sympathy. In other words, if they got rid of their cares, they wouldn't have those things to talk about. And for many people, that means they would just have to close down conversation entirely!

I do not mean to be unkind, but this is absolutely the truth. It is scriptural to cast your cares upon the Lord. You *can* do what God said to do.

I know God has helped us many times in spite of our failures, faults, and shortcomings. Some way or another He has seen us through. But consider what shape we were in when we got through the crisis! It is much better to come God's way, to practice His Word, and to have His best.

Worry Is a Sin

I remember when God first began to deal with me along this line of worry. I don't know whether or not you have ever thought about the sin of worry in connection with faith and receiving answers to prayer. But I had to begin to deal with this problem before I could receive healing for my body. Worrying and being hindered in faith are both tied in together.

You see, prayer, faith, and receiving healing or answers to prayer are all tied in together. I am satisfied that this is the reason some people do not get healed in their bodies. Sometimes their worry and anxiety is what is keeping them sick. If they got healed of the symptoms that existed in their bodies, those symptoms would just come back because the *cause* of their physical condition — the worry and anxiety — is still there.

God dealt with me on the bed of sickness more than sixty years ago, in the city of McKinney, Texas. I was just a boy and yet worry was the first thing God dealt with me about as He began to bring me into the light of the truth of His Word. I had never heard faith and healing preached. I was raised in a denominational church. But when the light began to come to me concerning faith and healing, God began to deal with my heart about this sin of worry.

You may say that a child couldn't worry (I was just a fifteen-year-old boy). But, yes, children *can* worry. Children are just replicas, so to speak, of their parents and what they see and hear in their homes from their parents.

My grandmother and my mother were world-champion worriers, and even as a little child, I knew they were always worrying. I had a critical heart condition, so I couldn't get out of the house to run and play like other children. I had to constantly be around my mother and Grandma. And I would constantly hear them worrying and fretting out loud.

So, you see, I learned to worry at a very early age. They were world-champion worriers, and I probably came in about third place right behind the two of them myself! As I began to read the Scriptures, I got bogged down in Matthew chapter 6, which talks about worry, and it took me six months to get out of that chapter because I was under such conviction about it.

I was born again on that bed of sickness, and I promised God that I would never doubt anything I read in His Word.

You may say, "Well, I never made any promise like that to God."

But if you are saved, you are not supposed to doubt what you read in His Word. So whether or not you made a promise like I did to God, He still requires faith of you, and you are wrong to doubt God's Word. Some people think if they don't commit themselves to be faithful to God's Word, then they're safe. But if you are a child of God, God still requires faith of you whether you've committed yourself to believe Him or not.

I had said to the Lord, "I'll never doubt anything I read in Your Word. And when I read Your Word and understand it, I promise You that I will put it into practice." But when I got to Matthew chapter 6 where Jesus said, "Take no thought for your life" (v. 25), the light seemed to become dimmed because I didn't begin to practice this. I didn't obey this scripture and begin to walk in the light of it. I was still taking plenty of thought for my life!

The Bible I was reading had a little footnote down at the bottom that told me that the Greek read, "Do not be anxious about tomorrow." And then it listed other Bible references, which basically all said the same thing: "Do not worry; do not be filled with anxiety."

I was full of anxiety and full of worry and full of fear. Not only was I nearly dead with a serious heart condition, but I was about to worry myself the rest of the way to death! My conscience smote me when I read Matthew 6:25 because I was not practicing the Word.

Matthew 6:25 said, "*. . . Take no thought. . . .*" I thought, *I'm not even supposed to think about tomorrow.* That is, I knew I was not supposed to be worried or to be anxious about the future. And that is exactly right.

As these words in Matthew 6:25 seemed to leap off the page at me and the Lord began to deal with me, I said to the Lord in astonishment, "Why, Lord, if I have to live like that, I'll never make it as a Christian; I'll never be able to live a Christian life." And, yet, living without worry and anxiety is to be a vital part of the Christian life. But I thought I couldn't live without worry or without being anxious. I thought I just couldn't do it, so I shut my Bible.

When I did that, the light dimmed and I went into darkness. I opened my Bible again and tried to read and just skim by that chapter in Matthew. I said to myself, *I'll just skip Matthew 6. I'll just bypass this one.*

Up until then, everything in God's Word had been all clear and light and a blessing to me. But when I chose not to walk in the light of what God showed me in His Word, everything became dark and fuzzy to me. You see, you are not going to get any more light until you walk in the light you already have.

Don't be worried about the things you don't understand in God's Word; just see to it you practice and do what you *do* know. The rest of it will take care of itself.

I kept on reading. I even began to study about the antichrist! The subject of the antichrist was not a problem area with me, so it didn't convict me when I studied about it. But worrying was a problem, and it bothered me to study that subject because I wasn't dealing with my sin of worry.

My conscience smote me because I was not practicing the Word. But I finally made a commitment to God on the fourth day of July in 1933 at 8:00 in the evening.

I said to the Lord, "Lord, forgive me. Forgive me for worrying. Forgive me for being full of anxieties. Forgive me for fretting. Forgive me for being discouraged as I've lain here bedfast. The doctors said I had to die. But forgive me for being discouraged. Forgive me for having the blues. Forgive me for feeling sorry for myself. Forgive me for having a 'poor-old-me' attitude."

I told the Lord, "Now I know that You will forgive me, Lord, because You said You would if I would confess my sin [1 John 1:9]. And I confess my sin of worry and ask You to forgive me. From this day on, because You've now forgiven me, I promise You the longest day I live, I'll never worry again. I'll never be filled with anxiety again. I'll never have the blues again. I'll never fret again. I'll never be discouraged again."

God as my witness, many years have come and gone, and even though I have been sorely tempted — just like you have — I have not worried. I have not fretted. I have not been filled with anxiety at any time, nor have I become overly anxious. I have not had the blues in all these years. I *have not* been discouraged. And no matter what happens, I *will not* be discouraged. Glory to God!

You see, all this goes together — walking in the light of the Word and developing triumphant faith.

I was holding a meeting once for a pastor of a rather large church in a large city. They would average from 550 to 570 in Sunday school. In the Sunday service they would have anywhere from 600 to 700 people. The lower floor would seat about 550 people and the balcony would seat 300 people. On Sunday evening the lower floor would always be filled and there would be from 50 to 150 in the balcony.

But in the revival meetings on the weeknights, the crowd would run anywhere from 90 to 150. That number on weeknights seemed a little slim compared to the average Sunday morning attendance. During the week it was hard to find 90 people in that large auditorium!

It was also a wonder that this particular pastor would even have me hold a meeting for him. You see, he had asked me several times to hold a meeting, and I had never agreed to hold one for him. He would walk up to me at conventions or different meetings and invite me to come to his church, and I wouldn't really answer him. I was afraid God would tell me to go to his church to preach. And I didn't want to go because I knew he'd had nearly every big-name minister in the country, preach in his church.

I'm not a sensational type of preacher or teacher and sometimes when you are not sensational, it is rather hard to get through to the people. So I just didn't want to go. I was holding a meeting at another place and as I was praying about my meeting, God spoke to me very definitely and said, "I want you to go to that other pastor's church."

The pastor had written me sometime before and asked me again if I would come, so I wrote him a letter and said, "Now I can come."

So I went to his church and as I said, we had a big crowd on Sundays, but the crowds looked so small on weeknights. The pastor and the associate pastor would say to me, "Brother Hagin, although our church is fairly large, we have never been able to have a day service in any revival. Our people are working people, and sometimes both husband and wife work." In a large city of that kind, people live over a wide area, and I could understand why they might find it hard to come to the day services.

So we started out with day services in that big church with two people in attendance! The next morning we had six. Every day the pastor and the associate pastor had been trying to boost me up and encourage me.

"Now, Brother Hagin," they would say, "don't get discouraged and leave us. You are doing well. You are helping us more than you realize. Now don't let the small weekday crowds bother you. You are drawing more people than Brother So-and-so (and they would name some big-name evangelist). We count the crowd every night and you're drawing more than he did."

Then the next day they would tell me all of this again. I never thought anything about it. I would just say, "Yes, yes," and go on. They kept that up for a week or two.

Finally I said to them, "Brethren, there is no reason for you to try to boost me up and encourage me. I'm not going to leave until God says 'Leave.' "

"Oh, you'll stay with us another week then?" they responded.

I said, "Yes, I'll stay because God hasn't told me to leave yet. If you or God tells me to leave, I'll leave. But I'm not going to be discouraged. God told me to come here. I wouldn't have come if He hadn't. And I'm not going to bother about it or worry if no one shows up for the services but two old snaggle-toothed women."

I thoroughly meant that. We started off with two people in the daytime services. I didn't look to see if they were snaggle-toothed or not, but we did start off with two women in the daytime services! But before the meeting was over, I counted 120 in the morning services. Praise the Lord! And that was during the week.

The pastor replied, "We've had other 'faith' preachers come to preach here and you're the only one we've invited who practices what he preaches. We talked it over and felt we needed your ministry, as we have never had a teaching minister come here before. We knew that we needed your teaching ministry in our church, but we were afraid that you would get discouraged and leave.

"Every other preacher we've invited here would just preach up a storm about faith during the night services. Then in the daytime his face would be long with discouragement, and he would say, 'Well, I'm going to leave!' Then we'd have to boost him up and encourage him and even promise him more money if he would stay."

But I believe that the Word of God is to be practiced by all of us, whether we are preachers or lay members — or whoever we are. And God's Word works. I would not encourage you to do anything I would not do or have not done myself.

PHILIPPIANS 4:6 (*Amplified*)
6 Do not fret or have any anxiety about anything [Well, what are you going to do about your problem then?], **but in every circumstance and in everything by prayer and petition** [definite requests] **with thanksgiving continue to make your wants known to God.**

Or we could say it this way: Whether it is burdens, cares, anxieties, worries, or concerns, we are to commit them to Him, cast them on Him, and roll them off on the Lord. And we are to do it *once and for all* (1 Peter 5:7 *Amp.*).

We sin in this area when we don't obey the Word and take our burdens to the Lord and leave them there. Leave your burdens with the Lord! As I've said, we come to the altar sometimes and pray and pray and pray. But when we get up from the altar, we pick our burdens back up off the altar and carry them away with us.

Learning To Cast Your Cares Upon the Lord

I started out in the ministry as a young Southern Baptist boy preacher. I got the revelation of divine healing on the bed of sickness, and I was healed. In the early days of my ministry, I was pastor of a community church, a country church. Nearly everyone in the whole community came to church. In April 1937, I received the baptism of the Holy Ghost and spoke in other tongues.

In those days when a person received the baptism of the Holy Ghost and spoke in other tongues,

he was ostracized by the denominational churches. On the other hand, I know many pastors who received the baptism of the Holy Ghost and still continued to pastor their churches. In fact, many of these pastors led their congregations into the baptism in the Holy Ghost. Most of the people in my church also received the baptism of the Holy Ghost.

Do you know what I found out when I began to fellowship with these Pentecostal people? I found out that they knew more about the Holy Ghost than I did, but that I knew more about faith than they did. We make a mistake when we think we can't learn from others.

So I switched over and started pastoring a Pentecostal church. I didn't know church problems existed until I got into a Full Gospel church! We didn't have any problems at all in that denominational community church I had previously pastored. If a fellow was *ever* tempted to worry, I was tempted to worry about this Full Gospel church I was pastoring!

Here I was, just a twenty-one-year-old boy, and I was the pastor of a church that was twenty-three years old. There were people in that church who had had the baptism of the Holy Ghost and had been talking in tongues more years than I had been alive! You can understand that one as young as I was would feel a sense of inadequacy.

Also, there were problems in that church. I knew something should be said to the people, but I didn't know what to say. I was afraid that if I said anything I would say the wrong thing. There were conditions that existed in that church that had existed for twenty-three years. I knew something ought to be done about the problems, but I didn't know what to do. And if I did something, I was afraid I'd do the wrong thing.

I remember I had gotten up early one Sunday morning, and I became burdened about all the problems in the church. I suppose this was the only time in my life that I momentarily succumbed to a burden or care of this nature. I became so taken up with thinking about the problems in that church and wondering what to do, that when I came to myself, I was out walking in the yard (the parsonage was right next to the church). I don't remember going out there. When I came to myself, I didn't even know how I got out there.

Out there walking that yard, I realized what I was doing, and I asked myself, *What am I doing out here?*

Then I thought, *Now, Lord, as the pastor, I have some responsibilities in this church. Something ought to be done, but I don't know what to do. I feel my inadequacy.*

Then I said, "Lord, You forgive me. I know better than this. I know better than to worry. I shouldn't be overly concerned and full of anxiety about anything. I was tempted and momentarily I succumbed to anxiety, but I refuse to worry."

I could sense the Spirit of God saying to my spirit, *"Casting all your care upon him; for he careth for you"* (1 Peter 5:7).

I said, "Lord, I know that I have responsibilities as pastor, but I am going to turn all these church problems over to You. I'm not going to worry about them. I can't fix them anyway.

"Lord, I'm going to preach the Word. I'm going to treat everyone right. I'm going to visit the sick, and I'm going to leave everything else to You. And I'm going to eat every meal and have a good night's sleep every night because I'm not carrying these burdens — You are."

When I said that, it was just like something lifted from me. I went to church happy and singing, and the Spirit of God met us and we had a glorious service. Marvelous things happened in that service.

We would have a district fellowship meeting among pastors on the first Monday of each month. I'd go to these meetings, and the preachers would all be talking about their cares, their anxieties, their burdens, and their responsibilities.

These ministers would say to me, "How goes the battle?" They were all in a battle, but I didn't have any battle. Praise God! I had the victory! Men in battle haven't won the victory yet. The battle is the Lord's, but the victory is ours. As I walked along carefree, here these ministers stood with long faces, talking about cares, burdens, and problems in their churches.

One of them said to me some time later, "I'll tell you, I got mad about it because your faith really convicted us. You would just wave your hand and say, 'Men, I don't have a care! I couldn't be better,' and just go right on by." He said those pastors would just stand there and blink their eyes and look at one another. Some of them would shake their heads and say, "The poor boy. He doesn't have enough sense to worry." No, I had *too much sense* to worry — too much Bible sense, that is.

I want to illustrate something to you. Can you see that if I had cast my cares about the church over on the Lord, I didn't have those cares anymore? I didn't have them; the Lord did. I didn't say that no cares existed. I just said, "*I* don't have a care," because *I* didn't; *the Lord* did. Praise God!

If I had three dollars in my billfold, and I gave them to you, I wouldn't have them anymore. Then if someone came along and said, "Brother Hagin, I'm a little short on money. Could you loan me a dollar? I'll pay you back tomorrow," I would have to say to you, "My brother, I would gladly loan you a dollar, but I don't *have* a dollar." I'd be telling the truth, wouldn't I? How could I loan that person a dollar if I didn't have a dollar? Those three dollars I did have *existed*, all right, but I didn't have them anymore. I had given them away.

In much the same way, if I cast my cares and anxieties on the Lord and someone says, "How goes the battle?" I'd have to say, "I don't have a care." Wouldn't I be telling the truth? Of course I would!

Some of these preachers said later, "I know better. He is lying. I know he *does* have a care." But I didn't say cares didn't *exist*; I just said *I* didn't have them. If someone asked me for a dollar and I didn't have any money with me, I wouldn't tell them that a dollar doesn't exist. I would only tell them that *I* don't have one. Cares do exist, but I've given mine away. I don't have them; the Lord has them!

One particular pastor, who was a neighboring pastor, would say, "He is lying. I know him better than any of the rest of you. And I know about all the problems in his church." He'd mention about four or five of the problems he knew about, and they were even worse than anything he had in his church. But I'd still just breeze by and say, "Men, I don't have a care." Hallelujah! I *didn't*. The Lord had all of my cares.

You *Can* Cast Your Cares Upon the Lord

When I took that twenty-three-year-old Pentecostal church I was telling you about, there was no one else who would take it except me. No one else had applied for the pastorate. No one else tried out for it. I went because God said, "Go."

After we left that church, however, they tell me forty preachers applied for the pastorate of that church. God moved on the scene and took care of those problems in the church because I gave those problems and those cares to Him. He worked every one of them out.

The Scripture says, *"Be careful for nothing . . ."* (Phil. 4:6). I don't know about you, but sometimes I have to talk to myself. Sometimes in pastoring a church, and I pastored for about twelve years, you are more tempted to be worried and anxious about things. But sometimes I'd just take myself by the ear and lead myself right over to the church door, put myself right down at the altar and say to myself, *Now, Kenneth, you know better than this. You are beginning to fret. Don't you do it! It's not right.* And I would cast all of my cares upon the Lord.

And many times in the nighttime, I would awaken and the devil would bring the picture to my mind of certain conditions that existed in the church, and I would be tempted to worry about them.

But instead of worrying, I'd start laughing right out loud, saying, "I don't have that care! Praise God, I'm carefree. No, I don't have the care of that, devil. You can bring a picture of it to me and show me a picture of it, but I don't have it. The Lord has it."

It is just amazing what the Lord can do with your problems when He has them. But as long as you are going to hold onto them, as long as you are trying to figure out how the Lord can work it out and trying to help Him work out your problems yourself, then He doesn't have your problems — you have them. As long as you hold onto your problems, you are going to have them — the Lord won't have them — and He's not going to be able to help you do a single thing about them.

Praise God, I'm glad in the midst of adverse circumstances, in the midst of the storms of life, in the midst of the winds of adversity that blow, we can do just exactly what the Word of God says: Do not fret or have any anxiety about anything (Phil. 4:6 *Amp.*). We can cast our cares upon the Lord (1 Peter 5:7).

If the devil tries to bring a picture of your problem to your mind, put it out of your mind immediately and say, "No, I don't have that, Mr. Devil. I don't have a care. I have turned that over to the Lord. He has it."

And God will work on your problem even while you are sleeping. He never slumbers or sleeps (Ps. 121:3,4). Praise the Lord! You need to sleep, but the Lord doesn't. And the Lord gives His beloved sleep (Ps. 127:2). You are His beloved because you are accepted in the Beloved, the Lord Jesus Christ (Eph. 1:6). So you should sleep, and your sleep should be sweet!

Someone may say, "Now, Brother Hagin, I've tried and tried and tried to do what you've said. I've tried to cast my cares on the Lord, but I just can't."

That is where you've missed it. Peter did not say to *try* to cast all of your cares on the Lord. He said we are to *do* it. He did not say *to try* not to fret or be anxious about anything. He said we are simply not to fret or be anxious about anything.

That is where the trouble is. It seems to me that folks would be glad to know they can cast their cares on the Lord and be free of those cares. In this day and hour, we need to know this. And it would help our lives tremendously if we would make a practice of casting our cares on the Lord.

It makes a difference when you believe the Bible, because when you believe God's Word, you'll practice it. The majority of church people do not believe the Bible, because if they did, they would practice it.

Most people just mentally assent that God's Word is true. They just mentally agree and say that the Bible is true, but they don't really believe it in their hearts. For example, if you are really walking in the light of God's Word, then you wouldn't worry even if you returned home and found your house had burned down while you were gone! You wouldn't worry or fret about it. You would say, "Bless God, we'll get a better house."

My wife used to get a little aggravated with me at times early in our marriage because I wouldn't worry. She was brought up in a denominational background, and at first she didn't understand this faith walk. We had two children, and once she said to me, "I don't believe you would worry if both of our children and I fell dead instantly."

I said, "I'd be a fool to worry then, after you were already dead. What good would that do?" Wouldn't that be foolish to worry about it after it already happened? And although my wife didn't understand what I was saying at that time, since then she has also learned to live free of worry as she casts her cares upon the Lord.

As I said, the Bible says you can't add one cubit to your stature by worrying about it (Matt. 6:27). In other words, worrying won't change anything for the better. So don't worry about anything! That is where God wants you to be as a Christian. He wants you to be carefree, trusting Him.

Remember, this casting your cares upon the Lord is a once-and-for-all proposition. So cast your cares once and for all upon the Lord. You *can* do it. There is no use saying you can't. Some of you are saying in your minds that you can't do this, but you *can*. The Lord wouldn't tell you to do something you couldn't do. As you learn to practice faith, your life can be beautiful and blessed. So purpose in your heart to practice God's Word and to practice faith.

If you haven't done it yet, there is no better time than now to turn loose of all of your cares and sleep peacefully tonight. Whatever cares, anxieties, or concerns are weighing you down, you can cast them on the Lord right now.

Close your eyes and name your cares one by one and give them to the Lord. They are too heavy for you to bear, but they are not too heavy for Him. And as you cast your cares upon the Lord and *leave* them there, you will see God begin to work mightily on your behalf to bring about the answers to all your problems and concerns.

Purpose in your heart to practice God's Word and to practice faith.

Questions for Study

1. What is the prayer of commitment?

   _____

   _____

2. What is one way that people can eliminate some of the problems they are praying about?

   _____

   _____

3. Name one thing that we _don't_ need to pray about?

   _____

   _____

4. Some people don't receive deliverance from their problems or situations because they still _____ _____ to their _____?

5. When will God do something about your worries and anxieties?

   _____

   _____

6. After you've prayed and committed your situation to the Lord, what does it mean if you're still lying awake at night trying to figure out the problem?

   _____

   _____

7. What will happen if you choose not to walk in the light of the Word that you already have?

   _____

   _____

8. When will God work on your problem?

   _____

   _____

9. When you believe God's Word, what will you do?

   _____

   _____

10. What is mental assent?

   _____

   _____

Chapter 10

Praying With Tongues

But the manifestation of the Spirit is given to every man to profit withal.

For to one is given by the Spirit the word of wisdom; to another the word of knowledge by the same Spirit;

To another faith by the same Spirit; to another the gifts of healing by the same Spirit;

To another the working of miracles; to another prophecy; to another discerning of spirits; to another DIVERS KINDS OF TONGUES; to another the interpretation of tongues:

But all these worketh that one and the selfsame Spirit, dividing to every man severally as he will.

— 1 Corinthians 12:7-11

In this chapter we will discuss *praying with tongues*. Believers receive the gift of tongues when they receive the baptism in the Holy Spirit.

Listed in First Corinthians 12:8-10 are the nine gifts of the Spirit, or the nine manifestations by which the Holy Spirit demonstrates Himself. Three of these gifts of the Spirit are utterance or inspirational gifts. These gifts, which are sometimes called the vocal gifts, are designed to be an inspiration in public worship.

Of these vocal gifts, the gift of tongues is the most predominant. Speaking with other tongues is important to the believer because tongues is the gateway into the supernatural.

Denominational people sometimes ask us, "Why do you Pentecostal folks emphasize tongues to such a great extent?" The answer is, of course, "*We* don't." You see, *the Bible* discusses the importance of tongues and the prominence tongues is supposed to have in the life of the believer.

The reason it seems we sometimes overemphasize tongues is because folks are always asking us about this gift of the Holy Spirit and compelling us to discuss it. And in discussing it, thank God, we always stand ready to give them an answer according to the Word of God.

Speaking in tongues is always manifested when believers are baptized in the Holy Ghost. In fact, speaking in tongues is the Bible evidence for receiving the baptism in the Holy Spirit (Acts 2:4). But once the believer is filled with the Spirit, he is to maintain a continual experience of speaking in tongues which will enrich his life immeasurably.

Also, there is a private use of speaking in tongues (1 Cor. 14:13,14), as the believer communes with God. And there is a public use of speaking in tongues in the public assembly or group (1 Cor. 14:27,28). In other words, there is a difference in purpose and use between simply speaking with tongues in one's private devotions, and in ministering tongues in a public assembly or group.

On the other hand, the essence of tongues is the same, and the source of the tongues is the same. The gift of tongues comes from the Holy Ghost. If people are being filled with the Holy Ghost in our midst, then we are going to have people talking in tongues. Not only that, but the Spirit-baptized believer does not have to stop speaking with tongues after his initial experience. He can continue to speak with tongues, although he may not be used to publicly minister or speak forth a message in tongues in a church assembly. Tongues can and should continue to be used by the Spirit-filled believer in prayer and in his worship of God.

I quote from Howard Carter, a well-known Pentecostal Bible teacher and founder of the oldest Pentecostal Bible school in the world:

> We must not forget that the speaking with other tongues is not only an initial evidence of the Holy Spirit's indwelling, but speaking with other tongues is a continual experience for the rest of one's life to assist in the worship of God. Speaking with tongues is a flowing stream that should never die out, and that will enrich the life spiritually.[1]

Tongues: The Initial Evidence Of the Baptism of the Holy Spirit

So notice first of all that speaking with tongues is always manifested when folks are filled with the Holy Ghost.

ACTS 2:4
4 And they were all filled with the Holy Ghost, and began to speak with other tongues, as the Spirit gave them utterance.

I would not argue and fuss about whether or not tongues is the evidence of the infilling of the Holy Ghost. According to Acts 2:4, it is. On the other hand, I know that Christians who do not speak with tongues have experiences in the Holy Ghost, too, because, after all, the new birth is effected or wrought by the Holy Ghost (John 3:3-8). And God's Spirit, the Holy Spirit, bears witness with our spirits that we are the children of God (Rom. 8:16).

Years ago while reading the New Testament as a young pastor, I felt that if I received the same Holy Ghost the Early Church did on the Day of Pentecost, then I wanted the same accompanying sign — tongues. If I didn't have the same accompanying sign — speaking with tongues — then I had no scriptural evidence that I was filled with the same Holy Ghost with which they were filled. Thank God, when I received the Holy Spirit, I did speak with tongues as the Spirit gave utterance (Acts 2:4).

Over the years, I've read in several accounts that before Smith Wigglesworth actually received the Holy Spirit with the evidence of speaking in tongues, he would argue with people that he was already filled with the Holy Ghost. Then he heard that Christians were speaking in tongues in a local Episcopal church, and he went to see about it. He found that the pastor and his wife had received the baptism in the Holy Ghost. Many church members, as well as others from all over Europe, had also received this New Testament experience.

The pastor and his wife asked Wigglesworth, "Have you received the Holy Ghost?"

Wigglesworth replied, "Yes."

Then they asked, "Did you speak with tongues when you were filled?"

Wigglesworth said, "No, but I'm just as much filled with the Holy Ghost as you are." Wigglesworth was so adamant about it, he almost disrupted their meetings.

Wigglesworth finally went to the parsonage or rectory to get the Episcopal pastor to pray for him to receive the Holy Ghost, but the pastor wasn't there. So the pastor's wife said, "I'll pray for you."

Wigglesworth replied, "Just pray for me that I'll get the tongues."

She said, "No, you don't want the tongues, you want the Holy Ghost. The tongues will take care of itself."

He said, "I have the Holy Ghost."

She said, "Never mind. Kneel down here." (She was tired of arguing with him.) So he knelt down, and she laid hands on his head. He said that when she laid hands on him, the Holy Ghost power came upon him. Just then there was an interruption, so she left the room, pulling the door closed so Wigglesworth wouldn't be disturbed. As the power of God came upon him, God gave him a vision.

Wigglesworth said, "In this vision I saw a stream of blood flowing from Calvary like a mighty river. I saw myself in that stream. I began to cry out, 'Clean, clean, clean. I'm clean; the blood has cleansed me. I'm clean because of the blood of Jesus.' In a few moments I noticed that I wasn't saying, 'Clean' in English, I was talking in some kind of language I had never spoken before. I was speaking in tongues."

"Then I had another vision," Wigglesworth related. "In it I saw the mighty power of Pentecost and of God. The Holy Ghost settled all my arguments for me. I had been arguing with Spirit-filled believers every day that I had the Holy Ghost just as much as they did. In a moment's time I saw that I had never really been filled with the Holy Ghost until then.

"Certainly," Wigglesworth said, "I'd had some wonderful experiences before as a minister. God had blessed me and had anointed me to preach. My wife and I had gotten many saved and even healed. But I had never really been filled with the Holy Ghost until then. When you get an experience inside the Word of God, you have an experience outside the realm of argument. Before, I had an argument, but now I had an experience with God."

Well, a Bible-based experience is always better than an argument! And the initial evidence of the baptism in the Holy Spirit according to the Word is speaking with other tongues. (For a further study of this subject, *see* Rev. Kenneth E. Hagin's study course, *The Holy Spirit and His Gifts.*)

We also need to realize that the gift of tongues with interpretation is distinctive of this dispensation, the New Testament era, the Age of Grace. All the other gifts of the Spirit were manifested in the Old Testament as well as in the New Testament. Even in the life and ministry of Jesus, all the other gifts of the Spirit were manifested except tongues and interpretation.

Because tongues and interpretation of tongues are distinctive of this Church Age dispensation, that is one reason they are more frequently distributed and used in the Church than the other gifts of the Spirit. That is another reason it seems we have an abundance of this particular manifestation.

Divers Kinds of Tongues

Divers kinds of tongues are supernatural utterances given by the Holy Ghost, which are languages never learned or understood by the speaker. However, divers kinds of tongues are not always unknown to the hearers. I say that because sometimes folks are present who understand a language one might receive when he is initially filled with the Holy Ghost or even when he ministers in tongues in a public assembly or group.

A minister once told me about taking a trip to Mexico. He and his wife spent several days there, and this minister had the opportunity to preach in one of the mission stations in Mexico. This minister had taken a load of provisions from his church to the needy folks in Mexico.

He said, "I preached about five nights, and the missionary interpreted my sermon to the people in Spanish. One night, I saw the most beautiful sight I had ever seen in my life. There was a large, homely woman who came to receive the Holy Ghost. The power of God fell on her and she began to speak in the most perfect English I had ever heard in my life. I understood everything she said."

The woman had not been to school a day in her life. She spoke only Latin-American Spanish. In other words, Spanish was her native language or tongue. In the natural, she couldn't speak a word of English. But when she received the Holy Spirit with the evidence of speaking in other tongues, she was given an utterance in a known tongue — *known* to some, but *unknown* to her. That did something for me spiritually! I have never been the same since."

Because it is called divers kinds of tongues, that is, different or diverse kinds of tongues, occasionally someone present may know the tongue which is spoken by another. However, this will not always be the case. Sometimes the diverse tongue is absolutely unknown to man. Sometimes the believer is speaking with heavenly languages because in another scripture we read, ". . . *NO MAN UNDERSTANDETH HIM; howbeit in the spirit he speaketh MYSTERIES*" (1 Cor. 14:2). But, thank God, God understands.

I have also been enabled by the Holy Spirit in ministering tongues in public, and sometimes even in praying in other tongues, to speak in a known tongue — that is, *known* to man, but *unknown* to me.

For example, I was in a prayer meeting with two Spirit-filled denominational pastors one time, and it was one of the greatest prayer meetings I have ever been in. We had been praying in tongues for a long time. As we were praying, I noticed that one of the pastors looked at me several times. I continued to pray in tongues. Afterwards, I asked him why he was looking at me.

He asked, "Did you know what language you were speaking?"

I said, "No, I was just praying."

He said, "You were speaking Spanish."

I said, "If I was, I didn't know it. I was just praying."

The pastor said, "I speak Spanish and I understood what you said. Actually, not only did you pray, but you quit praying and began talking to me in Spanish. I understood what you said."

The Holy Spirit was talking to this pastor in a language he could understand. The tongue was unknown to me, but not unknown to this pastor. I didn't know one word I said because I don't speak Spanish, but I did know that I was inspired by the Holy Ghost to speak forth that message. It was inspired utterance in a *known* tongue, but it was *unknown* to me.

Just after I spoke that message in tongues to him, the power of God came upon him, and he fell on his face on the floor. The Holy Spirit gave him a vision. He lay there about forty minutes.

This pastor had a church of about two thousand members. A Spirit-filled deacon in his church had offered to pay this pastor's way to this convention. This denominational pastor had accepted the deacon's offer and had become convinced of the truth of God's Word and the reality of God's Spirit!

You see, sometimes tongues are unknown to man; that is, only God understands the tongues. But sometimes tongues are known by man. Another example of this is an incident that occurred once with a woman who was a missionary to India. She was home on furlough and didn't know whether or not she should go back to India. While she was at a Bible institute, one of the students got up in an assembly and began to speak in tongues.

There was no interpretation at all. As they waited and wondered about it, she arose and said, "That student was speaking one of the dialects which is spoken in India. I understood every word that was said. That message was for me and that is the reason there was no interpretation. In that message, God spoke to me and said He wanted me to go back to India, and He was telling me what to do."

She understood the language and she knew that the Bible school student had no knowledge of that language. Thank God for the supernatural gifts of the Spirit.

The Importance of Speaking in Tongues

Some people say, "What is the use of speaking with tongues?" There are some folks who have been filled with the Holy Ghost with the evidence of speaking with tongues. But then they see no reason to continue speaking with tongues after their initial experience.

I have to question such a person's intelligence. It seems to me that anyone who is capable of reading could read the Word of God for himself and readily see what the Word says on the subject of tongues (Jude 20; 1 Cor. 14:2,4,5,18). Too many times we can read the Word of God with glasses that are colored with tradition. In other words, many times we do not get the full import of what God's Word says because we believe we already know what it says.

I want you to notice that in First Corinthians 14, Paul devotes almost an entire chapter to the subject of speaking with tongues. Paul talks a little about prophecy and a little about interpretation, but for the most part, the chapter is primarily about tongues. There are not too many subjects in the Bible on which an entire chapter has been entirely devoted to that subject alone. For example, prayer is a subject of utmost importance. But nowhere in the Bible do you find an entire chapter on prayer.

Paying tithes and giving offerings are very important, too, aren't they? You couldn't carry on the work of God without them. Yet there is not an entire chapter in the Bible devoted to the subject of giving tithes and offerings.

Water baptism is also a very important Bible subject. But do you know anywhere in the Bible where there is a whole chapter on the subject? No, you don't.

The new birth — the born-again experience — is an all-important subject. But do you know anywhere in the Bible where an entire chapter is devoted to the subject of the new birth? No, you don't because there isn't one!

There are many verses about the new birth, of course, and this subject carries great import in the Bible and is indirectly the subject of much of the New Testament, for it is to this end — the redemption of mankind — that Jesus came. Yet as important as the new birth is, we do not find an entire chapter devoted to this subject alone.

There are many Bible subjects that are very important. Just because there is not a whole chapter on them does not mean that they are not important. On the other hand, we must also realize that when we see an entire chapter on a subject, it must carry some significance because God did not put unnecessary words in the Bible. He does not fill up His Word with unnecessary statements. Therefore, this teaching on tongues must be important because God devoted an entire chapter to it in His Word.

Notice First Corinthians 14:2, *"For he that speaketh in an unknown tongue speaketh not unto men, but unto God. . . ."* Paul is not talking here about ministering tongues in a public assembly. He is talking about the individual Spirit-filled believer speaking in tongues in his own private prayer life.

It is also proper to pray in tongues at the altar because you go there to talk to God and to seek Him. When tongues are ministered in a public assembly or group, it is God speaking to us.

Speaking With Tongues Is Not Always Prayer

Even in Pentecostal circles, there are all kinds of ideas and teachings about tongues that do not line up with the Word. For example, sometime ago I heard a pastor speak on the subject of tongues before a large crowd of about nine hundred people. He said something that wasn't scriptural. I thought, *I'm so sorry he said that because it isn't true.*

This pastor misled the whole crowd because he said that all speaking with tongues are prayer. But all speaking with tongues is *not* prayer. He took that verse in First Corinthians 14 where Paul said, *". . . he that speaketh in an unknown tongue speaketh not unto men, but unto God. . . ,"* and applied that verse to *all* speaking in tongues. It is true that when we pray in tongues in our private prayer lives, we are praying directly *to* God. But this pastor failed to take into account other uses of tongues which are *not* prayer.

For example, diverse tongues is a means whereby the Holy Ghost can speak through the believer in a *known* tongue. The tongue may be unknown to the speaker, but known to someone else. But by saying that all tongues is prayer, this pastor was also discounting the gift of interpretation of tongues whereby *God* speaks unto *man.* That is not prayer, but it is God speaking to man. Therefore, this pastor's statement that all tongues is prayer does not line up with what the Word says.

Tongues are manifested in other ways besides just prayer. As we said previously, tongues may be a manifestation of a *known* tongue. For instance, I gave you the example of the pastor who heard me speak in Spanish under the anointing of the Holy Ghost.

If you were to ask me to speak in Spanish, I could not do it. I can count up to nine in Spanish, and I can say three or four words, but that is all. But I was speaking very rapidly and fluently in Spanish by the unction of the Holy Spirit.

This denominational pastor said that first I was praying, but then I began to talk to him in Spanish; that is, the Spirit of God was talking to him in a language that was *known* to him. That was not praying. And yet it was a manifestation of an inspired utterance given in a known tongue.

I held a meeting for a minister who had been a missionary years ago in China. In the meeting, I spoke in a language that I did not know. I realized that it seemed to be Oriental. Later he and his wife spoke to each other in Chinese and I recognized that I had spoken some of those words.

The woman later said to her husband, "Did you understand what Brother Hagin said?" Her husband said that he had understood at least half of it. His wife had understood most of it. It had been a good number of years since they had been to China, and the minister said I was not speaking the dialect of the area where they had lived. He had interpreted by the Holy Spirit the message in tongues, but he understood with his mind fifty to sixty percent of what I said in Chinese. The Holy Spirit was using me to give a message in a diverse tongue that was not prayer at all, but was a message to men, to the hearers.

One time I was preaching at a camp meeting in southeastern Oklahoma. As we were leaving one evening, it began to rain. My wife and I gave a woman who was standing there a ride home.

The woman said, "I belong to another church, but we live nearby so I have been coming to this church. I want to ask you a question. First of all, let me tell you that my son was in the Army, and after the war he stayed in Germany for a while in the occupational forces. He came to get me the other night at this meeting and he asked about you, Brother Hagin, because at the end of your sermon you spoke in tongues.

"My son asked me, 'Who was that fellow talking in German?' "

The woman said, "I told him, 'That was Brother Hagin.'

"Then I asked my son, 'Was Brother Hagin speaking in German?'

"My son said, 'Yes.' "

The woman continued, "Then my son said, 'Then another fellow got up and translated the message for him.' My son could speak quite a bit of German himself, so he understood the message you gave in tongues, Brother Hagin.

"I asked my son, 'Did the fellow who translated for Brother Hagin do all right?'

"My son said, 'He did fine. He did not translate it exactly — word for word — but he gave the meaning of what was said.' "

The woman said, "I told him you didn't know German. You don't, do you, Brother Hagin?"

I said, "No. I don't know a word in the German language."

The woman continued, "I told my son that you didn't know German and that it was tongues with interpretation. I told him that you were speaking under the inspiration of the Holy Ghost and that this other man was also inspired by the Holy Spirit of God to interpret what you said.

"When I told him all of this is in the Bible, he asked, 'Are you sure?'

"I told him, 'Yes, I don't know much about it, but I have been learning since I have been coming these few nights to the camp meeting.'

"My son said, 'I believe I will keep on going to these services.' "

The woman concluded, "My son isn't a Christian, but that made a great impression on him." Thank God for the supernatural gift of diverse tongues.

I was holding a meeting in 1960 in Mesa, Arizona. The pastor told me about a young Jewish boy who attended their church. This Jewish boy had joined the Air Force. He didn't have too many friends, so a young Pentecostal boy befriended him and began to associate with him some. He invited the Jewish boy to go to church with him, but he wouldn't go because he didn't believe in Christ — that He was the Messiah.

But then the Jewish boy said, "Well, I shouldn't be that way. After all, you are the only one here who has befriended me. I'll go with you."

So he came to that Pentecostal church. A woman there got up and spoke in tongues. The pastor who was usually used in interpretation said that he didn't get any interpretation. He waited, and no one else got the interpretation. This same woman was also used in the gift of interpretation of tongues, yet she never interpreted the message.

The pastor said, "After I waited for a few minutes, we just went on with the service. After the service was over, I was shaking hands with the folks at the front door, when this Jewish boy said to me, 'Who was that woman who talked to me?'

"I said, 'What do you mean?' "

The boy said, "That woman who got up in the service talked to me. She talked my language. She even called my name! She told me what I had been thinking. She told me that Christ was the Messiah and that I should believe on Him."

The pastor told the young Jewish boy, "That dear woman is a widow. She only has about a fifth-grade education. She takes in washings for a living. She doesn't speak any foreign languages."

The pastor called the woman over and introduced her to the Jewish boy so he could tell by talking to her that she was a very uneducated woman.

The Jewish boy said, "I'll have to think about this." He came back the next Sunday night and was born again.

This young Jewish boy received Christ as the Messiah and his Savior as a result of that woman standing up and giving a message in tongues. She wasn't praying; she was delivering a message in a *known* tongue. All talking in tongues is not prayer, regardless of what someone may tell you.

It is true that one phase of speaking with tongues is prayer. Tongues can be used in prayer. In fact, no one will ever have a completely successful prayer life without praying in tongues. You may have been mighty in God without praying in tongues, but you will be more powerful in God by praying in tongues: *"For he that speaketh in an unknown tongue speaketh not unto men, but unto God: for no man understandeth him; howbeit in the spirit he speaketh mysteries"* (1 Cor. 14:2).

Moffatt's translation of First Corinthians 14:2 says when a person is speaking in tongues, ". . . he is talking of divine secrets in the Spirit." God has devised a means whereby we may speak supernaturally to Him. By speaking in tongues, man can talk divine secrets with God.

Tongues: A Means of Edifying Yourself Spiritually

Tongues is also a means of building yourself up spiritually. In First Corinthians 14:4, Paul said, *"He that speaketh in an unknown tongue edifieth himself. . . ."* That means he builds himself up spiritually.

JUDE 20
20 But ye, beloved, building up yourselves on your most holy faith, praying in the Holy Ghost.

This verse does not say praying in the Holy Ghost will give you faith, but it says that praying in the Holy Ghost will *build you up* on your most holy faith. Praying in tongues builds you up on the faith you already have; it is a means of spiritual edification.

I had an experience when I was pastor of a community church that helped me a great deal. I happened to be staying in a good Christian home. The doctors said the woman of this home had an ulcerated stomach, and they confided to her husband that they thought it would probably turn into cancer of the stomach. She could not eat anything except baby food and a few raw eggs mixed in sweet milk, and she had trouble keeping even that on her stomach. She was desperately ill.

I wasn't there when she later received the baptism in the Holy Ghost, but she told me about her experience of being filled with the Holy Ghost and speaking with tongues. No one prayed for her healing, but from the moment she received the Holy Ghost, she was automatically healed and ate anything she wanted. She was perfectly healed!

I believed in divine healing because the Word of God talks about it and because I myself had been raised up off a deathbed. One surely could not find fault with an experience that could bring both healing *and* blessing. The woman was a believer, a child of God, and I considered her to be a very wonderful Christian. In fact, I thought she was one of the most wonderful Christian women I had ever met. After this woman received the Holy Spirit and began praying in tongues, she built herself up on her most holy faith, and her faith began to operate.

I have seen that happen many times. Many times people with incurable conditions receive the baptism of the Holy Ghost and speak with tongues and are healed. I had prayed for some of these same people before, and they did not receive their healing when I prayed for them, for one reason or another. We know that speaking with tongues is a tremendous spiritual boost to a person. It does edify him and build him up.

Tongues: A Means of Magnifying God

Speaking with tongues is also a way we can magnify God. It says in Acts 10:46 concerning Cornelius and his household, *"For they heard them speak with tongues, and MAGNIFY GOD. . . ."*

I was a Christian minister for several years before I received the baptism in the Holy Spirit. I used to go down to the barn and get up in the hayloft to pray. I prayed and had some wonderful times with the Lord in prayer.

However, I still went away from those times disappointed, although I was blessed. I would try to tell God how much I loved Him. I would use all the descriptive adjectives I had at my disposal to tell God how wonderful He is. I would exhaust my vocabulary and leave that place of prayer feeling disappointed in my spirit that I had not said what I wanted to say. My spirit felt like I had cheated it.

It's just like going to a restaurant to get something to eat. I don't mind paying for food when I get something to eat. But I don't like walking up to the cash register to pay for something when my stomach is still crying, "You cheated me!"

I would go away from the place of prayer unsatisfied, with my spirit crying, "You cheated me." I didn't know what it was that I was missing. I knew that I was a child of God. I knew that I had been healed by the power of God. I knew that I had been raised up from the deathbed. I knew God called me to preach; I preached and saw many people get saved. I even saw some get healed. But I would go away from that place of prayer with something on the inside of me saying, "You cheated me!" because my spirit wanted to pray, too, apart from my understanding — my mind.

1 CORINTHIANS 14:14
14 For if I pray in an unknown tongue, MY SPIRIT PRAYETH, but my understanding is unfruitful.

One thing I appreciate about being filled with the Holy Ghost is speaking with tongues. From the day I was Spirit filled to this day, I have worshipped and magnified God, praying and singing in tongues, and I have communicated with God by this means every single day.

I have never again left the place of prayer with my spirit crying, "You cheated me." I have never left the place of prayer with the feeling that I didn't say what I wanted to say because my spirit had been divinely enabled to say what it wanted to say by the Holy Spirit who indwells me.

I would not argue and fuss about it, but I simply feel sorry for folks who can't see the truth of the Bible about praying in tongues. I want them to enjoy the blessings of God too. Praise the Lord! If I have something good, I want others to enjoy it. I don't want to be selfish, do you?

I used to eat quite a lot of ice cream. My wife had a recipe for cherry nut ice cream, and I thought it was the best ice cream I had ever tasted, so I wanted to share it. Another woman wanted the recipe, so my wife shared it with her.

When I have something good, I want to share it with someone else. I wouldn't argue with anyone about whether that ice cream is the best; I would just share it with him and give him the recipe. And, spiritually speaking, if I have something good, I want to share it with others too.

I want to invite you to come on in to this biblical experience of speaking with other tongues and begin to communicate with God supernaturally through praying in the Spirit. God wants to do so much more for you. He wants to communicate with you in a more effective means than just by your native language; He wants to communicate with you supernaturally through the precious Holy Spirit.

Tongues: A Means of Praying Supernaturally

I want every Christian to know the joy of fellowshipping with the Lord in the Spirit. As we discussed earlier, the Holy Spirit in you can help you with your praying. The Bible says, ". . . my spirit [by the Holy Spirit within me] prays . . ." (1 Cor. 14:14 *Amp.*).

I cannot overestimate what this kind of praying has meant to my life personally. There is no way in the world to estimate its value. I simply could never overestimate the value of praying in tongues.

For example, I have traveled for many years away from home. And again and again, if anything was happening at home about which I needed to be aware, the Holy Spirit would immediately alert me in my spirit. I would wake up in the night and something on the inside of me would say, "Something is not right. One of the family members is in trouble. Something is wrong."

Immediately I would say to the Holy Ghost (no, I do not pray *to* the Holy Ghost. But He is a Person, a Divine Personality, and He is within me, and I do talk to Him), "I don't know what is wrong, but You know everything. You are in me as my Helper. Help me pray about this condition or situation the way it should be prayed about."

Then I would begin praying in tongues. I would pray on and on in tongues. I have prayed as many as six hours in tongues. Many times He will let me know what I am praying about and give me the answer to my prayer in my spirit. Whether He shows me the answer right then or not, in a few days I see the situation work out fine. We can do work for God praying supernaturally in tongues.

I do fifty percent of my praying in tongues. For instance, if my son or daughter or members of their families are having some trouble, I might not know what the trouble is. I will tell the Lord that I don't know for what to pray as I ought, but that I am looking to the Holy Spirit to help me. Sometimes I pray for my children for an hour in tongues.

Sometimes I'll have a revelation or God will show me the answer. He will show me just exactly what to do. But whether or not you have any revelation about the situation you are praying about, just continue to pray in tongues because the Holy Spirit knows and He is taking hold with you against the problem. That kind of praying gets the job done when nothing else will.

A friend whom I had known since he was a child, became a minister when he grew up. When he was in his early twenties he went to preach a service one night, and on the way back home, a fellow who was weaving all over the highway in his automobile hit this minister's car head on.

At this time the young minister and his wife were living with the minister's father who was a pastor. The father got a call from the hospital and was told that his son had been in a car wreck.

When the father got there, the doctors told him that his son's neck and back were broken, and that he was paralyzed from his waist down and was unconscious. The doctor said the young minister would always be paralyzed to some extent, and they doubted if he would ever make much improvement. Actually, the doctors couldn't understand why he wasn't dead. They put him in a full-body cast. His neck and his back were broken, and he was unconscious. The father stayed by his son's bedside all night. At one point, his son had temporarily regained consciousness but had again lapsed back into unconsciousness.

The next night when the father went to the hospital, the young man was still unconscious. The father told the nurses he was going to stay and pray at his son's bedside.

The young minister regained consciousness for a little while again that night. The father told his son to blink his eyes if he could understand what he was saying to him, so the son blinked his eyes. Then the young man lapsed back again into unconsciousness. The father stayed by his bedside and prayed. He began to pray at 8:00 in the evening. At 12:00 midnight, the father was still praying in tongues. He heard the nurse come in, but he never opened his eyes; he just kept on praying. He prayed about ten hours in tongues.

Early the next morning at about 6:00, the father got up and went over to his son. He saw that his son was lying there with his eyes open. He asked his son if he could hear him, and his son spoke up and said

he could. The young man told the father that he was all right and that God had healed him. The young man began to wiggle his fingers and toes; he had feeling all over his body.

The nurse and the doctor came in, and they both said it was truly amazing; it was a miracle! The young minister told them that God had healed him and that he wanted the doctor to take the cast off. He told the doctor that he would find that the two breaks in his back and neck were healed and that he was all right.

After much persuasion the doctor took the young minister and x-rayed his spine. The doctor came back and said he just couldn't believe it! He couldn't even find where his back had been broken. God had mended it so that it was just as normal as it was before! The doctor examined the X rays again and still couldn't find anything. So they kept the young man hospitalized for a day or two and kept checking him. They told him to wear a neck brace for a little while, but he went home and took it off.

Years later this man was still all right. He's been out preaching the gospel for years. The church had prayed about it, but the father got the job done when he began to pray in the Spirit. He got the help of the Holy Ghost. You increase your power in prayer one hundred percent by praying in other tongues!

Many times I have prayed in tongues for hours, and in that time the tongues have changed and I have spoken half a dozen different tongues or languages. Many times as the tongues would change, God would let me see foreign people. I would see foreign houses and buildings. That vision would stay before me all the time I was praying in tongues. I didn't know what tongues I was praying in, but I knew I was praying for those foreign people in their native tongue.

In some cases, I would later pick up a Pentecostal magazine and see the picture of the very folks for whom I was praying. I would read about a revival that broke out in that area. I believe the Spirit of God enabled me to have a part in it. You can stay home and have a part in the work of God around the world. There are more ways than one to "go" and take the gospel around the world.

Praying in Tongues Is Unselfish Prayer

Also, there are representatives in other countries whom we need to back up in prayer. Our praying does not need to be so self-centered. Sometimes the extent of our praying is for our families. Some churches pray *only* for the local church; those people's prayers are selfish. We should be interested in everyone *everywhere*. We need a worldwide vision.

I believe we should be interested in our local church, and, certainly, we should be praying for our own families. But we should not pray only for our families and our churches and neglect everything else.

Some people are not concerned about others. I can remember when in Pentecostal circles we were just after the saving of souls. We didn't care who they were — whether they came out of the denominational church or not — we just wanted to see souls saved and baptized in the Holy Ghost. I am still that way. I have never changed.

Also, there are many who always have the attitude in life, *What am I going to get out of it?* That, too, is selfish and shows a lack of praying in the Spirit and walking in the light of His Word.

For example, once I was supposed to hold a meeting in a certain city, and six other churches were going to cooperate. A man who was the manager of my meetings at the time set the meeting up. We spent several hundred dollars on advertisement. Each of these churches was going to share the cost of the advertisement. However, at the last minute, five out of the six ministers backed out of the meeting. My manager asked these ministers why they were not going to participate in these citywide meetings.

The minister replied, "We have been thinking about it. If we go over to that church meeting, some of our church members might like it better over there and they might decide to stay. So we are not going along with the meetings."

My manager said to them, "Why, Brethren, what am I going to do? I have told Brother Hagin that you were all cooperating and he has already spent all of this money advertising for the meetings!"

They said, "We can't help that. We are not going to support the meetings."

My manager said, "Brother Hagin is going to think you are all liars. If that is not lying, please tell me what it is. If a man is selling an automobile, for example, and he said to you, 'This automobile is perfectly all right. I just drove it and it is just fine. There's not a thing in the world wrong with it. This has been my own personal car.' Then if you buy it and find out it was not his own personal car and he didn't know what he was talking about — that the automobile needed a lot of repair — wouldn't you accuse that fellow of lying?"

They replied, "Yes."

He said, "Well, that man didn't lie about that car any more than you did about these meetings!"

But every one of those fellows backed out of the meeting anyway. We went ahead and had a great meeting anyway. The house was full, and some of those ministers' church members attended the meetings anyway.

We should never go to prayer with the attitude, *What am I going to get out of it?* If we do that, whether we are a preacher or layperson, we are wrong. Those ministers could not have been doing very much praying in tongues and feeding on the Word.

We cannot spend time praying in tongues and fellowshipping with God without the very love and nature of God permeating our being. And the more we pray in tongues, the less selfish we will become in our praying and it will show up in our relationships with our fellow man.

As I said, tongues is the gateway into the supernatural in our Christian walk. There are wonderful blessings in store for believers who receive the Holy Spirit with the evidence of speaking in tongues. And once you've had that initial experience, you continue to keep tongues a "flowing stream" in your life. To reach the potential we have in Christ for supernatural praying and supernatural living, we cannot neglect this precious gift of speaking with tongues.

---

[1] Howard Carter, *Questions and Answers on Spiritual Gifts* (Tulsa, Oklahoma: Harrison House, Inc., 1976), p. 120.

Questions for Study

1. When do believers receive the gift of tongues?

    _____

    _____

2. What are the inspirational or vocal gifts of the Spirit designed to do?

    _____

    _____

3. Why is speaking with other tongues important to the believer?

    _____

    _____

4. Speaking in tongues is the Bible evidence of what?

    _____

    _____

5. How does maintaining a continual experience of speaking in tongues affect the life of a believer?

    _____

    _____

6. Why are tongues and interpretation of tongues more frequently distributed and used in the Church than any of the other gifts of the Spirit?

    _____

    _____

7. One use of speaking in tongues is prayer. Name some other uses of tongues.

    _____

    _____

8. How can man talk divine secrets with God?

    _____

    _____

9. Why should you keep praying in tongues about a situation whether or not you have received any revelation about it?

    _____

    _____

10. We cannot spend time praying in tongues and fellowshipping with God without the very _____ and _____ of God permeating our being.

Chapter 11

The Prayer of Intercession
And the Prayer of Agreement

Let's look at two other kinds of prayer in this chapter: the prayer of intercession and the prayer of agreement.

First we'll look at the *prayer of intercession*. The word "intercede" means *to act between two parties with the thought of reconciling the two of them.* Therefore, the prayer of intercession is standing in the gap in prayer on behalf of another. Normally, we intercede for the unsaved.

God said something to Israel through the prophet Isaiah which shows that God desires His people to intercede on behalf of others.

ISAIAH 64:7
7   And there is none that calleth upon thy name, that stirreth up himself to take hold of thee: for thou hast hid thy face from us, and hast consumed us, because of our iniquities.

This verse implies that if someone had stirred himself up to pray and intercede and to call upon God, judgment on the nation of Israel could have been stayed or stopped! Let's look at a similar statement by Ezekiel.

EZEKIEL 22:30
30 And I sought for a man among them, that should make up the hedge, and STAND IN THE GAP before me for the land, that I should not destroy it: but I found none.

Do you realize what these verses are saying? God *looks* for people of prayer to stand in the gap, to make up the hedge, and to intercede so that people's lives can be spared.

Abraham's Intercession

In Genesis chapter 18, we see the example of Abraham as one who stood in the gap on behalf of others. When Abraham became aware of the impending judgment upon the inhabitants of Sodom and Gomorrah, he interceded for them. Let's look at the example of Abraham in Genesis chapter 18, who interceded or stood in the gap for others.

GENESIS 18:23-32
23 And Abraham drew near, and said, Wilt thou also destroy the righteous with the wicked?
24 Peradventure there be fifty righteous within the city: wilt thou also destroy and not spare the place for the fifty righteous that are therein?
25 That be far from thee to do after this manner, to slay the righteous with the wicked: and that the righteous should be as the wicked, that be far from thee: Shall not the Judge of all the earth do right?
26 And the Lord said, If I find in Sodom fifty righteous within the city, then I will spare all the place for their sakes.
27 And Abraham answered and said, Behold now, I have taken upon me to speak unto the Lord, which am but dust and ashes:
28 Peradventure there shall lack five of the fifty righteous: wilt thou destroy all the city for lack of five? And he said, If I find there forty and five, I will not destroy it.
29 And he spake unto him yet again, and said, Peradventure there shall be forty found there. And he said, I will not do it for forty's sake.
30 And he said unto him, Oh let not the Lord be angry, and I will speak: Peradventure there shall thirty be found there. And he said, I will not do it, if I find thirty there.
31 And he said, Behold now, I have taken upon me to speak unto the Lord: Peradventure there shall be twenty found there. And he said, I will not destroy it for twenty's sake.
32 And he said, Oh let not the Lord be angry, and I will speak yet but this once: Peradventure ten shall be found there. And he said, I will not destroy it for ten's sake.

When Abraham asked the Lord to spare the city if He should find fifty righteous people, the Lord said, ". . . *If I find in Sodom fifty righteous within the city, then I will spare all the place for their sakes*" (Gen. 18:26).

Then Abraham said, "Lord, I'd just like to speak a little further to you, if you don't mind. (I'm putting this in my own words, but this is the essence of what Abraham said.) If there are forty-five righteous people there, would you spare the place for forty-five?" (v. 28).

In effect, the Lord answered Abraham, "Yes, I'll do it — just because you asked Me. For forty-five righteous, I'll spare the thousands who are there" (v. 28).

Then Abraham continued to ask the Lord to spare Sodom and Gomorrah, even if there were only forty, thirty-five, thirty, or twenty righteous inhabitants.

Finally, Abraham asked God to spare Sodom and Gomorrah for the sake of ten righteous people, and God agreed to stay judgment if ten righteous were found. I believe Abraham surely thought there would be at least ten righteous in Sodom and Gomorrah.

Think about that! God would have spared that city which was full of corruption and immorality for the sake of ten righteous people. The Bible says God never changes — He is forever the same (Mal. 3:6). Will He not do in our day what He did in Abraham's day?

If under the Old Covenant Abraham interceded for other people and God heard him, how much more will God hear our prayers under the New Covenant? Will He not hear our prayers for cities and nations for the sake of His children who live in them? He will, if we'll intercede as Abraham did!

We are covenant children, just as Abraham was. However, we have an even better Covenant established upon better promises (Heb. 8:6). And we have the authority in the Name of Jesus to help others through prayer and intercession and to effect a change in nations to the glory of God!

The Holy Spirit Helps Us Intercede

We discussed in the last chapter how praying in tongues can enhance our prayer life and enable us to pray supernaturally as the Holy Spirit gives us utterance.

Now we'll see how the Holy Spirit will help us as we intercede for others. We can intercede with our understanding, as Abraham did, or we can intercede with our spirits in tongues or in groanings and travail. But we must keep in mind that intercession can only be accomplished by the leading and guiding of the Holy Spirit.

Let's look in Romans chapter 8 to gain insight on the Holy Spirit's role as we intercede for others.

ROMANS 8:26
26 Likewise the Spirit also helpeth our infirmities: for we know not what we should pray for as we ought: but the Spirit itself maketh intercession for us with groanings which cannot be uttered [in articulate speech].

Dr. P. C. Nelson, a Greek scholar, told me that the actual Greek reads, ". . . with groanings that cannot be uttered in articulate speech." Articulate speech means your regular kind of speech; your native language. Therefore, Romans 8:26 also includes praying in tongues and praying with groanings. That agrees with what Paul says in First Corinthians 14:14.

1 CORINTHIANS 14:14
14 For if I pray in an unknown tongue, my spirit prayeth, but my understanding is unfruitful.

1 CORINTHIANS 14:14 (*Amplified*)
14 For if I pray in an [unknown] tongue, my spirit [by the Holy Spirit within me] prays, but my mind is unproductive — bears no fruit and helps nobody.

Can you see the connection between Romans 8:26 and First Corinthians 14:14? In both of these verses, the Holy Spirit enables our spirit to pray apart from our understanding.

According to Romans 8:26, we don't always know for what to pray as we ought. We think we do sometimes, but we don't. We can't possibly know in our natural mind everything we should pray about in every situation and circumstance.

Therefore, praying with our understanding sometimes falls far short of what we ought to do in this kind of praying. We should pray as much as we know in our understanding, of course. But sometimes just praying a few words in general for others really just salves a person's conscience.

Ephesians 1:3 says, *"Blessed be the God and Father of our Lord Jesus Christ, who hath blessed us with all spiritual blessings in heavenly places in Christ."*

You can say what you want or desire and even quote scriptures, but when it comes to prayer, many times, especially in praying for others, we don't know what to pray for as we ought. But, thank God, the Spirit helps our infirmities. An infirmity is any weakness, which would include a lack of knowledge about how to pray. He makes intercession for us with groanings which cannot be uttered in articulate speech (Rom. 8:26).

Again, this scripture does not mean prayer is something the Holy Ghost does apart from you. That would make the Holy Ghost responsible for your prayer life, and He isn't. *You* are responsible for your own prayer life.

Notice also the Bible says in Romans 8:26 that the Holy Spirit *helps* the believer in prayer. The Holy Ghost is not sent to actually do your praying for you. He is sent to help you in every aspect of life and to help you in your prayer life as well.

Groanings in the Spirit

Groanings that come out of your spirit and escape your lips are the Spirit of God *helping* or assisting you in prayer. There are some things that come out of your heart that can't be expressed in words and are therefore expressed by groaning too deep for articulate speech.

These groanings are inspired by the Holy Ghost. They come from within you and escape your lips. Praying with groanings is one way of making intercession. Remember, intercession is praying for another, not for yourself. An intercessor takes the place of *another*.

Charles Finney, who began his ministry as a Presbyterian minister and later became a Congregationalist, knew something about prayer and intercession. He was known as a man who prayed down revivals.

Finney was once holding a revival meeting in a certain town. In that town there was a leading doctor who had never gone to church. The doctor's wife, on the other hand, was a wonderful Christian leader. The doctor claimed to be an infidel; he'd make fun of his wife and would never go to church.

Finney was an educated man who was trained to be a lawyer. This woman thought if her husband could talk to Finney, Finney would be able to help him. So she kept insisting that Finney come to the house on one of his days off. After much persuasion, Finney finally agreed to go to their home for a noon meal.

This doctor had a brother who was a farmer and a deeply spiritual man. The brother would come and stay in their home and go to Finney's meetings. This farmer brother was staying there at the time Finney came to lunch. Actually, the doctor was a little ashamed of his brother because his brother wasn't educated.

At the time appointed, Finney went to this doctor's house, and as the four of them were at the table, the woman asked Finney to pray. Finney bowed his head and began to pray, but was checked in his spirit. He stopped praying and said that the Lord wanted the farmer brother to pray.

The brother began praying, but suddenly he just grabbed ahold of his stomach and started groaning and weeping and crying. He jumped up from the table and ran up the stairs to his bedroom. Finney said he jumped up and followed him.

The doctor thought that something was physically wrong with his brother, so he jumped up too. He reached his brother's room before Finney. As Finney started to go into the room, the doctor was coming out of the room to go get his medical bag. He said his brother had some kind of stomach cramps.

But Finney took the doctor by his arm and said, "Doctor, there's not anything physically wrong with him. Your brother has a spirit of travail and intercession. He's praying and interceding for someone who is lost, and I think it's for your soul." The doctor jerked loose from Finney and said he didn't believe in that.

The doctor left and Finney went into the bedroom and shut the door. There the brother was just in an agony of prayer, in the Spirit. Finney knelt down beside him, and he began to groan in the Spirit too.

You see, you can help lift a spiritual load just like you can a physical load. In other words, if someone else is groaning and interceding in the Spirit, as the Spirit wills, you can pick up that prayer burden and begin to groan and travail just as the other person is groaning and travailing.

Finney began to feel part of the prayer burden coming off on him. So for forty-five minutes they knelt and groaned in the Spirit in prayer.

I know from experience that when you're interceding for someone whose soul is lost, it feels like your own soul is lost when it actually isn't. But because you're taking someone's burden upon you, you actually feel on the inside of you as if you were lost. Some people have had that burden and didn't know what it was. But that is intercession for a lost soul. If you have a burden given to you by the Spirit of God, go ahead and groan and travail as the Spirit wills and pray it out.

Finney said that the brother and he were praying, and the doctor's wife was downstairs just wringing her hands. The doctor had gone into his study angry and had shut the door.

Then after forty-five minutes of groaning, they quit groaning and started laughing. You see, you should always continue to pray until you have a note of praise or victory. You'll either start laughing or start praising or singing. Then you know you have the answer to whatever it is you're praying about.

Finney related that he and this brother rejoiced and laughed for a while. Then they got up from praying and went downstairs, and the woman asked Finney how the brother was doing. Finney told her what had happened and asked her where the doctor was. She told him that he had gone into his study and locked the door and wouldn't let her or anyone else in.

Finney went to the door and knocked. There was no answer, so he called to the doctor. He asked the doctor if he would open the door because he had word for him about his brother. Finally, the doctor opened the door and asked Finney how his brother was doing.

Finney stepped into the room and told the doctor that it was just as he had suspected; the brother had been praying for the doctor's poor, lost soul and that Finney had joined him in prayer. Finney told the doctor he was just as good as saved.

When he finished talking, the doctor dropped his head. The doctor then looked up and Finney saw tears streaming down the doctor's face. The doctor got down on his knees and asked Finney to pray with him. The doctor told Finney he had been full of pride. Then he accepted Jesus and was gloriously saved.

Yes, there is a prayer of intercession for the lost — prayers of travail and groanings. It's to be regretted that we don't know more about intercession and travail anymore. But don't be afraid to yield to groanings and travail if the Holy Spirit leads you that way. Of course, you can't do these things in the flesh; they are accomplished *in the Spirit*, by the leading and assistance of the Holy Spirit.

Notice that Finney and the brother were groaning. They could also have been speaking with tongues and not have understood that's what it was. Finney speaks in other places about unutterable gushings coming out of his heart. He would not have known what to call them. But "unutterable gushings" could certainly describe tongues too.

Why do I say that? Because according to P. C. Nelson, the Greek reads, ". . . with groanings that cannot be uttered in articulate speech" (Rom. 8:26). Articulate speech is your regular kind of speech, that is, speech in your native language.

So praying with groanings too deep for articulate speech could also include praying in tongues because speaking in tongues is inarticulate speech.

That agrees with what Paul said. Paul said that when he prayed in an unknown tongue, it was his spirit that was praying. And we read the *Amplified* translation of that verse, which says, ". . . my spirit [by the Holy Spirit within me] prays . . ." (1 Cor. 14:14).

In other words, praying with your spirit by the help of the Holy Spirit is prayer that is not coming out of your mind; it's coming out of your *spirit*. It may be prayer in a known tongue — that is, unknown to you but known to man — or it may be prayer in an unknown tongue, understood only by God. But it is prayer that is inspired and directed by the Holy Spirit.

The Holy Spirit *helps* the believer to pray. And He helps us to intercede for others. However, the Holy Spirit does *not* do the praying apart from the believer. It is our responsibility to take the time to pray and intercede for others and to obey the gentle urgings of the Holy Spirit to do so. As we yield to the Holy Spirit we may pray *in* groanings according to the will of God.

We can also pray in other tongues at will; we do not need to wait for the Holy Spirit to prompt us. As we yield to the Holy Spirit, He will give us utterance according to the will of God. That utterance may be in groanings or it may be in intercession in tongues, or it may be intercession in our understanding in our native language.

The Prayer of Agreement

Now let's look at *the prayer of agreement* as Jesus taught it in Matthew chapter 18.

MATTHEW 18:19
19 Again I say unto you, That if two of you shall agree on earth as touching any thing that they shall ask, it shall be done for them of my Father which is in heaven.

Don't put any limitations on that scripture. Jesus didn't. Let's just take Him at His Word. It's like the story I sometimes tell about the young girl whose father kept insisting that the Scriptures didn't mean what they said. She replied, "Well, if Jesus didn't mean what He said, why didn't He say what He meant?"

I believe Jesus said what He meant and meant what He said! In order for Matthew 18:19 to work there just has to be two of us to agree, and we have to be on the earth. That fits us. Then all we have to do is agree in line with God's Word as touching anything that we shall ask. And the Bible says it shall be granted us.

Notice that Jesus said, ". . . *it SHALL BE DONE for them of my Father which is in heaven*" (Matt. 18:19). The strongest assertion one can make in the English language is to say, "I shall" or "I will." You can't make any stronger statement than that. In the Book of John Jesus said, *"If ye shall ask any thing in my name, I WILL DO it"* (John 14:14).

P. C. Nelson, who was a Greek scholar, was talking to some of us ministers between services at a convention I once attended. He was reading his Greek New Testament. He said he always did all of his personal reading and private devotions from the Greek because he said the Greek language was more beautiful than the English.

Rev. Nelson said that there were a number of Greek idioms that could not be translated in the English language. He said the English language doesn't have any counterpart for those words.

The translators made the strongest statement they could in the English language, but Rev. Nelson said the more literal rendering of John 14:14 in the

Greek is, "If you shall ask anything in My Name, and I don't have it, then I will make it for you." Praise God! It's just more beautiful to say it this way!

I believe it is important that we read Matthew 18:18-20 in order to get the full import of what Jesus is saying.

MATTHEW 18:18-20
18 Verily I say unto you, Whatsoever ye shall bind on earth shall be bound in heaven: and whatsoever ye shall loose on earth shall be loosed in heaven.
19 Again I say unto you, That if two of you shall agree on earth as touching any thing that they shall ask, it shall be done for them of my Father which is in heaven.
20 For where two or three are gathered together in my name, there am I in the midst of them.

Binding and Loosing

We usually take verse 20 and apply it just to gathering together in Jesus' Name for a church service. You can do that, but actually, that is not what this scripture is talking about.

Jesus is saying that wherever there are two people who are agreeing in prayer, He is right there to make it good. Jesus is bringing out the fact that whatever we bind on earth shall be bound in heaven and whatever we loose on earth shall be loosed in heaven. Heaven will back us up in what we pray on earth in agreement, as long as it is in line with God's Word. We have the authority to loose and to bind.

Instead of using that authority, however, many folks just let the devil bind them. They say they can't help it and that the devil is after them. They seem to think they can't do anything about the devil's attacks. But they *can* do something about it. Every believer has authority over the devil in Jesus' Name. If you don't know how to use your God-given authority over the devil yourself, then get into agreement with another believer and bind the devil from harassing you.

The prayer of agreement is for us today. What is Matthew 18:19 doing in the Bible anyhow if it's not for us to use to get our needs met? Is it in there for us to use? Or is it in there just to hold the rest of the Word together! No, it belongs to us. We can use it.

Acting on God's Promises Brings Results

It's amazing how we can just go along and leave these scriptures unacted upon and unrealized in our own lives. Yet they are in the Bible all of the time for our use and benefit. They belong to us.

I was preaching in Oregon in 1957 during a time of an economic recession in the nation. Oregon was one of the states that felt the recession desperately, especially in their lumber business.

A man and his wife had been in my meetings and had heard me preach on Mark 11:23: ". . . *whosoever shall say . . . and shall not doubt in his heart, but shall believe . . . he shall have whatsoever he saith.*" I'd had everyone in the service come forward to the altar and declare by faith what they wanted from God's Word. In other words, they were to make a confession of their faith in God's Word.

The wife said that when they started home, she asked her husband what he had declared or confessed by faith. This husband and wife had some property that they had been trying to sell for a couple of years, and they discovered that they had both *said* or *confessed* that they would be able to sell that lot. This husband and wife were in agreement for the sale of this property in Jesus' Name. They hadn't been able to sell it in economically good times, and since the recession came along, it seemed that it would be impossible to sell it.

The next morning the owner went to the real estate agent to have him list the lot again. The real estate man said he had been trying to sell the lot for two years and it just wouldn't sell. But the owner said he thought it would sell and he wanted to list it again.

The real estate man suggested that the owner go talk to a man who lived next door to the property who had been interested in the lot previously and had wanted to buy it. He said if that man didn't want to buy it, then he would list it again.

So the owner went and talked to this man, and the man told him that he was still interested in the property. The owner of the lot still wanted the same price for it, and the man said that he would buy it.

This couple told me they had been in financial trouble for a couple of years, but then they realized they could have had the money all this time if they had only *said* or declared God's Word over that property in faith.

But instead of *believing* with their hearts and *saying* what they desired, they had only been praying that God would do something about the situation. They said they ought to have done something about it themselves earlier; but they didn't know what their privileges were in Christ.

You see, we have our part to play. When we make our move which includes declaring God's Word in the situation, then God moves in our behalf. If we fail to act upon God's Word in this way, then God has nothing to make good in our lives.

But that wasn't all of the story. The owner of this property, who had heard me preach on faith, worked in the woods. And in severe wintertime weather, he couldn't work. Therefore, he could only work certain months out of the year.

Another fellow was in the trucking business and he asked this man if he would like to work for him, since one of his employees was leaving. He could give him work twelve months out of the year, plus $100 more a month than what he was already making. The man accepted the job.

He and his wife were quite thrilled at this new job. They said they had always known Mark 11:23 was in the Bible, but that this was the first time they had ever acted on it. Yet they had been saved and filled with the Holy Ghost for years.

Isn't it strange that Pentecostal Christians can go through life, knowing the Word, but never acting on it. Thank God, His Word is true!

The Prayer of Agreement Works!

Jesus said, "*. . . That if two of you shall agree on earth as touching any thing that they shall ask, it shall be done for them of my Father which is in heaven*" (Matt. 18:19).

Jesus didn't say that there was a *possibility* that it would be done. He said that it *would be done*! If two of you can agree on anything you ask for according to God's Word, it will be done. *Jesus* made that statement. Instead of arguing against the Bible, why not just side in with it?

Years ago when I was a young Baptist boy, I had a friend whom I had grown up with. We played together as children and I would preach to him. I would corner him and preach to him and wouldn't let him go. He is an ordained minister today. He told me after he became a minister that he would never have made it in the ministry if it hadn't been for me preaching the Word to him.

This boy was working in his brother's garage back in 1935 in the worst of the Depression Days. There weren't any jobs to be found. He was nineteen years old, working with his brother, who paid him $3 a week and fed him. He didn't have good clothes. Both boys also tried to help their parents. So because of that added financial strain, the boys were very poor; they were just barely scratching out a living.

I stopped by to see this friend of mine, and he was down under the car. He was working on a '34 Chevy. His brother had left to go to the bank, and the boy motioned for me to kneel down and talk to him. He told me that he wanted me to pray with him about something.

This fellow had been going steady with a girl whom he wanted to marry. A person can hardly get married on $3 a week, and he wanted me to pray that God would give him a better job. He said he had already proposed to this girl and she had accepted. But he didn't even have the money to buy decent clothes to wear, much less have money to support a wife. He even had to wear khakis to church. He needed to buy a couple of suits of clothes and other things.

He had applied for a certain job, but when he put his application in, the man had told him they would take his application but that there were 2,000 people in line ahead of him for the same job. He was applying for a job at the cotton mill. He wanted me to agree with him that he would get that job, as there weren't any other jobs to be had.

So we agreed in prayer based on Matthew 18:19 that he would have this job in ten days. On the tenth day they called him, and he went to work for $10 a week. In a little while he bought himself a couple of suits of clothes. (In those days suits were very inexpensive.)

In about nine months' time, he and his girlfriend got married and they were able to live on $10 a week. He stayed at the cotton mill and was promoted and became one of the bosses and made a good salary. God eventually called him to preach and he went into the ministry.

That was my first experience of acting upon this scripture in Matthew 18:19. The prayer of agreement will work because it is God's Word.

Two Can Put Ten Thousand To Flight

You may be mighty in prayer alone, but you can be mightier with someone joining you. The Bible says that one will put one thousand to flight, but two will put ten thousand to flight (Lev. 26:8; Deut. 32:30).

In other words, you can do ten times as much with someone agreeing with you as you can by yourself. That's a good thought for you to meditate on. There doesn't have to be a great number of people for the prayer of agreement to work. For example, a husband and wife can become mighty partners in prayer. The prayer of agreement requires just two of you on earth, agreeing according to God's Word.

Wigglesworth and the Prayer of Agreement

Some time ago, I read the following account in one of Smith Wigglesworth's sermons. Wigglesworth said that in England a woman from a Presbyterian church had come to their little mission, had received the baptism of the Holy Ghost, and had spoken in tongues.

You may remember that when you were first filled with the Holy Ghost, you felt so wonderful you thought everyone would be glad to know about it. You thought all your friends and family would just be tickled to know about this New Testament experience.

Well, this Presbyterian woman thought that those in her Presbyterian church would be glad to know about the baptism in the Holy Spirit too. She went back to her church, and when God began to move in the service, she began to speak in tongues. But the elders got up and threw her out of the church. Her husband happened to be on the church board, and they had a meeting and informed him that he was going to have to put a stop to his wife's speaking in tongues in church, or they were going to have to excommunicate her from the church.

The man went home angry and stormed in and laid down an ultimatum to his wife. He informed her that she was either going to have to give up this Holy Ghost business and this tongue talking, or give him up. He wasn't going to put up with it! He was going to give her ten days to make up her mind whether she wanted him or the Holy Ghost.

This woman sent word for Wigglesworth to come and pray with her. She needed his advice. Wigglesworth didn't come to visit her as fast as she thought he should. One day he finally knocked on her door, and when she answered the door, Wigglesworth could see that her face was red and that she had been weeping. She immediately told him that he was too late. Wigglesworth didn't know why she had invited him to visit her. He just responded that God had never sent him anywhere too late.

The woman told Wigglesworth her story. The tenth day of her husband's ultimatum was up that very day. Her husband had asked her at the breakfast table what her decision was. She had said she couldn't give up the Holy Ghost, so her husband left.

Wigglesworth told this distraught woman that if they would agree in prayer according to Matthew 18:19, her husband would be back. She said, "Yes, but you don't know my husband." Wigglesworth agreed he didn't know her husband, but he told the woman he did know *Jesus*. He showed her Matthew 18:19. The woman said she had been living with her husband for twenty-five years, and in all that time he had never gone back on his word. When he made up his mind, that was it; it was a settled matter!

Wigglesworth exhorted the woman that God's Word is true. He told her if she would agree with him, her husband would be back that very evening. It took Wigglesworth a little time to get her to the place of agreeing because she was looking at the situation from the natural standpoint. When Wigglesworth finally got her to see what the Word says, she consented to agree with him in prayer. So they prayed and agreed.

He told her that when her husband came back, she should be sweet and lovely and act like nothing had happened. Wigglesworth told her when her husband went to bed, she should start praying quietly to herself, in the Spirit. When she was in the Spirit, she should go quietly and lay her hands on him and claim his soul.

You see, you have authority in your house. There's something here that we've failed to see as we ought to have. You can change things in prayer.

Wigglesworth left, and, of course, the man came back that evening. She and Wigglesworth had agreed on it! His wife had his favorite supper cooked and everything was fine and dandy. After he went to bed, she got off by herself to pray. She got to praying in tongues, and then very quietly went into the bedroom and knelt and laid her hands on him and claimed his soul for the Lord. She also claimed his complete deliverance.

The minute she did that, he awakened and jumped out of bed. He dropped to his knees and lifted his hands and asked the Lord to save him. He was saved and in a few minutes' time was filled with the Holy Ghost. His salvation occurred after his wife took the authority in her house that belonged to her (*See* Acts 16:31).

Dr. George Truett And the Prayer of Agreement

When you begin to teach scriptural truths like this, it almost sounds farfetched to some people. But I was in the office of a minister some time ago and saw on his desk a book of sermons by Dr. George Truett, who for so many years was pastor of the First Baptist Church in Dallas, Texas.

This book contains twelve of Truett's sermons, all of which were on the subject of faith. They sounded just like what I'm teaching. He even talked about healing. He brought out the fact that God can do any kind of a miracle, even today.

In one chapter, Truett wrote about the prayer of agreement. He told that when he was going to seminary, he would go out in the summertime and hold revivals. He was single at that time. He was preaching in west Texas once under a brush arbor, and they had made an altar bench where people could come and kneel to pray.

Truett preached his first sermon and afterwards a big rancher who was about six feet, six inches tall, came forward to talk to him. The rancher asked Truett if he believed the Bible. Truett said he surely did. The rancher then asked Truett if he believed the New Testament. Truett said he did.

The rancher then asked if Truett believed everything that was in it. Truett said that he surely did. The rancher asked him if he believed Matthew 18:19. Truett said he didn't know what it said, but whatever it was, he believed it. (We can all be sure that we believe the Word, but we have to act on it to get results.)

So Truett said he believed Matthew 18:19. This rancher showed Truett Matthew 18:19, and said Truett was the first preacher he'd ever met who believed it. The rancher wanted Truett to agree with him that his ranch foreman and family would be saved the next night in the service. He had been witnessing to his foreman. He said he would see to it that his foreman and his family were in church. Dr. Truett said that he would agree.

This big fellow reached out and grabbed Truett's hand and shook it, and said, "Lord, thank You, that I finally found someone to agree with me. I've been looking for someone for years. This little preacher and me agree that John and his wife and family will be saved tomorrow night."

Dr. Truett said he went home and could hardly sleep. He had agreed with the rancher because he said he would and because he said he believed Matthew 18:19. But in the nighttime Truett began struggling with thoughts to the contrary. Yet he knew he had to stay in agreement that the entire family would be saved because the prayer of agreement he and the rancher had prayed was in line with the Word. And Truett had said he believed the Word. But he was having an awful battle in his mind. The devil was trying to talk him out of the blessing they had agreed on.

Truett related that the next night he went to the meeting, and he looked around and didn't even see the rancher, much less anyone else who was there

for the first time. He thought they weren't coming. Finally, when the congregation was singing, the big rancher came in and behind him was a man and a woman and three children. Truett figured this must be the man — this ranch foreman — they had agreed about.

Truett preached right to that man and his family that night — he really gave them the works! And when they began to sing the invitation for salvation, Truett gave an altar call, but it just didn't seem to move this ranch foreman. Finally, Truett told the Lord he had done all he could do. He said that he was going to just turn the situation over to Him and sing one more verse of the invitation song.

They sang one more verse, and the foreman's oldest child, who looked to be about thirteen years old, came down to the altar. She knelt at the altar, and then one of the other children followed. Finally, all three of the man's children were down at the altar praying. Then the mother came, and finally the ranch foreman came and knelt too.

Dr. Truett said when the service was over, the rancher came up to him and said he knew if he could just find someone to agree with him, Matthew 18:19 would work. The rancher grabbed Truett's hands and nearly squeezed them off, shaking them in gratitude. He asked the preacher then to agree with him in prayer about his neighbor.

Truett said that after all this had happened, if that rancher had asked him to agree with him that the sun would rise in the west, he would have agreed! He was ready for anything!

Truett said he was young and didn't know any better than to believe God's Word. That was part of the reason he got so many results — by acting on the Word in simple faith. In other words, he said many times we can get our head educated at the expense of our heart, but that people who are in faith just believe God's Word and receive results from it.

Every sermon in Dr. Truett's book was on faith. In this story about the rancher, Truett and the rancher agreed on one family's salvation every night, and they were all saved! All the people they agreed upon were people who were coming to the meetings. In other words, they didn't agree for the salvation of people who were not hearing the message of the gospel. For two weeks they had the meeting, and the prayer of agreement worked every single night.

God's Word works! The prayer of agreement will work for you and for any believer who will dare to believe it and act on it. And that is true for every promise God gives us in His Word. You can be from any denomination and still act on the Word. And when you act on God's Word, the Word works!

In the last several chapters, we have discussed seven different kinds of prayer: the prayer of faith, the prayer of consecration, the prayer of worship, united prayer, the prayer of commitment, praying with tongues, the prayer of intercession, and the prayer of agreement.

As I've said, each of these kinds of prayers have different rules. We need to follow the Bible's teaching regarding all these kinds of prayer, and commit ourselves to *"Praying always with ALL PRAYER and supplication in the Spirit . . ."* (Eph. 6:18).

God wants us to understand the important subject of prayer and to learn how to pray more effectually and bear much prayer fruit for the Kingdom of God. As we endeavor to pray according to biblical principles, we will grow closer in fellowship to our Heavenly Father, and we will cause our prayer life to become more and more effective.

Questions for Study

1. What is the prayer of intercession?

   _____

   _____

2. Isaiah 64:7 emphasizes that the judgment on the nation of Israel have been stopped. How?

   _____

   _____

3. How is intercession accomplished?

   _____

   _____

4. What are groanings in the Spirit?

   _____

   _____

5. When praying for others, what does the Holy Spirit do and what is our responsibility?

   _____

   _____

6. What is required for Matthew 18:19 to work?

   _____

   _____

7. When will Heaven back up our prayers of agreement?

   _____

   _____

8. When does God move in our behalf?

   _____

   _____

9. Why does the prayer of agreement work?

   _____

   _____

10. How can we make our prayer life more effective?

   _____

   _____

Chapter 12

The Seven Most Important Things in Prayer Part 1

And in that day ye shall ask me nothing. Verily, verily, I say unto you, Whatsoever ye shall ask the Father in my name, he will give it you.

Hitherto have ye asked nothing in my name: ask, and ye shall receive, that your joy may be full.

— John 16:23,24

New Covenant Prayer

We discussed praying under the New Covenant in a previous chapter, but let's just review the subject of New Testament praying.

Jesus spoke the words in John 16:23 and 24 while He was on the earth. He was talking about the day in which we now live under the New Covenant. Jesus had not yet gone to Calvary when He made this statement. Jesus had not died. He had not been buried. He had not yet arisen from the dead.

The New Testament was not in force when Jesus said this because Jesus' blood had not been carried into the Holy of Holies. Jesus' blood is the seal of the New Covenant (Heb. 9:12-16; Heb. 10:19).

Before Jesus died and rose again, man had the promise of redemption, but had not yet received it. Eternal life had been promised, but not yet provided. Before Jesus went to the Cross, no one had received the new birth — people only had the promise of it. The new birth only became available under the New Covenant.

The new birth was foretold by the prophets in the Old Covenant. But as I said, the new birth was not available to those living under the Old Covenant. Certainly, Old Testament saints could receive the atonement of their sins through the blood of bulls and goats (Lev. 5:6; 16:16-18; Heb. 10:4-22) which were types of the shed blood of Jesus. But under the Old Covenant, men's *hearts* were never changed; their natures were never changed. That's the reason they kept on sinning; they couldn't help but sin because they didn't have a new nature (2 Cor. 5:17; Heb. 10:16).

Some of the greatest saints in the Old Testament sinned. Even after they were forgiven for some wrongdoing, they would go and do something else that was wrong. That's because their nature was all wrong. Their heart was all wrong. The heart is the inward man. The Old Testament saints only had a covering for their sins through the blood of bulls and goats. They did *not* have a change of heart or nature.

But in the Old Testament, God said that He would take that old heart out of us and give us a new one (Jer. 31:33; Ezek. 36:26). He said He would put a new spirit in us — He said He would put *His* Spirit in us (John 3:3-7; 2 Cor. 5:17; Rom. 8:14-16; Heb. 10:16).

All of this became available under the New Covenant in the new birth. But the new birth — the change in man's heart or nature — wasn't available while Jesus was on the earth, because the New Covenant wasn't in force then. Jesus hadn't shed His blood yet. So in John 16:23 Jesus is telling His disciples how to pray after He goes to Calvary and is raised from the dead. They were to pray *to* the Father *in Jesus' Name* (John 16:23).

As I already discussed in a previous chapter, we are not supposed to pray to Jesus. When it comes to prayer based on legal grounds, it should be addressed to the Father in the Name of Jesus. These are Jesus' instructions.

The Lord's Prayer Is Not a New Covenant Prayer

Even what we call The Lord's Prayer is not New Testament praying. The disciples asked Jesus to teach them to pray. Jesus gave His disciples The Lord's Prayer to pray for that period of time when He was on earth.

You see, Jesus came to the earth, and when He died on the Cross, He said, *". . . It is finished . . ."* (John 19:30). That meant that the Old Covenant was finished. Jesus ushered in the New Covenant by His death, burial, and resurrection. So Jesus gave His followers The Lord's Prayer for them to pray during this interim time — between the time the Old Covenant would be finished and the New Covenant would be ratified or established in His own blood.

Therefore, there are principles of prayer we can learn from The Lord's Prayer, but technically this is still a prayer under the Old Covenant. We know that because there is no mention of praying in Jesus' Name in The Lord's Prayer. Jesus just said, "When you pray, say, '. . . *Our Father which art in heaven . . .*'" (Matt. 6:9; Luke 11:2). This prayer is beautiful, but it is a prayer that Jesus taught folks to pray back before the Old Covenant went out and the New Covenant came in.

But Jesus said that when the New Covenant came into effect, they should pray to the Father in His

Name: "... *IN THAT DAY ye shall ask me nothing . . . Whatsoever ye shall ask the Father IN MY NAME, he will give it you*" (John 16:23). "In that day" is the day of the New Covenant. At this point, Jesus had not yet died for the redemption of mankind, so the disciples could only pray to the Father. They could not pray in the Name of Jesus.

The Lord's Prayer says, "*Thy kingdom come. Thy will be done . . .*" (Matt. 6:10). The Kingdom of God *has* come. The New Testament tells us that now under the New Covenant, the Kingdom of God is in the hearts of men (Luke 17:21). We have the Kingdom of God in our hearts, if we're born again. We are in the Kingdom of God *now* if we're born again.

Yes, the Kingdom of *heaven* will eventually come on the earth, but that's not the Kingdom of God which is already in us through the new birth. We make a mistake to say that the Kingdom of God and the Kingdom of heaven are the same. The Bible says that the Kingdom of God is *in* you.

Therefore, a portion of The Lord's Prayer has already come to pass: "Thy Kingdom come" has already come to pass if you are born again. With religious people who are not born again, this verse is still in the future tense. But with those who are born again, the Kingdom of God has already come into our hearts.

I am not saying that The Lord's Prayer isn't beautiful. And I am not saying you can't learn something from it, because you can. I am simply saying that it is not the New Testament norm for praying. The New Testament norm for praying is prayer addressed to the Father in the Name of Jesus. In The Lord's Prayer, Jesus didn't tell His disciples to make their requests to the Father in the Name of Jesus.

We need to realize that Jesus gave this prayer to the disciples at the beginning of His ministry, when they were still technically under the Old Covenant. But at the end of His ministry, Jesus changed their way of praying because He was about to go to the Cross and institute the New Covenant.

Jesus told the disciples in John chapter 16, "*And in that day ye shall ask me nothing. Verily, verily, I say unto you, Whatsoever ye shall ask the Father in my name, he will give it you*" (v. 23). Jesus went on to say, "*HITHERTO have ye asked nothing in my name . . .*" (John 16:24). "Hitherto" means *up to that time*. Up until then the disciples hadn't prayed in Jesus' Name, but now Jesus said to ask of the Father in His Name.

Number One:
Pray to the Father in Jesus' Name

Therefore, the first of the seven most important things in prayer is *to pray to the Father in the Name of Jesus.*

Look at the expression, "*. . . in my name . . .*" (John 16:23). As we discussed, we are not to ask for something for Jesus' sake. We hear so many people conclude their prayers by saying, "For Jesus' sake," but we don't find that expression anywhere in the Bible. It's not for Jesus' sake that we are to pray. There is a difference between praying in His *Name* and asking for something for His *sake.*

The reason we pray in Jesus' Name is that no one has any standing in heaven but *Jesus!* You and I don't. The only standing we have up there is *in Him.* So it's for our *own* sake that we pray, because of *Jesus'* standing. And it's because of Jesus' standing in heaven that we can receive the answers to our prayers.

For example, if you have a stomachache and are praying for healing, you're not praying for Jesus' sake; you're praying for your own sake. *You* are the one who is hurting, not Him! If you were hungry and didn't have anything to eat, you would pray for food for *yourself* to eat. *You're* the one who is hungry, not Him. There is a vast difference in praying in the *Name* of Jesus and for the *sake* of Jesus.

Let's be aware of this in our prayer lives, as it does make a difference how we pray. God may have helped us and heard us, and He may have done some things for us in the past in spite of our ignorance. But the more scriptural we are in prayer, the more help we're going to receive from heaven.

You'll get more answers to prayer by praying in line with God's Word. And if you pray in the Name of Jesus, then you'll be scripturally correct in your praying.

I know from my own experience that it did something for me spiritually when I quit ending my prayers, "For Jesus' sake." It was a hindrance in my own spiritual life to pray that way. So I quit saying, "For Jesus' sake." After just a little while I noticed a difference in my prayer life. I began to see answers to prayer. I believe you will too.

Whatsoever We Ask

JOHN 16:23,24
23 And in that day ye shall ask me nothing. Verily, verily, I say unto you, WHATSOEVER ye shall ask the Father in my name, he will give it you.
24 Hitherto have ye asked nothing in my name: ASK, and ye shall receive, that your joy may be full.

Focus on the word, "whatsoever" in verse 23. Then in the very next verse, Jesus says, *"Hitherto have ye asked nothing in my name: ASK..."* (John 16:24).

Jesus is talking in John 16:23 about our asking for whatsoever we would, according to God's Word — *in the Name of Jesus.* For a moment, put the word "whatsoever" after the word "ask" in John 16:24. Therefore, we could read verse 24: "Hitherto have you asked nothing in My Name: ask *whatsoever* in My Name, and you shall receive."

We read this verse, but sometimes we let the full significance of what Jesus is saying slip by us. So many times when we read the Bible, we read things into it that are not there.

For example, notice in John 16:23 and 24 that there is no "if" in those verses. Jesus didn't say to pray, *"If it be Thy will."* He used the word, "whatsoever." And He said, *"... WHATSOEVER ye shall ask the Father in my name, HE WILL give IT YOU"* (John 16:23).

Of course, what you ask must be in line with God's Word. God cannot violate His own Word. But the point I am making is that if you are praying scripturally based on God's Word, you don't need to ask, *"If it be Thy will."* You can just ask "whatsoever" you would that is in line with God's Word, and it shall be granted to you!

The word "whatsoever" means more to some people than it does to others. "Whatsoever" to some people just means a little bit of something. Some people believe that "whatsoever" in John 16:23 means whatsoever you ask for *spiritually.* They imply that God won't meet any of their *material* needs.

Similarly, some people look at Mark 11:24 where it says, *"... What things soever ye desire, when ye pray, believe that ye receive them, and ye shall have them,"* and they believe that the verse only refers to receiving *spiritual* blessings.

But you wouldn't call *"... What THINGS soever YE DESIRE ..."* just spiritual blessings. What *things* soever you *desire* refers to the desires of your heart.

Jesus isn't only talking about what *spiritual* blessings you desire. Spiritual blessings are included, of course, because elsewhere in the Bible we are told that we are blessed with *all* spiritual blessings in Christ (Eph. 1:3).

But Mark 11:24 includes *spiritual* blessings as well as *material* and *physical* blessings because it is talking about the desires of your heart. Therefore, Mark 11:24 includes *any* desire a believer would have — spiritually, materially, or physically, as long as that desire is in line with the Word.

So spiritual blessings are included in John 16:23 and Mark 11:24, but Jesus didn't limit this verse just to what *spiritual* blessings you desire. Jesus said, *"... What THINGS soever ye desire ..."* (Mark 11:24). He is talking about things in the spiritual *and* in the natural realm — spiritual, physical, and material blessings that you desire.

Then there are others who go so far as to say that the Lord doesn't answer personal prayers — prayers that are for our personal needs and desires. Nothing could be further from the truth!

That kind of wrong thinking reminds me of something I once heard. I was holding a meeting, and a certain woman came to be filled with the Spirit, and she received the Holy Spirit. I was quite interested because of her religious background. She had been brought up in a church where she was taught against miracles and healing and receiving these things from God.

She told me that in this little city where I was preaching, she had been under the care of a family physician who had found some alarming symptoms in her body. Her doctor had sent her to Ft. Worth, Texas, to a specialist.

The specialist finally informed her that she had a tumor, but he wasn't sure whether it was malignant or not. They were preparing her for surgery, but for some reason or another, she said she just didn't want to be operated on. She decided to talk to a certain nurse in that particular hospital about this, and this woman who had the tumor said that if there were any way out of the operation, she wouldn't have the operation.

The nurse said to her, "Well, why don't you let the Lord heal you?" The woman answered that she didn't know the Lord *would* heal her. She didn't think miracles were for us in these days. The nurse happened to be a Full Gospel Christian, and she arranged to have her pastor come and talk to the woman, as the nurse was not permitted to do too much talking while on duty.

Her pastor came and prayed for the woman, and the tumor disappeared. They took other X rays and couldn't find the tumor at all. The doctors couldn't understand it. They finally sent her back home, but before she left, she asked the nurse the name of this pastor's church and found that it was a Full Gospel church. So she began attending this kind of church in her own town. All of this had happened just before I came along.

This woman told me about her mother-in-law, who was about seventy years old at that time and who for several years had been living with the woman and her husband. The woman was thrilled about what God did for her and every time she and her husband prayed at the dinner table, they thanked God for her healing.

She went on to say that at almost every meal, she and her mother-in-law would get into a little spat. Her mother-in-law would say that the Lord didn't heal her — that she'd probably never had a tumor to begin with. But the woman would remind her mother-in-law about the X rays which proved she'd had a tumor.

The mother-in-law would respond that it was just her time to get well and that the preacher and God had nothing to do with it because God just didn't do things like that today. She said God does *not* heal today, and God didn't even hear that preacher's prayer! This mother-in-law said she had been praying herself for more than fifty years and hadn't received an answer to prayer yet and didn't know anyone else who had either.

There are people like that — even preachers — and you can't blame them when they believe that way because they are ignorant of spiritual things. I once heard a preacher on the radio say that God didn't hear individual people praying; He only heard the church praying corporately.

I boldly dispute that because it is unscriptural. I say that preacher lied. I say that he told a bald-faced lie. I'd rather accuse that minister of being a liar than to accuse Jesus of being a liar because Jesus said, "*. . . Whatsoever YE shall ask the Father in my name, he will give it YOU*" (John 16:23).

Our Joy Is Full When Our Prayers Are Answered

Notice in John 16:24 Jesus said, "*. . . ask, and ye shall receive, THAT YOUR JOY MAY BE FULL.*" This verse has to apply to everything that touches your life and everything you need or Jesus would have put a qualification in that verse. For instance, how in the world could your joy be full if your children are sick? It couldn't be. How could your joy be full if your rent was not paid, or if your bills were unpaid?

If creditors were about to foreclose on your home or take your automobile away from you, or your little children were crying for something to eat, your joy couldn't be full. You couldn't receive any kind of a *spiritual* blessing whereby your joy could be full under those conditions. No, you need a *material* blessing.

Bless God, John 16:23 and 24 includes *material* as well as *spiritual* blessings (Phil. 4:19; Eph. 1:3)!

However, it is quite obvious that many Christians still do not have fullness of joy.

We see Christians going around with long faces, burdened down, with fear written all over their faces and with perplexity and confusion on their countenances. Their joy isn't full because they either don't know about this verse of scripture, or they aren't taking advantage of what they know and what rightly belongs to them. But if a person's joy is full, you can tell it.

I related earlier the account Smith Wigglesworth told of an incident that happened when he was still a plumber. The woman he was working for asked him, "What in the world is it that causes that wonderful expression on your face? You look as if you're full of joy."

Wigglesworth told this woman that just that morning at breakfast his wife had come downstairs and had told him that two of their children were very ill. He said that before they ate, they went upstairs, laid hands on their children in Jesus' Name, and they were instantly healed. The children then came down and ate breakfast with them. Wigglesworth told this woman that it was just so wonderful to have such a wonderful Jesus.

"Ask, that your joy may be full" (John 16:24). Wigglesworth's joy couldn't be full if he had two sick children. How could his joy be full? He would have looked worried and distressed. But instead he had a light and a radiance on his face. Something seemed to be flowing out of him; it was the life of God. It was so obvious that the woman wondered what it was. And she was born again because she desired to have the joy she saw in Wigglesworth's life.

I believe it ought to be that way with all Christians. People should recognize the joy of the Lord in the lives of believers. John 16:24 says, "*. . . ask, and ye shall receive, that your joy may be full.*" Praise the Lord!

Remember, too, that when you ask, you have to maintain that joy even before the manifestation of your answer comes. But just knowing you've received the answer by faith and that you shall have whatsoever you asked, will thrill your heart. Your joy will be full or complete because you know that you'll see the answer come to pass.

Number Two:
Believe You Receive When You Pray

The second most important thing in prayer is *to believe that you receive when you pray.*

MARK 11:23,24
23 For verily I say unto you, That whosoever shall say unto this mountain, Be thou removed, and be thou cast into the sea; and shall not doubt in his heart, but shall believe that those things which he saith shall come to pass; he shall have whatsoever he saith.
24 Therefore I say unto you, What things soever ye desire, WHEN YE PRAY, BELIEVE THAT YE RECEIVE THEM, and YE SHALL HAVE THEM.

Notice you are not to believe that you *shall* receive. That's believing in the future. You can't believe God will answer your prayer off in the future *sometime*, and then expect to receive the desired result.

Faith is believing that God is immediately working on your behalf, the moment you pray in faith. You have to believe you receive the answer *now*. God puts emphasis on faith and on believing because He is a faith God. Faith is what pleases God.

HEBREWS 11:6
6 But without faith it is impossible to please him. . . .

You can have good works and right deeds and not have faith and, therefore, not please God. You would be more pleasing to God by having more faith, and have your good works be a result of your faith. Faith is what pleases God.

Wigglesworth said that there's something about believing God that will cause Him to pass over a million people to get to you. I like that. God is a faith God. And we are faith children of a faith God. We're saved by faith. *"For by grace are ye saved through faith. . . . Not of works, lest any man should boast"* (Eph. 2:8,9). We walk by faith and not by sight (2 Cor. 5:7).

It is praying in faith that works with God. That is the only prayer that does work. When you pray, believe that you receive. Jesus said you shall have the desires of your heart, if you'll believe that you receive them. You'll have them *after* you believe that you receive. But most folks miss it because they want to receive *before* they believe.

Believe you receive from God *when* you pray. There are not too many people who do believe they receive from God *when* they pray. You can tell by the way they keep praying for the same need over and over again. If they really believed they had received their answer, they wouldn't have to keep on praying for it.

After you have prayed in faith, you're supposed to continue to believe and thank God for your answer. You're not to ask again and again in unbelief for that same need to be met. When you come to God for the same petition the second time, come in faith that God heard you the first time.

You can always put God in remembrance of His Word, of course, and thank Him in faith that He is working on your behalf. That's the kind of faith that produces results in prayer. Of course, we must also realize that there is a prayer of intercession that is prayed over a period of time. We discuss this kind of prayer in another chapter.

I am convinced that if folks would quit praying about many of the things they're praying about and begin thanking God for the answer, the answer would come right away. But instead they keep on praying in unbelief.

If a person makes the same petition more than once, that means he didn't believe that he received the first time he prayed. (Of course, a person can always come to God and put God in remembrance of His Word.) If a person believed he received when he prayed, he would be thanking God for the answer. Then the answer would be made manifest.

The difference between Bible faith and natural human faith is that the faith Jesus is talking about in these scriptures is a *heart* faith — a spiritual faith — not a *head* faith. We get so used to walking by head faith. But here in Mark 11:24, it says we are to believe in our heart that we receive our answer the minute we pray, even though the answer has not yet manifested in the natural.

The same thing is true of a physical healing. However, it seems that it is more difficult to practice this heart faith with physical healing than with anything else because we have a body and feelings and symptoms with which we have to contend. The body with its symptoms will try to pull us back into the natural realm, into a head faith, or believing what our senses tell us.

Most people want to believe that God healed them when they can see that the condition has grown better or when the symptoms are gone. Then they will believe they are healed. But anyone can believe what he can see! What Jesus is saying here is that we should believe *when we pray*, and *then* we will receive.

Believe You Receive
Before You See the Answer

MARK 11:23,24
23 For verily I say unto you, That whosoever shall say unto this mountain, Be thou removed, and be thou cast into the sea; and shall not doubt in his heart, but shall

believe that those things which he saith shall come to pass; he shall have whatsoever he saith.
24 Therefore I say unto you, What things soever ye desire, when ye pray, BELIEVE THAT YE RECEIVE THEM, and ye shall have them.

Mark 11:24 is the verse that brought me off the bed of sickness. It is the verse I've used as an individual in prayer more than any other verse in the Bible. I've preached and taught on this verse more than any other text in the Bible.

Mark 11:24 was such a great blessing to me as I lay sick in bed. I had been given up to die by medical science. In those dark days on the bed of sickness, five doctors came and went, shaking their heads, saying that I had to die. They said I didn't have even one chance to live, not even one chance in a million.

Then the preacher came and said I should be patient because in a few days it would all be over. It may seem funny, but I can't tell it without tears coming to my eyes.

It was between 2:00 and 3:00 in the afternoon on a hot August day in Texas. The sun was shining brightly and there was hardly a cloud in the sky. But when that preacher left my room, telling me it would all be over in a few days, that room was dark. It was as though someone had pulled the blinds and had just put out the sunlight. It was so dark. The preacher said I had to die.

But thank God for this Word that fell from the lips of the Master as He walked the old dusty roads of Judaea long ago. Thank God, Jesus was talking to me when He said those words in Mark 11:24.

I wrote in the margin of my Bible that this verse is for me. The word, "whosoever" in Mark 11:23 applied to me. So beside the words, *". . . WHOSOEVER shall say unto this mountain . . ."* I wrote: "This means *me*."

Mark 11:24 says, *"Therefore I say unto you . . ."* and I put my name where it says "you." Jesus said, "Therefore I say unto *Kenneth Hagin*." I just took God at His Word! He said it, and I believed it. And you can put your name in that verse too.

My heart leapt within me when I read this verse of Scripture and something on the inside of me was overjoyed and thrilled with these words from the lips of Jesus. It seemed that someone had turned on a light inside of me. On the inside of me something lit up.

Jesus is talking in this verse about what *you* desire. He's telling you how to get the desires of your heart. He's discussing the subject of prayer. He's talking about how you through prayer can receive the desires of your heart.

This is the verse of Scripture that brought healing and strength to my body and to my poor deformed heart. This verse has enabled me, through these more than fifty years, to go almost constantly day and night without sickness, disease, or pain.

For the first thirty years of my ministry, I never really stopped to take a vacation. I would hold two to four services almost every day. Minister friends told me they didn't see how I held up under it. They said it surprised them that I didn't wear out. But I live by what I preach. It's not a chore and it's not a job to teach the Word of God. It's a thrill to do it. The Word works!

Jesus is talking about how you as an individual can receive the desires of your heart. Many times, people read something else into Mark 11:24. They think God might answer their prayer *if* it's His will.

Well, it must have been His will to answer their prayers or Jesus never would have said to ask! If it wasn't God's will that you have the desires of your heart, then Jesus lied about it by saying believers were to ask. I would much rather believe that someone else lied about this verse, than to believe that Jesus lied.

For about a month after that preacher left my room as I lay on the bed of sickness, I never even looked at the Bible. I didn't even ask to have the Bible brought to me because I thought I was going to die at any minute. I thought, *Surely if the preacher knew of any help for me, he would have told me.* But he just told me that in a few more days it would all be over.

In October following that day in August when the preacher came to see me, I asked Momma to bring the Bible to my bed. I opened it to this verse in Mark 11:24 and I read it again. Then I told the Lord that the doctors said I had to die; in fact, *five* of them had said I had to die.

The last doctor spent forty-five minutes talking to me one day explaining my condition to me. He told me nothing could be done for me. He did say that unless a Higher Power intervened, I would die. He told me to stay ready to go. When the preacher came, he wasn't even as kind as the doctor was about my condition! He didn't even ask me whether I was ready to go or not. He just said that in a few more days it would all be over.

So I told the Lord what the preacher had said. Then I pointed out to Jesus that when He was on the earth He had said, *". . . What things soever ye desire, when ye pray, believe that ye receive them, and ye shall have them"* (Mark 11:24).

I told Jesus that the desire of my heart — the one main consuming desire of my heart — was to have a well body. I told Jesus that I was going to take Him at His Word. I told Him that if I didn't get off that bed, it would be because He told a lie in His Word. I said that if His Word didn't work, then I was going to have my folks throw my Bible in the trash can.

But I knew that His Word wasn't a lie, and I also told Him this. I knew it was the truth. I told Him that I was going to get off that bed. I didn't get off the bed that day, but you can see I made it!

Don't try to put some kind of an interpretation on the Word of God. Just take it for what it says. In Mark 11:24, Jesus is talking about *your* desires. I can't make this scripture work for someone else. I can help the other fellow with my faith sometimes, and get the blessing of God to work for him to some extent, but there is a part that he has to play in answered prayer.

I can't always make God's Word work for the other fellow; it depends on what He does with the promises in God's Word *himself*. But I can make God's Word work for *me*, and you can make it work for *you* too.

Jesus is talking about what things soever *you* desire. He's talking about *your* praying. This verse does apply to the other fellow, but he has to appropriate it himself. You can't do it for him.

Keeping What You Have Received by Faith

Too many times we're trying to get someone else to do our praying and believing for us. We're great at that, aren't we? In the final analysis, all you will ever receive from God and *keep* will be that which you believed for yourself. And it will take faith to maintain what you receive after you have received it! If you don't have faith to maintain it, then you won't keep it. Satan will try to take it from you.

For example, as I have ministered in America these many years, teaching and preaching on the subject of faith by the Lord's direction, many times I've seen people lose the healing they had received from God.

I have followed up on people who were healed in some great healing meetings. I personally know some people who came to the meeting totally deaf, and they were so completely healed that they could hear a pin drop. Yet in a few weeks, they lost all of their healing and couldn't hear a thing.

Why did these people lose their healing? Because for the most part these people were healed by someone else's faith. Or they were healed by mass faith; that is, by corporate faith of all the people attending the healing meeting. But in many cases, those people failed to develop their own faith, and when the symptoms tried to return, they just accepted the symptoms, and the sickness or disease came back on them.

I know some who were in healing meetings who were crippled and were totally healed. One woman in Pueblo, Colorado, had just gotten healed before we were there preaching and teaching. She was a young married woman who had had polio as a child, and one foot was deformed. She had never worn a regular shoe on her foot; she had to have a specially made shoe.

This woman was in a meeting a few days before we came and had been healed. But by the time the preacher with the healing ministry had left town, she had lost her healing. Her foot had become deformed again and she couldn't walk.

After I taught one night, this woman went to the store and got a regular pair of shoes. We prayed for her, and she put on the shoe and walked normally. She said she finally knew how to keep her healing.

You see, the first time this woman received healing, when she got back home on her own away from the meetings, the devil came to tempt her with symptoms, and he defeated her. Because she didn't know how to stand against him and maintain her healing, she allowed Satan to rob her of her healing.

I know a woman minister friend who was still quite active in ministry at fifty-three years of age. She and her husband were in the insurance business as well. She developed a condition that pulled her head to one side, and it got progressively worse. Also, sometimes as she walked across the floor, her feet would suddenly go out from under her and she would fall.

This woman had been prayed for and, finally, they sent her to specialists who told her that it was a deterioration of certain nerves of her body. They said she would never be one bit better but would steadily grow worse and then be bedfast until she died.

I remember when she came to my meeting, she sat over against the wall holding her purse up against her head. She had asked a doctor if he could put a brace on her head, but he said if they put a brace on it, it would break her neck. He said she would just have to live with it, accepting the fact that her condition would grow steadily worse. Someone always had to walk with her because of the danger of her falling.

She had gone to a particular healing meeting and had received instant deliverance when the preacher laid hands on her and prayed for her. She returned home and was perfectly normal for several weeks. Then the same symptoms gradually and slowly came back on her, until she became worse than she had ever been before her healing.

I saw her come into my meeting, and I just happened to be teaching on how the believer is to keep his healing. She came forward in the healing line, saying she now understood how to keep her healing. She said she had lost it because she hadn't resisted the devil with his symptoms. It wasn't the other preacher's fault who had prayed for her; it was her fault.

In the final analysis, all you are going to keep in life is what you believe for yourself, based on God's Word.

If this woman had exercised her own faith in the first place, she would have kept her healing. Well, I prayed for her again and she received her healing.

Sixteen years came and went, and she and her husband were still more active than most ministers (although they were retired from the insurance business and in a sense had retired from the ministry). They got more people filled with the Holy Ghost in their home than all the Full Gospel churches in their city put together in any given week. They were constantly praying with people. Some of the most marvelous healings happened in their ministry because they had learned the secret of faith.

Each Believer's Responsibility

That's the reason I'm telling you these scriptural truths, so that *you* can begin to believe and teach and hold fast to that which you have learned. The Bible says, *"Therefore I say unto YOU, What things soever YE desire, when YE pray, believe that YE receive them and YE shall have them"* (Mark 11:24). This is primarily an individual faith affair.

How can I help someone else permanently with my faith if the other person doesn't exercise his own faith to receive from God? I wouldn't be able to help him. That person wouldn't be able to receive even if I prayed the prayer of faith because his lack of faith would nullify my faith. When it comes to praying for someone else, that other person's faith can nullify the faith of the one praying.

The Bible says, *"Can two walk together, except they be agreed?"* (Amos 3:3). Two of us couldn't walk together in faith unless we were in agreement with God's Word.

MATTHEW 18:19
19 . . . if two of you SHALL AGREE on earth as touching any thing that they shall ask, it shall be done for them of my Father which is in heaven.

If I were praying with another person for that person's need to be met, and that person was not in faith, then we would not be in agreement with God's Word. That person's unbelief would nullify the effects of my faith.

Even though people can sometimes temporarily receive something through someone else's faith, especially if they are baby Christians, if they listen to the devil's lies, they'll lose it. One person's unbelief nullifies the effects of the other person's faith in the prayer of agreement.

You need to know the Word for yourself and learn how to develop your own faith. That's how you maintain the blessings of God in your life. Then when the devil tries to defeat you, you can resist him with the Word — with your faith in God's Word.

I was holding a meeting in Tucson, Arizona, many years ago, and the pastor told me that several years before, a man came to his church who had a healing ministry. They started out the meeting in the pastor's church, since his church building was fairly large.

Many people go to Tucson because the climate is dry. (In fact, I have never seen so many people with arthritis before in one city!) There was a Methodist woman who had arthritis and was brought in to this church meeting on a stretcher. For three years she had been bedfast and the doctor had told her that she was going to grow steadily worse. She was unable to walk a step. This man with the healing ministry laid hands on her and ministered to her. Instantly she was free, and she walked up and down the aisles.

The local paper carried a front-page story of her healing, along with a picture of her walking. The doctor testified that it was a miracle of God because she had been stiff as a board. After she was healed, doctors couldn't find any trace of arthritis! Every night after that, the crowds got so big they had to continue the meeting at the city auditorium. For three weeks they had a mighty move of God in the meeting.

When I was there, this pastor told me that the meeting closed and about six weeks afterwards, the woman again became bedfast. She couldn't walk anymore at all. I went into her home and she told me she believed the other preacher had just hypnotized her.

What actually happened, however, was that she had been in a meeting where the gifts of the Spirit were operating through that evangelist. She was really healed by the power of God, but when she got back home on her own, it was up to her to maintain her healing with her own faith. And since she didn't know how to do that, she had lost her healing. The devil will always try to return with his symptoms. We see that principle in the Word.

MATTHEW 12:43,44
43 When the unclean spirit is gone out of a man, he walketh through dry places, seeking rest, and findeth none.
44 Then he saith, I WILL RETURN into my house from whence I came out; and when he is come, he findeth it EMPTY, swept, and garnished.

The Bible tells us in this verse that when the unclean spirit has gone out of a man, he walks through dry places, seeking rest, and finding none, it says, he'll go back to the house he came out of.

There is a scriptural principle involved in those verses. The devil is going to try to get back in again if he can — even in the case of sickness and disease. Sickness and disease are of the devil, and you can be sure that Satan is going to try and return to a person who's been healed and try to put that same sickness and disease back on them. He'll be back unless you stand your ground against him with the Word.

When the devil came back to this woman with symptoms of arthritis, it made her think she wasn't really healed. Therefore, she lost her healing. When we came along to preach in that city three years later, there she was, still bedfast.

The reason I'm preaching and teaching these biblical truths is that in the final analysis, prayer and faith are primarily the individual believer's responsibility. I could have ministered differently than I have over the years, and I could have had much larger crowds with more people healed at the moment; but I have found that by the third and fourth week of healing services, many people have lost their healing unless they are also taught the Word.

I hate to lose my labor! I'd rather do a more thorough job of teaching people the Word so they can learn to stand on it for themselves. Then those who do receive healing will be able to keep it.

Our wrong thinking defeats us so many times. That's why people need to be taught the Word in order to get their thinking straightened out. Some people say that if God really healed that woman who had arthritis, then she would still be healed.

But if God didn't heal her, then who did? How come when the man laid hands on her, she was able to walk instantly? A twelve-year-old child would have enough sense to know that *God* had healed her. If you can't see that, then you're in bad shape.

Listening to Doubt
Can Rob You of God's Blessing

I preached in a town one time, and a thirty-year-old man came to the meetings who had some kind of peculiar disease; his nerves were deteriorating. He related that he had become totally paralyzed and couldn't work. He heard about a healing meeting in Dallas and although he belonged to the Methodist church, he went to that meeting.

When hands were laid on him, he was instantly healed and had gotten up out of his wheelchair and walked. He went to his house and was able to pull off his clothes by himself and get himself ready for bed; he had been totally helpless before that time. However, then he made the mistake of beginning to question himself if he was really healed.

This Methodist man had never been in a Full Gospel meeting before in his life. He wondered if God had really healed him, or if the minister had some kind of a "power" that had made him well. When he began to ask himself such questions, he could feel his paralytic condition sweeping over him again. In a little while he was just as helpless as he had ever been! He could talk, but he couldn't move.

Then he said, "Lord, if this is really of You, then let that same power come over me again that came over me in the meeting."

He felt the power come over him again, and he was loosed, and he got up, walking freely. He went to the bathroom, got some water, walked around, and then got back in bed. When he awoke the next morning, he dressed himself and the news about his healing was soon all over town.

Later that morning, there was a knock at the door and when he answered the door, there stood his pastor. This man was up and walking around, but his pastor came over to warn him about this "healing business." This pastor told the man not to let people hoodwink him. The pastor told the man God doesn't heal today. By the time the pastor got through talking, the man couldn't move a finger!

Later on this man who was paralyzed and his wife moved to Dallas. I held a meeting in the church where his wife was a member. She had sought God and had received the Holy Spirit with the evidence of speaking in other tongues. She told me the story of what happened to her husband, and she said she knew her husband's healing was of God. She said that by his own admission, the man knew he had been healed by the power of God. But then he had listened to that pastor and lost his healing.

After that, her husband just lay in that bed continually and couldn't do one thing for himself.

"He'll curse God for his condition, and yet claim he is saved," his wife told me. "He says his healing was of the devil."

But if this man's healing was of the devil, how come that's never happened to him again? How come it never happened until a man of God laid hands on him and prayed for him?

I'm talking about prayer. Jesus said, ". . . *WHAT THINGS SOEVER YE DESIRE, when ye pray, believe that ye receive them, and ye shall have them"* (Mark 11:24).

That man was healed by a manifestation of God. However, when he got back on his own, it was up to him to maintain his healing with his own faith. But he let someone talk him out of it. From that day to this, if he's still alive, that man is probably still in a wheelchair.

That's the reason people need to be taught what the Word of God says and to believe God for themselves. You need the fellowship of people who believe God, people of like-precious faith. If the people peddle doubt and unbelief where you go to church, then you had better leave and find a church where they preach faith, because the principle of faith is taught throughout the Word of God. And as we believe that we receive when we pray, and act on our faith in the Word, we will see the Word work in our own lives!

We're discussing the seven most important things about prayer. We've seen that the correct way to pray under the New Covenant is to pray to the Father in Jesus' Name. We've also seen that in order to receive what we've asked for in prayer, we must believe that we receive *when* we pray. We'll continue our discussion of these important prayer principles in the next chapter.

Questions for Study

1. What is the seal of the New Covenant?

   _____

   _____

2. Why couldn't the people under the Old Covenant keep from sinning?

   _____

   _____

3. Why is The Lord's Prayer technically still an Old Covenant prayer?

   _____

   _____

4. How does the Kingdom of God differ from the Kingdom of Heaven?

   _____

   _____

5. What is the reason we pray in Jesus' Name?

   _____

   _____

6. What desires of the heart does Mark 11:24 state that a believer can have?

   _____

   _____

7. When should you believe that you receive the answer to your prayer?

   _____

   _____

8. How can you maintain the blessings of God in your life?

   _____

   _____

9. Wrong thinking defeats us so many times. What will straighten out wrong thinking?

   _____

   _____

10. Name one thing that can rob you of God's blessings.

   _____

   _____

Chapter 13

The Seven Most Important Things in Prayer
Part 2

And in that day ye shall ask me nothing. Verily, verily, I say unto you, Whatsoever ye shall ask the Father in my name, he will give it you.

Hitherto have ye asked nothing in my name: ask, and ye shall receive, that your joy may be full.
— John 16:23,24

As we've discussed in earlier chapters, the first and most important thing we need to learn about prayer is that we are to pray to the Father in the Name of Jesus. The second most important thing about prayer is found in Mark 11:24.

MARK 11:24
24 Therefore I say unto you, What things soever ye desire, when ye pray, believe that ye receive them, and ye shall have them.

When you pray, believe that you receive your answer. You don't wait until after your answer is manifested to believe God heard you. No, you believe you receive your answer *before* you see it or get it.

I keep going over this because it is important. This is what faith, true Bible faith is — believing God and taking Him at His Word — *before* you actually see the answer. These truths about faith will gradually dawn on you if you hear them enough; they will eventually get through to you and down into your *heart*.

Head Faith vs. Heart Faith

We need to constantly be reminded about spiritual things because everything around us in this natural world is trying to pull us back to walk by natural, human sense knowledge, or head faith, instead of by spiritual heart faith.

Many times, everything in your everyday life is so natural that it will pull you back into walking in the natural instead of walking by faith. If you're not careful, the church to which you go can also try to do that. Some churches take faith *out* of you, instead of putting faith *into* you.

Some people will also try to make you doubt and try to make you walk by head knowledge or sense knowledge. But we must learn to walk by Bible faith, or heart faith; that is, by faith that is of the heart or spirit, not the head. I wouldn't tell you something that isn't scriptural. And I wouldn't encourage you to practice something that I haven't practiced and that doesn't work.

I have practiced walking by faith for years, and Mark 11:24 has always been my mainstay. It says when you pray for the desires of your heart, believe that you receive them, and you shall have them. That's exactly the procedure I use.

Not only is it true of healing, but it is true in every other aspect of life. No matter what the need is — spiritual, physical, material, or financial — this is the way you receive from God. Faith is what pleases God (Heb. 11:6).

Some people say that they pray and pray, but things don't get any better in their lives. But when I received healing for my body, at first I had no evidence whatsoever of healing. I couldn't see it or feel it, but I began to say out loud in the room by myself I believed I received my healing. When I began to say that, it wasn't very long until I had it.

Jesus said that if you believe you receive, then you'll have it. So believing you receive before you see the answer with your physical eyes is the important thing. When you pray — not the next hour, the next day, or the next week — but *when you pray*, believe that you receive, and you shall have your petition. Hebrews 11:1 says, "*. . . faith is . . . the evidence of things NOT SEEN.*"

You won't become perfect in walking by faith overnight. Spiritual growth is very similar to physical growth. No one is born a full-grown human being, and no one is born a full-grown Christian. People are born babies and they grow up. You didn't learn everything you know overnight. Your teachers didn't put you in the fifth grade when you started school; they put you in kindergarten. And after you got to the fifth grade, they didn't put you in the twelfth grade. No, you grew gradually and learned.

Spiritually, it's the same way. People will work hard in the natural realm and finally earn certain degrees in areas of study where they want to work, but when it comes to spiritual things, if they don't reach their goals in a week, they think they might as well give up! But let's not be ignorant! Paul himself said he didn't count himself perfect, but that he was constantly pressing forward, as there was still more to be learned (Phil. 3:12-14).

The person who thinks he is already perfect and that he already has everything there is to get, deceives himself. I've run into folks who think like that. I would just as soon hear a donkey bray at midnight in a tin barn, as to listen to people like that talk. Thank God, we can grow! And when it comes to this faith life, we shouldn't expect to get there overnight.

Smith Wigglesworth said that some people are ready to give up if that for which they claim to be believing doesn't come overnight. But Wigglesworth says that this proves they never did believe God to begin with.

Many times God will permit you to be tried and tested in faith right up to the end. But when you believe God, you can stand firm, even though you are tested right up to the last moment. I've been there and I know. God will let you be tested right up to the end, when it looks as though the answer is not coming. But if you'll stand firm in your faith in God's Word, the answer will come every time. It seems that I've been there more times than not!

I got started in my faith walk that way, because my healing was like that. I was supposed to die, but I read the words of Jesus and believed them. It seems that I always do my best when I'm in difficult places. I learned years ago just to laugh all the more when the going gets rough. I don't always feel like laughing, but I make myself laugh right in the face of the devil. I just smile and say that I believe God and His Word.

We read an example in Acts 27 of someone believing God even though he was severely tested and tried. Paul was on board a ship headed for Rome when a treacherous storm arose on the sea. To lighten the ship and keep it from sinking, the people threw all of the merchandise and cargo overboard. But the storm raged on, and eventually the men on the ship lost all hope that they would be saved (Acts 27:20).

But one night an angel of God stood before Paul and told him there *was* hope. The angel said that the Lord would deliver all those aboard the ship. So the next day, right in the midst of the storm and the chaos, Paul stood up and said he believed God that it would be even as it was told him (Acts 27:25).

The storm that Paul was experiencing on that ship can be compared to the storms we face in life. We might not be in a storm out in the sea, but we all face storms in life in the form of tests and trials.

You and I can stand on God's Word in the storms of life, just as Paul stood on the Word of the Lord that was given him in that storm at sea. We can say,

with Paul, "I believe God, that it shall be even as it was told me!"

Many times when it seemed like all hope was gone, I have said to the devil and to God and to myself and to others, "I believe God! God told me in His Word that when I pray, I am to believe that I receive my petition. *Then* I will have it."

We need to be just as definite and specific about spiritual things as we are about natural things. How many of you can believe what your mother tells you? How many of you would believe what your father told you? How many of you husbands would believe what your wives told you? How many of you wives believe what your husbands tell you? You usually believe them, don't you? Well, you may or may not believe what others say, but I'll tell you, you *can* believe what Jesus said in His Word.

You *can* believe God's Word! Thank God, I can believe it. Jesus wouldn't tell us to do something we can't do, and He said we are to believe Him and take Him at His Word. If He asked us to do something we couldn't actually do, we would have a right to challenge His justice. He would be unjust. But, thank God, we *can* believe His Word: *". . . when ye pray, believe that ye receive . . ."* (Mark 11:24).

Stir Yourself Up in Faith

I know from experience that we need to be continually reminded and stirred up along this line. As I said before, everything in this world in this natural realm, will try to pull us back into the natural, sense realm. We need to be stirred up in the faith and in the things of God. We need to stir ourselves up.

In the last church I pastored, I invited a friend of mine to come and conduct some revival services for us. During the Depression Days, that friend and I had agreed in prayer that he would get a job so he could get married, and he got one in ten days. Later on he was filled with the Holy Spirit and God called him to preach. This was years later when I invited him to come and hold a meeting in my church.

We were eating one day in the parsonage and he told me that I was slipping spiritually. No one likes to hear that, even though it may be the truth. I didn't even answer him at first, but I later told him that I wasn't slipping.

He told me, however, that I was not where I used to be with God. He told me that I was not exercising the faith that I'd had at one time. He had known me very well because we had lived within two blocks of each other when we were younger and had played together as children. I suppose I had started preaching to him way back then. He said that through the years, he doubted he would have stayed saved if it hadn't been for me, for I was always preaching the Word to him.

He remembered some of the times in my life when no matter what the circumstances were, I would just laugh about them and say I believed God. I asked him what this had to do with my having slipped spiritually. He said he knew me when I would get on my knees in the church and pray for the Lord to send a revival. Then I would stand up and say I had it, and that it was on the way.

He thought I wasn't doing much of that anymore. Really, I *had* gotten busy with church work and with pastoring the church. If we're not careful, we can get to the place where we're praying, but we're not really believing and claiming the answer and the promises of God.

If you believe you receive, then you *claim* that you receive it. You *say* that you receive your answer. You receive your answer by faith.

My spiritual pride rose up when my friend said I was slipping spiritually, and I denied it. We went ahead with our meal, but I began thinking about what he said, and it dawned on me that he was right.

So I went out to the church and got on my knees and told the Lord that I believed I received revival in our church. I told God I knew revival was here and that I had it now. Do you know, while that friend of mine was there, we had one of the best revival meetings we'd ever had. We don't have to be defeated, if we'll say what the Word says.

Believing Is Not Hoping Or Struggling in Prayer

We have expressions we use about praying that are not in the Bible. These are expressions man has made up. For example, we don't have to "fight" our way through to the answer. We *believe* our way through. Prayer is not the struggle that many people would have you believe it is. Prayer is a matter of acting on God's Word. It's a matter of believing God's Word.

Certainly, we have to stand our ground against the devil. But we call that the "*. . . good fight of faith . . .*" (1 Tim. 6:12). It's not a fleshly struggle. It's a *good* fight of faith because if we're standing on God's Word, we win!

I remember on the bed of sickness I struggled and "fought" for a long time, but it was in the flesh.

You see, I was trying at first to do it in the natural, struggling in my own strength to be healed.

When I just stopped struggling and began *resting* on God's Word, saying that I believed I received my healing, it was the easiest thing in the world to get healed. Within ten minutes my paralysis had disappeared and I was on my feet. I've seen it happen again and again and again through these more than sixty years of ministry. God's Word is just as true today as it ever was.

Many times I have asked people what they believe when they get up from praying. Some look at me with a strange look and ask what I mean by that. I ask them again what they believe. Many times they answer, saying they *hope* God heard them. I tell them that He didn't because Jesus said, "*believe* you receive," not "*hope* you will receive." He didn't say to keep keeping on until you get the answer. He said *when* you pray you should believe you receive.

When you believe you receive, you don't have to pray all night long. You can go to bed and go to sleep. I do believe in praying all night long if you have enough to pray about and if you are inspired by the Holy Spirit to do so.

One time the Spirit of God said to me, "It is natural human reasoning that defeats people. Men in their own minds think that if they tediously and successfully seek long enough, eventually they can change the mind of God." But the Lord's mind will never be changed. He is ever the same. He stands ready at every moment to make His Word good in your life.

The Master said that when you pray, believe that you receive your desires, and you shall have them (Mark 11:24). And if you believe you have received, you can go to bed and go to sleep.

Even if the situation looks contrary to what God's Word says, all you really have to do is pray and believe God. Then go to bed at night and sleep peacefully because you *know* God heard you, and you know you've received your answer.

You will be able to do this if you believe God's Word. Jesus said you could. I've done it many a time, even when insurmountable obstacles were facing me in life.

I had severe heart symptoms that disappeared when I first received my healing. But later on, some of those same symptoms came back on me and I had some of the most alarming symptoms in my body. But, bless God, I went to God and prayed and believed that I received healing and then told God that I was going to believe His Word and go to sleep.

The devil kept telling me I would die, and he warned me not to go to sleep because I would probably die in my sleep. But I told the devil I believed that I received and that I was going to go to sleep. I wasn't going to bother about his symptoms anymore. It wasn't me that said I was healed — *Jesus* said it in His Word. I don't have to make God's Word good; God makes it good!

We need to quit trying to help God's Word. Many times that's what's wrong to begin with. We're trying to make God's Word good. Take your hand off of trying to make the Word work. You don't have to make God's Word good. He'll tend to His own Word. You don't have to perform God's Word.

All you have to do is the believing part. He didn't tell you to do a thing about getting His Word to work for you. He said you are to believe you receive, and He's the one who will watch over His own Word to perform it (Jer. 1:12). Then you will have your petition!

It's the most wonderful thing in the world to be able to pillow your head on the promises of God at night without a care in the world. It's wonderful to be able to sleep like a baby. Everything around you might be in turmoil but, bless God, right in the midst of it, if you will take God at His Word, you will have peace.

A Table of Blessings for Us
In the Presence of Our Enemies

Someone once said to me that he would be happy if he could just get away from Satan so he wouldn't be bothered by him anymore. I asked the man if he wanted me to pray that he would die and go to heaven!

That's the only way we'll ever get away from our enemies. The world is an enemy and the devil is an enemy, and the devil is the god of this world (2 Cor. 4:4). The flesh, or the carnal nature, is an enemy (Rom. 8:7) and we're living in the flesh. We have to contend with all of these things while we live on this earth. The only way to get away from them is to die and get out of this world.

A fellow came to me one time saying he wanted me to pray that he would never have any more trouble with the devil. I told him that if we could do that, I would have already done it for myself! I don't know anyone who has been free from trouble with the devil.

It's not scriptural to pray that you'll never have any more trouble with the devil. But you can learn to take authority over the devil. The Bible says, "*. . . Resist the devil, and he will flee from you*" (James 4:7). You can learn to do something about the devil — exercise your authority over him in Jesus' Name.

The Bible also says that God prepares a table before us in the presence of our enemies (Ps. 23:5). That means right in the presence of the devil God prepares a table of blessing for us! In other words, the devil is always present in this world we live in, but he does not have dominion over us as believers.

You can't get away from the devil without dying and going on to heaven. Also, the flesh, or the carnal nature, is an enemy (Rom. 8:7). Jesus Himself said that the spirit is willing, but the flesh is weak (Matt. 26:41; Mark 14:38). The flesh has not yet been sanctified or redeemed. Therefore, you must daily keep your flesh under the dominion of your spirit (1 Cor. 9:27).

Keeping the flesh under the dominion of your spirit is an ongoing process. In other words, we never get to the place as long as we are in our bodies, where our flesh doesn't need to be put under subjection to our spirit.

Just when I think I'm about sanctified, something will happen that will knock my head right where my feet were a few minutes earlier! I come to find out that I'm not nearly as sanctified as I thought I was. About the time I think the flesh is dead, I find out it's not nearly as dead as I thought it was!

We all have the same trouble because we're all human. Your old flesh is not any better than mine is. You know that just as well as I do. You might as well "fess" up and admit it.

So these are our enemies — the world, the flesh, and the devil. But, thank God, God prepares a table before us in the presence of our enemies (Ps. 23:5). Right in the presence of these enemies, we can sit at the table of victory and deliverance with Jesus!

Look at the second most important thing about prayer in relation to our enemies: *When you pray, believe that you receive your desires, and you shall have them.* Right in the face of adverse circumstances, you can believe God's Word. You can believe you receive according to Mark 11:24.

I've prayed for loved ones and Mark 11:24 has worked for me. A man has authority in his own house. God deals with households (Acts 16:15,31). For example, that centurion in Matthew chapter 8 had authority in his house and came to Jesus on behalf of his servant (Matt. 8:5-13). The man in his household was just a servant, but the centurion had authority over him.

The centurion came and told Jesus that his servant was lying at home sick. Jesus said He would come to the centurion's house, but the centurion said he was not worthy for Jesus to come to his home. The centurion asked Jesus to speak the Word only and his servant would be healed. Jesus told the centurion to go his way and as he had believed, so it would be done unto him.

I've believed that I've received, and then afterwards I've seen conflicting conditions come up. I've seen kinfolk in my own household get worse.

For example, my niece lived with us for a time. Before she came to live with us, she had gotten into trouble because she had gotten in with the wrong crowd. At first she wasn't open to the gospel, but I just stood my ground in faith, and eventually she was saved.

So when you've prayed for your kinfolks and it seems like they're getting worse instead of getting better, don't ever say your faith isn't working. Just laugh, no matter what the circumstances are. Just keep saying you believe you received. Then the answer will always come.

Don't Take Sides Against the Word

If you're going to keep saying your faith isn't working, you're taking sides against the Word; you're not walking by faith. You're not believing you have received. You're believing you *didn't* receive and that is what undoes your prayer.

Hold fast to your confession and say that you believe you have received your petition. Once I do that, I never go back on it. Hold fast to God's Word and stand fast on it, and God will stand by you. You're going to have to side in with God's Word if you're going to get the Word to work for you. You can't take sides against the Word and expect it to work for you. Many people unconsciously take sides against God's Word.

One minister who was holding a meeting in Arkansas went with the pastor of the church to call on a businessman who had had two heart attacks. The man had been home in bed because of his heart condition, and then he'd had another attack. The man was unconscious and the doctor said he would never regain consciousness but would die.

So the evangelist and the pastor went to the man's house and laid hands on him and prayed over him. Instantly, he regained consciousness. He sat up in bed, and all of his symptoms were gone. He got up and went down to the living room and visited with his friends.

When the pastor and the evangelist left, the wife of this man followed them out while her husband stayed at the door. The wife told the pastor and the evangelist to be sure and keep on praying for her husband. The evangelist asked her what for. She said the devil would come right back and put an attack on her husband. The minister told her that she had more faith in the devil than she did in God!

Certainly, the devil may try to bring back symptoms on a person to see if he really believes what he says he believes about God's Word. But many Christians are believing the devil more than they are believing God. They magnify the devil's works more than they do the works of God. You always hear them talking about what the *devil* is doing.

This evangelist told this woman to confess and believe that the devil *wasn't* going to come back with his symptoms, and that he *wasn't* going to put that heart trouble back on her husband. He told her to stand on the promises of God.

She replied, "Why, I wouldn't say that for anything in the world because the devil might hear me say it." Some Christians have more respect for the devil and fear of the devil than they do for God. I believe that God is bigger than the devil!

I've even had Full Gospel preachers get upset when I talk like this because they are worried that the devil is going to hear them. But I always tell them that I *want* the devil to hear me! I'm saying it out loud for his benefit! I want the devil to know that *I* know the Bible is true!

I want the devil to know that I have authority over him in the Name of Jesus. Jesus told us that as believers we have authority over the devil (Luke 10:19). I want the devil to know that I'm not afraid of him. I want the devil to know that I'm not going to shake in my boots every time he comes around, and I'm not going to run and hide every time he sticks his head up. It's practicing God's Word and practicing faith that gets the job done!

It's amazing how much faith believers can have in the wrong thing. They are always saying they can't believe. What they are really saying is they can't believe the right thing, the Word of God, because they *are* believing something. They are believing the wrong thing.

For instance, that woman believed that the devil would come back and put another heart attack on her husband. That's why she said it. Her own words had her located. She wasn't in faith at all.

People should take the faith they exercise in the devil and use it instead to believe in the right thing — what *God* has said in His Word. Then they'll get positive results.

I've had people ask me to pray for them because they believed they were getting the flu. They had already made the statement that they believed they were getting the flu. Why don't they take that belief and put it on the positive side and believe that they *won't* get the flu?

People can pray with them and believe they are healed. But they'll still have the flu if they keep on believing they'll have it. Jesus said you can have what you believe for (Mark 11:24). You *can* believe right, so do it. It's right believing and right confessing in this area of prayer that get results. We *can* believe God hears us and that we receive *when* we pray.

Number Three:
Forgive If You Have Ought Against Any

MARK 11:25
25 And when ye stand praying, forgive, if ye have ought against any: that your Father also which is in heaven may forgive you your trespasses.

This is point number three. The third most important thing in prayer is *to forgive if you have ought against any.*

Prayer won't work unless you have a forgiving heart. Mark 11:25 says, "When ye stand praying, *forgive*, if ye have ought against any."

MARK 11:26
26 But if ye do not forgive, neither will your Father which is in heaven forgive your trespasses.

A person told me one time that he had some prayers answered, but that he still had some things in his heart against people. I told him that he was a liar. I told him that if he could pray and get results with unforgiveness in his heart, then Jesus lied. But I'd believe that this man lied before I'd believe that Jesus lied.

I told him that some good things may have happened, but it wasn't his praying that caused them to happen. They were probably natural things that might have happened anyway.

No one can have an effective prayer life and have anything in his heart toward another. You can't have revenge in your heart, and you can't have

hatred in your heart. You can't have that old "get even" spirit and continue to prosper.

And you're not responsible for that other person's life; you're responsible for *your* life. In other words, another person's heart and what is in it can't hinder you, but what you have in *your* heart against another *can* and *will* hinder you. That means any grudge or ill will at all will hinder your faith.

You have to guard your heart. You have to watch your inward man with all diligence (Prov. 4:23). Do not allow a root of bitterness, a bit of envy, or a bit of revenge to get into your heart. It will wreck your spiritual life. It will stall your prayer life. It will mar your faith. It will eventually shipwreck you.

I've known preachers whom I've tried to help who let bitterness get into their heart. Sometimes it was toward a fellow minister, and it cost them their ministry. For some of them, it cost them their life. There's no doubt in my mind at all that they would be alive today if they had not let bitterness get into their heart.

I'm just not going to let any ill will get into me; I'm not going to let anything evil get into my heart.

I have known men and preachers who were afflicted because they would not forgive and they became bitter. Some of them were Full Gospel preachers who couldn't carry on their own ministry successfully because of unforgiveness. Some of them suffered greatly physically and have never received healing because of bitterness and unforgiveness.

These ministers became physically ill when they became bitter. And they'll live and die without being able to receive their healing, and yet it wasn't God who afflicted them. It's God's perfect will that they be healed. So keep your eyes on Jesus. He's the Healer.

I talked to a fellow minister along this line, and I knew in my heart what was wrong with him. After a division in his church, he left and another man took over his pastorate. After a year or so the new pastor left, and my friend wanted to come back to pastor the church. About half of the people wanted him back and half didn't. Finally the half that didn't want him to return as pastor went across town, rented a store building, and started another church.

This pastor was talking to me and was very bitter because these people had left and started another church. He was even mad at the leaders of that movement because they permitted these people to do it, although the new church was several miles away from his church, and a new work was really needed there.

This pastor just ranted and raved about all of this. He was much older than I was at the time, and I wanted to tell him that he was going to bring sickness on himself, but I didn't feel at liberty to talk to him about this because of our age difference.

That fellow has been sick nearly ever since then. The Spirit of God told me that unless he got that bitterness out of him, he would continue to be sick. He developed an ulcerated stomach and has had it ever since, as well as other illnesses. I knew it was the bitterness in his spirit that caused all of this, and I knew it would mar his life.

This minister was upset because some of the people in his former church didn't want him to be their pastor. He had become bitter because part of his congregation had left his church and had started another church. And his bitterness hurt him spiritually and physically.

During the years I pastored, it never bothered me if folks didn't want me to be the pastor and didn't vote for me. What is an election for in the first place?

Every man is bound to obey his own conscience and to vote according to what he feels God is telling him. I've always determined that I would never permit the least bit of ill will or animosity in my heart toward anyone because one step out of love is a step into sin. I would not allow myself to be side-tracked in the ministry by bitterness and resentment.

It costs much more to be out of the will of God than it does to be in the will of God. Being out of the will of God will cost you your health. It will cause sickness and sometimes premature death. It'll cost you money and rest.

I'm just not going to let bitterness get into my heart toward my brother and my fellow preacher.

Don't *ever* let a root of bitterness grow in your heart because you have refused to forgive someone who has offended you. Follow the Bible's command to "forgive one another, even as God for Christ's sake has forgiven you" (Eph. 4:32). As you do, you will keep the channels open for your prayers to be answered and the blessings of God to come into your life.

Questions for Study

1. What is true Bible faith?

   _____

   _____

2. When your faith is being tested, what should you do in order to receive the answer from God?

   _____

   _____

3. Why is it important to stir yourself up in faith?

   _____

   _____

4. Instead of struggling in prayer, what should we do?

   _____

   _____

5. Even if a situation looks contrary to what God's Word says, what should you do?

   _____

   _____

6. The Bible tells us that believers have three enemies. Who or what are they?

   _____

   _____

7. If you keep saying that your faith isn't working, what are you really doing?

   _____

   _____

8. What are some reasons to make faith confessions out loud?

   _____

   _____

9. How does having hatred or revenge in your heart affect your prayer life?

   _____

   _____

10. Name one way a root of bitterness grows in a person's heart.

   _____

   _____

The Seven Most Important Things in Prayer
Part 3

We saw in Chapter 13 that the third most important thing about prayer is that you must forgive when you pray if you have ought against any. You must have a forgiving heart if you are going to pray effectually.

Number Four:
Depend on the Holy Spirit's Help in Prayer

The fourth most important thing in prayer is *to depend on the Holy Spirit to help you in your prayer life*. As we've discussed in previous lessons, one important way the Holy Spirit helps us in prayer is to give us utterance in other tongues. Paul discusses praying in tongues in First Corinthians chapter 14.

1 CORINTHIANS 14:14,15
14 For if I PRAY IN AN UNKNOWN TONGUE, MY SPIRIT PRAYETH, but my understanding is unfruitful.
15 What is it then? I WILL PRAY WITH THE SPIRIT, and I will pray with the understanding also: I will sing with the spirit, and I will sing with the understanding also.

1 CORINTHIANS 14:14 (*Amplified*)
14 For if I pray in an [unknown] tongue, MY SPIRIT [by the Holy Spirit within me] PRAYS, but my mind is unproductive — bears no fruit and helps nobody.

The Apostle Paul said in these verses that to pray in tongues is to pray *with* one's spirit by the help of the Holy Spirit within us. If Paul is correct in that statement, then we need to know about it.

We need to pray with our spirit as well as with our understanding. I suppose all Christians everywhere pray with their understanding, but not all pray with their spirit by praying in other tongues. Many do not even know that it is possible to do so.

Some people in their haste and ignorance have said that tongues have been done away with. But, you see, praying in tongues is your spirit praying by the Holy Spirit within you.

If tongues have been done away with, then just how are you going to pray with your spirit today as the Corinthians did, as stated in First Corinthians 14:14,15? Corinthian Christians didn't have a means of praying that we don't have. We have the same biblical means they had — praying with our spirits in tongues with the help of the Holy Spirit. The ability to pray with our spirits is available to us today just as much as it was available to the Early Church.

ROMANS 8:26,27
26 Likewise the Spirit also helpeth our infirmities: for we know not what we should pray for as we ought: but the Spirit itself [Himself] maketh intercession for us with groanings which cannot be uttered.
27 And he that searcheth the hearts knoweth what is the mind of the Spirit, because he maketh intercession for the saints according to the will of God.

Romans 8:26 includes praying with tongues because according to the late Dr. P.C. Nelson, the Greek translation reads, "The Spirit Himself makes intercession for us with groanings that cannot be uttered *in articulate speech*."

Articulate speech means your regular kind of speech. Speaking with tongues is not your regular kind of speech — speech in your native language. So this verse includes groanings and it also includes speaking and praying with other tongues.

We must not forget that speaking with tongues is not only an initial sign or evidence of the Holy Spirit's indwelling, but it is a continual experience for the rest of one's life. Speaking in tongues assists one in the worship of God. Howard Carter once said that praying in the Spirit is a flowing stream that should not dry up, but it will enrich your life spiritually.[1]

Paul was talking about the Holy Spirit helping us in our prayer life. *"Likewise the Spirit also HELPETH our infirmities . . ."* (Rom. 8:26). He was talking about prayer, because he also said in Romans 8:26 that we know not for what we should pray as we ought. So the subject in this verse is prayer, and Paul was talking about the Spirit helping us in prayer.

If speaking with tongues and praying with tongues isn't for us today, then that would mean this is one help of the Holy Spirit which the Body of Christ has been denied today. Some people try to tell us that tongues have been done away with, but, thank God, tongues haven't been done away with. This gift of the Spirit is for this entire Church Age dispensation.

On the Day of Pentecost *". . . they were all filled with the Holy Ghost, and began to speak with other tongues, as the Spirit gave them utterance"* (Acts 2:4). If speaking with tongues was the Spirit giving them utterance, then praying with tongues is the Spirit giving us utterance today. If the Spirit is giving us utterance, He is *helping* us pray; He is helping us worship God.

ACTS 10:44-46
44 While Peter yet spake these words, the Holy Ghost fell on all them which heard the word.
45 And they of the circumcision which believed were astonished, as many as came with Peter, because that on the Gentiles also was poured out the gift of the Holy Ghost.
46 For they heard them SPEAK WITH TONGUES, and MAGNIFY God....

Therefore, speaking with tongues helps us to magnify God. And the Holy Spirit is available to help us magnify God in our prayer life.

Let me say a few things here. Many people read Romans 8:26 casually and jump to their own conclusion and miss what it says. Some people believe this verse says that the Holy Spirit does your praying *for* you.

One woman told me that after reading this verse, she just didn't pray anymore because she was going to let the Holy Spirit do it for her! But that is not what this verse says. Romans 8:26 doesn't say that the Holy Spirit does our praying *for* us; it says that He *helps* us pray. The Holy Spirit does not pray apart from the believer.

If the Holy Spirit did your praying for you, then He would be the One who would be responsible for your prayer life. You wouldn't even have to pray because you know He could do a better job than you could. But if someone *helps*, he doesn't do the job by himself; he just gives assistance to the one being helped.

Likewise the Holy Spirit is in you *to help* you. You can depend upon Him to help you: *"Likewise the Spirit also HELPETH our infirmities: for we know not what we should pray for as we ought . . ."* (Rom. 8:26). This is the fourth most important thing about prayer: *We must depend upon the Holy Spirit to help us pray.*

Depend upon the Holy Spirit to help you! If I know about things for which I ought to pray, then I can pray with my understanding and I can believe I receive when I pray, and I will receive them. There are things, however, about which we should pray, but we do not know how to pray as we ought. But the Spirit knows, and He can help us, and we can receive answers from God.

We all need the necessities of life, such as being able to pay the rent and buy groceries. And we can believe for the necessities of life because the Bible promises that God will meet all of our needs: *". . . my God shall supply all your need according to his riches in glory by Christ Jesus"* (Phil. 4:19). When we pray for the necessities of life, we know *what* we are

praying for; therefore, we have definite scriptures on which to base our prayer.

But there are needs and situations that may arise in our lives about which it is not quite so easy to pray, because we don't know how to pray as we ought. That's when we need the Holy Spirit's help.

Too many times we pray for the Lord to bless people, and about all that does is salve our conscience to make us believe we have prayed for people. That is not sufficient.

Actually, God has already blessed His people, but many of them just don't know it. If they are believers, they are already blessed with all spiritual blessings in heavenly places in Christ Jesus (Eph. 1:3). But many of God's people just don't know it, or they haven't appropriated what rightfully belongs to them.

Praying in Tongues
When You Don't Know What To Pray For

But believers can enlist the Spirit of God to help them pray about things without even knowing exactly what the needs are. For example, many times in my own life I have told the Lord I didn't know exactly what I should pray for concerning my own children. But as I began to pray, the Holy Spirit would give me utterance to pray out the perfect will of God for them.

If you're going to wait to believe that God heard your prayer until *after* you see something in the natural, you are never going to get it. No, *you* must begin to pray, and then the Holy Spirit will take hold and begin to help you, giving you the utterance. God hears us when we pray!

When I know there is a problem, I begin praying in tongues, and most of the time before I get through praying, I have the answer to the problem in my spirit. Many times I've received answers for loved ones while praying in tongues.

Actually, it is best to pray in tongues when you're praying for someone else, especially if you don't know what the problem or need is. You can pray in your understanding as far as your knowledge goes, of course. And you can also plead your case for your loved ones with the Word of God.

EPHESIANS 6:18
18 Praying always with all prayer and supplication in the Spirit, and watching thereunto with all perseverance and supplication for all saints.

This is a way to pray for your brothers or sisters in Christ. This is prayer that is prayed in the Spirit for all believers — all saints.

On occasion I have told the Lord that I didn't know what to pray for. I knew I should pray because I sensed that a certain person was in need or in trouble, but I didn't know what the need was. So I depended on the Holy Spirit to help me, and I would begin to pray in tongues.

The Holy Spirit Communicates With Our *Spirits*

Therefore, the best way to get answers is to get into the Spirit when you pray. The best way to get into condition spiritually so you can hear the Lord is to pray in tongues. Since praying in tongues is praying with your spirit, and God is a Spirit (John 4:24), then God will communicate with you through your spirit as you pray in tongues.

God very seldom speaks to man through the physical senses. He only does that as a last resort when people are either spiritually dead or too dense to receive from Him any other way. So many have missed it by wanting God to manifest Himself in the physical realm through the physical senses. But Satan is the god of this world (2 Cor. 4:4).

Therefore, if you try to rely on hearing from God in the physical realm through the physical senses, you can quickly get in trouble and throw yourself wide open for satanic deception.

The only times I've ever missed God is when I've wanted Him to do something for me in the sense realm; I wanted something to register on my physical senses. But all the time on the inside of me, in my spirit, I knew the Holy Spirit was telling me something different. That's the reason we get confused sometimes; we try to do things ourselves, and we try to hear from God apart from the way the Bible teaches us that God speaks to His people.

If you want your spirit to be more keen to spiritual things, then you're going to have to exercise your spirit. God isn't going to talk to your head because He doesn't live in your head. The Holy Spirit doesn't come into your *head;* He comes into your *heart.* He comes into your spirit to dwell. When you speak in other tongues, you are not speaking out of your head, you are speaking out of your spirit. It is your spirit speaking.

Paul said that when he prayed in an unknown tongue, his spirit prayed (1 Cor. 14:14). So when you pray in tongues, it is your spirit praying by the Holy Spirit within you. And if you groan by the unction of the Holy Spirit, you do it by the Holy Spirit within you.

Have you ever prayed and been so burdened down in prayer that you couldn't think of adequate words to express what you felt? All you could do from way down inside of you was to groan in prayer until the burden lifted. Paul said that is the Spirit helping you. The Holy Spirit is helping you pray.

From the natural standpoint, I know that the mind says this is silly. The natural mind looks at praying with groanings from the natural standpoint and says it's foolish. That's why so much of our praying and worship is in the natural and not in the Spirit at all. It is so sad that in many of our churches we are not even taught spiritual things (that also applies for Full Gospel churches too). Sometimes we only have *a form* of worship, and the people of God are missing out on so much.

Paul says that these groanings which escape our lips, come up from our spirit. They come up from the innermost being, from what the Bible calls your heart. It's not talking about your physical heart, the organ that pumps blood throughout your body. Most of the time when the Bible talks about the *heart* of man, it is talking about the *spirit* of man.

In these days, because of advanced medical technology, many people are having heart transplants. I once heard on the news that someone asked one of the heart-transplant patients how it felt to have someone else's heart. He said that he didn't feel any different at all. Of course, he wouldn't feel any different because he just had someone else's *physical* heart organ. He didn't have another person's spiritual heart, or spirit.

It wouldn't be any more wrong to have a heart transplant than it would be to have a kidney transplant. The heart and the kidneys are just physical organs. Doctors couldn't transplant what the Bible calls a man's heart — that is, the real man — the spirit man on the inside. The inward man of the heart can't be transplanted as medical science does in heart transplants. God, of course, recreates man's heart in the new birth, thereby giving man a new heart (Jer. 31:33; Ezek. 37:26).

I have actually heard religious leaders discuss heart transplants as if it is a moral issue. Some of these religious leaders were well educated, yet they did not know the difference between the physical heart, a physical organ, and the spiritual heart — the inward nature of man.

I think some of these dear souls educated their heads at the expense of educating their spirits! In some cases, I have almost decided that Ph.D. stands for "post-hole digger"! It seems to me that a common posthole digger would know more than some of these so-called religious experts!

It is no wonder church people are not more spiritual when you see some church leaders being so natural-minded and materialistic, focusing only on the physical realm. All the worshipping many of them do is only in the natural realm; they never get into the Spirit.

Many church leaders don't even know they are spirit beings. They think they are just soul and body; that is, just mind and body. But man is not just mind and body. Man *is* a spirit; he *has* a soul; and he *lives* in a body. The Holy Ghost comes to dwell in *man's recreated human spirit.*

When you are born again, your body becomes a temple of the Holy Ghost because the body is the temple for your spirit, and the Holy Ghost lives in your spirit. He communicates with you or with your spirit, the real you, not with your head.

That inward voice of the Holy Spirit ofttimes tries to give us direction, but our mind is many times so cluttered with everything else, that we fail to lean on the Holy Spirit's direction. Our mind has been educated through the physical senses or the sense realm. That is the reason the mind needs to be renewed with the Word of God (Rom. 12:1,2).

If your mind is not renewed with the Word of God, even though you are born again and Spirit filled, you will always be a carnal Christian and a baby Christian. You will be body-ruled and sense-ruled.

Too many times our prayers are prayed out of our minds, but we should also pray in the Spirit with other tongues. Praying in the Spirit with other tongues serves multiple purposes.

First, praying in tongues is a means of spiritual edification. That means it affects us individually and personally. Second, praying in tongues is a means of praying for things about which we have no knowledge. Third, the Holy Spirit gives us utterance in tongues to help us make intercession and supplication for others. Fourth, praying in tongues provides us with a means of worshipping and magnifying God.

Number Five:
The Holy Spirit's Help In
Intercession and Supplication

The fifth most important thing in prayer is *to depend upon the Holy Spirit to help you pray the prayer of intercession and supplication.* The Bible speaks about intercession and says that the Spirit makes intercession for us (Rom. 8:27).

Remember, the prayer of intercession is not prayed for yourself. An intercessor is one who takes the place of another. You intercede for *others*, not for yourself.

Actually, to "intercede" means *to act between two parties with a thought of reconciling the two of them.* In other words, the two parties are at odds with one another. Therefore, we usually intercede for the lost, although one can intercede for the backslider as well.

On the other hand, to "supplicate" means *to make a humble entreaty* or *to implore God; to entreat for; to ask humbly and earnestly.* Therefore, we make supplication for the saints.

By praying in the Spirit in intercession, we can and oftentimes do intercede for unsaved loved ones or even unsaved people we know nothing about. In praying in tongues, I've prayed by the help and the inspiration of the Holy Spirit for people who were lost.

To make intercession also means to take the place of another. So sometimes in intercession I have felt that my own soul was lost because I was taking the place of another. This may not happen to you and it does not always happen with me. It's not necessary that it happen, but if it does, yield to the prompting of the Holy Spirit because He is the One who helps us to pray. That is biblical.

Then there is an area of groaning in prayer by the inspiration of the Holy Spirit. These groanings come out of our spirits, and they escape our lips. It is the Holy Spirit helping us pray (Rom. 8:26).

We can make intercession and supplication in groanings and in other tongues as the Holy Spirit helps us. Intercession is usually for the lost. Supplication is praying for the saints — for believers.

It is important to note that *all* intercession and supplication is not done by groanings and by praying in tongues. You can also pray and should pray with your understanding as far as your knowledge goes. And remember, praying *in the Spirit* is praying by the inspiration and the direction of the Holy Spirit, whether in tongues or in your native language.

Also, after a while of praying in the Spirit, you will know whether you are praying as a means of building yourself up spiritually and worshipping God, or whether it is intercession or supplication for someone. Many times you can also tell when you are in intercession or travail for someone who is lost.

As I said, if you are taking the place of a lost one and crying out in groanings and tongues in prayer for the lost, many times you will have the same feeling of being lost in your own spirit, even though you are saved and Spirit filled. You may experience these feelings yourself because you are taking the place of another in prayer.

I am convinced that the reason more of the lost are not being saved is that we don't pray in this manner as we should. During times of praying in tongues, I have also cried out in English, "Lost! Lost!" It would seem in my spirit that I had such agony, as if I were lost too. (At one time I *was* lost, too, so I know how a lost person feels.) When I was praying like this, I wasn't lost but I was carrying the burden, so to speak, as I interceded or took the place of another in prayer.

At one time we all had that burden of guilt and sin in our own spirit and in our own heart. It has been so long for some of us that we have almost forgotten how that felt.

But, yet, when you intercede for the lost, many times you will have a burden of guilt and of sin — that lost feeling — in your own spirit, in your own consciousness. That's because you are in a sense taking that lost person's place in prayer. You are interceding for them.

Once in a great while I will have a burden of intercession before I am aware of who it is I am praying for, and then later God will reveal it to me. I have had that experience at times in revival services. On the other hand, many times after praying in that manner with groanings and travail for someone who was lost, I would never find out who it was for.

And then sometimes in praying that way, the Lord would let me know for whom I was praying. At times, I've even had a vision about what or for whom I was praying. I knew at times that I was praying for someone who was lost. I prayed with travail.

When you have this travail in your spirit, very often you feel a great upheaval inside of you, like a woman in travail who is about to have a baby. When you travail in the Spirit, you can have similar "birth pangs," so to speak, on the inside of you in your spirit, as you intercede for the lost.

These days even many Full Gospel people have not experienced this kind of intercession for the lost and do not know what we are talking about. There was a time when Full Gospel folks had experienced this kind of travail with groanings, but this is now almost a lost practice among us. And most people coming from denominational circles don't know a thing about it at all.

Let me share one experience I once had in interceding for the lost. I was holding a meeting one time and was praying in the Spirit for my service. For a long time I groaned and prayed in tongues and then began to cry out, "Lost! Lost!" I felt inside like a lost soul in hell. Then as I continued to pray this way, I had a spiritual vision.

In this vision I saw men and women and it looked like they were floating down a river. There were thousands of them. Some were happy and were singing as they just glided down this river, unaware of what awaited them.

Suddenly they came to a place like a cliff, and they just plunged off into the depths below. Down, down, down they went into the eternal fires of hell. I could see smoke and fire coming up from that fiery cavern below. I saw those people going down into that eternal fire. I saw them screaming and crying out for mercy as they plunged into those flames.

I was praying in the parsonage when this vision occurred, and some others were also praying in the room with me. I would cry out, "Lost! Lost!" And I would cry out for water, as if *my* tongue were parched from the intense heat of that flame.

It was like that rich man in hell who cried out for Lazarus to dip his finger in water to cool his tongue (Luke 16:24). It felt like I was in flames. I was interceding for the lost. This vision happened many years ago, but it is still just as real to me now as it was then. Spiritual things never grow old.

That evening I only preached about fifteen minutes, and every unsaved person in that service came to the Lord! No one invited them to come. No one talked to anyone, but every single lost and backslidden person in that building came as one man to the altar and was saved. Praise the Lord!

In another case, I was praying several days before my Sunday night service and in a vision, I saw a man come to one of my services. I saw how he was dressed. I saw him come to the altar and be saved. When the Sunday night service came, it happened just as I saw it. He was about seventy years of age and had never been to church in his life. No one in that church knew him to pray for him, so no one even knew he would be in the service, but the Holy Spirit did. And that man was gloriously saved!

At one church I pastored during World War II, I went out to the church while it was still light outside to pray for my Saturday night service. I had a sermon; I had been reading the Bible and praying, and I had something in my spirit. I had outlined this sermon and thought I'd preach it that night. But somehow, I didn't feel it was exactly what the Lord wanted for that particular service, so I felt I should spend some extra time there praying.

So I began to pray in tongues, and as I walked up and down the aisle praying I noticed a change in the tongues. I wasn't praying in tongues, I was "preaching" in tongues. I went to the pulpit, not knowing a word I was saying, but I preached a sermon, making gestures with my hands. I knew when I came to the end of my sermon. It was all in tongues. I knew when I gave the invitation, because I held my hand out as if I were inviting people to come forward to the altar. But I was there by myself in the church preparing for my service.

Then I had a vision. In the vision, all the people were sitting in place in the church, when I suddenly saw a young woman step out into the aisle. She came down front, knelt at the end of the altar, and was saved. Then I saw a man leave another section and kneel at the altar and he was also saved. I stepped off the platform and it was as if I was laying my hands on the woman's head. I was seeing all of this in a vision. I prayed over the young woman and then I prayed over the man. Then the vision ended.

Suddenly I realized that it had gotten just about dark outside. This was still wintertime and it was before we went to daylight saving time, so it got dark earlier than usual.

I thought to myself, "This can't be right. This man I saw in the vision lives just outside of town, and he could already be saved, for all I know. He does come to church sometimes. But that young woman, she doesn't even live around here. Her parents come to church, but she doesn't live in this town. She doesn't even live at home."

So I said to myself, "What I saw in that vision can never come to pass because that young woman isn't even in this area anymore! How could she even come to church? Why am I seeing all this?"

About that time someone drove up to the church, so I turned the lights on in the church and opened the doors. This young woman drove up to the church with her father! It was the very young woman I'd seen in the vision! I thought, "Well, the Lord knew more than I did, didn't He?"

Now I wouldn't have thought to pray for her because her father had said she didn't live in the area anymore, but the Holy Spirit knew she would be at that service.

I went home to get ready for the evening service, and then I came back to church. When I walked in, I saw the fellow I had seen in the vision sitting right over where I had seen him sitting in the vision. And the young woman was sitting right where I had seen her sitting. I preached my sermon that night, and I held my hand out to give the invitation, just as I had done when I was praying, and they both came forward to be saved. It happened just like I had seen it in the vision.

Intercession and supplication in the Spirit doesn't just belong to the preacher. It belongs to all of us. It is for every single one of us. Thank God for the results that have been accomplished, but can you see the results that could be accomplished if there were more of us praying that way?

The Holy Spirit Helps Us Pray for the Sick

I've learned that we can also make intercession and supplication for the sick. An example of this occurred in Wigglesworth's ministry regarding the case of a sick man named Lazarus.

Wigglesworth loved to go into people's homes and pray for them. In his day, there weren't as many hospitals as we have today, so people were confined more to their homes.

One time there were a couple of young men who came up from Wales to visit the Wigglesworth's mission. These young men saw God moving there, and they said they wouldn't be surprised if God sent Wigglesworth to Wales to raise up Lazarus.

Then they explained that Lazarus was a coal miner who had worked in the mines during the day and preached at night, until he had finally broken himself down physically. He had tuberculosis and had been bedfast for four years.

Two years later, Wigglesworth did hold a meeting in Wales. One day on his day off Wigglesworth went up on a mountain to pray. As he prayed, the Spirit of God told Wigglesworth that He wanted him to go raise up Lazarus.

Wigglesworth could have gotten back in the natural and said that Lazarus was probably dead by then. But he didn't. He took a postcard from his pocket and wrote a message to these men saying that God told him to come and raise up Lazarus. He told them when he would be there.

The next week at the appointed time, Wigglesworth knocked on the door of the house where Lazarus lived. A man came to the door and asked Wigglesworth if he was the one who had sent the postcard. When Wigglesworth answered yes, the man threw the postcard in his face and said they didn't believe in things like that.

You see, folks had prayed for nearly five years for this fellow, Lazarus, and when he didn't get healed, they had lost faith and confidence. Lazarus himself had become discouraged and bitter about not getting healed.

But Wigglesworth said to himself that it would never do to give in to the devil when *God* had spoken. Most people would have given up, but Wigglesworth didn't. He had a friend with him, and they decided to go find several more people who could pray with them.

His friend knew some people with whom they could stay that night, so they went there. These two agreed to join them in prayer and that made four people. They said that the next day they would try to find more people to go back to the house with them and pray for Lazarus.

In the nighttime, Wigglesworth was awakened with all the symptoms of tuberculosis, the disease that afflicted Lazarus. Wigglesworth said he was so weak, he couldn't lift a hand, and even his lungs were affected. Somehow Wigglesworth managed to roll out of bed onto the floor. He began crying out to God until he got deliverance over that thing. Actually, Wigglesworth was making prayer and supplication for Lazarus.

The next day Wigglesworth and seven other people went to Lazarus' house. Wigglesworth told the others to make a circle around the sick man's bed and to just say the Name of Jesus over and over again. As they did, the power of God fell in that room five different times and then lifted.

The sixth time the power of God fell, the man Lazarus cried out, "I have been bitter in my heart, and I know I have grieved the Spirit of God." As Lazarus repented, both he and the bed shook with the power of God, and Lazarus rose out of his bed completely healed! The prayers of Wigglesworth and the others helped to bring deliverance to this man who had been so close to death. [2]

I've made intercession and supplication for the sick in much the same way as Wigglesworth interceded for Lazarus. For instance, I've prayed for people who have had tumors, and something would swell up on the inside of my own body like a tumor when I was praying for them. I would pray until it disappeared. When it left me, it left them.

You can't do this whenever *you* want to do it; you can't put on something. This kind of prayer comes by the unction of the Holy Spirit. You have to depend upon the Holy Spirit. We are helpless by ourselves.

I was holding a meeting years ago, and my friend and I were praying about my evening service in a trailer near the church. And as I was praying, I began to have symptoms of sickness in my body,

including symptoms in my right ear. I told my friend that three people would come to the service that night with these three different conditions I had felt in my own body, and each of these people would be healed. The very symptoms I was experiencing in my body, I had prayed through, and those people were healed!

These manifestations are as the Spirit wills and not as man wills (1 Cor. 12:11). We need to realize that. At the service that night, I spoke about each one of these cases, and the first two people came forward and were healed. I was reluctant to speak about the ear symptoms because I *knew* there was a certain woman in the church who had had problems with her ears. Therefore, I simply said that there was someone present who had the feeling of something plugging up the ear. I knew that because that's the sensation I had when I prayed.

My hearing had been impaired in the right ear and I had prayed in the Spirit until the impairment left. I said that the person who had this impairment could receive his healing too. The woman stood up and asked if that had happened at 3:00 that afternoon. I told her it had.

My friend and I had both looked at our watches at the time it happened that afternoon. She said that in the doctor's office that afternoon when the doctor examined her ears, her right ear had popped open. She said that now she was hearing one hundred percent out of that ear.

Can you see how much more the supernatural could be in demonstration if we were all praying that way? Paul infers in Romans 8:26 and 27 that every Spirit-filled believer can expect the Holy Spirit to help him in making prayer and intercession. This prayer can be in the area of healing as well as for the lost. And praying in the Spirit includes praying for things about which we are not sure or for which we have no knowledge.

A missionary I knew from England came down with cancer. Although he was an older man, the doctors decided to operate on him. After he came out of the operation, they told him that they couldn't get all of the cancer and that he had only a limited time to live. He got well enough to leave the hospital, but he wasn't able to return to the ministry.

A Pentecostal periodical published a request for prayer for this missionary, but it didn't say exactly what was wrong with him. One night a woman in Australia was awakened and had a burden to pray. She began praying in the Spirit and spent two or three hours praying in other tongues. Then she had a vision of what she was praying about, and she saw this man and saw his name and his address.

Although she had never heard of him before in her life, she wrote down accurately everything she saw. She knew this man had an inward cancer and was operated on, but that the doctors didn't get all of it and that this man was dying. She prayed this burden through, and she knew that the man was healed. She received all of this knowledge of the missionary's situation by a revelation of the Holy Spirit. She wrote all of this down and sent it to the man and told him that he was healed.

By the time the letter got to the man, he was already up and completely healed. The doctors had examined him and said the cancer was gone. He was sixty-five years old. He lived many more years before he went on to be with the Lord.

These are facts of what praying in the Spirit can accomplish. This woman knew what the Holy Spirit had told her in prayer. You may not always know what you are praying for. You don't have to know. But yield to the Holy Spirit when He prompts you whether you know all the facts or not. Sometimes He'll let you know.

God Seeks Those Who Will Give Themselves To Prayer

Can you see that those who don't have the baptism of the Holy Ghost are really missing something, especially in this area of prayer? When we don't give ourselves to the things of God as we ought, we miss out on many of the blessings of God that are rightfully ours in life. Isn't it sad that we have to wait until some kind of tragedy strikes before we really give ourselves to prayer? Then sometimes it's too late to start praying.

If we would just be more sensitive to the Spirit, we could know ahead of time of things to come so we could pray (John 16:13). I believe the Holy Spirit is searching for those who will give themselves to this kind of praying. But many times the Spirit searches through entire church congregations and can't find anyone to yield to Him and give themselves to prayer.

When we get up to heaven and the rewards are passed out, many people are going to be surprised. There will be many who will want to step forward to receive rewards, but they are not going to get them. And there will be many who were little known by the world, but who gave themselves to prayer and fasting, and they will be rewarded for their obedience to God.

A seventy-nine-year-old woman lived in a little town near the first Full Gospel church I once pastored. There wasn't a church in her town so she attended ours. Some of us would go out to dinner together for the noon meal after church and then sit around visiting. She would sit and visit awhile and then she would always excuse herself and say that she had to go to prayer. She would get off in a bedroom by herself and get down on her knees and pray all Sunday afternoon.

At times during her life she and her husband had lived where there wasn't a Full Gospel church. At those times she would take upon herself a burden of prayer and would pray and intercede for that town until someone would come and build a Full Gospel church. Then she would pray for God to raise up another church. She prayed a church into every town throughout that whole area! She's going to get the reward for praying in those churches!

A pastor friend of mine didn't have a parsonage where he pastored a few miles away from me, and this same woman did have her own home. Her husband was dead, so she let the preacher and his wife live in one part of the house free of charge, and she lived in another part of the house.

He said that every single day this woman got up at 4:00 a.m. and would dress and prepare for the day. This woman would pray from 5:00 a.m. until 8:00 a.m. Then at 8:00 a.m. she would eat. At about 10:00 a.m. she would start praying again until about 5:30 p.m.

Then this woman would eat supper and she might come in and sit down and visit with the preacher and his wife for a while, but by 8:00 p.m. she was praying again and would pray until about midnight. She was always praying and making intercession and supplication. She wasn't praying for herself. There's no doubt in my mind that she was the only one in a wide area on whom the Spirit of God could have rolled such a prayer burden. I wonder if you are one, too, whom God can trust with a burden of prayer.

Number Six: Edify Yourself by Praying in Tongues

The sixth most important thing in prayer is *to take time to build up yourself by praying much in the Holy Ghost, with other tongues.*

JUDE 20
20 But ye, beloved, BUILDING UP YOURSELVES on your most holy faith, PRAYING IN THE HOLY GHOST.

Praying in the Holy Ghost is praying in the Spirit or in tongues. Paul made a statement similar to Jude 20 in First Corinthians 14:4, which says, *"He that speaketh in an unknown tongue EDIFIETH himself; but he that prophesieth edifieth the church."* The word "edifieth" in First Corinthians 14:4 means the same thing as "building up yourselves" in Jude 20.

One element of speaking with tongues in our prayer lives does not involve praying for someone else, but is purely a means of personal and spiritual edification. It does something for us spiritually to pray in other tongues. We need that kind of praying. We are not going to be able to edify others without being edified ourselves.

The more we pray in other tongues and build up our spirits, the more keen we will be in the Holy Spirit and in the things of the Spirit. Praying in tongues helps make us sensitive to the Holy Spirit when He desires to manifest spiritual gifts through us.

We must stay sensitive to the Holy Spirit so He can manifest the gifts of the Spirit through us as He desires. This is especially true if we are to be used in the operation of the vocal gifts of the Holy Spirit (1 Cor. 12:10) — prophecy, tongues, and interpretation of tongues — for we have a role to play in order for the vocal gifts to be manifested through us.

The believer must yield to the promptings of the Holy Spirit and speak out what the Holy Spirit has given him. That is, the believer must exercise his own vocal chords, but the Holy Spirit gives the utterance.

In other words, we have something to do to cooperate with the Holy Spirit in the manifestation of vocal gifts because we are the ones doing the talking. We don't operate those gifts at will or apart from the Holy Spirit, but we're the ones who must yield to the Holy Spirit's utterance and do the actual speaking.

Because believers have something to do with the vocal gifts — tongues, interpretation of tongues and prophecy — the Bible instructs us in the use of these gifts, telling us how and when to exercise them (1 Cor. 14:26-33).

However, you will notice that there are no instructions given to us at all about the operation of the other gifts of the Spirit. That's because a believer can't give himself or make himself have a manifestation of one of the gifts of the Spirit. He can only stay sensitive to the Holy Spirit and be available if the Holy Spirit desires to manifest a spiritual gift through him.

For example, a person can't make himself have a revelation. And God doesn't prompt a person to step out in faith and receive a revelation. No, the revelation just comes spontaneously by the Holy Spirit as the Holy Spirit wills. But it is up to the person to do something with a revelation after he receives it.

However, with the vocal gifts, the believer himself has a role to play in these spiritual gifts being manifested. While it is true the believer must be prompted by the Spirit, it is also true that the believer must yield to the Holy Spirit's promptings and step out in faith and speak forth what the Holy Spirit has given him.

For example, if I am being used in a vocal gift, I'm the one who has to do the talking. I'm the one who has to speak forth what the Holy Spirit has given me. I have something to do with prophecy or tongues and interpretation, because I'm the one who does the talking; however, the Holy Spirit is the One who gives the utterance.

Did you ever notice how sometimes interpretation of tongues can be so "dead," with not much anointing on the interpretation? That happens when the speaker has not taken time to edify himself by praying in the Holy Ghost, and he doesn't have much unction or anointing to bring forth the message. One who has not prepared himself sufficiently by spending time with God and His Word will not be very keen in the things of the Spirit.

Praying in the Spirit Helps You Grow Spiritually

Spiritual things are very similar to natural things. Jesus took natural things to explain spiritual things. No one is going to be an expert or keen in any area without working at it. In the area of sports, for instance, a person who is known for his high batting average, for his hitting ability, did not get to his position without many hours of batting practice.

On the news I once heard about a fellow whose batting average had been way down, but by much hard work and practice he had brought it up. The reporter talked to the baseball player about how he had been working on it. It seemed everyone else would practice at regular times, but this fellow would come to the park early every morning and have someone throw balls for him. He would practice two or three hours every day on just batting, and the more he practiced, the keener he became.

Once I heard someone on television play the piano. He was just a young person, about nineteen or twenty years old, but he was tops in his field. He could play all of those marvelous classical pieces.

When the young man was interviewed, he said he started playing the piano when he was four years old, and from the time he was nine years old, he practiced from four to six hours every day. (As a child he didn't run and play as much as the other children his age because he was always practicing the piano.) He had missed much in that respect, but look where all his practice had taken him. He couldn't have become keen and expert in natural things without putting in time practicing.

We know these things don't just fall on us like ripe cherries off a tree. Likewise, you needn't think that in the spiritual realm, you are going to become expert overnight in praying either. You won't be able to. You needn't think that you can just sit around and wait for something to fall on you either. The only thing that will fall on you is disappointment and discouragement.

No, you will have to put some effort into the things of God. You won't be able to become proficient in any area, without some effort and personal diligence.

If you want to become expert in any area, you must be dedicated. Men have become expert because they gave themselves to achieve a goal. They took time to become expert and keen in a certain field. They denied themselves a lot of good activities, even legitimate things in life, to give of themselves to become proficient in a certain area.

What about us? We are not going to be expert in the area of prayer unless we give time to prayer, unless we make prayer a habit and a way of life. We are not going to be expert in spiritual things unless we take time to dedicate ourselves to the things of God.

For eighteen months after I received the baptism of the Holy Ghost in 1937, as a young Baptist boy preacher and pastor, I didn't do a lot of praying in tongues. There wasn't much teaching on that subject back in those days. We had to discover much about it ourselves. So I began to examine the Word on the subject.

At first I didn't think a person should pray in tongues, unless he was almost forced into it or urged or prompted by the Holy Spirit to do so. I thought a sort of spirit of "ecstasy" had to fall upon a person, until he was just so overflowing that you couldn't help but pray in tongues.

But then I came to realize the Bible didn't teach that. Paul said, ". . . *I WILL pray with the spirit, and I WILL pray with the understanding* . . ." (1 Cor. 14:15). Therefore, the believer can pray in tongues at will. I determined within myself that I was going to

spend a certain length of time in prayer every day. Once I decided that I was going to, I started doing it, and it has paid rich dividends.

When I first started praying regularly in tongues, it took me about an hour to really get to that place in the Spirit where I was just lost in the Spirit. Being "lost" in the Spirit is when you just forget about the mental and natural realms. Time slips by and you think you have only prayed fifteen minutes, when really you have been praying perhaps an hour or more.

I have never really been able to understand these people who talk about what a job or chore it is to pray in the Spirit. Some believers say that it just wears them out. It never wore me out, and sometimes I would pray five and six hours at a time that way.

People who say praying in tongues wears them out are trying to put too much of the flesh into it and they are wearing their flesh out. But if you'll get into the Spirit, and get lost in the Spirit, so to speak, it is really a rest.

Isaiah said, *"For with stammering lips and another tongue will he* [God] *speak to this people. To whom he said, THIS IS THE REST wherewith ye may cause the weary to rest; and this is the refreshing . . . "* (Isa. 28:11,12). Praying and speaking with tongues is a rest.

The Spirit of God says, "And if you will give yourself unto these things, if you will freely give yourself unto these things and pray in the Spirit as you should, surely you shall find rest, not only in the inward man but in your mind and in your body. And there shall be a refreshing in your entire being from the top of your head to the soles of your feet, and you shall be edified and built up and you shall be a blessing unto many."

No wonder the devil fights praying in tongues so hard. He wants to make you weary; he wants you to wear yourself out. There is a side of praying in tongues that edifies us. It edifies us spiritually and builds us up.

I've had the Lord tell me when I wasn't so dull in spiritual things that I was just not keen in the Spirit because I hadn't given myself time *in the Spirit*. I would get busy with other natural things, and I wouldn't take time to wait upon Him. The Lord would tell me this.

As I said, when I first started praying like this in other tongues, it would take me an hour to get over into that area of getting lost in the Spirit, where the natural realm would seem to fade away. But now I can get there almost immediately. You can too if you'll practice it long enough.

As we have discussed in this chapter, it is so important to our own spiritual walk to learn how to depend on the Holy Spirit to help us in our prayer life.

As we pray much in the Spirit, we will build up our spirits and become sensitive to the voice of the Holy Spirit. And as we give ourselves to prayer with the help of the Holy Spirit, we can enter into a realm of prayer where people can be delivered from the chains of sin and sickness that have kept them bound, and the supernatural works of God can be wrought!

---

[1] Howard Carter, *Questions and Answers on Spiritual Gifts* (Tulsa, Oklahoma: Harrison House, Inc., 1976), p. 120.

[2] Smith Wigglesworth, *Ever Increasing Faith* (1924; Springfield, Missouri: Gospel Publishing House, 1971), pp. 28-32.

Questions for Study

1. When praying for someone else, especially if you don't know what the problem or need is, what is the best way to pray?

   _____

   _____

2. What is the best way to get into condition spiritually?

   _____

   _____

3. When does God speak to man through the physical senses?

   _____

   _____

4. If you want your spirit to be more keen to spiritual things, what do you have to do?

   _____

   _____

5. What is the definition of the word "supplicate"?

   _____

   _____

6. How can we know ahead of time about things to come so we can pray about them?

   _____

   _____

7. Why is it important to stay sensitive to the Holy Spirit?

   _____

   _____

8. How can we become expert in the area of prayer and spiritual things?

   _____

   _____

9. Why do some people say that praying in tongues wears them out?

   _____

   _____

10. In Isaiah 28:11 and 12, what does the phrase "*. . . This is the rest . . .*" refer to?

    _____

    _____

Chapter 15

The Seven Most Important Things in Prayer Part 4

Praying always with all prayer and supplication in the Spirit, and watching thereunto with all perseverance and supplication for all saints.
— Ephesians 6:18

The *Moffatt's* translation of this verse says, "Praying at all times in the Spirit, with all manner of prayer and entreaty. . . ." Another modern translation says, "Praying with all kinds of prayer." The *King James Version* says the same thing in effect: *"Praying always with all prayer. . . ."*

So Paul infers that there is more than one kind of prayer. If there weren't, he would have just said, *"Praying always . . ."* and let it go at that. But he said, *"Praying always with ALL* [kinds of] *prayer . . ."* (Eph. 6:18).

How desperately our nation needs all kinds of prayer! How desperately the Church needs prayer! How desperately we individually need prayer! And to ensure the happiness and welfare of our families, nothing can take the place of prayer.

In this chapter we will discuss the seventh most important thing in prayer. But first let's review six of the seven most important things in prayer, which we covered in the preceding chapters.

Number One:
Pray to the Father in Jesus' Name

The first most important thing in prayer is *to pray to the Father in the Name of Jesus.*

JOHN 16:23,24
23 And IN THAT DAY [the day of the New Covenant] ye shall ask me nothing. Verily, verily, I say unto you, Whatsoever ye shall ASK THE FATHER IN MY NAME, he will give it you.
24 Hitherto have ye asked nothing in my name: ask, and ye shall receive, that your joy may be full.

Number Two:
Believe You Receive When You Pray

The second most important thing in prayer is *to believe that you receive when you pray.*

MARK 11:24
24 Therefore I say unto you, What things soever ye desire, when ye pray, believe that ye receive them, and ye shall have them.

Number Three:
Forgive If You Have Ought Against Any

The third most important thing in prayer is *to forgive if you have ought against any, for prayer won't work unless you have a forgiving heart.*

MARK 11:25,26
25 And when ye stand praying, FORGIVE, if ye have ought against any: that your Father also which is in heaven may forgive you your trespasses.
26 BUT IF YE DO NOT FORGIVE, neither will your Father which is in heaven forgive your trespasses.

Number Four:
Depend on the Holy Spirit's Help in Prayer

The fourth most important thing in prayer is *to depend upon the Holy Spirit to help you in your prayer life.*

ROMANS 8:26
26 Likewise the Spirit also helpeth our infirmities: for we know not what we should pray for as we ought: but the Spirit itself [Himself] maketh intercession for us with groanings which cannot be uttered.

1 CORINTHIANS 14:14 (*Amplified*)
14 For if I pray in an [unknown] tongue, my spirit [by the Holy Spirit within me] prays, but my mind is unproductive — bears no fruit and helps nobody.

Remember, the Holy Spirit *helps* you in your prayer life. Praying with other tongues and groaning in and by the Spirit is not something the Holy Spirit does apart from you. These groanings and words escape your lips as *you* speak them out *in cooperation* with the Holy Spirit. So depend upon Him to help you in your prayer life.

When you don't know for what to pray as you ought, that is when you particularly need the Holy Spirit's help. If you do know for what to pray, then as you pray as an individual for your own needs to be met, believe that you receive your needs met and you will have them (Mark 11:24).

Number Five:
The Holy Spirit's Help In Intercession and Supplication

The fifth most important thing in prayer is *to depend upon the Holy Spirit to help you pray the prayer of intercession.*

As we desire to pray for others, and begin to do that, the Bible says the Spirit of God will help us because we do not always know how to pray as we ought. Therefore, the Holy Spirit makes intercession for us with groanings which cannot be uttered (Rom. 8:26). As we discussed earlier, these groanings inspired by the Holy Spirit can also include praying in tongues. You can also make supplication and intercession in your own language, with your understanding.

Number Six:
Edify Yourself by Praying in Tongues

The sixth most important thing in prayer is *to take time to build yourself up by praying much in the Holy Ghost with other tongues.*

JUDE 20
20 But ye, beloved, BUILDING UP YOURSELVES on your most holy faith, praying in the Holy Ghost.

Also, remember in First Corinthians 14:4 Paul said, *"He that speaketh in an unknown tongue edifieth himself. . . ."*

As I've already mentioned, praying in tongues has multiple benefits and value to the believer. First, it is a means of spiritual edification. That means it affects us individually — personally. Second, it allows our spirit to pray apart from our understanding for things about which we have no knowledge. Third, the Holy Spirit gives us utterance in tongues to help us make intercession and supplication for others. Fourth, it is a means whereby we can worship and magnify God.

Number Seven:
Interpretation of Tongues In Your Private Prayer Life

The seventh most important thing in prayer is *to interpret your tongues, as the Holy Spirit wills, in your private prayer life.*

As we discussed earlier, the Bible says we do not know what to pray for as we ought (Rom. 8:26). But the Holy Spirit helps us to pray for those things about which we are unaware and for which we do not know how to pray.

That is why First Corinthians 14:13 tells us to pray for the interpretation of our prayers in tongues. Then when it is necessary, we will know what we are praying about in tongues.

1 CORINTHIANS 14:13-15
13 Wherefore let him that speaketh in an unknown tongue PRAY THAT HE MAY INTERPRET.
14 For if I pray in an unknown tongue, my spirit prayeth, but my understanding is unfruitful.
15 What is it then? I will PRAY WITH THE SPIRIT, and I will PRAY WITH THE UNDERSTANDING also. . . .

It is true that it is not always necessary for us to know what we are praying about in tongues; but when it is necessary, the Holy Spirit will tell us.

Notice in verse 13: *"Wherefore let him that speaketh in an unknown tongue PRAY THAT HE MAY INTERPRET."* Actually, the Holy Spirit through Paul is telling us to pray that we can interpret our prayers in tongues. And God is not going to tell us to pray for something we cannot have.

I am convinced that every single believer should be able to pray in tongues, for we are encouraged to do so (1 Cor. 14:5). Also, every believer should be able to interpret his own prayers (1 Cor. 14:13), as the Spirit wills, even though he may never interpret tongues publicly (1 Cor. 14:27,28). It is my observation that one can interpret his own private prayers without being a public interpreter; that is, without being used in the gift of interpretation in a public assembly.

But think about it. What point would there be for God to tell you to pray to interpret your prayers if you couldn't do it? If the Spirit of God told you to pray for something you couldn't have, that would be foolish, wouldn't it?

We can see from First Corinthians 14:13 that many of those people in the Church of Corinth could interpret their prayers that were prayed in the Spirit in their private prayer lives. Therefore, First Corinthians 14:13 is referring to the fact that any believer can interpret his own prayers in his private prayer life.

Notice *why* God wants us to be able to interpret our prayers: *". . . let him that speaketh in an unknown tongue pray that he may interpret. For if I pray in a unknown tongue, my spirit* [by the Holy Spirit within me] *prayeth, but my understanding is unfruitful"* (1 Cor. 14:13,14).

Verse 14 begins with the word "for." The word "for" is a conjunction and it shows that Paul is continuing his discourse in verse 14 to explain why he said in verse 13 that we should pray to interpret our tongues. Paul said, *"For if I pray in an unknown tongue . . . my understanding is unfruitful"* (1 Cor. 14:14).

If you could interpret your own prayers, your understanding would no longer be unfruitful; your understanding would be fruitful. It would help you sometimes to know what you are praying about.

That's why First Corinthians 14:15 says, *"What is it then? I will pray with THE SPIRIT, and I will pray with THE UNDERSTANDING also. . . ."* This verse means more than what we thought it meant. It means we can pray both ways — by our *spirit* with the help of the Holy Spirit and with our *understanding*, with our own native language. But this verse also means something else.

First Corinthians 14:15 also means that if you pray to be able to interpret your prayer, you cannot only pray with your spirit, but you can understand what you prayed with your spirit in tongues.

If you interpreted what you prayed in tongues, you would also know what you prayed in your understanding. You would then be praying with your spirit and with your understanding (1 Cor. 14:15). In other words, every believer can pray not only with his spirit, but as the Holy Spirit wills, he can understand what he prays in the Spirit too! He is praying out the perfect will of God.

Of course, it is not necessary to interpret tongues when you are simply praying to edify and build yourself up (1 Cor. 14:4). Such prayers need not be interpreted. But there are some things about which you would be praying that you would need to know the interpretation. You need to know because if your mind were enlightened, it would greatly help you. This may be new for some of you, but if you keep an open heart and mind to the Word, you can grow spiritually.

I have been doing that since 1938 when I was baptized with the Holy Ghost. We didn't have any teaching on it in those days. In most churches, there still needs to be more teaching on the subject. Some people have even said that if you were filled with the Holy Spirit and spoke in tongues when you were initially filled, it is not necessary for you ever to speak in tongues again.

When I first received the Holy Spirit back in 1938, I noticed that many times when I was praying, I would begin to speak in tongues. But I would stop myself from praying in tongues because I didn't know whether it was right or not. But, thank God, it's right because it's scriptural!

Then about a year later I began to study the Word on this subject, and I began to see some of these Bible truths. I saw that it was not only scriptural to pray often in tongues, but it was scriptural to pray to interpret what you prayed in tongues (1 Cor. 14:13).

I interpreted my prayers a long time before I did any interpreting in public. I didn't always interpret *all* the prayers I prayed in tongues in my personal devotions. But as the Lord willed, and as it was necessary, I would interpret them. I know from the Word and from experience the difference it makes to be able to understand some of the things you're praying about in other tongues.

Romans 8:26 says, *". . . for we know not what we should pray for as we ought. . . ."* If you don't know for what to pray as you ought, prompted by the Holy Spirit, you can pray for "what you ought" in groanings and tongues. Then if the Holy Spirit gives you the interpretation, you'll know what you prayed for.

In some of the first experiences I had along these lines, I was seeking God, waiting before Him in prayer just because I loved Him, not because I was a minister seeking Him for a sermon. I would be praying about my services and the message I was to preach.

I was interpreting my prayer. I would pray in tongues a few words, then pray out the interpretation. We make a great mistake by thinking that tongues and interpretation is just a gift for public use. It isn't. In fact, the main use of tongues and interpretation is for the believer's private use.

Since these things are scriptural, and they belong to us as believers, then you as a believer should know about them, too, so you can enjoy the benefit of what is yours, freely given to you by God.

Sometimes we feel spiritually satisfied — we feel that we have arrived — because we have been baptized in the Holy Ghost and have spoken in tongues for a while. Actually, God has much more for us!

For example, a pastor once told me about a young man in his church who had been seeking the baptism of the Holy Ghost. They were having revival services in that church, and this young man came to the service every night. One night he received the baptism in the Holy Ghost. After that he stopped coming to the revival services. When the pastor asked him why he stopped coming to the services, he said, "Why, I finally got *through*."

But we don't "get through" when we receive the Holy Spirit. That is just the beginning of the Spirit-filled walk!

There are many amazing things I received by praying in tongues and then interpreting what I prayed about. I believe that every believer should be praying in tongues and interpreting with his understanding. This is not just a prayer out of his understanding; it is praying the interpretation of what the believer is praying about in tongues, so he can understand it. Then his understanding is fruitful.

The Public Use of Interpretation of Tongues

We've talked about the importance of a believer interpreting his tongues in his private prayer life (1 Cor. 14:13). However, the Bible also refers to the gift of interpretation of tongues that operates in a public setting.

1 CORINTHIANS 14:27,28
27 If any man speak in an unknown tongue, let it be by two, or at the most by three, and that by course; and let one interpret.
28 But IF THERE BE NO INTERPRETER, let him keep silence in the church; and let him speak to himself, and to God.

In this passage in First Corinthians 14:27,28 Paul is referring to one who is called of God to interpret tongues in the public assembly — in the local body. Paul said, *". . . if there be no interpreter, let him keep silence in the church. . . ."* inferring that there are those who are used as *public* interpreters.

Sometimes it is difficult to illustrate spiritual truths. When Jesus taught people in His earthly ministry, He took natural things to illustrate spiritual things. To illustrate the difference between interpreting tongues in your own private prayer life and being used to interpret in a public assembly, I will use this same principle of teaching.

For instance, a car and a bus are both in the same class, so to speak; they are both motor vehicles. You may have driven a car but not a bus, or vice versa. Driving a car is similar to driving a bus, because they are both motor vehicles. And yet just because you have driven a car is no sign you are qualified to drive a bus.

In the same way, just because a believer may interpret tongues in his own personal prayer life does not mean he is called by God to be an interpreter in a public or group meeting.

So we see that there is a *public* side to interpretation of tongues under certain conditions (the qualifying and equipping by God), and a *private* use of it. I have experienced both and I know the difference between the two.

As I said, I interpreted my own prayers in private a long time before I ever interpreted publicly. To go back to my illustration, when I began to interpret my own private prayers, it was like driving a car. When I began to interpret publicly it was like driving a bus. It was partly the same, yet it was a different thing entirely. One who interprets tongues publicly stands on a different plane and in a different office than one who only interprets in his private devotions.

When I first began to interpret my prayers (and, of course, I still do interpret my prayers), all I could interpret was my own private prayers in tongues. I could not interpret tongues in the public assembly. I never interpreted a message in public; I didn't do anything along that line.

But later I received the ability to use this gift of interpretation of tongues in a public assembly. The gift of interpretation of tongues is the same gift whether used privately or publicly, but the difference is one of *operation*. One operation of the gift of interpretation of tongues is for *private* use, and one is for *public* use.

I want you to notice something here that I am convinced is right. Paul did not say in First Corinthians 14:13, "Let him that speaks in an unknown tongue pray that he may have the *gift* of interpretation." No, he said, "Let him pray that he may *interpret.*" Interpret what? Interpret his praying in tongues.

Therefore, one can pray with his spirit and with his understanding also (1 Cor. 14:15). However, interpreting his own prayers would not make a believer a public interpreter; that would simply make him one who prays with his spirit and with his understanding, interpreting his prayers that he has prayed in tongues. Of course, one interprets his prayers as the Spirit of God wills, not as he wills (1 Cor. 12:11).

When I received the gift of interpretation and later became a public interpreter, I still couldn't interpret what other people prayed. That was between them and God. But I could interpret all public utterances and still can, although I don't always do it, for it is not always necessary that I be the one to interpret. God may have someone else He desires to use as well. Again, I interpret as the Spirit wills.

1 CORINTHIANS 14:26-28
26 How is it then, brethren? when ye come together, every one of you hath a psalm, hath a doctrine, hath a tongue, hath a revelation, hath an interpretation. Let all things be done unto edifying.
27 If any man speak in an unknown tongue, let it be by two, or at the most by three, and that by course; and let one interpret.
28 But IF THERE BE NO INTERPRETER, let him keep silence in the church; and let him speak to himself, and to God.

As I said earlier, these verses are talking about tongues and interpretation in the *church* — in a public assembly or group. And in these verses, the word "interpreter" is talking about someone used in the gift of interpretation of tongues in a public setting.

I learned from experience that if someone speaks in tongues in the public assembly, if I am sensitive and responsive to the Holy Spirit, I can always interpret the message. Paul infers in First Corinthians 14:26-28 that an interpreter could do this. He said, "... *if there be no INTERPRETER* ..." (1 Cor. 14:28), inferring that some people are interpreters.

An interpreter might not be present in every meeting. The believer wouldn't necessarily know that, of course, but the Holy Spirit would. And according to what Paul says in First Corinthians 14, when there is no interpreter present, those who *could* give out a message in tongues should be sensitive enough to the Holy Spirit to flow with Him accurately and keep silent. If they followed the Holy Spirit's leading perfectly, they wouldn't speak out when there was no interpreter present, for the Holy Spirit would know that.

You see, if it were just up to the Holy Spirit, the operation of this gift would be perfect. If it were just up to the Holy Spirit, we wouldn't need instruction in the operation of this gift. But it isn't just up to the Holy Spirit; the Holy Spirit operates through imperfect vessels — human beings. Therefore, instructions must be given. Believers have to learn how to yield to the Holy Ghost in a more perfect way; that's why God gives instructions to believers in His Word regarding the use of these vocal gifts.

The fact that Paul said in First Corinthians 14:28, "... *if there be no interpreter.* ...," also implies that an interpreter could always interpret any message given in tongues.

If all of this is new to you, don't set your mind against it. Just keep open to the Spirit of God and the Word of God.

Supernatural Praying and Praising

Just as believers can pray out the interpretation of their *praying* in tongues as the Spirit wills, they should be able to *sing* praises to God in the same way: with their spirits and with their understanding. This should be going on in the daily prayer life of every believer. Paul said, "... *I will pray with the spirit, and I will pray with the understanding also: I will SING with the spirit, and I will SING with the understanding also*" (1 Cor. 14:15).

I was never much of a singer. I took music lessons in high school, and even after I was preaching, I took voice lessons, but my voice teacher gave up on me.

My teachers would tell me that I had a good ear for music, however. I can tell if someone else is hitting the notes right. I practiced and practiced and practiced, but I never hit the notes correctly myself. But when I got filled with the Spirit, I sang three songs in tongues! I *can* sing in tongues. Every believer ought to. It is all prayer and praise to God.

In the Book of Ephesians, Paul talks about believers praising God in song by the inspiration of the Holy Spirit as they are continually being filled with the Holy Spirit.

EPHESIANS 5:18,19
18 And be not drunk with wine, wherein is excess; but BE [being] FILLED WITH THE SPIRIT;
19 SPEAKING TO YOURSELVES in PSALMS and HYMNS and SPIRITUAL SONGS, SINGING and MAKING MELODY IN YOUR HEART to the Lord.

Paul is writing this to the church at Ephesus where the people were already born again and filled with the Spirit. We know that they were already believers because it is recorded in Acts 19:1-6 that these Ephesians had already been saved and filled with the Holy Spirit. We also know that they were born again because Paul addresses his epistle, "... *to the SAINTS which are at Ephesus* ..." (Eph. 1:1).

Yet here in Ephesians 5:18 and 19, Paul is writing a letter to these believers telling them to be filled with the Spirit. In other words, he was telling them, "Be drunk on the Spirit." In the literal Greek it says, "Be *being* filled" with the Spirit.

Paul was not only writing this to the Church at Ephesus, but he was writing it to all Spirit-filled believers. Paul was telling believers to maintain a constant experience of *staying* filled with the Spirit.

We are to keep on drinking of the Holy Spirit after our initial experience of being filled with the Spirit. In the Bible, water is a type of the Holy Spirit. We can see this principle of staying filled with the Holy Spirit in John 7.

JOHN 7:37-39
37 In the last day, that great day of the feast, Jesus stood and cried, saying, If any man THIRST, let him come unto me, and DRINK.
38 He that believeth on me, as the scripture hath said, out of his belly shall flow RIVERS OF LIVING WATER.
39 (But this spake he OF THE SPIRIT, which they that believe on him should receive: for the Holy Ghost was not yet given; because that Jesus was not yet glorified.)

Jesus is saying that believers are to drink all we want of the Holy Spirit. Jesus is encouraging us to drink of and to stay filled with the Holy Spirit.

Then in Ephesians 5 we are given the characteristic of the Spirit-filled life. Verse 19 says *"Speaking to yourselves in psalms and hymns and spiritual songs, singing and making melody in your heart to the Lord."* This is a part of praying and praising supernaturally by the help of the Holy Spirit in the believer's own private prayer life.

These psalms, hymns, and spiritual songs are not songs you get out of a songbook. They are given to the believer by the inspiration of the Holy Spirit at the spur of the moment. They are a manifestation of the gifts of tongues and interpretation or the gift of prophecy in operation.

A psalm is a spiritual poem or an ode that can be recited, chanted, or sung. It may rhyme or it may not rhyme, but there is an element of poetry about it. Spiritual songs and hymns are, of course, sung. People who are given to singing will be more used in this way.

The Gift of Prophecy in Prayer

We've discussed how tongues and interpretation can and should be used in prayer and in "speaking to ourselves in psalms and hymns and spiritual songs" (Eph. 5:19). Let's see how the gift of prophecy can also be used in our private prayer life as the Spirit wills.

In First Corinthians 14:1, Paul said to the Church at Corinth (and that applies to believers everywhere), *"Follow after charity* [love], *and desire spiritual gifts, but rather that ye may prophesy."* The Spirit of God through Paul told us to desire the gift of prophecy above all other spiritual gifts (1 Cor. 14:5).

A very learned man who was teaching against the Pentecostal experience once said, "To prophesy only means to preach." Well, prophecy may include some preaching, because prophecy in its most general sense is inspired utterance. However, if all prophecy is simply preaching, Paul told the whole Church at Corinth that every one of them should desire to be preachers!

That learned man wasn't thinking correctly when he said that to prophesy only means to preach. If prophesying only meant to preach, then in First Corinthians 14:39, Paul was telling believers to covet to preach!

1 CORINTHIANS 14:39
39 Wherefore, brethren, COVET TO PROPHESY....

Paul was not telling believers to covet to preach. He said, *". . . covet to PROPHESY. . . ."* The Bible says, *". . . he that PROPHESIETH speaketh unto men to edification, and exhortation, and comfort"* (1 Cor. 14:3).

But that is not all of it. In the Old Testament, in the Book of Psalms, there are psalms and prayers which David prayed under the inspiration of the Holy Spirit. The Psalms were the Israelites' prayer and songbook.

There is a prophetic element to these psalms because they minister edification, exhortation, and comfort (1 Cor. 14:3). David and other writers were inspired by the Holy Spirit to write these psalms.

The Bible says all Scripture is given by inspiration of God (2 Tim. 3:16). But every believer should be filled with the Holy Spirit and have a measure of this prophetic element operating in his life so he can speak to himself in psalms and hymns and spiritual songs (Eph. 5:19). In that way, the believer can be edified, exhorted, and comforted even in the midst of tests or trials through the gift of prophecy expressed in his own private prayer life. This is the *private* use of the gift of prophecy in the believer's prayer life.

Then there is the *public* use of the gift of prophecy. Paul told the whole Church at Corinth that they should desire to prophesy. Why? One reason is that through the public use of the simple gift of prophecy, believers can speak to men and women supernaturally unto edification, exhortation, and comfort as the Spirit wills (1 Cor. 14:3).

In the ministry of a prophet or prophetess, however, at times there might be revelation given through an utterance; therefore, it is not just the simple gift of prophecy in operation.

In other words, a prophet may prophesy and a revelation may come forth that exceeds the simple gift of prophecy. That's because a prophet is equipped with certain spiritual gifts to stand in a fivefold ministry office or calling (Eph. 4:11,12). Certain revelation gifts of the Holy Spirit, as well as certain vocal gifts, qualify the prophet to speak forth revelation under the unction and direction of the Holy Spirit.

Every believer will not speak forth revelation in prophecy. But every believer should desire to prophesy — to speak forth edification, exhortation, and comfort. One reason a believer should desire to prophesy (1 Cor. 14:1) is that any believer can have prophecy operating in his *private* prayer life.

After I had been praying and interpreting my prayers for a time, I saw this in the Word. I began to covet to prophesy in my own prayer life. Then many times, after privately praying in tongues and interpreting, I began to go into prophecy. And since then I have prayed with prophecy sometimes for an hour or more. Praying with prophecy is praying out the perfect will of God in a *known* tongue (1 Cor. 14:1-5 *Amp.*). Praying in tongues is praying out the will of God in an *unknown* tongue.

You see, tongues is supernatural utterance in an unknown tongue. Prophecy is a supernatural utterance in a *known* tongue, but it is still supernatural. If prayer came from your own understanding, it would not be supernatural; it would be natural. But it isn't coming from your understanding; it is coming from your spirit.

Whether you prophesy in prayer or whether you pray in tongues and interpret your prayers, it is the Holy Spirit enabling you to pray supernaturally. You are praying out the interpretation of your prayers in a known tongue.

When I interpret my tongues or prophesy in prayer, I am praying out of my spirit. My mind has nothing to do with it. My mind is not praying; it is quiet. Sometimes the interpretation of my tongues or what I prophesy in prayer surprises me. Very often God will comfort or encourage me in the midst of a test or a trial as I prophesy in my private prayers.

There are so many spiritual blessings that belong to believers that they don't know about, and there are so many spiritual benefits they could be enjoying but are not. A fellow could legally have something that was available to him, but if he didn't know about it, it would not do him any good. For example, if there were $10,000 in the bank in a person's name, and he didn't know about it, he could starve to death and yet have $10,000 in the bank!

I believe many believers have done this spiritually. The Bible proclaims the rich inheritance we have as children of God, yet it seems that only a few believers are taking advantage of what really belongs to them.

Part of our rich inheritance is this ability to pray supernaturally by the inspiration of the Holy Spirit in tongues and interpretation and in prophecy in our own private prayer lives. This blessing belongs to us as believers. However, it is up to us to obey the Bible's instructions in order to experience this kind of supernatural praying.

We need to *pray that we may interpret* our prayers in tongues (1 Cor. 14:13), and we need to *desire to prophesy* (1 Cor. 14:1). Then we will begin to understand what it is to enter into this supernatural realm of prayer, where we pray with our spirit and our understanding under the inspiration and direction of the Holy Spirit.

Questions for Study

1. What are the seven most important things in prayer?

   _____

   _____

2. What does the Holy Spirit do for us when we don't know what to pray for as we ought?

   _____

   _____

3. Why should we pray to interpret what we pray in other tongues?

   _____

   _____

4. When is it not necessary to interpret tongues?

   _____

   _____

5. Explain the difference between the public side of interpreting tongues and the private side.

   _____

   _____

6. If there is no interpreter present in a meeting, what should those who _could_ give out a message in tongues do?

   _____

   _____

7. In Ephesians 5:18, why did Paul instruct the already Spirit-filled believers in Ephesus to _". . . be filled with the Spirit"_?

   _____

   _____

8. Why should every believer desire to prophesy?

   _____

   _____

9. How does praying with prophecy differ from praying in tongues?

   _____

   _____

10. When will we begin to understand what it is to enter into the supernatural realm of prayer?

    _____

    _____

Chapter 16

What Jesus Said About Prayer — Part 1

In the next few lessons we will be discussing various principles that Jesus taught about prayer. In this chapter we'll look at the following prayer principles found in Matthew chapters 6 and 7:

1. Don't pray to be seen of men.
2. Ask in faith because God responds to faith, not to 'much speaking.'
3. Pray to the Father in Jesus' Name.
4. Put the Kingdom of God first.
5. Ask and you shall receive.

First, let's look in Matthew chapter 6 at several prayer principles that Jesus taught.

MATTHEW 6:5-8
5 And when thou prayest, thou shalt not be as the hypocrites are: for they love to pray standing in the synagogues and in the corners of the streets, that they may be seen of men. Verily I say unto you, They have their reward.
6 But thou, when thou prayest, enter into thy closet, and when thou hast shut thy door, pray to thy Father which is in secret; and thy Father which seeth in secret shall reward thee openly.
7 But when ye pray, use not vain repetitions, as the heathen do: for they think that they shall be heard for their much speaking.
8 Be not ye therefore like unto them: for your Father knoweth what things ye have need of, before ye ask him.

Don't Pray To Be Seen of Men

First, Jesus said in Matthew 6:5, *". . . when thou prayest, thou shalt not be as the hypocrites are. . . ."* I am sure none of us want to be like hypocrites, and we certainly don't want to be hypocritical in our praying.

Jesus went on to explain how the hypocrites in His day prayed. He said they loved to pray standing in the synagogues and in the corners of the streets, so that they could be seen of men (v. 5). But Jesus told us how we should pray. He said, *"But thou, when thou prayest, enter into thy closet, and when thou hast shut thy door, pray to thy Father which is in secret; and thy Father which seeth in secret shall reward thee openly"* (Matt. 6:6).

This doesn't mean that all of our praying should be done privately. For instance, we can see the Early Church at prayer in the Acts of the Apostles. We can see them as a group praying together again and again throughout the Book of Acts.

What Jesus was saying is simply this: There is a possibility in public praying, when people are gathered together to pray in a group, that we might be like the hypocrites, only praying publicly to be seen of men. We might be praying so that folks will think we are really spiritual and that we are real prayer warriors. We can fool folks sometimes, but we can't fool God. God, who sees in secret, is the One who hears and answers our prayers.

The thought Jesus is trying to get over to us in these verses is not to pray in order to be seen of men and to receive the accolades of men. If that is your only reason for praying, then that is all the reward you will ever get — the accolades of men.

Certainly, Jesus did not say *not* to pray publicly, nor did He say we are not to pray with others in a group. If Jesus had said that, then He violated His own teaching, for Jesus Himself prayed with His own apostles. No, the thought is simply one of *motive* — not to pray to be seen of men.

Let me say this before I go further, however. You cannot get by in your Christian walk just on public prayer or praying with others in a group. You must have a private prayer life of your own if you are going to develop and grow spiritually and enjoy fellowship with God.

Build a private prayer life of your own. Also, we should pray with our families, particularly if we have children and have family devotions. And we should offer thanks for the food which we eat.

But you as an individual can't just get by on praying with your families or praying with others. You are going to need to have regular prayer times, not just those times when one is driven to prayer out of despair because of trying circumstances.

Your own private prayer life is really the place where you are going to grow spiritually. That is where you are going to learn to pray and have sweet fellowship and communion with God. But too many times this is where people fail. So let me encourage you to maintain the practice of getting alone with God.

God Responds To Faith, Not to 'Much Speaking'

Jesus said something else about prayer in Matthew chapter 6. He said, *". . . when ye pray, use not vain repetitions, as the heathen do . . ."* (Matt. 6:7). Here in Matthew 6:5 and 7 we have two admonitions from the Lord. Jesus said, "Don't be like the hypocrites in your praying, and don't be like the heathen in your praying." Jesus said the heathen thought they would be heard because of their repetitions, or because of their "much speaking." That's the way the heathen or the unsaved in the world think.

You can readily see that some of this worldly thinking has even sifted into the Christian way of thinking. Many Christians have the idea that they will be heard by God because of their much speaking. Yet that is exactly what Jesus condemned here, when He said, ". . . *they* [the heathen] *think that they shall be heard for their much speaking*" (Matt. 6:7).

"Vain repetition" means just repeating the same prayer — saying the same words or phrases over and over again by rote. Some think they will be heard by God by doing that, but they won't. Faith is what pleases God, not vain repetition.

We will see in a moment that Jesus said it is *the prayer of faith* that God hears. God is not going to respond to your prayers simply because you repeated the same prayer over and over again — because of your "much speaking." God responds to faith! Some have the idea, "If I could just pray long enough and loud enough, eventually I could talk God into the notion of hearing me." That may not be the way they put it, but that seems to be the way they act.

I have actually heard people tell others who were praying around the altar or in prayer meetings: "Louder — pray louder, so God will hear you"!

Certainly, vocal prayer is scriptural, as I've discussed in an earlier chapter. But God is not going to hear you because you holler loudly, nor will He hear you just because you pray quietly. No, God hears you because you *believe Him* when you pray, and because you come to Him according to His Word.

It is also certainly true that sometimes in prayer, by giving expression to the inward longings and yearnings of your heart in the Spirit, you will unconsciously get a little loud about it. But that's not the same as praying loudly just so that God will hear you or to try to talk Him into the notion of answering you! For example, I am a rather quiet person, and yet there are times when I get loud in prayer. But God doesn't hear me any more readily just because I get loud.

MATTHEW 6:8
8 Be not ye therefore like unto them [the heathen]: for your Father knoweth what things ye have need of, before ye ask him.

The Father knows your needs before you ask, but yet He wants you to ask for your needs to be met because He said in His Word we are to ask. We discuss this in another chapter.

Prayer Principles In The Lord's Prayer

Now let's look at Matthew 6:9-13 which we call The Lord's Prayer. What Jesus is saying to us in this passage of Scripture is not necessarily a prayer for us to pray word for word. But in it Jesus does give us some principles in connection with prayer that *will* work for the Church today.

MATTHEW 6:9-13
9 After this manner therefore pray ye: Our Father which art in heaven, Hallowed be thy name.
10 Thy kingdom come. Thy will be done in earth, as it is in heaven.
11 Give us this day our daily bread.
12 And forgive us our debts, as we forgive our debtors.
13 And lead us not into temptation, but deliver us from evil: For thine is the kingdom, and the power, and the glory, for ever. Amen.

Some things that people have said about The Lord's Prayer are a little misleading. You see, this prayer is not The Lord's Prayer in the sense that Jesus taught *the Church* to pray this way. It is called The Lord's Prayer in the sense that Jesus gave this prayer to *His disciples* when they asked Him to teach them to pray.

Certainly, dispensationally speaking, this prayer is not how the New Testament Church of the Lord Jesus Christ should pray, for Jesus told His disciples to pray this way *before* His death, burial, and resurrection. In other words, Jesus gave this prayer to His disciples to use at a time when they were still technically under the Old Covenant.

Actually, The Lord's Prayer was given to the disciples as a way to pray during the transition between the fulfillment of the Old Covenant and the establishment of the New Covenant. In that sense, Jesus was giving His followers a way to pray during that interim period between covenants. Jesus' followers had a promissory note on their salvation because they believed on Jesus.

Under the Old Covenant, no one asked anything in the Name of Jesus. But as we discussed in earlier chapters, under the New Covenant when the Church prays, they are to pray to the Father in the Name of Jesus (John 16:23,24). There are some things, however, that we can learn from The Lord's Prayer.

Pray to the Father

For example, Jesus began by saying, *"After this manner therefore pray ye: Our FATHER . . ."* (Matt. 6:9). First of all, we know that everyone is not a child of God. Under the New Covenant, only those who have been born again are children of God.

Jesus' followers could pray this way, saying, "Our Father. . . ," because, as I said, they had a promissory note on their salvation. The unsaved today could pray this prayer with their lips, but only as one could recite a poem or a verse, or sing a song. The word "Father" is not for the unsaved; it is for those born-again children who are in the Kingdom of light.

You see, if you are really going to pray effectually and fellowship with God from your heart, then you must actually be a child of God. If you are not a child of God, you cannot say from your heart or spirit, "Our Father," as Matthew 6:9 instructs.

We hear much teaching these days about the "Fatherhood of God" and the "Brotherhood of Man." Some would try to make us believe that as human beings we are *all* the children of God and that God is the Father of all of us. But, really, He isn't. God is the *Creator* of all mankind.

Therefore, we as human beings are all *fellow creatures*, but God isn't the Father of all human beings. We are not all "brothers" in that sense. As I said, God is only the Father of those who have been born again — of those who are in His family — the Kingdom of Light (Eph. 3:15).

Jesus said to some very outstanding religious people, *"Ye are of your father the devil . . ."* (John 8:44). Jesus was talking to the Pharisees, who if you were to examine their lives as far as good works were concerned, were some very "religious" people. Yet Jesus said, "You are of your father the devil," because they did not accept Jesus as God's Son and therefore did not submit to God's Word from their hearts.

So to really be able to address God as Father, you must be born again. He may be addressed as God to the world, but He is more than God to us. He is also our Father.

I like something that Paul said in Ephesians chapter 3. He was praying a prayer for the Church at Ephesus. In verses 14 and 15 Paul writes, *"For this cause I bow my knees unto the FATHER of our Lord Jesus Christ, of whom the whole FAMILY in heaven and earth is named."*

I don't know about you, but many times — in fact, most of the time — when I kneel in prayer I start off praying just that way. I say, "I bow my knees unto the Father of our Lord Jesus Christ, of whom the whole family in heaven and earth is named."

To me, this brings prayer down to a personal, more intimate level. Many people have the idea that when they pray they are talking to God like He is far away somewhere. But if they do that, they have the wrong picture of praying to the Father. The truth about it is, God may only be *God* to those people, but, thank God, He is *Father* to me!

That is one reason the Jews couldn't understand Jesus. For instance, if Jesus had come along like some of the prophets of the Old Testament, proclaiming judgment against them and presenting to them a seemingly faraway God whom they couldn't approach in any way, they might have understood Him because that's what they were used to. That was the kind of God they had understood in the Old Testament.

But Jesus didn't do that. Jesus came along and introduced God as a *Father*. Jesus said to those who believed on Him, *". . . what man is there of you, whom if his son ask bread, will he give him a stone? . . . how much more shall your FATHER which is in heaven give good things to them that ask him?"* (Matt. 7:9,11). But for the most part, the Jews couldn't understand that kind of God. That wasn't the kind of God they had known under the Old Covenant.

For instance, when God came down and talked to Moses on the mountain, there was fire, thunder, and lightning, and God's Voice was heard. And if anyone touched that mountain, he died instantly. The people feared and trembled at the sight of the supernatural power of God (Exod. 19:12-16).

And when the Presence of God moved into the Holy of Holies, if anyone intruded into that place who wasn't supposed to be there, he fell dead instantly (Num. 18:7). So you see, the Jews as a whole understood a God who was unapproachable. They knew about a God who was High and Holy and who dealt in awful judgment, and they feared Him.

But Jesus came along and began to talk about God as His Father and about approaching God as a Father. They couldn't understand that kind of talk. The same attitude is carried over to our day, especially among religious people. To many, Christianity is just another religion centered around a faraway God. Many don't really *know* Him. They have never come to God the Father by Jesus Christ, to know Him as their Father. That's why many are trying to approach Him in the wrong manner.

Certainly, we should fear God; that is, we should reverence Him and worship Him. But, thank God, He is also our Father. Jesus is saying in Matthew 6:9-13 that the right approach to God is to come to Him because He is your Father and to come to Him in praise and worship. The Bible says, *". . . Our Father which art in heaven, Hallowed be thy name"* (Matt. 6:9). Glory to God! Come first with praise and worship into His presence because He is your Father.

Put the Kingdom of God First

Notice the next verse of this prayer: *"Thy kingdom come. Thy will be done in earth, as it is in heaven"* (Matt. 6:10). There is a principle involved here which says we are to put the Kingdom of God first in our lives, even before ourselves. Jesus says this again later in the same chapter. *"But seek ye first the kingdom of God, and his righteousness; and all these things shall be added unto you"* (Matt. 6:33).

Notice what Jesus said prior to this.

MATTHEW 6:25,27
25 Therefore I say unto you, Take no thought for your life, what ye shall eat, or what ye shall drink; nor yet for your body, what ye shall put on. . . .
27 Which of you by taking thought can add one cubit unto his stature?

Jesus was talking about material things, and He was telling us not to worry. We discussed the subject of worry in a previous chapter. To worry will actually destroy the effectiveness of your praying. God's Word tells us what to do about our worries and our problems. We are to cast them on the Lord and let Him solve them for us (1 Peter 5:7).

1 PETER 5:7
7 Casting all your care upon him; for he careth for you.

MATTHEW 6:31,32
31 Therefore take no thought, saying, What shall we eat? or, What shall we drink? or, Wherewithal shall we be clothed?
32 (For after all these things do the Gentiles seek:) for your heavenly Father knoweth that ye have need of all these things.

Your Heavenly Father knows, just as a natural father would know, when His children have need of something to wear and when they need the other material things of life too. God knows about these needs, just as you who are fathers know about such things. Jesus said, *"But seek ye first the kingdom of God, and his righteousness; and all these things shall be added unto* [not taken away from] *you"* (Matt. 6:33).

Jesus didn't say, "It is God's will that you not have much of anything to eat. Jesus didn't say you will have to go through life with the soles of your shoes worn out, the seat of your britches worn out, the top of your hat worn out, and that you will have to drive an old beat-up car."

No, that is not what Jesus said. He said, *". . . seek ye first the kingdom of God, and his righteousness; and all these things shall be ADDED unto you"* (Matt. 6:33). Material things won't be taken away from you if you put God first, they will be *added* unto you!

A denominational preacher who had been filled with the Holy Ghost and had come over into Full Gospel circles once said to me, "Brother Hagin, don't misunderstand me. I have the baptism of the Holy Ghost and speak in other tongues every day. I believe in the supernatural. I believe in divine healing. But on the other hand, I just can't find very much in the Bible about divine healing. Yet you preach so much on the subject of healing."

I said, "Well, I find divine healing in nearly every chapter of the Bible! It is just according to how you look at it."

For example, we can find divine healing right here in Matthew chapter 6: *". . . your heavenly Father knoweth that ye have need of all these things"* (Matt. 6:32). The Father knows if we need healing. And the words of The Lord's Prayer in Matthew 6:10 tell us it is His will to heal us: *"Thy kingdom come. Thy will be done in earth, as it is in heaven"* (v. 10).

Is it God's will that any be sick in heaven? No, of course not. We know better than that! If we are to pray for God's will to be done on the earth as it is in heaven, then His will in heaven involves His will for His children on the earth too. You see, it is a *family* matter.

There may be some of God's children who may be ill, but sickness is still not the will of God. The Scripture says, "God knows we have need of all of these things," including healing!

Also, if we would follow this principle of prayer that Jesus has outlined in Matthew 6:5-15, we wouldn't even have to be praying for some things we are praying about and asking for. For example, too many times our praying is so selfish. It is like the story that is told about the old farmer who prayed, "God bless me and my wife, my son John and his wife — us four and no more."

We may not pray like that word for word, but when you analyze it, that is about the extent of our praying much of the time. We spend most of our prayer time praying selfishly. We spend most of our prayer time praying about our own needs — material, financial, and physical.

There is nothing wrong with asking God to meet our needs, for in His Word God promises He will meet our needs (Phil. 4:19). And God does say we are to ask (John 16:23,24). And yet Jesus tells us in Matthew 6:33 that if we seek the Kingdom of God first, all of these things will be added unto us. Therefore, if our priorities are right in prayer, we shouldn't have to do so much praying about our own needs.

It has been years and years since I have prayed about money by asking God for it. I learned this secret of putting the Kingdom of God first many years ago. I never pray about material things, but they are always added unto me. I am not particularly concerned about getting a blessing. I don't pray, "God bless me." I pray, "Lord, make me a blessing. Help me to help someone else. Help me to bless others with that which you have given me."

Unforgiveness Hinders Your Prayers

Jesus gives us another important principle as He finished The Lord's Prayer.

MATTHEW 6:14,15
14 For if ye forgive men their trespasses, your heavenly Father will also forgive you:
15 But if ye forgive not men their trespasses, neither will your Father forgive your trespasses.

What Jesus is talking about in Matthew 6:14 and 15 is the principle we discussed in Chapter 8. Prayer will not work in an unforgiving heart. You just simply cannot hold things against people in your heart and maintain a prayer life that is successful and gets results. This is of utmost importance.

It is so natural, so human, to hold things against people; it is part of our carnal nature. I have had people who were saved and filled with the Holy Spirit, but who were not walking in the best fellowship with the Lord, tell me just how badly they had been treated by someone. They would tell me in great detail what So-and-so did to them.

Then they would say, "Oh, yes, I have forgiven him, all right. But I never will forget how that old devil treated me" (talking about their brother or sister in the Lord). So, you see, they really hadn't forgiven that person. Unforgiveness was still in their hearts because it showed up in what they said.

In many cases people need help because they're frustrated and mentally confused because they are harboring offenses on the inside of them against people. They just need to forgive. Their frustration and confusion can many times be attributed to their unforgiveness.

I have read that medical doctors have found that resentment causes some people to be more prone to certain types of diseases. The doctors said that when they could get these people to get rid of resentment, in many cases their ailments cleared up, when before they hadn't responded to any medical treatment.

We are learning more and more how unforgiveness is connected with sickness and disease and ultimately with unanswered prayer. These things are all related. We don't want *anything* to hinder our prayer lives.

Ask and You Shall Receive

Jesus said something else about prayer in Matthew chapter 7.

MATTHEW 7:7-11
7 Ask, and it shall be given you; seek, and ye shall find; knock, and it shall be opened unto you:
8 For every one that asketh receiveth; and he that seeketh findeth; and to him that knocketh it shall be opened.
9 Or what man is there of you, whom if his son ask bread, will he give him a stone?
10 Or if he ask a fish, will he give him a serpent?
11 If ye then, being evil, know how to give good gifts unto your children, how much more shall your Father which is in heaven give good things to them that ask him?

I call your attention to the fact that this discourse is a continuation of what Jesus had already said in Matthew chapter 6, when He said, "*. . . pray ye: Our Father which art in heaven . . .*" (v. 9). Here in Matthew 7:7-11, Jesus is painting the picture of a father and a son. Jesus asked the question, "*. . . what man is there of you, whom if his son ask bread, will he give him a stone?*" (Matt. 7:9).

In other words, Jesus was saying, "What father is there of you, whom if his son ask bread, will instead give him a stone?" Jesus continued, "*If ye then, being evil,* [or natural] *know how to give good gifts unto your children, how much more shall your Father which is in heaven give good things to them that ask him?*" (v. 11). Praise the Lord!

I believe we all know that these verses in Matthew 7 are in the Bible whether we use them or not. It says, "*Ask, and it shall be given you; seek, and ye shall find; knock, and it shall be opened unto you*" (Matt. 7:7). But instead of just accepting what Jesus said, so many times we get on the negative side of doubt and unbelief, and fail to get what we are asking for and fail to receive what we are seeking. Therefore, the door on which we are knocking is not opened. It is because we are on the negative side and are not coming to God in prayer based on His Word.

Notice verse 8: *"For EVERY ONE that ASKETH RECEIVETH; and he that SEEKETH FINDETH; and to him that KNOCKETH IT SHALL BE OPENED."* Too many times people have gotten on the negative side, and they seem to think that what Jesus is saying is, "You just keep on asking, seeking, and knocking. You just keep on and maybe you'll get through to God." No, that is not what Jesus is saying. He is saying that if you ask, you receive. If you seek, you find. And if you knock, the door shall be opened unto you.

I read about some of our missionaries who went out at the turn of the century to the Holy Land to preach the gospel. They stayed there until about 1931 or 1932. When they returned in 1932, after spending the first thirty-two years of the twentieth century there in the Holy Land, they wrote a book which is one of the best ones I have ever read on the Holy Land and customs of the Bible.

You understand that these missionaries went out at the turn of the century before the changes occurred that are taking place today in that land. For instance, Jews have since gone back to their homeland from every country of the world and have taken some of the foreign customs back with them. But Matthew 7:7-11 is one passage of Scripture these missionaries commented on in their book and I thought it was good.

First, these missionaries made this observation: You cannot naturally understand the Bible with the Western mind. We have read and tried to interpret the Scriptures intellectually in the light of the Western mind. But you can't do that.

One of these missionaries said, "My wife and I were both educated and trained as missionaries and as ministers of the gospel. I had the idea before I went to the Holy Land that when Jesus said, 'Ask, and it shall be given you; seek, and ye shall find; knock, and it shall be opened unto you,' He meant that if you asked and didn't get it, to just keep on asking and just keep at it."

The man continued, "But then when I went to Israel, I found out something different. The people understood in their minds (and after all, the events of the Bible took place in the Eastern world) that the minute you asked, you received your answer. In other words, once you ask, you should immediately thank God in faith because you had the answer." In other words, the minute you ask, you receive. The

minute you seek, you find. The minute you knock, the door is opened to you.

This missionary went on to say, "In some areas, the people of the East still have some of the same customs they had hundreds of years ago. For instance, if someone came to the door of the outer gate of someone's home and knocked, seeking entrance, the wealthier people would send their servants to the gate.

"The servant would call out and ask for the visitor to identify himself. If the visitor was a friend or someone who was known by the owner of the house, he could enter immediately. But if he was a stranger, the servant would go back to the master of the house and ask if he wanted to let him in."

The thought here is this: When you knock, if you are known, thank God, you receive an immediate entrance! The Bible says, *". . . to him that knocketh it shall be opened"* (Matt. 7:8). As God's children through the new birth, we are known by God! We are in His family, and He is our Father. And we have immediate access into His Presence whenever we desire!

Jesus summarized what He said about asking and receiving by saying, *"Or what man is there of you, whom if his son ask bread, will he give him a stone? Or if he ask a fish, will he give him a serpent? If ye then, being evil, know how to give good gifts unto your children, HOW MUCH MORE . . ."* (Matt. 7:9-11).

I don't know about you, but those three words, "how much more," just send a thrill through my spirit. How much more! Jesus said, *"If ye then, being evil* [natural, carnal, or human], *know how to give good gifts unto your children, HOW MUCH MORE shall your Father which is in heaven give good things to them that ask him?"* (Matt. 7:11).

To me, a person could easily preach divine healing from that passage of Scripture. How many of you parents want your children to go through life with their nose to the grindstone, never having anything, poverty-stricken and poor, downcast, and downtrodden? How many of you want your children to go through life sick and suffering? Not a single one of you! Well, Jesus said that if you feel that way, being evil, or natural, *how much more* do you think God feels that way as your Father because He is holy!

Are these blessings such as healing, that we talk about so many times, good or are they evil? Healing is good; it's not evil. The Bible says that sickness and poverty are a curse (*see* Deuteronomy 28 and Galatians 3:10,13,14). So if sickness and poverty are a curse, then they can't be good, can they? No. If you don't believe that, read Deuteronomy chapter 28 and you will find that poverty and sickness are a curse.

A curse is not a good thing, is it? I mean, if sickness came from God, and God put sickness on people, then that would make sickness the will of God. In that case, people should pray, "God, make my children sick, because that's Your will. I want them to be blessed. Sickness is such a blessing, so You make them sick. The sicker they are, the more blessed they will be. So, God, just make them as sick as You can."

That sounds ridiculous, doesn't it? And yet in the religious world as a whole, many times the impression is given to people that sickness is from God, and that God is some way or another working out His holy will in people's lives by making them sick! The impression is given that God is helping folks become better Christians by making them suffer with sickness and disease.

Isn't it a strange idea that people could actually be better Christians living under the curse? Yes, it is strange! It is certainly not God's will that His people be under a curse. It is His will that they be under a blessing. The Bible says that God wants to give us good gifts, not evil gifts such as sickness and disease: *"If ye then, being evil, know how to give GOOD GIFTS unto your children, HOW MUCH MORE shall your Father which is in heaven give good things to them that ask him?"* (Matt. 7:11).

This same illustration is recorded in Luke chapter 11.

LUKE 11:11-13
11 If a son shall ask bread of any of you that is a father, will he give him a stone? or if he ask a fish, will he for a fish give him a serpent?
12 Or if he shall ask an egg, will he offer him a scorpion?
13 If ye then, being evil, know how to give good gifts unto your children: how much more shall your heavenly Father give THE HOLY SPIRIT to them that ask him?

The words in Matthew 7:9-11 are similar to this passage in Luke, but Matthew didn't refer to the Holy Spirit. Matthew simply said, *". . . HOW MUCH MORE shall your Father which is in heaven give GOOD THINGS to them that ask him?"* (v. 11).

The Holy Spirit is one of the "good things" referred to in Matthew 7:11, even though He is not specifically mentioned in this passage of Scripture.

I am sure that the Spirit of God prompted Matthew to write this passage the way he did for a reason. The Holy Spirit, as He inspired Matthew, didn't want us to get our minds only on spiritual things. He wanted us to see the goodness of a loving Heavenly Father who gives the good things of life — including *natural* things — to His children. He wanted us to know that God loves us just as we as natural parents love our own children. And God the Father wants His children to have good things.

The Holy Spirit inspired Luke to write this illustration in a slightly different way, specifically mentioning the Holy Spirit as a good gift of the Father. I believe the Holy Spirit did that for a reason because Luke 11:11-13 settles once and for all that to receive the Holy Spirit with the evidence of speaking in tongues is to receive a *good* gift.

According to Luke 11:11-13, if we ask for bread, God the Father won't give us a stone instead. And if we ask our Father for a fish, He won't give us a serpent. And if we ask for an egg, He won't give us a scorpion.

Remember in Luke 10:19 Jesus refers to serpents and scorpions as *evil* spirits. But when we ask God for something good, He doesn't give us something bad in answer to our prayers. No, He gives us good things. And He will give the Holy Spirit, "a good thing," to those who ask Him. He is a loving, gracious Heavenly Father!

We are discussing principles Jesus taught about prayer. In this chapter we saw that we are to pray, but we are not to pray as the hypocrites or the heathen pray (Matt. 6:5,7). We also saw that our prayer to the Heavenly Father will not work with unforgiveness in the heart (Matt. 6:14,15; Mark 11:25,26). If we have the slightest bit of ill will or bitterness or resentment against someone else, our prayers will be hindered until we forgive others.

Then we discussed that we should not pray selfishly. Certainly, we are to pray for our own needs to be met. The Word instructs us *to ask* for the things we have need of, and we *shall receive* those things we ask for. But we shouldn't pray only for ourselves and our loved ones. We should pray for others too.

And in this chapter we have also seen that the Bible also declares that we must have our priorities right in order for "all things to be added unto us": *". . . seek ye first the kingdom of God . . . and all these things shall be added unto you"* (Matt. 6:33).

What Jesus said about prayer is vitally important for us to understand and obey if we are to have a successful prayer life. In the next chapters, we'll continue looking in the Gospels for other principles Jesus taught about prayer.

Questions for Study

1. According to Matthew 6:5, if you're only praying to be seen of men, what reward will you get?

   _____

   _____

2. Why must you have a private prayer life of your own?

   _____

   _____

3. Why do some Christians keep repeating the same prayer over and over again?

   _____

   _____

4. Why did Jesus give The Lord's Prayer to His disciples?

   _____

   _____

5. What prayer principles can be learned from The Lord's Prayer?

   _____

   _____

6. Name one reason why the Jews of Jesus' day couldn't understand Him.

   _____

   _____

7. In His Word God promises He will meet our needs and says we are to ask. Read Matthew 6:33 and name another way that God _meets_ our needs.

   _____

   _____

8. How are unforgiveness and resentment connected with sickness and disease?

   _____

   _____

9. As God's children, when do we receive access into His Presence and why?

   _____

   _____

10. Name one of the "good things" referred to in Matthew 7:9-11.

    _____

    _____

Chapter 17

What Jesus Said About Prayer — Part 2

Let's look at some other principles of prayer which Jesus taught during His ministry here on earth. In this chapter, we'll see that Jesus taught us to pray for our enemies and for laborers to be raised up for the harvest of souls.

We'll also see how the Book of Matthew records Jesus' teaching on the prayer of faith — believing we receive *when* we pray. And, finally, we will look in the Book of Luke to understand what it means to pray the prayer of importunity as Jesus taught it.

Pray for Your Enemies

In Matthew chapter 5, Jesus tells us for whom to pray. Sometimes folks are in doubt in this area, but here we find some information that will help us.

MATTHEW 5:44,45
44 But I say unto you, Love your enemies, bless them that curse you, do good to them that hate you, and PRAY FOR THEM WHICH DESPITEFULLY USE YOU, and PERSECUTE YOU;
45 That ye may be children of your Father which is in heaven: for he maketh his sun to rise on the evil and on the good, and sendeth rain on the just and on the unjust.

Do you want to know for whom to pray? Jesus said in Matthew 5:44 to *". . . pray for them which despitefully use you, and persecute you."* Jesus did not say to *criticize* and talk about those who despitefully use you and persecute you. He said to *pray* for them. How many of us are doing that?

Notice the next verse: *"That ye may be the children of your Father which is in heaven: for he maketh his sun to rise on the evil and on the good, and sendeth rain on the just and on the unjust"* (Matt. 5:45). Jesus is inferring here that if you are a child of your Father, a child of God, that you are going to do the things He said to do in the previous verse, in verse 44.

Pray for Laborers

Let's look at another statement Jesus made concerning who we are to pray for. We've seen that we are to pray for those who despitefully use us. But here is something else we are to pray for.

MATTHEW 9:36-38
36 But when he saw the multitudes, he was moved with compassion on them, because they fainted, and were scattered abroad, as sheep having no shepherd.
37 Then saith he unto his disciples, The harvest truly is plenteous, but the labourers are few;
38 PRAY YE therefore the Lord of the harvest, THAT HE WILL SEND FORTH LABOURERS INTO HIS HARVEST.

It is very significant that nowhere in the New Testament are we told to pray that the Lord would *save* the lost. That may sound strange, but it is absolutely the truth.

Certainly, Paul prayed and said, *". . . my heart's desire and prayer to God for Israel is, that they might be saved"* (Rom. 10:1). But the Bible gives us no instruction at all to pray that the Lord would save the lost.

Why? Well, to begin with, God has already saved the lost by sending Jesus to the earth to die for the sins of mankind. Now all the sinner must do is *accept* this salvation that is so freely provided for him through Jesus' work on the Cross, and he must confess the Lordship of Jesus (2 Cor. 5:19,21; Rom. 10:9).

But the lost can't be saved unless someone takes the gospel to them. We could pray forever that the lost would be saved, but they will never be saved unless they hear the gospel (Rom. 10:14). That is why Jesus said, *"Pray ye therefore the Lord of the harvest, that he will send forth labourers into his harvest"* (Matt. 9:38). Are we praying that prayer? Jesus told us to.

I have found this scripture in Matthew chapter 9 to be helpful in praying for loved ones. I didn't always know it, and I'm sorry I didn't. We are so bound by religion and so blinded by religious teachings sometimes that it hinders us in our Christian walk, which should be a walk of faith.

I am ashamed that I didn't know about this verse in prayer for the unsaved. I prayed so desperately about certain relatives — not in my immediate household, but other relatives. I had a right to claim those in my own household for God, for that is biblical (Acts 16:15,31-34).

I have scriptural grounds for claiming the souls of those in my own household. I did claim those in my own household, and every one of them was saved. (My wife was already saved, of course. But my children were also saved early in life and have always served the Lord. In the course of time, my niece came to live with us, and she was also saved.) The Bible says, ". . . *Believe on the Lord Jesus Christ, and thou shalt be saved, AND THY HOUSE*" (Acts 16:31).

So I had a right to claim those in my own household. I never prayed about them; I just claimed their souls for God.

But there are other kinfolks that are not of my immediate household — my aunts and uncles and so forth. I prayed for years, fifteen years or more for some of them, fasting for some of them as much as three days at a time. If any of them were saved by my praying that way, I don't know it.

But do you know what happened? I began to see results the minute I changed my praying. I began to bind the power of Satan over their lives and claim their souls for the Kingdom of God. Then I would pray, "Lord, send someone to talk to them. I can't talk to them. If You said 'Go,' I would go. But send a laborer to share the good news with them." This is scriptural because it's according to Matthew 9:38.

Sometimes God wants you to speak to your own kinfolks, and you can be a great blessing to them. But on the other hand, many folks have driven their relatives away from the gospel by nagging them all the time. Some folks who were trying to witness to their relatives didn't have wisdom enough to know how to approach them about the things of God.

I didn't detect any leading in my spirit at all to deal with my own kinfolks myself, so I prayed, "Lord, send someone to talk to them." The minute I started praying that way, God did it. It worked. It worked so quickly and so wonderfully, it was amazing! My eyes opened then to the truth of the Word, and how to pray for unsaved loved ones.

You see, there is someone (and God knows who that someone is) who *can* reach your unsaved loved ones. There is someone who can influence them. So why don't you pray that way? You can pray, "Lord, send someone to speak to this loved one." Or "Lord, send someone to speak to this friend." If He sends you, then you go. But the Bible says, *"Pray ye therefore the Lord of the harvest, that he will send forth labourers into his harvest"* (Matt. 9:38). It is scriptural to pray this way about the unsaved.

Someone said, "Well, if the Lord wants to send forth laborers into His harvest, why doesn't He just send them?" But God can't do any more on earth than we will permit Him to do. We permit God to move in our lives and in the earth by obeying His Word and by praying.

God Is Limited by Our Prayers

You might ask, "Why is God limited by our prayers? Why can't God move in our lives without us permitting Him to move?" If you will go back to the book of beginnings, the Book of Genesis, you will know why.

We know that God made the world and the fullness thereof (Ps. 50:12), and God gave the first man, Adam, dominion over all the works of God's hands (Gen. 1:28; Ps. 8:6). In the beginning Adam not only had dominion over the earth — over the animals and all creation — but he had dominion over the angels. Adam had dominion over *all* the substance of God's handiwork. Adam even had dominion over Lucifer, called Satan after his expulsion and fall from heaven (Luke 10:18). Adam was the second in line to the Godhead — the Father, the Son, and the Holy Spirit.

PSALM 8:4-8
4 What is man, that thou art mindful of him? and the son of man, that thou visitest him?
5 For THOU HAST MADE HIM A LITTLE LOWER THAN THE ANGELS, and hast crowned him with glory and honour.
6 Thou madest him to have dominion over the works of thy hands: thou hast put all things under his feet:
7 All sheep and oxen, yea, and the beasts of the field;
8 The fowl of the air, and the fish of the sea, and whatsoever passeth through the paths of the seas.

Verses 4 and 5 say, *"What is man, that thou art mindful of him? . . . For thou hast made him a little lower than the angels. . . ."* One of the Hebrew words translated "angels" in verse 5 is "Elohim," or *God.* God actually created Adam to be the god of this world and to have dominion over all the works of His hands.

Certainly, those verses don't mean that Adam was God or even that he was created in the same capacity as God. God is the *Creator;* Adam was only the *creature* (Rom. 1:25). Adam was a created being (Gen. 1:27).

But Adam was given dominion over all of God's handiwork (Gen. 1:26). But then Adam sold out to Satan in the Garden of Eden (Gen. 3:6). Adam committed high treason (Rom. 5:14). God gave Adam dominion over the earth, but through sin Adam forfeited his authority and transferred the lease he had on this earth to the devil; and now the devil is called the god of this world (2 Cor. 4:4).

How did Satan get to be the god of this world? Because Adam was the god of this world to begin with, but Adam sold his rights out to Satan by transgressing the positive command of God (Rom. 5:14 *Amp.*).

In Matthew chapter 4 and Luke chapter 4 it is recorded that Jesus was tempted by Satan in the wilderness. The Bible says that Satan took Jesus up on a high mountain and showed him all of the kingdoms of the world in a moment of time (Matt. 4:8; Luke 4:5).

LUKE 4:5-7
5 And the devil, taking him up into an high mountain, shewed unto him ALL THE KINGDOMS OF THE WORLD in a moment of time.
6 And the devil said unto him, All this POWER [authority] **will I give thee, and the glory of them: FOR THAT IS DELIVERED UNTO ME; and to whomsoever I will I give it.**
7 If thou therefore wilt worship me, all shall be thine.

The devil told Jesus that he would give Jesus the authority to reign over the kingdoms of this world. Who is reigning over the kingdoms of this world? Satan is! He legally had that authority because Adam turned it over to him when Adam sinned.

You hear people say, "God is ruling the world right now."

How ignorant can people be? If God is reigning over the kingdoms of this world, He sure has things in a mess, doesn't He! No, Satan is the god of this world, and Satan said to Jesus, "*. . . All this power* [authority] *will I give thee, and the glory of them* [the kingdoms of the world]*: FOR THAT IS DELIVERED UNTO ME; and to whomsoever I will I give it*" (Luke 4:6).

Notice that phrase, "*. . . for that is delivered unto me. . . .*" Who delivered the dominion or authority of the kingdoms of the world into Satan's authority? Adam did.

Did you notice that Jesus did not dispute what the devil said to Him? Jesus did not dispute it when Satan said the power or authority of all the kingdoms of the world belonged to Satan. That's because Jesus knew Adam had turned over his original dominion in this earth to Satan, and that now Satan was the god of this world.

Also, if Satan didn't have the authority and power over those kingdoms, this would *not* have been a temptation to Jesus. But the Bible says, "Jesus was *tempted* forty days by the devil" (Luke 4:2). Therefore, the Bible calls it a bonafide *temptation*. But notice that Jesus didn't dispute the fact at all that Satan had that authority to give.

I believe any intelligent person can see that there is a force, a power in this world behind the govern-

ments of this world, which is ruling and reigning. That's what the Bible teaches (Eph. 6:12). I believe we can see the effects of Satan ruling as the god of this world to some degree in the government of every nation on this earth.

People ask, "Why can't God do something about Satan's being the god of this world?"

But the point I want to make is that God can't just destroy Satan as the god of this world because Adam made a legal transaction with Satan when he disobeyed God. At that point, Adam forfeited his dominion or authority as the god of this world to Satan. Therefore, God can't just step in and take over on the earth and legally cure all the world's ills, because Satan is legally the god of the world through Adam's default.

Also, if God could just sovereignly cure all the world's ills, then God could have intervened back in the Garden of Eden, too, and stopped Adam from disobeying Him. But Adam had a choice, he had his own free will. And Adam chose to sell out his authority on the earth to Satan by his act of disobedience to God.

God could not violate Adam's free will. That's why God could not just move in and destroy Satan's authority on the earth once Adam committed that authority into Satan's hands. God couldn't do that because when Adam sold out his dominion on the earth to Satan, that was a legal transaction. And God does not do things illegally. God is a *just* God. God can't just illegally move in and destroy Satan's authority on the earth because that would have made it possible for Satan to point a finger at God and rightly say, "You are unjust. Adam legally gave me his dominion on earth."

Therefore, we can't hold God responsible for the suffering and the death of little children, for blinded eyes, and for the crippled and the maimed. If God were that kind of a God, then He would be meaner than the devil! But God is not responsible for all the suffering on the earth; Satan is. The one who is responsible for the suffering on the earth becomes even more clear by something Jesus said.

JOHN 10:10
10 The THIEF [Satan] **cometh not, but for to STEAL, and to KILL, and to destroy: I am come that they might have LIFE, and that they might have it MORE ABUNDANTLY.**

No, my friends, God is not responsible for the suffering that's in the world today; the devil is responsible because the devil is the god of this world. When Adam fell and Satan became the god of this world, everything that God had created as perfect began to become twisted and perverted. Satan began to rule and reign over man with poverty and sickness and disease.

But God in His mercy provided a means of redemption for man through Jesus Christ. Thank God, believers are redeemed from the hand of the enemy, and the enemy has no legal right to dominate us anymore (Col. 2:15)! We have been delivered out from under Satan's dominion.

ROMANS 6:14
14 For sin shall not have dominion over you: for ye are not under the law, but under grace.

It's been said that sickness and disease is the foul offspring of its mother, sin, and its father, Satan. We could also read Romans 6:14 this way: "*Satan* shall not have dominion over the believer." Therefore, we could also say, "*Sickness and disease* shall not have dominion over the believer."

COLOSSIANS 1:13
13 Who hath delivered us from the power of darkness, and hath translated us into the kingdom of his dear Son.

The whole world lies in darkness, but through Christ we are delivered from the power, or authority, of darkness.

God can only move here on the earth as we Christians ask Him to, or He would be moving into Satan's territory illegally. But God has a people down here on the earth who have authority because we have been redeemed. Only as we ask God to move through prayer can God legally move in the earth and in our lives.

To tell the real truth about it, Satan can't move in and work in a believer's life unless that person gives him the authority to do so. God works through man. Satan also works through man. When believers can learn to resist the devil and yield to God (James 4:7), and let God work through them, they will see the victory that has legally been purchased for them at Calvary.

To yield to God means to yield to His Word. And God's Word says that we as Christians are to pray. God's Word also tells us how to pray and for what or whom to pray. For example, in Matthew 9:38 Jesus says to pray that the Lord of the harvest would send forth laborers into the harvest fields of the world.

If God could just send forth laborers without our asking, and if He could do some other things in our lives without our asking, then why do we have to pray about those things?

If we don't need to pray and ask God to move in our lives, then we should just sit back and let God do something about the situations in our lives and about getting all the sinners in the world saved. But throughout the Bible we see God telling man to pray and to *ask* (John 16:23,24). We see God inviting man to call upon Him. Even in the Old Testament God said, "*Call unto me, and I will answer thee, and shew thee great and mighty things, which thou knowest not*" (Jer. 33:3).

Many scriptures, both in the Old and New Testaments, encourage us to pray. If God could move in our lives and in the earth like He wanted to without our praying, then what would be the purpose of our praying and asking?

When we pray, we open the door for God to move. That's the way God has ordained in His Word that it should be. Then Satan can't accuse God of being unjust. God will only move in line with His Word.

God *is* limited by the prayers of His children. Knowing that, we should be all the more diligent to pray as Jesus taught us to. We should pray for those who despitefully use us, rather than criticize and complain against them. And we should pray for laborers to be sent forth into the harvest, that many might be brought into the Kingdom of God.

Binding and Loosing And the Prayer of Agreement

Jesus said something about prayer in Matthew chapter 18 that believers need to understand in order to have a successful prayer life.

MATTHEW 18:18,19
18 Verily I say unto you, Whatsoever ye shall BIND ON EARTH shall be BOUND IN HEAVEN: and whatsoever ye shall LOOSE ON EARTH shall be LOOSED IN HEAVEN.
19 Again I say unto you, That IF TWO OF YOU SHALL AGREE on earth as touching any thing that they shall ask, IT SHALL BE DONE for them of my Father which is in heaven.

Here Jesus is talking about the prayer of binding and loosing and the prayer of agreement, which we discussed in another lesson. As I said, Jesus is bringing out the fact that heaven will back us up in what we pray on earth in Jesus' Name that is according to the will of God.

We have the authority in the Name of Jesus to loose the power of God on this earth and to bind Satan in his operations against us. We have the authority in the prayer of agreement to ask for what we need and know it shall be done for us.

Believe You Receive When You Pray

Then in Matthew chapter 21, Jesus said something else about prayer. Earlier we discussed from the Book of Mark this principle of believing you receive when you pray. More is said in the Book of Mark than in the Book of Matthew on the subject.

MATTHEW 21:18-22
18 Now in the morning as he returned into the city, he hungered.
19 And when he saw a fig tree in the way, he came to it, and found nothing thereon, but leaves only, and said unto it, Let no fruit grow on thee henceforward for ever. And presently the fig tree withered away.
20 And when the disciples saw it, they marvelled, saying, How soon is the fig tree withered away!
21 Jesus answered and said unto them, Verily I say unto you, If ye have faith, and doubt not, ye shall not only do this which is done to the fig tree, but also if ye shall say unto this mountain, Be thou removed, and be thou cast into the sea; it shall be done.
22 And all things, WHATSOEVER YE SHALL ASK IN PRAYER, BELIEVING, YE SHALL RECEIVE.

Jesus is talking about prayer here. He is talking about faith and prayer. You can't very well talk about faith without talking about prayer. And you can't talk about prayer without talking about faith because the two just go hand in hand.

Mark chapter 11 records this same incident. In fact, it is the only reference about prayer in the Book of Mark. Mark is saying the same thing as recorded in Matthew chapter 21. Matthew summarized the event in about five verses, but Mark took about twice as many verses to tell the same story.

MARK 11:12-14,20-26
12 And on the morrow, when they were come from Bethany, he [Jesus] was hungry:
13 And seeing a fig tree afar off having leaves, he came, if haply he might find anything thereon: and when he came to it, he found nothing but leaves; for the time of figs was not yet.
14 And Jesus answered and said unto it, No man eat fruit of thee hereafter for ever. And his disciples heard it. . . .
20 And in the morning, as they passed by, they saw the fig tree dried up from the roots.
21 And Peter calling to remembrance saith unto him, Master, behold, the fig tree which thou cursedst is withered away.
22 And Jesus answering saith unto them, Have faith in God.
23 For verily I say unto you, That whosoever shall say unto this mountain, Be thou removed, and be thou cast into the sea; and shall not doubt in his heart, but shall believe that those things which he saith shall come to pass; he shall have whatsoever he saith.

24 Therefore I say unto you, What things soever ye desire, when ye pray, BELIEVE THAT YE RECEIVE THEM, and ye shall have them.
25 And when ye stand praying, forgive, if ye have ought against any: that your Father also which is in heaven may forgive you your trespasses.
26 But if ye do not forgive, neither will your Father which is in heaven forgive your trespasses.

Once again, notice at the end of this passage that Jesus is telling us to forgive others who might have offended us. Forgiveness must be important, for unforgiveness is the only hindrance to answered prayer that Jesus mentions. He is just simply saying that our prayers are not going to work if we have an unforgiving heart. But if we will keep a forgiving attitude, we can be assured of answers to prayer when we pray according to God's Word.

In these two passages of Scripture, Jesus is talking about believing that you receive *when* you pray. In Mark 11:24, Mark is saying the same thing that Matthew records in Matthew 21:22. Sometimes to say something two different ways adds emphasis to what is being said.

MATTHEW 21:22
22 And all things, whatsoever ye shall ask in prayer, believing, ye shall receive.

MARK 11:24
24 Therefore I say unto you, What things soever ye desire, when ye pray, believe that ye receive them, and ye shall have them.

Jesus said in Matthew 21:22, *"And all things, whatsoever ye shall ask in prayer, believing, ye shall receive."* Well, that is the same as saying, *". . . What things soever ye desire . . . believe that ye receive . . ."* (Mark 11:24).

What if you didn't receive when you prayed? Then according to these two verses, you didn't ask, *believing.*

"Yes," someone said, "but what I asked for might somehow not be the will of God for me." We are so quick to excuse ourselves sometimes for our prayer failures. But these verses don't say to ask, believing, and if you don't receive, it must not have been the will of God for you.

Certainly, we must ask according to God's Word. That is, we must have Scripture for whatever it is we are asking God for. Since God's Word is God's will, we know that if we ask according to His Word, believing, then we know it is His will to answer us. And we shall receive whatever it is we asked for.

Jesus said that if you ask, believing, you shall receive (Matt. 21:22; Mark 11:24).

Jesus said it, I believe it, and that settles it! And Jesus said, ". . . *What things soever ye desire, when ye pray, believe that ye receive them, and ye SHALL have them*" (Mark 11:24).

I tell you, I have believed sometimes for some things that have seemed impossible, and I got them. Praise the Lord! I received those things which seemed impossible to receive by praying this prayer of faith that Jesus is talking about in Matthew 21 and Mark 11.

Faith and Prayer Go Hand in Hand

Like I said, faith and prayer go hand in hand. I learned early in my Christian walk that faith and prayer go together. I got my healing and was raised up from the bed of sickness. But after that in other matters, until I learned to walk entirely by faith for myself, I asked for prayer from others when I needed something from the Lord.

It is all right to depend on one another at times. We are all members of the same Body, the Body of Christ, and we should help one another. However, we all need to develop our own faith in God's Word.

For example, there was a flu epidemic in our town once and I became sick with the flu. I said to my youngest brother (I knew the church was having a Wednesday night service, but I was just not able to get out of bed), "Go to the church and ask the pastor and one of the men who is a great man of prayer and faith to come down here after the service and pray for me."

So my brother went and asked them to come and pray for me, and when the service was over, they came to our house. The pastor talked a little bit about active faith and passive faith; then he anointed me with oil, and they left.

I didn't feel a bit better. I had every ache I had to begin with. I had a fever just like I had to begin with. If anything, to tell you the truth about it, I felt worse.

I said to myself, *Well, if anything, from the natural standpoint I feel worse, but I want to thank God because I am healed.* I did that in faith. And I thanked God because I was healed. I didn't say it because it was already manifested, or because I could see it or feel it. I wouldn't have been making my confession *by faith* then; it would have been a confession based on what I could see or feel. I would have been walking by sight. Can you understand that?

You see, you have to talk about faith when you talk about prayer because faith and prayer go together. That fact has never dawned on many people.

For example, many people say, "If I say I have something that I don't see or feel, I would be lying about it."

But if you *believe* you have something that God's Word promises you, you are not lying about it. Believing really has nothing to do with seeing or with what your senses may tell you. Believing has to do with trusting that God's Word is so.

If I had been saying that I *looked* healed, then I would have been lying. But I didn't say, "I'm healed because I *look* like it." I could tell I had a fever because I was burning up. I also didn't say, "I am healed because my fever is gone." Or "I'm healed because I *feel* great."

I said, "I believe the minute the pastor and that other man anointed me and laid hands on me and prayed for me, I received my healing. I believe I have received my healing because the *Word* said so; not because I feel anything. Now I am going to sleep."

When the pastor and the other man left our house, Mama said to me, "How do you feel?"

I said, "I'm fine, Mama." I wasn't talking naturally; I was talking biblically. She may have interpreted it naturally, but I wasn't talking that way about it at all.

After the pastor and the other man left, I couldn't go to sleep right away, but I just praised God until I finally did go to sleep. I kept saying, "Praise the Lord. Hallelujah. Glory to God, I'm healed."

I was a denominational Christian and had never heard people praising God much before. The Full Gospel church where I attended was a new church, and at that time only the pastor and a few others had the baptism of the Holy Ghost. So they didn't have much praise and worship in the services.

But I just kept saying, "Praise the Lord! The pastor anointed me with oil and I am healed. Thank God for it. I believe I am healed because the Word says so." I finally drifted off to sleep.

When I woke up the next morning my fever was gone, and the aches were gone. But I tell you, I felt terribly weak. I felt as if I couldn't get out of bed. But I reasoned like this, *If I believe I am healed, I will get up. Well people should be up.* So I got up. I got a bite to eat and then said to my mother, "I am going over to see some friends."

I had to walk to see my friends, and they lived two or three miles away. They lived on the other side of the town square, and I had about a mile and a half to go just to get to the town square. Getting there was like climbing a hill.

The devil said, "You will never make it. You will never make it. You are not healed. You lied about it."

I said, "No, Mr. Devil, I didn't lie about it. I believe I'm healed. I am going by what I believe, not what I feel. I am walking by faith, and God's Word is a light unto my path. God's Word says I am healed, and I am walking in the pathway of light."

But I tell you it was like climbing a hill all the way to this courthouse square. At times I felt as if I weren't going to make it.

Once I got to the corner of that square, I had a supernatural experience. Although I didn't have the baptism of the Holy Ghost yet, I had a supernatural experience. The corner of the square was about the halfway mark to where I was going to visit my friends who also had the flu. I was going over there to pray for them to be healed too.

When I got to the corner of the square, I felt something come down over me. It was just like putting on a coat which covered me completely. When this happened, I never felt so strong in my life. The power of God just shot out the ends of my fingers and the ends of my toes. It was the power and anointing of God.

You talk about feeling good physically! I felt as though I'd never had the flu, a fever, or *any* ailment. I felt like I could run, whereas before I had been dragging along. I was so weak it had seemed like I might fall before I got to that place in the square. But now I felt like David did when he said he could run through a troop and jump over a wall (Ps. 18:29). Praise the Lord!

After that happened, I barely remember going the rest of the way! It seemed as if I floated. I went into the house where my friends lived (these folks were Full Gospel people too), and I told them about the Lord healing me.

I prayed for them, but I never did get them healed. They stayed in bed for two weeks because they stayed in the dark, spiritually speaking. You see, they didn't allow the Word to get in their spirits, so there was no action to their faith. The Bible says, *"The ENTRANCE of thy words giveth light . . ."* (Ps. 119:130).

I'm talking about things Jesus said concerning prayer. And I'm talking about faith, because faith and prayer go hand in hand.

The Prayer of Importunity

Luke recorded something about faith and prayer that neither Mark nor Matthew said. Luke talked about the prayer of importunity, that is, being persistent in your faith and in your praying. Again, so many people miss it when they hear that. They believe what Jesus is saying is this: "You just keep on asking, and eventually you will get it." Let's look at this passage of Scripture to see what it is actually saying.

LUKE 11:5-8
5 And he said unto them, Which of you shall have a friend, and shall go unto him at midnight, and say unto him, Friend, lend me three loaves;
6 For a friend of mine in his journey is come to me, and I have nothing to set before him?
7 And he from within shall answer and say, Trouble me not: the door is now shut, and my children are with me in bed; I cannot rise and give thee.
8 I say unto you, Though he will not rise and give him, because he is his friend, yet because of his importunity he will rise and give him as many as he needeth.

Here was a man who had a friend who came to his house in the nighttime to visit. The man didn't have any bread to set before his friend, so he went to another friend's house and said, "A friend has come to visit and I have no food. Please lend me three loaves of bread."

The second friend said, "But I am already in bed and my children are in bed too." And the Bible says, *". . . Though he will not rise and give him, because he is his friend, yet because of his IMPORTUNITY he will rise and give him as many as he needeth"* (Luke 11:8).

If you take this passage literally, then God would be likened to the friend who is in bed. However, we know that God never sleeps nor slumbers (Ps. 121:3,4). Therefore, we know this verse is showing us an analogy or a similarity to scriptural prayer because Jesus was teaching on prayer when He gave this illustration. He was proving a point.

Jesus was simply saying that even in the natural you could get results from a friend like the man did in Luke chapter 11, not necessarily because a person was your friend, but because of your urgent request. In other words, a person might not grant the favor because he is your friend, but he would grant you the favor because of your importunity; that is, you wouldn't take "no" for an answer.

Then Jesus said, *"And I say unto you, Ask, and it shall be given you; seek, and ye shall find; knock, and it shall be opened unto you"* (Luke 11:9). You see, it is the importunity of *faith*, not the importunity of *unbelief* that gets the job done. However, you could just keep on begging God, and be "importunate" all you wanted to, and you would never get an answer even if you lived to be a hundred years old! Why not? Because your importune praying must be in faith, not unbelief.

It is the importunity of faith that works. So believe God's Word that when you ask, it shall be given you. When you seek, you shall find. When you knock, it shall be opened unto you!

I like something Andrew Murray said that will help you to see what I am talking about. As I said, so many people have the idea that if they keep on asking the same thing over and over again, eventually they will get their request. They seem to think that is what Jesus is talking about in the passages of Scripture we've covered in Matthew 7 and Luke 11. But as Andrew Murray said, it is not good taste to ask the Lord for the same thing over and over again. It is just not good taste; actually, it is doubt and unbelief.

Murray said that if you pray to God about something you've already prayed for and it hasn't materialized, do not ask again the same way you did the first time. To do that would be a confession that you didn't believe God the first time you asked Him! You could get into doubt and unbelief by asking for the same thing over and over again.

But just remind God of what you asked for if it hasn't materialized yet. Remind Him of what He promised and put Him in remembrance of His Word (Isa. 43:26). Remind Him that you are expecting the answer. That way you are staying in faith, and you are being persistent in your faith. That is what it means to be importunate in your faith, and this kind of praying will bring results.

You can see then that Jesus is saying in this passage the very opposite of what most people think He is saying. So don't stay on the negative side of importunity in prayer — just asking and begging and crying and pleading in doubt and unbelief hoping that God has heard you. That kind of praying in unbelief will never bring any results.

Instead, ask God in faith according to His Word, and believe that you receive *when* you pray. Then be importunate in faith, continually thanking God for the answer to your prayers. *That* is the prayer of importunity that will always bring results!

God moves in this earth as His children pray in faith according to the principles in His Word. So pray for those who despitefully use you, and see God move in their lives for good. Pray for laborers to be sent into the harvest, and see your prayers answered as souls come into the Kingdom of God.

Never give up in prayer; never faint in your faith! As you continue diligently to pray in faith, more and more you will see God's will fulfilled both in your life and in the lives of others!

Questions for Study

1. According to Matthew 5:45, what makes a Christian want to do the things mentioned in verse 44?

2. Why is it that nowhere in the New Testament are we told to pray that God would save the lost?

3. What scriptural grounds do you have for claiming the souls of those in your own household?

4. How do we permit God to move in our lives?

5. Why didn't Jesus dispute what the devil said to Him in Luke 4:5-7?

6. Why can't God step in and take over on the Earth and cure all the world's ills?

7. According to Matthew 18:18 and 19, what authority do we have?

8. Read Matthew 21:22 and Mark 11:24. According to these two verses, why don't some people receive when they pray?

9. What is the prayer of importunity?

10. What is the negative side of importunity?

Chapter 18

What Jesus Said About Prayer — Part 3

And HE SPAKE A PARABLE UNTO THEM TO THIS END, that men ought always to pray, and not to faint;

Saying, There was in a city a judge, which feared not God, neither regarded man:

And there was a widow in that city; and she came unto him, saying, Avenge me of mine adversary.

And he would not for a while: but afterward he said within himself, Though I fear not God, nor regard man;

Yet because this widow troubleth me, I will avenge her, lest by her continual coming she weary me.

And the Lord said, Hear what the unjust judge saith.

And shall not God avenge his own elect, which cry day and night unto him, though he bear long with them?

I tell you that he will avenge them speedily. Nevertheless when the Son of man cometh, shall he find faith on the earth?

— Luke 18:1-8

Verse 1 says that Jesus spoke this parable to the disciples: *". . . to this end, that men ought always to pray, and not to faint."* Another translation says, *". . . that they should always pray and not give up."* Still another translation says, *". . . that men ought always to pray, and not cave in."*

We have pointed out that there are different rules that apply to different kinds of prayer. Some of us have put all kinds of prayer in the same sack, so to speak, and have shaken them all out together. That is the reason we have become confused and our prayers haven't worked for us. Too often we seem to think that everything that is said about *one* kind of prayer applies to *all* kinds of prayer. But saying that would be just as sensible as saying the rules of football apply to *all* sports. Of course they don't.

Football, baseball, basketball, and many other games all fall under the category of sports. But the same rules do not apply to all of these different games or kinds of sports. Each sport has its own individual set of rules.

Praying With Persistent Faith

As I said, many people have lifted this passage in Luke 18:1-8 out of its setting and have thought from the negative standpoint, "If I can just keep on praying — if I don't give up, and if I pray loud enough, and long enough — I will eventually talk God into the notion of hearing me and answering my prayer."

But let's ask ourselves the question, *What was Jesus really talking about in Luke 18?* Actually, Jesus was talking about praying with persistent faith. We know this because verse 1 says, *". . . he [Jesus] spake a parable unto them TO THIS END, that men ought always to pray, and not to faint"* (Luke 18:1).

To say that this passage is a strict analogy of believers praying to God is not entirely true, because that would be saying that God is an unjust judge. But we know that God cannot be unjust. However, in this passage, Jesus was encouraging believers that since the unjust judge in Luke 18 avenged the widow, *how much more* would *God* speedily avenge His own children, His own elect. Because God is just, He will *speedily* avenge His elect.

In Luke 18, Jesus is encouraging believers in prayer by telling them that even an unjust judge finally heard and answered the widow woman's cry, though he "feared not God and regarded not man." This widow woman had come before the unjust judge and had said, *". . . Avenge me of mine adversary"* (Luke 18:3). Then Jesus said that if the unjust judge avenged the widow, *". . . shall not GOD avenge his own elect. . . ?"* (Luke 18:7).

In this parable Jesus was not talking about praying to be saved. He was not talking about praying to be filled with the Holy Ghost. He was not talking about praying to receive your healing. He was not talking about praying to have your financial or material needs met. We have already covered scriptures which apply to praying for those things using the prayer of faith: *"And all things, whatsoever ye shall ask in prayer, believing, ye shall receive"* (Matt. 21:22). You receive those things I just mentioned by praying the prayer of faith.

But here in Luke 18:1-8, Jesus is talking about the people of God who are under persecution, crying out to God for deliverance.

LUKE 18:7,8
7 And shall not God avenge his own elect, which cry day and night unto him, though he bear long with them?
8 I tell you that HE WILL AVENGE THEM SPEEDILY. Nevertheless when the Son of man cometh, shall he find faith on the earth?

We have great liberty here in the United States, but in many other countries there is not the same religious freedom, and Christians are persecuted for their faith in Jesus Christ. And I am sure that Christians in many other countries are crying to God for deliverance and freedom.

But Jesus is saying here in Luke 18 that the time is coming when pressure is going to be put on all Christians, no matter where we live. The Book of Revelation talks about the end times and about the cry of God's people ascending up to Him. But Jesus said here, *"I tell you that he [God] will avenge them speedily. Nevertheless when the Son of man cometh, shall he find faith on the earth?"* (Luke 18:8).

What Jesus is saying here is that the believer is not to give up in prayer, and when the world waxes worse and worse and persecution comes so that we will almost despair of life, yet we will cry unto God and He will avenge us speedily. He won't be like the unjust judge was. The unjust judge did not avenge the widow woman speedily. The Bible says the woman troubled the judge, and finally when the judge avenged her, he did so, saying, *". . . lest by her continual coming she weary me"* (Luke 18:5).

But notice Jesus said that God would *speedily* avenge His own elect. This says just the opposite of what most people think it says.

For instance, most people think this passage of Scripture is saying that if we have unsaved loved ones, if we keep on praying long enough, eventually we will just wear God down, wear Him out, and worry Him as this woman did that unjust judge. Then after we do all of that, God will eventually save our loved ones, just so we'll stop petitioning Him about it!

Or people think this scriptural passage is saying that if they have some personal need, if they keep at it in prayer, they will eventually talk God into the notion of doing something for them. But that is not what Jesus is talking about in these verses at all. God stands ready and willing at every moment to answer prayer.

Jesus is not talking about persistent faith to wear God out so He will answer your prayers. He is simply saying if believers will be persistent in faith, *how much more* will God avenge them than the unjust judge avenged the widow. But as verse 1 says, it is the persistence of *faith*, not the persistence of *doubt*, that causes God to respond and avenge his elect.

To take scriptures and texts out of their setting and out of their context and try to apply them to other areas will cause us more harm than good. The main thought in Luke 18 is that men ought always to pray, and not to faint — not to cave in. It is easy to cave in sometimes in our faith.

Asking in Jesus' Name

Now let us look at the Gospel of John and see something here that Jesus said about prayer. John, strange as it may seem, does not record anything that the others do in regard to prayer. And what John says about prayer, the others — Matthew, Mark, and Luke — did not record.

Actually, in his Gospel, John said that if everything was written which Jesus said and did, the world itself couldn't contain the books that would have been written (John 21:25). However, many things are recorded in the Word that Jesus said and did which can help us. And regarding prayer, we've seen that Jesus taught many principles of prayer which can help us develop in our prayer life as we practice them.

Of course, the writers of the gospels — Matthew, Mark, Luke, and John — didn't all record the same thing. Luke recorded a part of what Matthew said about prayer. Mark didn't record much about prayer. He just recorded one instance in regard to Jesus' cursing the fig tree. Matthew covered that in Matthew chapter 21. But Matthew also recorded what Jesus said about the prayer of agreement: *". . . That if two of you . . . agree on earth as touching any thing that they shall ask, it shall be done . . ."* (Matt. 18:19). None of the other writers mentioned the prayer of agreement.

The Book of John covers the subject of prayer from an entirely different standpoint than any of the other gospel writers did. Actually, we have to put together all the things John said about prayer to get a clear picture of what God wants us to know.

JOHN 14:10-14
10 Believest thou not that I am in the Father, and the Father in me? the words that I speak unto you I speak not of myself: but the Father that dwelleth in me, he doeth the works.
11 Believe me that I am in the Father, and the Father in me: or else believe me for the very works' sake.
12 Verily, verily, I say unto you, He that believeth on me, the works that I do shall he do also; and greater works than these shall he do; because I go unto my Father.
13 And whatsoever ye shall ask [demand] IN MY NAME, that will I [Jesus] do, that the Father may be glorified in the Son.
14 If ye shall ask any thing IN MY NAME, I will do it.

We have used this passage of Scripture in regard to prayer. But Jesus is not talking about prayer here at all in the way we think He is talking about prayer.

As we look once more at John 16:23 and 24, we will be able to see the difference between these two passages of Scripture.

JOHN 16:23,24
23 And in that day ye shall ask me nothing. Verily, verily, I say unto you, Whatsoever ye shall ASK THE FATHER in my name, he will give it you.
24 Hitherto have ye asked nothing in my name: ask, and ye shall receive, that your joy may be full.

In John 14:13,14 the Greek word for "ask" implies *to demand as something due.* In other words, we could say, "And whatsoever you shall *demand* in My Name, that will I do . . ." (John 14:13).

When you demand something due you in the Name of Jesus, you are not demanding anything of God. God isn't the one hindering you; Satan is. You are exercising your authority over the devil in Jesus' Name. You are simply standing in your position of authority against Satan in the Name of Jesus.

Jesus said, *"And whatsoever ye shall ask* [demand] *in my name, that will I do . . ."* (John 14:13). Actually the Greek is more explicit than this. It reads, "Whatsoever you shall demand as your right in My Name. . . ." Based on your rights in Christ, you are demanding Satan to stop in his maneuvers against you. And you have the right to use the authority in the Name of Jesus as something due you because of your inheritance in Christ.

In John 14:13,14, the believer is standing against Satan and circumstances which do not line up with the Word of God. The believer is exercising his authority over Satan and the adverse circumstances affecting his life, and commanding Satan to bow his knee to the Name of Jesus (Phil. 2:9,10). The believer is also exercising the command of faith in that Name.

John 14:13,14 is *not* talking about prayer as is John 16:23,24. John 14:13,14 is the believer's right to exercise his authority over Satan in the Name of Jesus. It is a demand or command of something due the believer because of the rights and privileges God has already provided for him in Christ based on the authority invested in the Name of Jesus.

In John 14:13,14, Jesus is talking about something entirely different from what He said in John 16,23,24. In John 16:23,24, Jesus is giving us the principle for New Testament *prayer.* Jesus is telling us that all prayer must be addressed to the Father in Jesus' Name: *". . . Whatsoever ye shall ask the FATHER in my name, HE will give it you."*

Here in John 16:23,24 Jesus is talking about prayer *to the Father* in the Name of Jesus. We discussed this kind of New Testament prayer at length in earlier lessons. But in John 14:13,14, Jesus isn't talking about prayer. It is a demand of Satan to loose his hold on whatever he has tried to bind in your life: *". . . whatsoever ye shall ask* [demand] *in my name, that will I* [Jesus] *do. . . ."*

In the Acts of the Apostles, we see this principle of using Jesus' Name, not as a prayer, but as a demand and a command of faith. At that Name sickness had to go.

ACTS 3:1-8
1 Now Peter and John went up together into the temple at the hour of prayer, being the ninth hour.
2 And a certain man lame from his mother's womb was carried, whom they laid daily at the gate of the temple which is called Beautiful, to ask alms of them that entered into the temple;
3 Who seeing Peter and John about to go into the temple asked an alms.
4 And Peter, fastening his eyes upon him with John, said, Look on us.
5 And he gave heed unto them, expecting to receive something of them.
6 Then Peter said, Silver and gold have I none; but such as I have give I thee: IN THE NAME OF JESUS CHRIST OF NAZARETH RISE UP AND WALK.
7 And he took him by the right hand, and lifted him up: and immediately his feet and ankle bones received strength.
8 And he leaping up stood, and walked, and entered with them into the temple, walking, and leaping, and praising God.

At the Gate called Beautiful, Peter and John were going into the temple. There at the gate they met a man, a beggar, who had been crippled from birth. The man was begging alms, and Peter stopped and said, "Look on us."

The man looked on them, expecting to receive something from them. Peter immediately averted the man's attention from receiving silver and gold. Instead, by the unction and direction of the Holy Spirit, Peter said, *". . . Silver and gold have I none; but such as I have give I thee: In the NAME OF JESUS CHRIST of Nazareth rise up and walk"* (Acts 3:6).

Peter exercised his authority in the Name of Jesus. He demanded in Jesus' Name that the crippled man rise up and walk. Jesus said in John 14:13 that *". . . whatsoever ye shall ask* [or demand] *in my name, that will I* [Jesus] *do. . . ."* Notice Peter didn't pray that *God* would heal this crippled man. By the unction of the Holy Spirit, Peter said, *". . . In the name of Jesus Christ of Nazareth rise up and walk"* (Acts 3:6).

This account in Acts 3 is an example of what Jesus was talking about in John 14:13,14. Jesus was not talking about prayer, that is, asking of the Father in Jesus' Name. He was talking about the believer's command or demand that Satan and circumstances become subject to the Name of Jesus. He is talking about believers speaking forth the command of faith in that mighty Name. Sickness and disease must become subject to that Name (Phil. 2:9,10).

Let me go over the difference in these two passages of Scripture one more time to make sure you understand. As we discussed, Jesus said in John chapter 16 on the subject of prayer, *"And in that day ye shall ask me nothing . . ."* (v. 23). Jesus was not talking about praying to Him, or asking Him anything. He was talking about praying to the Father *in Jesus' Name.*

Jesus said to the disciples just before He went away, *". . . IN THAT DAY ye shall ask me nothing . . ."* (John 16:23). What day is that? It is the very day we now live in, the day of the New Covenant or the New Testament. Jesus was saying that under the New Covenant believers would pray to the Father in Jesus' Name.

One translation reads, "In that day you shall not pray to Me." In other words, you are not to pray to Jesus; you are to pray to God the Father in the *Name of Jesus.*

JOHN 16:23
23 . . . Verily, verily, I say unto you, Whatsoever ye shall ask the Father in my name, he will give it you.

This is talking about praying to the Father in the Name of Jesus. That is how we are to pray. In verse 24 Jesus says, *"Hitherto have ye asked nothing in my name* [you haven't prayed to the Father in My Name]: *ask, and ye shall receive, that your joy may be full."*

But in John 14:13 and 14, we have seen that Jesus is saying something different. Jesus said, *". . . whatsoever ye shall ask in my name, that WILL I DO, that the Father may be glorified in the Son. If ye shall ask any thing in my name, I WILL DO IT"* (John 14:13,14).

As I said, here Jesus is saying you are to use the Name of Jesus to demand what is rightfully due you. You are not demanding of the Father; you are demanding that Satan cease and desist in his operations against you in the Name of Jesus. You are exercising your authority over Satan and circumstances that are contrary to God's Word. And you are speaking forth the command of faith in that Name.

Whatever you ask or demand as your right, Jesus said, *"I will do it."* That is what I want to get over to you. It is the authority in the Name of Jesus that does it. I want you to think on the truth of that scripture until you see it with the eyes of your heart, or your spirit.

Doing the Works of Jesus

It is interesting that John 14:13,14 directly follows John 14:12 where Jesus talks about believers doing the greater works.

JOHN 14:12-14
12 Verily, verily, I say unto you, He that believeth on me, THE WORKS THAT I DO SHALL HE DO ALSO; and greater works than these shall he do; because I go unto my Father.
13 And whatsoever ye shall ask in my name, that will I do, that the Father may be glorified in the Son.
14 If ye shall ask any thing in my name, I will do it.

Notice that Jesus said in John 14:12, *"Verily, verily, I say unto you, He that believeth on me, the works that I do shall he do also. . . ."* Jesus is talking about the works that believers are to do here on the earth. How are believers going to do the works of Jesus? Through His *Name.*

Did you ever notice that Jesus didn't actually pray for people as He ministered to them? We talk about praying for the sick, but Jesus never prayed for the sick. Don't misunderstand me, it *is* scriptural also to pray for the sick (James 5:14,15). But that is not the *only* way to minister to the sick. Jesus said, *". . . the WORKS that I do shall he* [the believer] *do also. . ."* (John 14:12).

If we just ministered to the sick through prayer, even though we got results, we still wouldn't be doing the *works* that Jesus did in His earthly ministry. He laid hands on the sick, but He never prayed for them. He would *command* the devil to leave and take his hands off of them. He would just say, for example, *". . . Go your way; and as thou hast believed, so be it done unto thee . . ."* (Matt. 8:13).

Jesus exercised authority over the works of the devil and over circumstances while He was on this earth. And He was saying in John 14:13,14 that we can do these same works in His Name: *". . . whatsoever ye shall ask in my name, that will I do . . ."* (John 14:13). For example, we have a right to demand that Satan take his hands off our finances in the Name of Jesus.

What Are the *Greater* Works of Jesus?

There is another interesting fact involved here in John 14 that is important. Jesus said, *"Verily, verily,*

I say unto you, He that believeth on me, the works that I do shall he do also; and GREATER WORKS than these shall he do . . ." (v. 12). Believers are to do even greater works than Jesus did when He walked on the earth — through His *Name*. What are the greater works?

Someone said, "Let's just do the works Jesus did first; then we will do the greater works." But that explanation falls a little bit short of the thought Jesus wanted to get over to us.

Notice *why* Jesus said we would do greater works: *". . . because I go unto my Father"* (John 14:12). I don't know whether you know it or not, but the Church today can and is doing greater works than Jesus did.

You might ask, "How can it be true that the Church is doing greater works than Jesus did?" The answer becomes very obvious when we read the phrase, *". . . because I go unto my Father"* (John 14:12). Jesus had to go to the Father so He could send the Holy Spirit to us.

Notice what Jesus said in John chapter 16, speaking about the Holy Ghost.

JOHN 16:7-11
7   Nevertheless I tell you the truth; It is expedient for you that I go away: for IF I GO NOT AWAY, THE COMFORTER WILL NOT COME UNTO YOU; BUT IF I DEPART, I WILL SEND HIM UNTO YOU.
8   And when he is come, he will reprove the world of sin, and of righteousness, and of judgment:
9   Of sin, because they believe not on me;
10 Of righteousness, because I go to my Father, and ye see me no more;
11 Of judgment, because the prince of this world is judged.

What are the *greater works* the Church is doing? The greater works we do are getting people born again. Jesus did not get anyone born again in His earthly ministry until the few days' time following His resurrection before He ascended back into heaven. Someone said, "I thought those people following Jesus in His earthly ministry were saved."

Jesus' followers were saved in the same sense that the people in the Old Testament were saved; they had a promissory note on their salvation to be consummated in that day when Jesus would redeem mankind. But they were not born again. They couldn't have been saved because Jesus had not yet died on the Cross to redeem mankind.

"Well," someone asked, "didn't Jesus forgive people's sins in His earthly ministry?" Yes, He did, but there is a difference between forgiving people's sins

and making them new creatures in Christ.

You see, under the Old Covenant, the people could only obtain the *forgiveness* or *atonement* for sins through the sacrificing of bulls and goats (Lev. 16:21; Heb. 9:6-14). Their sins were only *covered* by the blood of bulls and goats.

But under the New Covenant, because of the redemptive work of Christ, we can have the *remission* of sins. That is, our sins can be *remitted* and wiped out through the blood of Jesus, as if they never existed (1 John 1:9). In other words, as Christians, our sins are not *covered*; they are remitted or taken away.

Certainly, after you are born again, if you sin, your sins can be forgiven, but that doesn't mean you are born again *again*. If that were the case, you could have been born again many times by now!

We know the new birth is one of the greater works Jesus was talking about in John 14:12. People were not born again under Jesus' earthly ministry. They were still under the Old Covenant until Jesus purchased our redemption at the Cross.

For instance, you've never read anywhere in the Old Testament or in the Four Gospels where it says, *". . . And the Lord added to the church daily such as should be saved."* But you do read that statement in the Acts of the Apostles (Acts 2:47). The Book of Acts was recorded after Jesus' death, burial, and resurrection.

You see, there wasn't any Church of the Lord Jesus Christ in Jesus' earthly ministry until Jesus breathed on His disciples and said, *". . . Receive ye the Holy Ghost"* (John 20:22). This is when the disciples were born again. Therefore, this was actually the beginning of the Church — a body of believers. But until that time, the only Body of Christ that was in the earth was Jesus' own physical body.

There were those who followed Jesus. They were believers because they believed on Jesus and they had the promise of their redemption. But man's redemption could not be consummated until Jesus Christ went to the Cross and the Holy Ghost came to baptize believers into one Body, the Body of Christ. The Body of Christ is formed as people become born again. Born-again believers make up the Body of Christ.

Today we are the spiritual Body of Christ. The only Body of Christ which is in the world today is the Church, which is made up of Christians — those who have been born again.

ACTS 2:47

47 . . . And the Lord added to the church daily such as should be saved.

We're talking about the greater works that Jesus spoke about, which the Body of Christ is to do in His Name (John 14:12). Besides the new birth, another "greater work" is getting people filled with the Holy Spirit.

Just as no one was born again under the ministry of Jesus, neither was anyone baptized or filled with the Holy Ghost under His ministry. That is why it's a greater work. We are going to do these greater works of getting folks born again and filled with the Holy Spirit because Jesus went unto the Father.

God's Word Should *Abide* in Us

In John chapter 15 Jesus says something else about prayer. He gives us important conditions that we must fulfill in order to receive the answers to our prayers.

JOHN 15:7,8
7 If ye abide in me, and my words abide in you, ye shall ask what ye will, and it shall be done unto you.
8 Herein is my Father glorified, that ye bear much fruit; so shall ye be my disciples.

In John 15:7 Jesus gives us two conditions to answered prayer. First He said, *"If ye abide in me . . ."* (John 15:7). The only way in the world a person can *abide* in Jesus is to be born again.

But notice Jesus didn't just say, "If ye abide in me." He gave another condition to answered prayer. He went on to say, *". . . and my words abide in you . . ."* (John 15:7). If He had just said, "If ye abide in me," we Christians would all automatically have it made. But He said, *". . . and MY WORDS abide in you . . ."* (John 15:7).

Here is an interesting thought. In these verses concerning prayer, not one single time does Jesus mention *faith* or *believing* in connection with prayer. Do you know why? It is quite obvious. Notice again verse 7: *"If ye abide in me, AND MY WORDS ABIDE IN YOU, ye shall ask what ye will, and it shall be done unto you."*

You see, there is no problem with having faith to receive the answers to your prayers if Jesus' words abide in you.

ROMANS 10:17
17 So then faith cometh by hearing, and hearing by the word of God.

There is only a problem of not having enough faith to receive the answers to your prayers when the Word doesn't abide in you, for if the Word is not abiding in you, in your heart, then faith is not abiding there. But if the Word abides in you, then faith abides in you too. If faith doesn't abide in you, the Word is not abiding in you. It's that simple.

Without the Word abiding in you, you could give mental consent to the Word. In fact, you could just stand up and shake your fist and declare with all enthusiasm and fervor that you believe that the Bible is God-inspired; that you believe it from cover to cover, from Genesis to Revelation.

You could even be willing to roll up your sleeves and fight for your beliefs, and yet never really have the Word abiding in you at all. You could do some things religiously in prayer, but without the Word of God abiding in you, your prayers wouldn't really amount to too much or bear much fruit.

No, only as the Word abides in you and causes your faith to increase are you able to receive the answers to your prayers. In Romans chapter 10, the Word of God is actually called the "word of faith."

ROMANS 10:8
8 But what saith it? The word is nigh thee, even in thy mouth, and in thy heart: that is, the WORD OF FAITH, which we preach.

This God-inspired Word is called the "word of faith." Hallelujah! And if this Word abides in you, it will cause faith to spring up in your heart. Remember, *". . . faith cometh by hearing, and hearing by the word of God"* (Rom. 10:17). That is the reason the Psalmist of old said, *"The entrance of thy words giveth light . . ."* (Ps. 119:130).

You see, when you know the Word, you won't be praying in the dark, because when you know the Word, you have light. Again the Psalmist said, *"Thy word is a lamp unto my feet, and a light unto my path"* (Ps. 119:105). When you know the Word, you are not walking in the dark. Your pathway is illuminated when you have the Word in your heart.

I didn't know those words in John 15:7 and Psalm 119:105 and 130 were in the Bible when I was first saved. I began to read more of the Word and I finally found out those words were in there. When I did find those scriptures, I remember thinking that my experience in receiving my healing was right in line with the Word. And I didn't know as much of the Word at that time as I do now. Of course, if your experience is of the Holy Spirit, it will be in line with the Word because the Spirit and the Word agree (1 John 5:7,8).

I remember when light from God's Word came to

me on the bed of sickness. Light came to me about faith, prayer, and divine healing. It seemed to me that when the light came, it just lit up the whole room, spiritually speaking. It seemed that before that time, my room was dark. It was daytime, yet it was spiritually dark.

It was dark, spiritually speaking, when five different doctors shook their heads and said, "You have to die. There is no hope for you." Five doctors said that. Sure it was dark. I didn't have the Word to stand on because I didn't know what the Word said concerning faith and healing. But when the Word came into my heart, it was light!

I had been reading the Word, but the truth concerning divine healing hadn't dawned on me — it hadn't really gotten into my heart. At first, the scriptures I read seemed to only be churning around in my head. But as I began to give the Word first place in my life and to spend time meditating on it, the Word got into my heart. When the Word got into my heart, my spirit, it began to produce results — I was raised from off a deathbed!

The Bible says, *"The entrance of thy words giveth light . . ."* (Ps. 119:130). The Bible also says, *"If ye abide in me, and my words abide IN YOU . . ."* (John 15:7). John 15:7 isn't talking about the Word abiding in your head, but in *you*, in your spirit. You see, the real you is your spirit, the inward man. The Word has to abide in your spirit before it will produce results in your life.

Some people have an argument against faith and divine healing. One reason for that is they only know the Word in their head. They have not allowed God's Word to abide *in* them, so that the entrance of God's Word can give light and illuminate their thinking. Therefore, the Word never produces any results in their lives.

I was saved and healed and raised up from the bed of sickness because the Word got into my heart. After I was healed, I began to go to a different denominational church from the one I had been raised in. The one I had been raised in would not accept my testimony of healing.

This other church I began attending was about two blocks from our house. So I decided, *I am not going to walk two miles to my old church when I could go two blocks to this other church where they accept my healing testimony.* (There wasn't a Full Gospel church in my town.) I hadn't found anyone really who believed as I did at that time.

I remember the first Sunday morning I went to visit this church. I was born within a block of the new church I would be attending, so the people knew me. As I came walking up the steps that morning, the pastor and the Sunday school superintendent were standing on the front steps greeting people. As I approached them, the Sunday school superintendent said to me, "Kenneth, I want you to teach the young people's class."

I wasn't a member of that church, and he knew that, but this superintendent had known me from the time I was born. He told me later, "You were born and raised right here. We all know it had to be God that raised you up from a deathbed. We accept that. Do you want to go to work for God?"

I answered, "Yes, sir." I was ready to do anything for God.

Some folks want to do something for God, but they want it to be on *their* terms. But I was ready to do anything for God that He wanted me to do. If He wanted me to sweep the church out, I would sweep it out. I would do anything for God. I believe it should be that way.

So this superintendent said, "All right, I want you to teach the young people's class."

Then the Sunday school superintendent said to me, "You can teach from the Sunday school curriculum, or you can do what the pastor does; you can just teach the Bible. In our adult men's class, the pastor just teaches the Bible. He doesn't use the literature at all. He just uses the Bible."

I said, "I believe I will teach the Bible then."

The superintendent said, "All right, just have at it." So I did. I started teaching that morning, and I had more young people in that one class than the rest of the Sunday school combined. It was a large class.

I was seventeen years old at that time and I began to teach and preach and I've been teaching and preaching ever since. Praise the Lord! I taught on the subjects of faith and healing and saw many wonderful results. None of this would have happened if I hadn't taken the time to get the Word to abide in my heart. And I would have died on the bed of sickness.

I know this much, you can have the Word of God in your head and not in your heart, and it won't amount to a thing in the world in your life.

For example, there was a man who attended this church where I taught Sunday school who was in church every time I was there. He never missed a service. He would talk to me after the services. I knew he was a good man, as far as being a good man is concerned, because he had lived within three blocks of this church, and I had really known him all of my life. He was an older man.

This man would draw me into discussing the Scriptures, and sometimes after Sunday night services, we would talk nearly all night long about the Scriptures. Very few preachers could discuss and quote them as well as he could. He had a knowledge of the entire Bible, both Old and New Testaments, that very few others had.

Finally one night I pinned him down (I could tell which direction he was going), and I said, "Have you ever been saved?"

He said, "Well, if I have, I don't know it."

"No," he said, "I will just be honest with you and tell you the truth about it, Kenneth. I claim to be an infidel. But I have studied the Bible and have read it through many times. I have discussed the Bible with some preachers and then gone home and laughed about it because they weren't very knowledgeable; I put them on the run. You are the first fellow that I haven't been able to put on the run. You stay with me. Instead of laughing, I go home thinking. You get me to thinking."

I am convinced that I helped that fellow to come to know God. I preached him under conviction. For example, once he started crying right on the street corner as I talked to him about the Word.

This man told me personally, "I have read the Bible through ten times and have studied portions of it more times than that. I have studied it from the standpoint of arguing it." He was very adept at that. He could argue against almost any church doctrine. But when he ran into me, I wasn't pushing any doctrine; I was just preaching the Word. I wasn't even a member of that church. I just taught the Word there.

You see, this man had the Scripture in his head, but there is a difference between a person having the Word in his head and having it abide in his heart — in his spirit.

If you want to receive answers to your prayers, you must first get God's Word to abide *in* you: *"IF ye abide in me, and MY WORDS ABIDE IN YOU, YE SHALL ASK what ye will, and IT SHALL BE DONE unto you"* (John 15:7).

How do you get the Word to abide in you? Whatever it is you are praying about, find scriptures that cover your case. Find scriptures that promise you the things you are desiring from God.

Then meditate on those scriptures until you get them down on the inside of you. Then you have a real foundation for faith. The devil will not be able to move you off of *that* foundation because it will be based solidly on the Word. It's easy to have faith when God's Word is abiding in you!

Walking in the Light of the Word

Jesus said in John chapter 15, *"If ye abide in me, and my words abide in you . . ."* (v. 7). Psalm 119:130 says, *"The entrance of thy words giveth light. . . ."* If you have a light on your path, then you can walk in that light and you can make progress and get results.

If there is no action, you are not walking, and your path will be dark. Light comes as God's Word abides in you. And the Bible says, *". . . if we WALK in the light, as he is in the light, we have fellowship one with another, and the blood of Jesus Christ his Son cleanseth us from all sin"* (1 John 1:7).

Notice this verse doesn't say a thing in the world about *standing* in the light. First John 1:7 doesn't say, "If we *stand* in the light, as he is in the light, we have fellowship one with another." It says, *". . . if we WALK . . ."* (1 John 1:7).

God's Word is a light unto the path that we walk. To walk implies action — faith. I had to walk in the light of God's Word that was shed on my path in order to receive my healing. First I had to *pray* and *ask*, then I had to *walk* and *act* in faith that I had received my healing. When I did, I got results. Thank God for the Word!

Then the Psalmist of old prayed, *". . . quicken thou me according to thy word"* (Ps. 119:25). Jesus said, *"If ye abide in me, and my words abide in you . . ."* (John 15:7). You see, God can't quicken us according to His Word, although He wants to, unless His words abide in us — unless we walk in the light of the Word.

I read many of the books by F. F. Bosworth years before I met him. I don't know about you, but when I hear someone teach or preach or I hear someone's testimony, I am interested in how that person turned out — how the Word worked for him. I am not much interested in following the *theory* of some fellow when it doesn't even work for him in his own life. I heard F. F. Bosworth say when he was seventy-five years old and still active, "I always start every morning by saying, 'Lord, quicken Thou me according to Thy word.'"

Bosworth went on to explain what it meant to him to be quickened according to God's Word. He said that he was still in good health, even though he was seventy-five years old at the time. All those many years he had trusted God and had never had to take any kind of medication or treatment.

Bosworth lived to be eighty-two years old. He said he knew about his death ahead of time. He had to get a doctor so that when he died the doctor could pronounce him dead. So he had his wife call the doctor, and the doctor said Bosworth was having a heart attack. But Bosworth knew in his spirit that the Lord was calling him home.

A leading evangelist flew down to Florida to see Bosworth because he was a great friend of Bosworth's. When the evangelist went into the house, Bosworth was sitting up in bed. His hands were lifted and he was praising God.

Bosworth said, "Brother, this is the day I have waited for all of my life. I am going home. Glory! I am ready and I am going home."

Bosworth had prayed daily, "Lord, quicken Thou me according to Thy word." And the Lord quickened him every day until Bosworth was ready to go home. He died without sickness or disease. He simply went home to be with the Lord.

Bosworth said, "The doctor told me I'd had a heart attack. But the Lord told me ahead of time that He was coming for me." After all, a fellow wouldn't die if his heart didn't quit beating, would he? The heart has to stop beating or a person wouldn't die. But Bosworth didn't die with sickness and disease. He remained healthy all of his life. Even at the age of eighty-two, he stayed active right until the end. I like to find out how a fellow turns out — how he practices what he preaches! Praise the Lord!

The Word is true whether we put it in practice or not. But there are going to be some of us who are going to practice the Word and, as a result, enjoy the full benefits of it.

I have been enjoying the blessings and the benefits of God's Word for more than sixty years. I have studied these principles of prayer which Jesus taught and which we have discussed, and I have put them into practice in my own life.

Won't you join me in receiving God's best for your life? Determine to practice what the Word teaches about prayer. Be persistent in your faith and never give up in prayer. Ask in Jesus' Name for those rights and privileges that are yours as a child of God. Then as you abide in Jesus and allow His Word to abide in you, you can ask of the Father and know that you have received the answers to your prayers!

Questions for Study

1. Why is it not entirely true to say that Luke 18:1-8 is a strict analogy of believers praying to God?

   _____

   _____

2. What is the main thought of Luke 18:1-8?

   _____

   _____

3. In John 14:13, 14, what does the Greek word "ask" imply?

   _____

   _____

4. What is the difference between the Scripture passages in John 14:13,14 and John 16:23,24?

   _____

   _____

5. How are believers going to do the works of Jesus?

   _____

   _____

6. Why did Jesus say we would do greater works than He did?

   _____

   _____

7. How is the _forgiveness_ of sins different from the _remission_ of sins?

   _____

   _____

8. What two important conditions did Jesus give in John 15:7,8 that we must fulfill in order to receive the answers to our prayers?

   _____

   _____

9. Complete the following sentence: If the Word is not abiding in you, in your heart, then _____ is not abiding there.

10. How do you get the Word to abide in you?

   _____

   _____

Chapter 19

What Paul Said About Prayer — Part 1

In this chapter we are going to look in detail at what the Apostle Paul said about prayer. Paul, writing to the Church, said in Romans 10:1 that his prayer for Israel was that they might be saved. But Paul said some other significant things on the subject of prayer.

We have used some of the verses Paul wrote as texts in some of our other lessons, and we have referred briefly to some of them in connection with another study course, *The Holy Spirit and His Gifts.* When we put together what Paul said to the various churches about prayer, the subject of prayer takes shape and form in a way that we do not see when we just use a text about prayer here and there.

The Holy Spirit's Help in Prayer:
God's Gift for This Dispensation

Let's begin our discussion of what Paul said about prayer by looking in the Book of Romans.

ROMANS 8:26,27
26 Likewise the Spirit also helpeth our infirmities: for we know not what we should pray for as we ought: but the Spirit itself [Himself] maketh intercession for us with groanings which cannot be uttered.
27 And he that searcheth the hearts knoweth what is the mind of the Spirit, because he maketh intercession for the saints according to the will of God.

Paul is saying something about prayer in this passage of Scripture that Jesus never talked about while He was on this earth. He is talking about the Holy Spirit helping us as we pray.

Jesus did teach many principles and guidelines about prayer. For instance, He talked about two agreeing together and receiving the desires of their hearts as they agree in prayer (Matt. 18:19). He talked about praying the prayer of faith (Mark 11:24). But in Jesus' teaching to His disciples in His earthly ministry, Jesus never said one word to the disciples about the Holy Spirit helping them in prayer, as Paul mentioned in Romans 8:26.

Jesus also never mentioned praying in the Spirit, that is, praying with other tongues. The reason Jesus never talked about praying in tongues was that the people He was talking to didn't have the Pentecostal experience of being filled with the Holy Spirit with the evidence of speaking in tongues. It wasn't available to them. They were still under the Old Covenant. They weren't even born again.

Jesus did promise the disciples that the Holy Spirit would come to dwell in them and in all of those who accepted Jesus Christ as their Savior (John 14:16,17,23,26).

He also promised them that they would be baptized in the Holy Spirit after He ascended to the Father (Luke 24:29; Acts 1:5,8). But that was all future tense. Jesus was saying this to His disciples when He was on the earth, and the promise of the Holy Spirit being given to the Church was yet to come.

The baptism of the Holy Spirit with the evidence of speaking in other tongues is exclusively promised to born-again people under the New Covenant. In other words, the gift of tongues is only for this Church-age dispensation. Jesus told His disciples before He went away — before He went to Calvary — that this Pentecostal experience would be available to them.

LUKE 24:49
49 And, behold, I send the promise of my Father upon you: but tarry ye in the city of Jerusalem, until ye be endued with power from on high.

ACTS 1:5,8
5 For John truly baptized with water; but ye shall be baptized with the Holy Ghost not many days hence. . . .
8 But ye shall receive power, after that the Holy Ghost is come upon you: and ye shall be witnesses unto me both in Jerusalem, and in all Judaea, and in Samaria, and unto the uttermost part of the earth.

The promise of the Holy Spirit that Jesus was talking about in these verses was fulfilled on the Day of Pentecost. The 120 believers gathered in the Upper Room *"were all filled with the Holy Ghost, and began to speak with other tongues, as the Spirit gave them utterance"* (Acts 2:4).

We must remember that in the New Testament it was the norm, not the exception, for believers to be Spirit filled. So Paul in his epistles was writing to born-again, Spirit-filled people. He was writing to the Church, the New Testament body of believers.

The *Indwelling* Presence vs.
The *Infilling* Power of the Holy Spirit

Let us stop long enough here to make an observation. We get so mixed up religiously sometimes that we miss God's plan and God's best. What a difference there would be in our lives if we would just walk in the light of what God's Word says!

For instance, a person once said to me, "Brother Hagin, I am a child of God. The Holy Ghost is already dwelling in me because I'm saved. There is no need for me to be filled with the Holy Spirit because I already have the Holy Spirit."

When folks say this to me, they usually quote First Corinthians 6:19, which says, *"What? know ye not that your body is the temple of the Holy Ghost. . . ?"* to prove that they have all of the Holy Spirit there is to have.

But have you ever noticed that some of the worst lies are those that are half lie and half truth? What this Christian said to me was partly true and partly false, and here is the reason why.

When the sinner receives Jesus Christ as his Savior, the Holy Spirit does the work of regeneration in the sinner's heart. But the sinner does set out to receive the Holy Spirit because the Bible says, *"Even the Spirit of truth; WHOM THE WORLD CANNOT RECEIVE . . ."* (John 14:17).

But the sinner *can* receive Jesus Christ as his Savior because John 3:16 says, *"For God so loved the WORLD* [the unsaved] *that he gave his only begotten Son, that whosoever believeth in him should not perish, but have everlasting life."* And when the sinner receives Jesus Christ as his Savior and is born again, he receives the *indwelling* Presence of the Holy Spirit — the Comforter — who was promised to those who would believe in Jesus (John 14:16,17,26). Therefore, it is certainly true that if one has been born again, he has the Holy Spirit in a measure.

The Bible teaches that the believer can also be endued with power from on High through the *infilling* or the baptism of the Holy Spirit (Luke 24:49; Acts 1:5,8). The sinner can receive the new birth and the Holy Spirit's *indwelling* Presence by accepting Jesus as his Savior. Then once a person is saved, he can receive the *infilling* of the Holy Spirit.

Therefore, it is only a half-truth when someone says, "Because I am born again, I already have the Holy Spirit. I don't need any other experience. I don't need to ask God for this experience of being baptized with the Holy Spirit with the evidence of speaking in tongues, for I already have all of the Holy Spirit there is to have."

When a person says that, he has not studied what the Word teaches about the Holy Spirit's twofold working in the believer's life.

Two Separate Experiences

Therefore, receiving Jesus as your Savior and the *indwelling* Presence of the Holy Spirit is not the same as receiving the *infilling* of the Holy Spirit. These are two separate experiences. Let's look at a passage in Acts chapter 8 which shows this twofold working of the Holy Spirit in believers' lives.

ACTS 8:5-8,12-17
5 Then Philip went down to the city of Samaria, and PREACHED CHRIST unto them.
6 And the people with ONE ACCORD GAVE HEED UNTO THOSE THINGS which Philip spake, hearing and seeing the miracles which he did.
7 For unclean spirits, crying with loud voice, came out of many that were possessed with them: and many taken with palsies, and that were lame, were healed.
8 And there was great joy in that city. . . .
12 But when they BELIEVED Philip preaching THE THINGS CONCERNING THE KINGDOM OF GOD, and THE NAME OF JESUS CHRIST, they were baptized, both men and women.
13 Then Simon himself believed also: and when he was baptized, he continued with Philip, and wondered, beholding the miracles and signs which were done.
14 Now when the apostles which were at Jerusalem heard that Samaria had RECEIVED THE WORD OF GOD [concerning salvation], **they sent unto them Peter and John:**
15 Who, when they [Peter and John] **were come down, prayed for them, that they might RECEIVE THE HOLY GHOST:**
16 (For as yet he was fallen upon none of them: only they were baptized IN THE NAME OF THE LORD JESUS.)
17 Then laid they their hands on them, and they RECEIVED THE HOLY GHOST.

We can see that salvation and the baptism in the Holy Spirit are two separate experiences in Acts chapter 8.

Philip first went down to Samaria and preached Christ to these people. They were saved as they received the Word of God concerning salvation.

ACTS 8:5
5 Then Philip went down to the city of Samaria, and PREACHED CHRIST unto them.

What did Philip preach to the Samaritans about? Philip preached about Jesus Christ. Preaching Christ is preaching the good news of the gospel of salvation through Jesus.

These Samaritans believed the gospel message Philip preached, so they were born again.

ACTS 8:6,12
6 And the people with ONE ACCORD GAVE HEED UNTO THOSE THINGS which Philip spake. . . .

12 But when they BELIEVED Philip preaching THE THINGS CONCERNING THE KINGDOM OF GOD, and THE NAME OF JESUS CHRIST, they were baptized, both men and women.

However, these Samaritans did not receive the baptism in the Holy Spirit until Peter and John went down and taught them about this subsequent work of the Holy Spirit.

ACTS 8:15,17
15 . . . when they [Peter and John] were come down, prayed for them, that they might RECEIVE THE HOLY GHOST. . . .
17 Then laid they their hands on them, and they RECEIVED THE HOLY GHOST.

We know that because when Peter and John went down to Samaria, the Bible says, *"For as yet he [the Holy Spirit] was fallen upon none of them: only they were baptized in the name of the Lord Jesus"* (Acts 8:16).

Therefore, the believer receives a *measure* of the Holy Spirit in the work of the new birth, but receives the *fullness* of the Holy Spirit in the baptism of the Holy Spirit. (For a more complete study of the dual working of the Holy Spirit in the life of the believer, *see* Rev. Hagin's study course, *The Holy Spirit and His Gifts*.)

Therefore, we can see that the new birth and the baptism of the Holy Spirit are two separate experiences. Having explained that, let me repeat that when Paul wrote the Book of Romans, he was writing a letter to a body of believers that had not only been born again, but that had received the baptism in the Holy Ghost.

The promise of the Holy Spirit's help in prayer in Romans 8:26 can only be fully realized in a believer's life *after* he is baptized in the Holy Spirit with the evidence of speaking in tongues.

The Holy Spirit Is Our Helper in Prayer

Paul was saying to the Church at Rome and to us as well, that *". . . the [Holy] Spirit also helpeth our infirmities: for we know not what we should pray for as we ought . . ."* (Rom. 8:26).

How many times have we proved that to be true in our own lives! How many times have we said about a certain situation, "I don't know how to pray about it. I don't know for what to pray as I ought." It may be concerning ourselves, our children, or concerning others.

It is certainly true that if a person had certain needs, he would know how to pray for them and he

could believe God to hear that prayer according to the Word. The Word says that the things which we need are provided for us.

For example, healing for our physical bodies is provided for us, for it is written, *". . . Himself took our infirmities, and bare our sicknesses"* (Matt. 8:17). But there are other things for which we do not know how to pray as we ought. It's that way with all of us. So what are we going to do?

Thank God, we have the Holy Spirit to help us! I am glad we are not left alone. How desperate we would be if we were left alone, just on our own. I don't know about you, but I feel so sorry for believers who don't know how to pray this way, with the help of the Holy Spirit.

I also feel sorry for believers, bless their hearts, who are born again and love the Lord, but the very thing that they need the most, very often is the thing of which they are most afraid. I'm talking about being filled with the Holy Spirit. You can talk to these believers about being filled with the Holy Ghost and speaking with other tongues, and they become frightened. Yet the infilling of the Holy Spirit is exactly what they need the most.

It is like the story that is told about the old farmer. He was driving his cart pulled by a mule along the road one moonlit night. The mule saw a shock of hay close to the road, and becoming frightened, wanted to run away. The farmer jerked the old mule using the reins and finally got him stopped. The farmer said to the mule, "Why, you poor ole mule! The thing you are afraid of is the thing you need the most."

So often that's like some Christians! Since I have been filled with the Spirit and have prayed much with other tongues, I know the great value that this Pentecostal experience has been in my own life. I know what a blessing the Holy Spirit has been in my life personally. I know what a blessing He has been in the lives of our family members and also in the lives of others.

God knows the future better than we know the past because God knows everything. And the Bible says He will show us things to come (John 16:13). And sometimes with the help of the Holy Spirit, I have been able to pray people out of horrible situations, even death. I have been able to pray and change a number of situations because the Holy Spirit who lives inside me has shown me things to come, so that I could pray about those things, and the people have been delivered.

The Bible says that in certain areas of life "*. . . we know not what we should pray for as we ought: but the Spirit itself* [Himself] *maketh intercession for us . . .*" (Rom. 8:26). How does He do that? The rest of that verse says, "*. . . with groanings which cannot be uttered.*"

The *King James* translation is not as explicit as it could be. The late Dr. P.C. Nelson, a Greek scholar, said the Greek actually reads this way, "*. . . with groanings that cannot be uttered in articulate speech*" (Rom. 8:26). That means groanings which cannot be uttered in your regular kind of speech — your native language.

Therefore, Romans 8:26 would include praying in tongues, as well as in groanings because praying in tongues is certainly inarticulate speech, isn't it?

1 CORINTHIANS 14:14
14 For if I pray in an unknown tongue, my spirit prayeth, but my understanding is unfruitful.

1 CORINTHIANS 14:14 (*Amplified*)
14 For if I pray in an [unknown] tongue, my spirit [by the Holy Spirit within me] prays. . . .

When I pray in unknown tongues, the Holy Spirit is inside of me, helping me to pray. I have said this before, but it needs repeating. The Holy Spirit is not going to do our praying for us. If He is, then He is the One who is going to be responsible for our prayer life. But the Holy Spirit is not responsible for our prayer life.

Each one of us is responsible for his own prayer life. The Holy Spirit inside of us is there to *help* us; that is, to help *us* pray. He is not going to do it Himself; He is only called alongside to *help*.

People have said to me, "Brother Hagin, when I first got filled with the Holy Spirit, I used to pray in tongues quite often. It seemed like I had a real 'ministry' of intercession. But now it seems that it has departed from me. Pray that the Lord will give it back to me."

I always say, "No, the Lord hasn't taken anything away from you. The reason the Holy Spirit has stopped helping you is that you have quit praying.

"You see, the Holy Spirit wasn't doing the praying to begin with. *You* were. And He helped you do it. And when you quit, He quit. There wasn't anything for the Helper to help you do."

The Holy Spirit Takes Hold Together With Us in Prayer

There is a very enlightening thought in Romans 8:26 that blessed me greatly spiritually. Perhaps it will bless you too. Romans 8:26 says, "*. . . the Spirit also HELPETH our infirmities. . . .*"

I was reading a book by a professor of Greek who taught at a theological seminary. He gave the meaning of the words translated from the Greek here, and it revealed a shade of meaning that is not obvious in English. (I am not a Greek scholar; I use study tools to help me study the Bible.)

This professor of Greek gave a long Greek word for "helpeth" which came from three different root words. He said "helpeth" literally means *to take hold together with against.*

Therefore, this professor said this phrase in Romans 8:26 would literally read like this: The Holy Spirit helps take hold together with us in prayer against our infirmities — whatever the infirmity may be — whether the infirmity is a lack of knowledge, a weakness, a need, or any situation we are facing in life.

By way of illustration, if I were to say to a group of men, "I want you to help me move a piano out of the church and help me move another one in," I think you would understand what I wanted them to do. I would want them to help me by taking hold together with me against the weight of that piano in order to move it.

In the same way, the Holy Spirit helps us in our infirmities. That is, He takes hold together with us against our infirmities for any situation we might be facing. An infirmity can be any weakness we might have, including ignorance about *how* to pray about a situation.

Many times the Holy Spirit can't do anything for us because *we* don't take hold together with *Him* or stand with Him against anything — our infirmities or our problems. When we don't take hold in prayer with Him, then He can't help us, because He is our *Helper.* He is not our *doer. We* are the *doer; He* is the *Helper.*

Jesus did not say, "I will pray to the Father, and He will send you another *doer*" (John 14:16). No, Jesus said the Father would send us another Comforter or *Helper.* The Holy Spirit is going to help *you* be the doer. He is going to help *you* pray.

In First Corinthians 14:14, Paul is talking to the Church at Corinth about praying.

1 CORINTHIANS 14:14
14 For if I pray in an unknown tongue, my spirit [by the Holy Spirit within me] **prayeth, but my understanding is unfruitful.**

It is necessary to keep reminding you of the spiritual blessing, benefit, and help that praying in other tongues brings. But in praying in other tongues, your natural mind is unfruitful. In other words, the natural mind can't enter into praying in tongues because the things of God are spiritually discerned (1 Cor. 2:14).

Your natural mind can't understand what you are saying to God when you pray in tongues. In fact, your natural mind will even try to hold you back from praying in other tongues. Praying in other tongues will seem like foolishness to your natural mind.

And the natural mind can't understand those groanings that come out of your spirit either, because that is done by the Holy Spirit within you, who is helping you pray. Those groanings come up from within your spirit and escape from your lips.

Sometimes when you get into the Presence of God, all you can do is groan. Has that ever happened to you? That is the Holy Spirit helping you to pray.

There are groanings prompted by the Holy Spirit which cannot be spoken or uttered in articulate speech — your native language. Also, words that cannot be spoken in articulate speech can include praying in tongues too.

I have found from experience that in praying with the help of the Holy Spirit, I will often have a combination of the two — groanings and other tongues. The greatest things that have ever happened to me — the greatest miracles I have seen in my ministry, the greatest revelations that have ever come to me from the pages of God's Word — have come during those times of waiting on God with groanings and praying in other tongues.

I believe we need to have more "prayer schools." We have a prayer school here at RHEMA Bible Training Center, where we don't just *teach* on the subject of prayer, but we actually spend time praying.

It is one thing for us to hear the Word of God taught and nod our heads as if to say, "Yes, that is all true." But it is another thing entirely to be a doer of the Word and to act upon what we've heard.

Praying in the Spirit

Many times we get busy in the affairs of life, and our natural minds instead of our spirits take over and dominate us. This will keep us out of that place of really praying in the Spirit.

EPHESIANS 6:18
18 Praying always with all prayer and supplication IN THE SPIRIT....

Notice the phrase, "*. . . in the Spirit. . . .*" Christians are doing a lot of praying sometimes, but not too much of it is in the Spirit. Many people are just going through motions of prayer.

What does it mean to pray *in the Spirit*? As I said earlier, praying in the Spirit is prayer that comes out of one's *spirit* rather than out of one's *mind*. It is prayer inspired and directed by the Holy Spirit, whether in a known or an unknown tongue.

We know that tongues can and should be used in prayer.

1 CORINTHIANS 14:2
2 For he that speaketh in an UNKNOWN TONGUE speaketh not unto men, but unto God: for no man understandeth him; howbeit IN THE SPIRIT he SPEAKETH MYSTERIES.

Prophecy can be used in prayer too. Prophecy is an inspired utterance in a *known* tongue; tongues is an inspired utterance in an *unknown* tongue. Both prophecy and tongues are inspirational gifts of the Spirit.

Prophecy is speaking supernaturally out of your spirit as the Holy Spirit gives utterance in a known tongue. Divers, or diverse kinds of tongues is speaking out of your spirit by the Holy Spirit in an unknown tongue — unknown to you, that is.

Prophecy is equivalent to tongues and interpretation of tongues. Tongues and interpretation of tongues is prophecy in its varied manifestation. Both prophecy and interpretation of tongues are inspired utterances.

Interpretation of tongues is speaking out of your spirit by the Holy Spirit the meaning of what was spoken in tongues. Prophecy is really tongues and interpretation in its varied form.

Paul said, "*. . . greater is he that prophesieth than he that speaketh with tongues, except he interpret, that the church may receive edifying*" (1 Cor. 14:5). This infers that if a person speaks in tongues and interprets, he is on the same level as he who prophesies. If words mean anything, that is what Paul was saying.

Interpreting Our Praying in Tongues

First Corinthians chapter 14 tells us something believers are to pray for. Believers are to pray to be able to interpret their own private prayers in tongues. Interpreting our tongues will greatly enhance our effectiveness in prayer.

1 CORINTHIANS 14:13
13 Wherefore let him that speaketh in an unknown tongue PRAY THAT HE MAY INTERPRET.

Paul is not talking here about interpreting messages in tongues in public. That is a different operation of this gift altogether. Paul is talking about the believer interpreting his own prayer that he prays in other tongues so he will know what he prayed. That way the believer will be more effective in prayer.

This is an area that even folks who have been filled with the Spirit for many years have missed. They can lose many valuable truths God would desire to show them because He promised believers He would show us things to come (John 16:13).

We are told in the Word that when we pray in tongues, we are to pray that we might also interpret. Have you ever done that? If you haven't experienced this, you are missing out on a valuable benefit God desires you to have through the Holy Spirit.

Praying Psalms, Hymns, and Spiritual Songs

Let's look in Ephesians chapter 5 to see something else Paul said about prayer.

EPHESIANS 5:18-20
18 And be not drunk with wine, wherein is excess; but be filled with the Spirit;
19 SPEAKING TO YOURSELVES in psalms and hymns and spiritual songs, singing and making melody IN YOUR HEART TO THE LORD;
20 Giving thanks always for all things unto God and the Father in the name of our Lord Jesus Christ.

Praying, singing, worshipping, praising, and thanking God all go together. All of these elements should make up our individual prayer life.

Earlier in this same chapter of Ephesians, Paul said, *"Neither filthiness, nor foolish talking, nor jesting, which are not convenient: but rather GIVING OF THANKS"* (Eph. 5:4).

If our prayer life and our fellowship with God through prayer is as it should be, we should be full of thanksgiving.

I don't like to hear Christians speak words that are contrary to the Word of God. When believers speak negative words, it is a dead giveaway that they are not fellowshipping with God as they ought to be. Some of the language they use gives them away or locates them.

For example, instead of saying something that will bless others, many believers murmur and complain about their circumstances. The ability to keep a right attitude no matter what the circumstance, comes from fellowshipping with God. The Bible says believers are not to speak words that don't line up with the Word, *". . . but rather giving of thanks"* (Eph. 5:4).

And then Paul said, *"And be not drunk with wine, wherein is excess; but be filled with the Spirit; Speaking to yourselves in PSALMS and HYMNS and SPIRITUAL SONGS, singing and making melody in your heart to the Lord"* (Eph. 5:18,19).

As we discussed in a previous lesson, these verses are talking about an aspect of praying in the Spirit in psalms, hymns, and spiritual songs, for you are speaking or singing as you are inspired by the Holy Spirit. This is something you do in your own private, individual devotions because the Bible says, *"Speaking to YOURSELVES . . ."* (Eph. 5:19).

I find it the greatest comfort sometimes to speak to myself in psalms. I have found that in the midst of trouble, tests, or trials that speaking to myself in psalms is one of the greatest spiritual benefits, helps, and encouragements in the Christian walk.

Then as you stay filled with the Spirit and speak to yourself in psalms, hymns, and spiritual songs in your own private prayer life, you'll have something to bless others with when you come to church to worship with other believers. This is what Paul is talking about in the Book of Colossians when he mentions this kind of prayer once more.

COLOSSIANS 3:16
16 Let the word of Christ dwell in you richly in all wisdom; TEACHING AND ADMONISHING ONE ANOTHER in psalms and hymns and spiritual songs, singing with grace in your hearts to the Lord.

Psalms are spiritual poems or odes which may or may not rhyme and which are given by the inspiration and unction of the Holy Spirit. They are given to the believer to comfort and encourage him.

I usually just speak out the psalms I receive from the Holy Spirit. I don't sing them because I am not given to music. But a song is in my heart. Others who are more musically inclined might sing out their psalms. Sometimes I go to sleep talking to myself in psalms. And sometimes I wake up in the morning speaking out psalms.

Hymns and spiritual songs are songs that are also given by the inspiration of the Spirit of God. They are not just songs sung from a hymn book.

Some of the songs we sing out of songbooks might be Spirit inspired and some of them might not be. In fact, I believe most of them are not. Most of those songs are embalmed with unbelief. There is some truth to some of them, but have you ever just stopped and listened to some of the words of those songs!

Ephesians 5:18 and Colossians 3:16 are talking about the Spirit-filled believer praying and worshipping God in the Spirit, both in his own private devotions and with other believers. The believer needs to continually sing and make melody in his heart as he worships God. That is a vital part of a successful prayer life. One reason why many Christians seem to be spiritually "dead" is that they haven't been singing and worshipping God in their hearts.

So much of the time, (even Spirit-filled Christians) all we do is drop down on our knees and petition God like the old fellow who said, "Lord, my name is Jimmie; I'll take all You'll gimme."

I didn't say that to be funny. I said that to illustrate something. We may not pray in exactly those words, but all we do in prayer is say, "Gimme, gimme, gimme." Most Christians think that is all there is to praying.

But I want to tell you that when it comes to a successful prayer life, God doesn't want us to pray, "Gimme, gimme, gimme." He wants us to worship Him. And through worship and sweet fellowship and communion with Him, thank God, He can and will fill our spirits to overflowing. And He will help, bless, and encourage us.

ACTS 13:2
2 As they [certain prophets and teachers] **MINISTERED TO THE LORD, and fasted, the Holy Ghost said. . . .**

Notice it was *as* they ministered to the Lord that the Holy Spirit spoke to them. Let's go back to Ephesians 5:19 again: *"Speaking to yourselves in psalms and hymns and spiritual songs, singing and MAKING MELODY IN YOUR HEART TO THE LORD."*

You are not making melody to yourself or to one another. You are making melody to the *Lord.* Making melody to the Lord is ministering to the Lord. That is the kind of atmosphere in which the Holy Ghost can say something: *"AS they ministered to the Lord, and fasted, THE HOLY GHOST SAID . . ."* (Acts 13:2).

As these prophets and teachers ministered to the Lord, they received divine direction and illumination. Divine confirmation came to them as they ministered to the Lord.

In Ephesians 5:19 Paul says, *"Speaking to YOURSELVES in psalms and hymns and spiritual songs. . . ."* These psalms and hymns and spiritual songs are a part of our personal prayer life. They are to be a part of our devotional life, and a part of our communion with our Heavenly Father.

Speaking to yourself in psalms, hymns, and spiritual songs is something you can do when you are by yourself. But you can also do this privately to yourself even in the presence of others. You need not be loud about it or bother anyone else.

I speak to myself and to the Lord in psalms and hymns many times when I am running errands. I speak that way to myself sometimes in the barber shop. I speak often to myself in psalms and hymns and spiritual songs, singing and making melody in my heart to the Lord.

Acts 13:2 says, *"As they ministered to the Lord, and fasted, the Holy Ghost said, Separate me Barnabas and Saul for the work whereunto I have called them."* Barnabas and Saul received divine direction from the Holy Spirit *as* they ministered to the Lord.

If you want to hear the Holy Spirit speak, you have to put yourself in the place spiritually where He speaks. You are in a position to hear the Holy Spirit speak when you are ministering to the Lord in praise and worship — in psalms, hymns, and spiritual songs.

Thank God for this glorious privilege of praying in the Spirit in other tongues! Aren't you glad you learned about this supernatural means of edifying yourself and ministering to the Lord? Aren't you glad you don't have to struggle in prayer as you perhaps did in days gone by?

You have a means whereby you can interpret the prayers you pray in tongues. God has provided a divine means of communicating with His people. How few Christians take advantage of all that is rightfully theirs in Christ!

You have a Helper, the Holy Ghost within you. As you yield to Him, He will take hold together with you against your infirmities as you pray. And the Holy Spirit will also give you supernatural utterance in psalms, hymns, and spiritual songs as you minister unto the Lord.

Questions for Study

1. Name two principles and guidelines Jesus taught about prayer in Matthew 18:19 and Mark 11:24.

   _____

   _____

2. Why didn't Jesus mention praying in the Spirit when He taught on prayer?

   _____

   _____

3. Explain the difference between the _indwelling_ Presence and the _infilling_ of the Holy Spirit.

   _____

   _____

4. When can the promise of the Holy Spirit's help in prayer be fully realized in a believer's life?

   _____

   _____

5. In Romans 8:26, what is the literal meaning of "helpeth?"

   _____

   _____

6. Why does your natural mind try to hold you back from praying in other tongues?

   _____

   _____

7. What does it mean to pray _in the Spirit_?

   _____

   _____

8. What is the gift of prophecy equivalent to?

   _____

   _____

9. What elements should make up our individual prayer life?

   _____

   _____

10. What is "making melody to the Lord"?

    _____

    _____

Chapter 20

What Paul Said About Prayer — Part 2

In this chapter, we will continue our discussion about what Paul said about prayer. We discussed in the last chapter that the Holy Spirit helps us in prayer. One of the most important ways He helps us is by giving us utterance as we pray in tongues.

The Lord has given to the Church this divine, supernatural means of communication with Himself — that is, praying in other tongues. I fear we do not value it as highly as we ought, nor take advantage of praying in the Spirit as we ought.

ROMANS 8:26
26 Likewise the Spirit also helpeth our infirmities: for we know not what we should pray for as we ought: but the Spirit itself [Himself] maketh intercession for us with groanings which cannot be uttered.

The literal Greek says the Spirit makes intercession with "groanings which cannot be uttered in articulate speech."

1 CORINTHIANS 14:2
2 For he that speaketh in AN UNKNOWN TONGUE speaketh not unto men, but unto God: for no man understandeth him; howbeit IN THE SPIRIT he speaketh mysteries.

Moffatt's translation of First Corinthians 14:2 says he who speaks in an unknown tongue "is talking of divine secrets in the Spirit."

Let me see what else Paul had to say about praying in tongues.

1 CORINTHIANS 14:14
14 For if I pray in an UNKNOWN TONGUE, my spirit prayeth, but my understanding is unfruitful.

1 CORINTHIANS 14:14 (Amplified)
14 For if I pray in an [unknown] tongue, my spirit [by the Holy Spirit within me] prays, but my mind is unproductive — bears no fruit and helps nobody.

Paul was saying in this verse that when the believer prays in tongues, it is his *spirit* praying, not his *understanding* or *mind.* He said, "My spirit by the Holy Spirit within me prays, but my mind is unproductive." Praying in tongues is a *spiritual* exercise, not a mental exercise.

EPHESIANS 6:18
18 Praying always with all prayer and supplication IN THE SPIRIT, and watching thereunto with all perseverance and supplication for all saints.

Pray in the Spirit

Notice in Ephesians 6:18 that Paul didn't say a word to the Church at Ephesus about praying in tongues, but he did say something to them about praying *in the Spirit.*

But Paul told the Church at Corinth that praying in tongues was praying with the Spirit. He said, "*. . . he that speaketh in an UNKNOWN TONGUE speaketh not unto men, but unto God: for no man understandeth him; howbeit IN THE SPIRIT he speaketh mysteries*" (1 Cor. 14:2).

Do you suppose that Paul meant the same thing in Ephesians 6:18 and First Corinthians 14:2 when he said, "in the Spirit"? I believe he did.

Paul is encouraging the Church at Ephesus to follow the practice of praying and worshipping God in the Spirit, and that includes praying in tongues.

Notice something else about Ephesians 6:18. Paul is telling us how to pray for the saints. He said, *"Praying always with all prayer and supplication in the Spirit, and watching thereunto with all PERSEVERANCE and SUPPLICATION for all saints"* (Eph. 6:18). I have always followed this scripture in prayer.

We know we are to pray for one another. However, if we see a brother or sister who is going through a trial, we usually pray, "God bless Brother So-and-so," or "God bless Sister So-and-so." But too many times this kind of praying falls far short of getting the job done. Yet there is a way that we can effectively pray for folks, and that is in the Spirit, whether in tongues or in our known language. The Spirit of God knows how to pray for anyone. And He is in us as believers to help us pray (Rom. 8:26,27).

An Example of Praying in the Spirit

I read something once that is a good example of biblical experiences believers can have when they begin to pray in the Spirit. I was reading some articles which had been published years ago in a Pentecostal magazine. The articles were written earlier about events that had happened at the turn of the century, in about 1909. The articles were reprinted in the 1940s.

One article told of a minister who had helped build a church, but had since gone on to be with the Lord. This minister started out as a young man, really just as a boy, reaching out to others. He wasn't exactly a preacher, but he wanted to do something for God. In this Pentecostal magazine, this young preacher, who was then only nineteen, told some amazing experiences in connection with the move of the Spirit of God in those meetings.

Some folks were going to hold a revival in a certain place in Missouri. This young man attended the meetings just to pray as an altar worker. He was only a nineteen-year-old boy at the time.

There was a man in this town in Missouri who was from an old-time Holiness denomination. He wasn't Pentecostal, but he had been praying for revival in that town. So when these Pentecostal folks came to town, he put them up in his hotel free of charge, and he fed them. The Pentecostals put up a tent and started the meeting.

He said, "In those days the only communication we had was in the Spirit." And he went on to explain his statement with a testimony.

They did not have mass communication as we do today. (Sometimes I think maybe we would be better off if that were the way it was today.)

Anyway, several hundred people were saved in this meeting, and about two hundred were baptized with the Holy Ghost. So a church was started with the new converts.

After the church was built, the people decided they wanted this nineteen-year-old boy to pastor this church. Really, he was the only preacher of the bunch anyway. He had not only preached, but he had helped oversee the building of the church. They had built the church by faith.

When they would run out of lumber or nails, they would stop work on the church and pray. And God would send the materials to them! When they got the church built, it was all paid for.

About a year or two after this young man began to pastor this church, he became desperately ill. In those days Pentecostals trusted God completely for their healing and many did not go to doctors for treatment.

This pastor became so ill, the people in the congregation gave up on him because they thought he was going to die. To save themselves the trouble of an inquest, they called a doctor. The doctor came and examined this pastor, and confirmed that he was going to die.

The doctor said, "Yes, he is going to die. He won't be alive three days from now. You should have called me earlier if you wanted me to do anything. I can't do anything now."

They replied, "Well, we thought it was too late for you to help him. But we just wanted you to confirm the fact that he is sick. Then when he dies, you can indicate on the records how he died."

This pastor had been in a semi-conscious state. But about three days later he suddenly came to; he regained consciousness. (Some of the church folks had been with him praying all this time.)

When this pastor opened his eyes, he saw a man standing by his bedside. "Brother," the man said, "I have never met you before. I pastor a church down in Arkansas. But I was praying in my church, and the Lord told me to come up here and anoint you with oil, and you would be raised up."

So the pastor from Arkansas anointed him with oil, and instantly the young boy pastor was raised up, completely healed. This young pastor had never met this other man before, and the man didn't know him either.

But, you see, in those days, the only immediate communication people had was in the Spirit. The Holy Spirit communicated this young pastor's condition to this other pastor. God had given this pastor from Arkansas this young pastor's name and told him exactly where he lived in Missouri. The Arkansas pastor obeyed the Lord's instruction to go and anoint the young man with oil. He had enough money to take a train to Missouri, but he didn't have enough money to buy a round-trip ticket to get back home.

After the sick man got healed, he said to the pastor from Arkansas, "Please preach a few days here in my church for me." So they started a meeting that night in the church and took up an offering to send the pastor back home to Arkansas.

The point this superintendent was making was that the only communication they had in those days was in the Spirit. That pastor in Arkansas didn't even know this young pastor in Missouri. The pastor from Arkansas had heard from the Lord about this young pastor while he was praying. The Lord even told him exactly where the young pastor was. This is an example of the miraculous results of praying in the Spirit.

I think we miss much nowadays because of the modern means of communication that we enjoy. It's easier sometimes to utilize our own resources than to get in the Spirit and allow God to use us and make us a blessing to someone. But the Bible says, *"Praying always with all prayer and supplication IN THE SPIRIT, and watching thereunto with all perseverance and supplication for all saints"* (Eph. 6:18).

We're going to have to be *in the Spirit* in order to pray for the saints.

The Peace of God: A Result of
Prayer and Obeying the Word

Now let's see what Paul said about prayer in writing to the Church at Philippi. And we know that what applied to the Church concerning prayer then, whether it be the Church at Rome, Corinth, Ephesus, or Philippi, applies to the Church today as well.

PHILIPPIANS 4:6-8
6 Be careful for nothing; but in every thing by prayer and supplication with thanksgiving let your requests be made known unto God.
7 And the peace of God, which passeth all understanding, shall keep your hearts and minds through Christ Jesus.
8 Finally, brethren, whatsoever things are true, whatsoever things are honest, whatsoever things are just, whatsoever things are pure, whatsoever things are lovely, whatsoever things are of good report; if there be any virtue, and if there be any praise, think on these things.

Many people would like to have the peace of God that Paul is talking about in verse 7.

PHILIPPIANS 4:7 (*Amplified*)
7 And God's peace [be yours, that tranquil state of a soul assured of its salvation through Christ, and so fearing nothing from God and content with its earthly lot of whatever sort that is, that peace] which transcends all understanding, shall garrison and mount guard over your hearts and minds in Christ Jesus.

I like that last part: ". . . that peace which transcends all understanding, shall garrison and mount guard over your hearts and minds in Christ Jesus." The *King James* translation says, *"And the peace of God, which passeth all understanding, shall keep your hearts and minds through Christ Jesus."*

Notice the phrase in verse 7, "your hearts and minds." That means God can keep both your spirit and your soul in peace. Your heart is your spirit and your mind is your soul. This peace of God that keeps or guards our hearts and minds is a result of obeying verse 6: *"Be careful for nothing; but in every thing by prayer and supplication with thanksgiving let your requests be made known unto God."*

Therefore, the peace of God in our lives is the result of a successful prayer life and obeying the Word.

We get telephone calls at our ministry all the time from people who need help. We want to help folks, and we do pray with them. The Word of God tells us to pray one for another. We pray with them

and help many of them. And we receive mail from people with prayer requests.

This is well and good. We pray over those requests and we hear testimonies all the time about results people receive. But, actually, many times I think people go about trying to get help the wrong way. Human nature, or the flesh, would rather not do what the Bible says to do. From the natural standpoint, human nature has never really changed throughout the history of mankind.

For instance, in the Old Testament, a group of people decided to build a tower in order to get to heaven (Gen. 11:1-9). They wanted to get to heaven some other way than the way God had said.

And although we are saved, or born again, and even filled with the Spirit, in our natural minds sometimes we still try to get the blessings of God in some other way than the way God has told us in His Word.

Philippians 4:6 tells us how to have what verse 7 promises — the peace of God that passes all understanding. If you follow the instructions that verse 6 gives, you will enjoy the reality of verse 7. You can't just jump over verse 6 and ignore it and then pray that God will give you what verse 7 promises — that your soul and your spirit will be garrisoned by the very peace of God. Yet people request all the time, "Pray for me that I'll have peace."

But in the final analysis, I can't pray for you that you'll have peace unless you take that necessary step in Philippians 4:6 that ensures the peace of God. It would be like approaching three or four steps that lead to a door of a building. You could stand on the ground and ask me and everyone else to pray that you would get into the building. But until you take those steps — until you walk up those steps yourself — you are not going to get into that building!

In the same way, you could pray and ask us to pray that you will have this peace that passes understanding. But God has told you what steps to take in order to get it.

The Bible said, *"Be careful for nothing; but in every thing by PRAYER and SUPPLICATION with THANKSGIVING let your requests be made known unto God"* (Phil. 4:6).

Verse 7 begins with the word "and." It says, *"And the peace of God, which passeth all understanding, shall keep your hearts and minds through Christ Jesus."*

The word "and" is a conjunction; it is a connecting word. It links verses 6 and 7 together. In other words, if you do what verse 6 says to do, you will receive the benefit of verse 7: *"AND the peace of God, which passeth all understanding, shall keep your hearts and minds through Christ Jesus.*"

Notice this peace is beyond all natural understanding. The peace of God is a result of heart faith, it's a result of what you believe in your heart apart from your circumstances or apart from what your mind may be trying to tell you. You've probably experienced the peace of God and you probably know immediately if it leaves you. You know immediately when you *don't* have the peace of God which passes all understanding. It leaves you when you begin to worry and fret and have anxiety about something.

Believers do get into places where we lose the peace of God. Why do we? Because Christians can have the peace of God and then lose it if they fail to continue practicing Philippians 4:6. Even in the midst of tests and trials Christians can enjoy this peace of God that passes all understanding.

People out in the world, and even other believers sometimes, will look at us in amazement because they can't understand the peace we have in the midst of turmoil. They can't understand why some of us seem to enjoy more peace than others, even in the midst of tests and trials. They can't understand it because the Bible says this peace "*. . . passeth all understanding . . .*" (Phil. 4:7).

I have listened to some Christians, even Spirit-filled Christians, talk about their tests and trials, and I felt so sorry for them because they didn't know how to pray and have the peace of God in their lives. But this peace of God which passes all understanding will keep the believer's heart and mind through Christ Jesus if he will only obey the Word!

Paul's Instructions To Obtain God's Peace

Exactly what are the instructions that Paul gives in the preceding verse to be able to have this peace? First, he said, *"Be careful for nothing . . ."* (Phil. 4:6).

We don't talk that way in modern language. The *Amplified* translation says it a little more clearly. It says, "Do not fret . . ." (Phil. 4:6).

That is the reason many Christians don't have the peace of God in their lives. They are always fretting. But it says, "Do not fret or have any anxiety about *anything*. . . ." Fretting and anxiety seem to go hand in hand, don't they?

Refuse To Worry

So the first step to take to obtain God's peace is to refuse to fret or be anxious about anything. That is the number one reason why people don't have this peace which passes all understanding: they are fretful and full of anxieties. The Bible says, "Do not fret or have any anxiety about anything . . ." (Phil. 4:6 *Amp.*).

I have preached on those verses of Scripture to people and they have looked at me in astonishment. I am not talking about folks who didn't know the Word; I am talking about born-again, Spirit-filled people who should have known and *practiced* the Word better than they did. They would look at me and their eyes would get big, and they would say, "Well, if I'm not supposed to fret, what am I going to do then?"

If some folks can't worry about a situation or circumstance, they don't know what else to do about it. That leaves them almost frantic. One woman once said to me (bless her heart), "Why, I can't give up good ole worry." She thought she couldn't give it up. She had been practicing the habit of worrying too long, and she had been full of anxiety so long, she couldn't imagine life without it!

"I can't give that up," she said. However, I believe that we can do what God's Word says we can do. God's Word says, "Do not fret or have any anxiety about anything . . ." (Phil. 4:6 *Amp.*). Do you believe you can do that?

1 PETER 5:7
7   Casting all your care upon him; for he careth for you.

How do we cast our cares upon the Lord? I don't know how we could do it except through praying the prayer of commitment. The word "prayer" is not mentioned here, but I don't know any other way to be a doer of First Peter 5:7 than to do it through the prayer of commitment. We discussed this at length in another chapter.

What are you going to do about the anxieties and the things you are fretting about? You are going to have to do something about them. Why not *cast* them. Cast them where? Cast them upon the Lord: *"Casting all your care upon him; for he careth for you."* Hallelujah! "Be careful for nothing," or "in nothing be anxious." In other words, don't fret or have any anxiety about anything. What *are* you going to do then?

PHILIPPIANS 4:6
6   Be careful for nothing; but in EVERY THING by prayer and supplication with thanksgiving let your requests be made known unto God.

Does this verse say to let your requests be known to God in the little things? Yes, even in the little things. What about the big things? Yes, even in the big things. In the sort of middle-sized things? Yes, in *everything* we are to pray and make our requests known to God.

I have heard some people say, "Well, I wouldn't bother God with little cares and anxieties. I can handle them myself." Haven't you heard people say that? But God doesn't want you to fret or be anxious about *anything*, big or small. The Bible says, *". . . but in EVERY THING by prayer and supplication . . ."* (Phil. 4:6).

Then there are other folks who will take the little cares of life to the Lord in prayer, but without saying it, they seem to leave the impression that some cares are too big for Him to handle and they won't cast those big cares upon the Lord. But, thank God, He is interested in everything that concerns us because He is our Father. *"Casting all your care upon him; for HE CARETH FOR YOU"* (1 Peter 5:7).

Why in the world would we want to go on fretting and worrying and being full of anxiety about the circumstances of life when we can do something about our anxieties and worries?

I have seen this motto written: "Why pray when you can worry?" I know whoever wrote this was trying to be funny, but I sometimes think that is actually the motto of some Christians in life! But that should not be. The Lord is saying, "Pray and don't worry." The Christian's motto *should* be, "Why worry when you can pray?"

PHILIPPIANS 4:6
6 . . . but in every thing by prayer and supplication with thanksgiving let your requests be made known unto God.

Also, did you notice Paul said, ". . . *with thanksgiving let your requests be made known unto God"*?

Paul really said several things here. First, he said, "Don't worry." I don't care what the situation or circumstance, don't worry about it. Don't be full of anxiety about it; and don't be fretting about it.

Second, Paul said, "In everything pray and let your requests be made known to God." "Everything" includes *everything* — every problem, situation, circumstance, anxiety, care, or concern. *Nothing* is excluded. Pray about the situation but don't worry about it.

Third, he said, "Pray with thanksgiving." Some people don't pray with thanksgiving. Their prayers aren't closed with thanksgiving. They are more likely closed with a moan or a groan or a sigh which all indicate doubt and unbelief. But Paul said to pray with thanksgiving about the outcome of their prayers! That's praying in faith!

Thanksgiving is to be offered unto God before your answer has ever materialized. Paul said we are to pray *"with* thanksgiving." When you pray *with* thanksgiving, you are thanking God ahead of time because you *know* that He has heard you *and* answered you. You know He's heard you because His Word says so (Mark 11:24). This is something we have missed and have overlooked in receiving answers to prayers.

I believe that if people would stop asking God for the same thing over and over, and would begin to praise and thank Him for the answer, they would receive the answers to their prayers.

For example, in our discussion of the prayer of praise and worship, I mentioned the story of the young minister who was holding a meeting at a certain church and went with the pastor's wife to pray for a baby who was having convulsions. The young preacher said he did everything he had seen others do, such as anointing the baby with oil and rebuking the devil, but nothing worked.

It was only as they began to quietly praise and thank God from their hearts that the baby was completely healed. The healing came while they were praising and thanking God.

We need to be constantly reminded of some of these prayer secrets.

You remember we talked about Paul and Silas in earlier lessons (Acts 16:25,26). Paul and Silas had been put in jail. This incident in jail may be what Paul was referring to in Philippians 4:6 where he wrote, ". . . *IN EVERY THING by prayer and supplication with thanksgiving let your requests be made known unto God."* Paul wrote this letter to the Church at Philippi while he was in prison.

Paul and Silas were in jail and their feet were in stocks. Their backs were bleeding because they had been beaten. But the Bible says, ". . . *at midnight Paul and Silas prayed . . ."* (Acts 16:25). That scripture doesn't stop there though. That would be the story of some people, but not these disciples. It says that Paul and Silas prayed ". . . *AND sang praises unto God . . ."* (Acts 16:25).

You see, it was *after* they prayed that they sang praises to God. It goes on to say, ". . . *and the prisoners heard them."* God heard them too! You know the story. God wrought great deliverance for Paul and Silas as they praised Him.

Then writing to the church at Philippi, Paul wrote, ". . . *with THANKSGIVING let your requests be made known unto God"* (Phil. 4:6). Then it says, *"And the peace of God, which passeth all understanding, shall keep your hearts and minds through Christ Jesus"* (Phil. 4:7).

If you will do what verse 6 says to do — pray with thanksgiving — then verse 7 will be a reality in your life. I really don't know of any other way to get this peace, except to follow the instructions God has given us in His Word. *Then* the peace of God which passes understanding, or natural human reasoning, shall keep your heart and mind through Christ Jesus.

A minister once came to me who had had some things happen in his life which had robbed him of his peace. He was greatly disturbed and couldn't sleep at night. He couldn't eat and keep his food down. He came to me because he believed I could help him. I think he wanted me to pray all of his troubles away. He was being sued by someone over an automobile accident, and he didn't know just what the outcome would be. He knew it could ruin him if he lost the case.

I am sure he had not slept for at least three days when he came to me. He looked haggard and worn out. I got my *Amplified* translation and read Philippians 4:6 and 7 to him. The best way I could help even though he was a preacher, was to tell him what the Bible says. That made him mad.

He said, "Oh, everybody doesn't have as much faith as you. I can't do that."

I said, "Why, yes, you can. You have come to me for help, and I am just telling you what I do when I'm faced with tests and trials. I have been in troublesome situations before, too, and this is what I do. I just follow the instructions!

"I refuse to worry about it, but in everything by prayer and supplication, with thanksgiving, I let my requests be made known unto God. And I always receive the very thing you are seeking — the peace of God which passes all understanding."

He simmered down a bit and then said, "Just how do you do it?"

I said, "Do you have an *Amplified Bible*? In the *Amplified* translation the meaning is clearer. I just get on my knees with my Bible opened to this scripture, and I say, 'Now, Lord, this is Your Word. And You say that you can't lie. The Psalmist said, *"For ever, O Lord, thy word is settled in heaven"* [Ps. 119:89]. So I refuse to worry and be fretful about this. I bring this to You, Lord. This is a care and an anxiety. Peter said, *"Casting the whole of your care — all your anxieties, all your worries, all your concerns, once and for all — on Him . . ."* [1 Peter 5:7]. So I'm casting my care upon You.' "

I then referred this minister to First Peter 5:7. You would think that preachers would know this verse is in the Bible, wouldn't you? Then I went on to say to him, "So when I'm faced with difficult circumstances, I pray to the Lord, 'Lord, I cast this care over on You. Now I am going to sleep. And tomorrow I am going to eat, too, because I have the peace that passes all understanding.' Then I get into bed and go to sleep."

This minister then asked, "Well, are you ever troubled?"

I answered, "Yes, sometimes I have to go back a time or two in prayer and repeat this to the Lord for my own benefit. Then my mind begins to grow quiet because I give place to the Word instead of to worry. When I give place to the Word my spirit begins to dominate me. This peace will come as you walk in genuine faith, doing what the Bible says to do because God said this peace would guard or garrison both your mind and your spirit."

There have been times when I have cast all of my cares upon the Lord, and after falling off to sleep, for some reason or another I was awakened. The minute I was awakened, the devil brought to my mind again the critical situation I was facing at the time.

Do you know what I did when that happened? (This is a part of receiving the peace beyond all understanding.) I just started laughing right out loud. Right in the nighttime I would just burst out laughing. *That* is beyond our understanding or natural human reasoning, but the Lord always took care of the situation.

How in the world could a person laugh right in the midst of trouble? Yet when you have this peace, you can laugh right in the face of trouble — even death. After I was healed and raised off a deathbed, there was a time when death came and tried to fasten itself upon my body. I started laughing.

The devil said to me, "What are you laughing at?"

I said, "Well, you said I was going to die, but I'm not. I'm going to live. I'm not going to die. I'm going to live."

If you try to tell most people they can laugh in the midst of trouble because of the peace of God that's within, they can't understand it. (If you have been to the place where you stood your ground when your faith was severely tried and challenged, you *can* understand it. But if you haven't, it would probably be hard for you to understand it.)

Think on the Right Things

We talked about Philippians 4:6 and 7. God tells us in these verses how to pray — with *thanksgiving,* which includes having the joy of the Lord — and how to have the peace that passes understanding when we pray. But verse 8 goes right along with what we've been talking about concerning prayer.

After we pray and cast our cares upon the Lord, and this peace of God guards our hearts and minds, there is still something else we must do. If we aren't careful, our minds will try to slip back into thinking negative thoughts. The devil, through our minds, will endeavor to defeat us. So in verse 8, Paul sums up his instructions concerning prayer.

PHILIPPIANS 4:8
8 Finally, brethren, whatsoever things are TRUE, whatsoever things are HONEST, whatsoever things are JUST, whatsoever things are PURE, whatsoever things are LOVELY, whatsoever things are OF GOOD REPORT; if there be any virtue, and if there be any praise, THINK ON THESE THINGS.

Many times folks will say about a negative thought "Yes, but it's true!" Well, many things are true which are not pure or lovely.

You see, once you get to this place where you have this peace that passes all understanding, if you want to keep it, you are going to have to think on the right things. In other words, God's peace is not going to be able to guard your mind unless you think right. Isn't that what the Bible is saying?

ISAIAH 26:3
3 Thou wilt keep him in perfect peace, whose mind is stayed on thee: because he trusteth in thee.

Many people need to change their way of thinking in order to be successful in their Christian walk. Yet it scares some people if you teach about the mind. I have taught along these lines in some of our churches, and I have even had the pastor say, "Brother Hagin, that is a little like Christian Science, isn't it?"

As one medical doctor said, "No, that's not Christian Science; that's Christian *sense!*"

I noticed that the pastor who said this to me was always talking about the negative side of everything. He had a dark outlook on life. He saw something bad in all his fellow ministers and in everyone else. Everything was bad. He surely wasn't thinking about the right things. Some of it might have been true, all right, but it wasn't just, pure, lovely, or of a good report.

Sometimes we miss it in this world by looking at world conditions. Things look bad, it's true. The situations and circumstances we face in life are real. We all face trials of life and experience the unpleasant conditions that are in the world. All of these things are true, all right; but they are not necessarily just, and they are not pure or lovely. Yet some people let some of these things worry them to death, so to speak. But the Bible says, "*. . . if there be any VIRTUE, and if there be any PRAISE, think on these things*" (Phil. 4:8).

You see, right in the midst of trouble, instead of being overcome, thank God, we should overcome! We should be *victors*. Instead of being downcast, we should be *happy*. Instead of being discouraged, we should be *encouraged*. Can you see what I am talking about?

You can pray for people and help them temporarily. You can bring them into contact with God and His power. But as long as they don't change their thinking, they will get right back where they were and be defeated.

I have seen a number of people who were helped in some of my meetings. Yet in the process of time they got right back into some of the same problems they were in before because of their habit of thinking the wrong thoughts.

For example, I would pray for some folks and I knew they were healed. Others testified that they were healed. All the pain left their bodies and all the symptoms were gone. They even testified in my meeting for several days afterwards about their healing.

And yet I knew all the time in my heart that their sicknesses would come back on them. Why? Because the whine never left their voices. I knew they would go back to whining and complaining through life and that negativity would allow the devil to take advantage of them and bring that same condition back on them — or some other kind of sickness or disease.

In these chapters, we are looking at the different principles of prayer found in Paul's epistles to the churches. We've seen how important praying in tongues is when we're praying for things which we don't know how to pray for. And we've discussed how we are to refuse to worry about anything, but we are to allow the peace of God to rule in our hearts and minds.

As we study these different scriptures, we are learning what the Word of God says about prayer. If we will only put these principles of prayer into practice in our own private prayer lives, we will be able to rise above our circumstances and walk in victory in life!

Questions for Study

1. Complete this sentence: Praying in tongues is a _____ exercise, not a _____ exercise.

2. In Philippians 4:7, the phrase "your hearts and minds" refers to your _____ and your _____

3. The peace of God in our lives is the result of what?

   _____

   _____

4. The peace of God is the result of what kind of faith?

   _____

   _____

5. When does the peace of God leave you?

   _____

   _____

6. In Philippians 4:6, what three instructions did Paul give to be able to have God's peace?

   _____

   _____

7. How do we cast our cares upon the Lord?

   _____

   _____

8. When you pray _with_ thanksgiving, what are you really doing?

   _____

   _____

9. Once you get to the place where you have this peace of God that passes all understanding, what must you do to keep it?

   _____

   _____

10. In order to be successful in their Christian walk, what do many people need to do?

    _____

    _____

Chapter 21

What Paul Said About Prayer — Part 3

We are still discussing what Paul said about prayer. In this chapter we'll see that we are to give thanks in every situation in life. And we'll discuss how we can change nations through prayer as we pray for those in authority. Finally, we'll look at how we can sanctify our food by the Word and by prayer.

In Everything Give Thanks

Let's notice something Paul said about prayer, writing to the Church at Thessalonica.

1 THESSALONIANS 5:16-18
16 Rejoice evermore.
17 Pray without ceasing.
18 In every thing give thanks: for this is the will of God in Christ Jesus concerning you.

Notice verse 17: *"Pray without ceasing."* Some people seem to have the idea that what Paul is saying to us is that we should just pray all the time. But other translations of that verse say, "Never give up in prayer," or "Be unceasing in prayer." In other words, don't give up your prayer life. Maintain a prayer life. It doesn't mean pray with every breath you take. You can't pray with every breath. You know that as well as I do.

This exhortation to never give up in prayer is sandwiched in right between the command to "rejoice" in First Thessalonians and "give thanks" in verse 18. That's a good sandwich, isn't it? What did Paul say? He said, *"Rejoice evermore"* (1 Thess. 5:16).

How many of us are full of rejoicing? Then he said, *"Pray without ceasing"* (1 Thess. 5:17). Then Paul said, *"In every thing give thanks: for this is the will of God in Christ Jesus concerning you"* (1 Thess. 5:18).

Someone said, "Well, I can't thank God in everything." God said you can. In fact, He said this is His will for you in Christ Jesus. People want to be in the will of God, don't they?

You *can* thank God when you get the right perspective on this verse. This does not mean that we are to thank God *for* every test and every trial. But we are to thank God *in* the midst of every test and trial. For every test, I always find scriptures to stand on. I have done that for many years.

I have done it in the face of adversity and financial lack. I have gone down the road many, many times, having closed the last meeting I had on my agenda. I didn't know where my next meeting would be or where the money I needed was coming from. But I knew God's Word. And that was enough for me.

I had a wife and two children. Actually, at one time in our lives our little niece was living with us, so we had three children. Including my wife and I, we had five mouths to feed and five of us to clothe.

On one particular occasion, I had preached my last service. I had the last offering in my pocket, and it wasn't enough to pay my rent when I returned home, and I was already behind in paying it. I didn't have enough money to buy the necessary food to put on the table for my family. This happened more than once. I didn't have enough money, and I didn't have another place to preach; I didn't have another meeting scheduled.

When I first started out in the ministry — for about the first two years — I found myself in that position quite often. I would start my drive home after my meeting closed down and drive at night because the tires on my car were bald. Driving in the daytime might have caused the tires to burst because of the heat.

I didn't even have a spare tire. I drove all over Texas and parts of Oklahoma and Louisiana without a spare. I didn't do that because I wanted to. I just didn't have enough money to buy a spare! So I had to just trust God.

But, you see, I didn't drive without a spare to tempt God. I was just learning faith principles, and my faith was not developed to the level that I could buy a spare. God always gave me grace as I trusted Him.

I would start home from my meetings many times, and the devil would say, "What are you going to do now? What are you going to do now? What are you going to do now?" I didn't have an air conditioner, so I had the car windows rolled down.

You could hear those bald tires just singing; and it seemed as though one of the tires picked up on that: "What are you going to do now? What are you going to do now?"

Then the other tire picked it up, singing, "What are you going to do now?"

And then the other tire picked it up, singing, "What are you going to do now?"

It wasn't long before I had a quartet singing, "What are you going to do now? What are you going to do now?" That question just seemed to get louder and louder as I drove down the highway.

But, thank God, when you have the Word, and when you walk in the light of the Word, you have *victory* over those negative thoughts!

I said, "Mr. Devil, do you want to know what I am going to do? I'll tell you what I am going to do. I'm going to act just like the Word of God is so. I am going to act like the Bible is true. That is what I'm going to do."

I said, "Mr. Devil, God said, 'Rejoice evermore' [1 Thess. 5:16]. Thank God for the offering I did get. It was just $42, but thank God for it. Hallelujah! Thank God for the $42. I would be in a mess without it. I needed $102, but thank God for the $42. Glory to God! I am thanking God for it. I am rejoicing. I am giving thanks. And I'll tell you something else, Mr. Devil, I am thanking God in the midst of this test.

"You see, Mr. Devil," I continued, "this is just a good time to prove that God and His Word are true. This is an opportunity for me to believe God, and I am thanking Him in advance for my answer!

"And since you asked the question, I am going to answer it. You asked me what I'm going to do. I'll tell you exactly what I'm going to do! I am going to go home and go to bed and sleep like a baby. That's what I'm going to do." I said that, and I laughed right in the devil's face.

You can go through life like that, friends — laughing, rejoicing, and giving thanks regardless of circumstances, just trusting in the Word. Some unspiritual folks, even Spirit-filled people, will say, "My, my, my, that poor old boy doesn't have enough sense to worry." Thank God, the real truth about it is that I have too much sense to worry — that is, too much *Bible* sense!

On one occasion when I was on the road ministering, I got home about two or three o'clock in the morning. My wife said, "Well, how did you come out?" I knew what she was asking. She was concerned about our finances. She was staying home and paying the bills and she wanted to know if we had enough money to pay the rent.

I said, "Oh, everything is fine. We don't have a thing in the world to worry about. I'll tell you about it in the morning. Let's go to bed."

While I was still sleeping the next morning, she got up and got the kids off to school. The telephone rang, and it awakened me. I heard my wife say, "Well, he got in late, and he's sleeping."

I sat up and said, "Oh, that's all right; I'm awake. Who is it?"

She said, "It's a long-distance call from So-and-so."

I took the phone, and a man said, "Hey, Doc, when can you start a meeting for us?"

I answered, "Tomorrow night."

He said, "Oh, I couldn't start that fast. How about Sunday?"

I said, "Fine. I'll be there." And the man gave me directions to his church because I didn't even know him, but I knew of him and knew he was a good man.

I went to that pastor's church and we had a six-week meeting. Glory to God! And we had quite a meeting! But if I had griped and complained all the way home from my previous meetings, I'm not sure it would have worked out that way.

You see, it is as we praise and thank God in the midst of difficult circumstances, and as we stand our ground against Satan that God can move on our behalf. That's how victory comes.

Praying for Those in Authority

In writing to Timothy, Paul had some further instructions concerning prayer.

1 TIMOTHY 2:1,2
1 I exhort therefore, that, first of all, supplications, prayers, intercessions, and giving of thanks, be made for all men;
2 For kings, and for all that are in authority; that we may lead a quiet and peaceable life in all godliness and honesty.

Timothy at this time was the pastor of a New Testament local church. Paul is writing a letter to him. I like something that Paul said here. He said, *"I exhort therefore, that, FIRST OF ALL . . ."* (1 Tim. 2:1).

Also, in First Thessalonians 5:25 Paul said, *"Brethren, pray for us."* He invited the Church at Thessalonica to pray for him. It is scriptural to pray one for another.

Too often we put ourselves first in our praying, and sometimes that is as far as we ever get in prayer. In other words, most of the time we are just praying selfishly for ourselves or about our own personal lives and needs.

But Paul said, *". . . FIRST OF ALL, supplications, prayers, intercessions, and giving of thanks,* [should] *be made for all men"* (1 Tim. 2:1). Then lest we not understand exactly what he is talking about, Paul explained in verse 2 who "all men" pertained to: *"For kings, and for all that are in authority. . . ."*

In that day kings ruled over nations. That's why Paul said to pray for kings and for all who are in authority. In our day, instead of saying "kings," we would simply say "for the heads of the government and for all who are in authority."

Why did Paul want Christians to pray for kings and all who were in authority? Because whatever happens in the nation in which we live is going to affect all of us. Paul told us why we are to pray for our leaders: "... *that we may lead a quiet and peaceable life in all godliness and honesty*" (1 Tim. 2:2).

You see, God is concerned about us. And He will change things in our nation because we ask Him. Whether our leaders in government are Christians or not, God will still do more on our behalf and do some things in the government for our sake. You notice that the word, "intercessions" is mentioned here.

As I said in an earlier lesson, intercession means to stand in the gap on behalf of another (Ezek. 22:30). For example, we saw that when God planned to destroy the cities of Sodom and Gomorrah because of the great wickedness of the people, God came down and talked with His covenant friend, Abraham, first. Abraham made intercession for God to spare Sodom for the sake of a few righteous.

GENESIS 18:23-32
23 And Abraham drew near, and said, Wilt thou also destroy the righteous with the wicked?
24 Peradventure there be fifty righteous within the city: wilt thou also destroy and not spare the place for the fifty righteous that are therein?
25 That be far from thee to do after this manner, to slay the righteous with the wicked: and that the righteous should be as the wicked, that be far from thee: Shall not the Judge of all the earth do right?
26 And the Lord said, If I find in Sodom fifty righteous within the city, then I will spare all the place for their sakes.
27 And Abraham answered and said, Behold now, I have taken upon me to speak unto the Lord, which am but dust and ashes:
28 Peradventure there shall lack five of the fifty righteous: wilt thou destroy all the city for lack of five? And he said, If I find there forty and five, I will not destroy it.
29 And he spake unto him yet again, and said, Peradventure there shall be forty found there. And he said, I will not do it for forty's sake.
30 And he said unto him, Oh let not the Lord be angry, and I will speak: Peradventure there shall thirty be found there. And he said, I will not do it, if I find thirty there.
31 And he said, Behold now, I have taken upon me to speak unto the Lord: Peradventure there shall be twenty found there. And he said, I will not destroy it for twenty's sake.
32 And he said, Oh let not the Lord be angry, and I will speak yet but this once: Peradventure ten shall be found there. And he said, I will not destroy it for ten's sake.

Abraham said to the Lord, "... *Wilt thou also destroy the righteous with the wicked?*" (Gen. 18:23). And Abraham asked the Lord to spare Sodom and Gomorrah for the sake of fifty, then forty-five, then forty, then thirty, then twenty righteous people. Finally, Abraham said, "... *Peradventure ten shall be found there ...*" (Gen. 18:32).

And God responded to Abraham, "... *I will not destroy it for ten's sake*" (Gen. 18:32). God was willing to withhold His judgment for the sake of ten righteous people, just because Abraham asked him.

There are more than ten righteous people in your country. So pray boldly for kings and the heads of your government and for all who are in authority, knowing that your prayers can effect changes in this world to the glory of God.

I know we've heard a great deal about God's judgment and wrath, but there is another side of the story. God will move in our nations if we ask Him to, if we pray for the people who lead and govern those nations.

Changing a Nation Through Prayer

I was greatly moved some years ago to have two seminars in the summer on the subject of prayer. I was strongly impressed to do some praying for our nation, particularly about some things the Lord had shown me concerning the government and world events some years before.

Many times prophecies are conditional. In the case of world events, for example, prophecies of God's judgment don't always have to come; they can be averted if the people involved will repent. You can see that illustrated in the Bible in Isaiah chapter 38, for example.

God had sent the prophet Isaiah to King Hezekiah to tell him, "... *Set thine house in order: for thou shalt die, and not live*" (Isa. 38:1). But as it is recorded, Hezekiah didn't die.

Certainly, Isaiah was speaking under the unction and anointing of the Spirit of God, and what he said was certainly true under the present circumstances. But Hezekiah changed the present circumstances by repenting. Hezekiah humbled himself and that stayed the judgment of God. He turned his face to the wall, wept, and repented.

When Hezekiah turned his face to the wall and prayed, the Lord said to Isaiah, "*Go, and say to Hezekiah, Thus saith the Lord, the God of David thy father, I have heard thy prayer, I have seen thy tears:*

behold, I will add unto thy days fifteen years"
(Isa. 38:5).

I don't know whether you know it or not, but in much the same way as Hezekiah prayed, some Christians have been able to change some things through prayer. The Christians who are able to change things in prayer are those who know how to pray and who know how to pray in the Holy Ghost. We have been able to change some things in our own nations.

And I believe Christians are going to change some things yet, all over the world as they pray for their nations. And it will happen as a result of doing what these verses in First Timothy 2:1 and 2 says.

1 TIMOTHY 2:1,2
1   I exhort therefore, that, FIRST OF ALL, supplications, prayers, intercessions, and giving of thanks, be made for all men;
2   For kings, and for all that are in authority; that we may lead a quiet and peaceable life in all godliness and honesty.

Lifting Up Holy Hands

In First Timothy chapter 2 Paul says something else about prayer.

1 TIMOTHY 2:8
8   I will therefore that men pray every where, lifting up holy hands, without wrath and doubting.

I believe that men everywhere ought to pray. But there are more explicit instructions that Paul gives here. He said, ". . . *lifting up holy hands, without wrath and doubting.*"

Most of us as Christians should know that we are to pray without doubting. Jesus Himself told us to pray without doubting.

MARK 11:23,24
23   . . . verily I say unto you, That whosoever shall say unto this mountain, Be thou removed, and be thou cast into the sea; AND SHALL NOT DOUBT in his heart, but shall believe that those things which he saith shall come to pass; he shall have whatsoever he saith.
24   Therefore I say unto you, What things soever ye desire, when ye pray, believe that ye receive them, and ye shall have them.

So we encourage people to follow the instructions in First Timothy 2:8 — to pray without doubting. But Paul also said to pray, lifting up holy hands without wrath. Many who came from denominational church backgrounds may find it hard to lift their hands.

It's been a long time ago, but I remember when I first began to fellowship with folks who lifted their hands to pray and praise God. To lift my hands and pray was the hardest thing in the world I had ever done in my life.

Someone asked, "Well, do you *have* to lift your hands to pray?" No, you don't have to. But on the other hand, if Paul said not to doubt, and we obey *that* part of the scripture, then we ought to obey the rest of it too. And he also said to lift up holy hands.

Follow New Testament Instructions

I don't know about you, but I like to do things the New Testament style. If I find instructions in the New Testament, I like to obey God's Word and just do what it says. But if it is not in the New Testament, I am a little wary of it.

Paul said, ". . . *lifting up holy hands, without wrath and doubting"* (1 Tim. 2:8). That is a New Testament instruction. I like to have people lift their hands when they pray, and I ask people to do that in my services. I don't think anyone would object to following instructions that are given in the New Testament. If a person would object to New Testament instructions, something is not right in his spiritual walk.

For instance, years ago in a meeting I once heard a man object to something Paul said in one of his epistles. (I really felt sorry for this man because everyone in the entire congregation of about a thousand people found out how ignorant this man was of the Scriptures.) This man said, "Don't tell me what Paul said; I'm not following Paul."

I thought, *Well, then, why doesn't he just tear all of those epistles out of the New Testament that Paul wrote?* But if Paul was writing under the inspiration of the Spirit of God, and he was, then we ought to follow what the *Holy Spirit* was saying *through* Paul.

There are times when Paul said that he made statements ". . . *after my judgment: and I think also that I have the Spirit of God"* (1 Cor. 7:40). But Paul wasn't saying that he was just speaking out of his natural mind; Paul implied he was speaking by the unction of the Holy Spirit.

So if Paul was speaking under the inspiration of the Spirit of God, then I am under obligation to listen to it. If the Holy Ghost inspired him to write these letters to the Church of the Lord Jesus Christ, then they apply to the Church of the Lord Jesus Christ today too.

The reason this man said, "I'm not following Paul" is that Paul said some things that condemned what he was doing. It is easy for a person to say, "Well, I'm just following Jesus," when writers of the Books of the Bible say things that he may not want to hear.

Jesus didn't deal with some things in His earthly ministry that Paul dealt with in the Scriptures. The reason Jesus didn't deal with some things that Paul dealt with was that Jesus wasn't ministering to the *Church*. He was teaching and ministering to the *Jews*.

The Church wasn't even in existence when Jesus was on the earth, although in principle, much of what Jesus said applies to the Church. But the Church *was* in existence when Paul wrote his epistles under the inspiration of the Spirit, and he was writing his epistles *to the Church*.

Rightly Dividing New Testament Scriptures

Even leading theologians often don't understand this distinction between Jesus' and Paul's teachings, and therefore they can interpret New Testament scriptures incorrectly.

For example, I was preaching at a meeting in California many years ago, and the president of one of our leading seminaries in the east came to California about that same time. He was a man of such prominence that his picture was on the front page of the local newspapers.

This man's visit was unexpected, but when the local newspapers of this particular city learned he was on this plane, they sent a reporter and a photographer out to the airport to greet him and to take his picture. So you know that he had to be a man of some prominence. The reporter inquired why he had come to that city. He said that it was a combination of a vacation and a business trip.

While he was in that city, this man spoke at one of the seminaries in Los Angeles, and again the newspapers sent a reporter to report on his address to the seminary students. The coverage of this event took nearly one whole page in the local papers.

As I read the article, I thought, "Now here is a man who is very learned. He is a very intellectual and educated man. But it looks as if anyone with any sense who had been brought up in Sunday school, would know more about the Bible than he does."

In the course of his lecture, this theologian said, "I'm going to revive an old argument. You know that an argument has raged in the Church for the past four hundred years in theological circles. The argument is, 'Who is right, Jesus or Paul?'"

He went on to say, "Some things that Jesus said contradict what Paul said (and he gave a few Bible references). And some things that Paul said contradict what Jesus said."

However, this theologian didn't straighten out anyone's thinking or help anyone that I could tell. He just made a lot of unsupported statements.

"Well," he concluded, "I'm more prone to follow Jesus. After all, He is the Son of God. So I'll just follow Him."

I thought to myself, *Jesus didn't contradict Paul, and Paul didn't contradict Jesus.* It's the simplest thing in the world to understand this issue. Paul himself gives us the key. He said, *"Study to shew thyself approved unto God, a workman that needeth not to be ashamed, rightly dividing the word of truth"* (2 Tim. 2:15).

The reason that some things Paul said seemed a little different than what Jesus said, and what Jesus said in some small areas seemed different than what Paul said, is that Jesus was primarily teaching the Jews. He wasn't even talking to the Church. The Church wasn't even in existence yet. Some of the things Jesus said to the Jews under the Old Covenant don't apply to the Church, and there is no use trying to apply some of His statements to the Church.

And what Paul said applied to the Church — to born-again people under the New Covenant — not to the Jews who were not redeemed and were living under the Old Covenant. When you *rightly divide* the Word (2 Tim. 2:15), it all makes sense and there are no contradictions at all in it. It was some time ago when this theologian made these statements, but recently I thought how ridiculous it is for a man, particularly a minister, to make unscriptural statements. It only confuses folks.

So we see that Paul gave us specific instruction about prayer. In this chapter, we have seen that Paul said that we are to give thanks in every situation in life. We are to pray for those in authority. He also said we are to lift up holy hands, and we are not to doubt when we pray.

Sanctifying Our Food By the Word and Prayer

Paul also said we are to sanctify our food. Paul was talking about prayer. Let's read the entire context and find out exactly what he was saying concerning sanctifying our food.

1 TIMOTHY 4:1-5
1   Now the Spirit speaketh expressly, that in the latter times SOME SHALL DEPART FROM THE FAITH, giving heed to seducing spirits, and doctrines of devils;
2   Speaking lies in hypocrisy; having their conscience seared with a hot iron;
3   Forbidding to marry, and commanding to abstain from meats, which God hath created to be received with thanksgiving of them which believe and know the truth.
4   For every creature of God is good, and nothing to be refused, if it be received with THANKSGIVING:
5   For it is SANCTIFIED BY THE WORD OF GOD AND PRAYER.

In verse 1, Paul was talking here about people who had been in the faith, but who had departed from the faith. He was not talking about sinners or heathen because he said, *"Now the Spirit speaketh expressly, that in the latter times SOME SHALL DEPART FROM THE FAITH, giving heed to seducing spirits, and doctrines of devils"* (1 Tim. 4:1).

Have you ever come across those who have given heed to seducing spirits and doctrines of devils? Those who teach doctrines of devils teach believers that they are not to marry and that they are to abstain from meats. Have you ever come into contact with those who say you shouldn't eat any meat? I guess we all have, haven't we? How in the world can they say that in the light of such scripture?

Lest people would misunderstand, Paul said, *". . . the Spirit speaketh EXPRESSLY . . ."* (1 Tim. 4:1). In other words, Paul was saying that this is what the Holy Spirit is saying to us. So Paul was again saying that he was speaking under the unction of the Holy Spirit. Some people say, "Oh, that was just Paul talking!" When they say that, they are implying that Paul's statement is not inspired by the Holy Spirit. That is not biblical because the Word says, *"All scripture is given by inspiration of God, and is profitable for doctrine, for reproof, for correction, for instruction in righteousness"* (2 Tim. 3:16). Really, it is the devil who promotes and inspires that kind of thinking. And he does it to lead people astray and get them off course spiritually.

Doctrines of Devils

Let me give you an example of someone who gave heed to "doctrines of devils" in the area of diet. I knew of a man who was a denominational minister. He had received the baptism of the Holy Ghost. I had sweet fellowship with him over the years. He was on fire for God. That fellow could get more people saved accidentally than most people could on purpose! That was his ministry — reaching the lost.

But this minister got off in this area of diet, and after that he spent all of his ministry trying to regulate people's diets. If he ever got anyone saved after that, I don't know it!

I believe the devil simply undermined that man's ministry of reaching the lost by getting him off course into this area of food and diet. He finally began spending all of his time telling people how to regulate their diets — what to eat and what not to eat — and he used the Old Testament to substantiate his new doctrine.

God had told the Jews in the Old Covenant that there were certain creatures they were to eat and certain ones they were not to eat. No one is going to find fault with that, but wait just a minute. In the New Testament it says, *"For every creature of God is good, and nothing to be refused, if it be received with thanksgiving"* (1 Tim. 4:4).

In First Timothy 4:3, Paul told us what seducing spirits and doctrines of devils would teach: *"Forbidding to marry, and commanding to abstain from meats, which God hath created to be received with thanksgiving of them which believe and know the truth."* Praise God, I'm glad I know and believe the truth.

You see, if the devil can get people off doctrinally in all these side issues, he can keep the Body of Christ from preaching the gospel! That is the Great Commission that was given to the Church. Mark 16:15 says, *". . . Go ye into all the world, and preach the gospel to every creature."* The Word does not say, "Go ye and preach rules of diet to every creature"!

People have said to me, "Brother Hagin, do you eat pork?" I tell them, "Of course. I sanctify it by the Word and prayer." That is what Paul said here. When we receive our food with thanksgiving, it is sanctified by the Word of God and prayer.

I sanctify my food by the Word and prayer, bless God! Just sanctify the food you eat, and it won't hurt you. That is what Paul was saying. Someone said, "Well, I can't." Well, if you ever come to "believe and know the truth of God's Word," you can sanctify your food with the Word of God and prayer (1 Tim. 4:3)!

Then what about these cults and even members of the church world who delve into these areas of food and diet? We should be careful of getting off into a ditch in any area, including this area of diet.

Let's just continue to heed the Scriptures. *"For every creature of God is good, and nothing to be refused, if it be received with thanksgiving"* (1 Tim. 4:4). That is plain enough. The Bible says, *". . . nothing to be refused, if it be received with thanksgiving."*

Receiving the food you eat with thanksgiving makes a difference, as well as sanctifying it with the Word and prayer.

You can regulate your diet according to what you want or need, but just be sure you receive the food you eat with thanksgiving so that it will be sanctified by prayer. Then it won't hurt you. Nothing I eat ever hurts me. The reason the food I eat never hurts me is that I obey the Word; I'm a doer of the Word.

I'm not saying that we shouldn't be concerned about eating what is healthy for our bodies. Of course we should use wisdom in every area of our lives. I'm just saying to sanctify our food with the Word, prayer, and giving of thanks. I sanctify it with the Word and prayer. I receive it with thanksgiving.

This passage in First Timothy chapter 4 is specifically talking about meats, which the Bible says, *". . . God hath created to be received with thanksgiving of them which believe and know the truth"* (v. 3).

However, this principle applies to all the food we eat. We should sanctify all of our food, not only the meat, but all of our food. I don't mean this unkindly, but I believe that Christians should come to know the truth regarding this subject. And we will find the truth in God's Word, for God's Word *is* truth.

Many times people have told me, "Well, I can't eat this, and I can't eat that. That hurts me when I eat it."

I don't say anything to them, but I just wonder why they don't sanctify their food. If they'll sanctify it by the Word and prayer, the foods that bothered them before won't hurt them.

Why don't we just believe God and obey His Word regarding this subject of sanctifying our food? I always believe God's Word when it comes to food, or about anything else for that matter.

I learned the secret of sanctifying my food as a young boy on the bed of sickness. I didn't even know about divine healing when I learned this. I was dying on the bed of sickness, and there were things that the doctor said I should eat that were good for me. I had to be on a soft diet because I was bedfast. He said that he wanted me to drink milk. I tell you, I would just about have to hold my nose in order to drink one glass of milk.

So I prayed to the Lord, "All right, Lord, You just help me here. I am going to sanctify this." I drank milk there on that bed of sickness, and I have drunk milk ever since. These days, people have come up with the idea that adults shouldn't drink milk. Well, I can, praise the Lord, for I sanctify it through the Word and prayer.

There were other things the doctor said to eat that were good for me. I found this scripture back then as a boy, and I started sanctifying my food. When I did, no food bothered me to eat. From that day to this nothing I've eaten has hurt me or bothered me.

I would encourage you to begin sanctifying your food by the Word of God and prayer. And whatever food you eat, receive it with thanksgiving because you know and believe the truth!

In these last few lessons, we've discussed several principles of prayer that Paul taught in his epistles. In this chapter, we've discussed how believers need to *"In every thing give thanks . . ."* (1 Thess. 5:18). And we've seen that the Holy Spirit through Paul admonishes believers to pray for those in authority, and to lift up holy hands without wrath or doubting. Finally, we've discussed the need for believers to sanctify their food by the Word and prayer.

We are New Testament believers. Let's determine to follow New Testament instructions regarding prayer and continue to grow up spiritually, fellowshipping with the Lord and bearing much fruit in prayer to His glory.

Questions for Study

1. What did Paul mean in First Thessalonians 5:17 when he said, *"Pray without ceasing"*?
   _____
   _____

2. What happens as we praise and thank God in the midst of difficult circumstances?
   _____
   _____

3. Who are we to put first in our prayers?
   _____
   _____

4. Why did Paul want Christians to pray for kings and all who were in authority?
   _____
   _____

5. What does the word "intercession" mean?
   _____
   _____

6. Which Christians are able to change things in prayer?
   _____
   _____

7. Why didn't Jesus deal with some things in His earthly ministry that Paul dealt with in the Scriptures?
   _____
   _____

8. List four specific instructions that Paul gave us about prayer.
   _____
   _____

9. What happens when we receive our food with thanksgiving?
   _____
   _____

10. What are the benefits when New Testament believers follow New Testament instructions regarding prayer?
   _____
   _____

Chapter 22

What Others Said About Prayer

IS ANY AMONG YOU AFFLICTED? let him pray. IS ANY MERRY? let him sing psalms.

IS ANY SICK AMONG YOU? let him call for the elders of the church; and let them pray over him, anointing him with oil in the name of the Lord:

And the prayer of faith shall save the sick, and the Lord shall raise him up; and if he have committed sins, they shall be forgiven him.

Confess your faults one to another, and pray one for another, that ye may be healed. The effectual fervent prayer of a righteous man availeth much.

Elias was a man subject to like passions as we are, and he prayed earnestly that it might not rain: and it rained not on the earth by the space of three years and six months.

And he prayed again, and the heaven gave rain, and the earth brought forth her fruit.

— James 5:13-18

What James Said About Prayer

Let's find out what others in the Bible said about prayer.

We'll begin this chapter discussing what James said about prayer. Notice that James asks three questions in this passage of Scripture: (1) "Is any afflicted?" (2) "Is any merry?" (3) "Is any sick?"

James was talking about three different things. For example, "afflicted" and "sick" are not the same. These two words as they are used here can't mean the same thing because James gave one instruction for the afflicted and another instruction for the sick.

Let the Afflicted *Pray*

The Greek word translated "afflicted" in James 5:13 isn't referring to illness. It isn't referring to what we call physical afflictions at all. "Afflicted" in this verse means *to suffer trouble*. In other words, this type of affliction spoken of in James 5:13 is a test or a trial.

James was saying that if you as a believer are being tested or tried by what we call the storms of life, you are to do your own praying. It says, *"Is any among you afflicted? let HIM pray . . ."* (James 5:13). However, not too many Christians do that. In the midst of a test or trial, most Christians usually try to find someone else to do their praying for them.

But notice James didn't say a word about getting someone else to pray for you if you are afflicted. Did you ever stop to think about that? James said, "Let *him* — the one who is afflicted — pray" (James 5:13). In other words, if *you* are afflicted, *you* are to pray.

I have always followed that rule. I believe in doing my own praying when I am in the midst of a trial. That's scriptural.

Actually, I discovered this on the bed of sickness, and I have never asked anyone else to pray for me in the midst of a trial or a difficulty or a storm since. I have done what the Bible says to do; I do my own praying. I don't mean that we are not to pray one for another, but God wants us to learn to do our own praying too.

When you learn to do your own praying, you will gain great victories. But if you have to depend on someone else to pray you out of a test or trial, then the next time you find yourself in difficult circumstances, you won't know the way out. You'll have to find someone to pray you out of that test or trial again. And if you can't find someone to pray for you, you might not make it through that affliction victoriously.

But God wants you to triumph in every situation and circumstance. The way you do that is through prayer: *"Is any among you afflicted? let him PRAY . . ."* (James 5:13).

Let Those Who Are Merry *Sing*

Then James asks, *". . . Is any merry? . . ."* (James 5:13). The rest of that verse says, *". . . let him sing psalms."* That's easy. We don't have to comment on that too much because that's clear enough. It's easy to sing when you are merry, isn't it? That is, if you have singing ability. But even those of us who can't sing can make some kind of joyful noise unto the Lord!

Let the Sick Call for the Church Elders

Finally James asks, *"Is any sick among you? let him call for the elders of the church; and let them pray over him, anointing him with oil in the name of the Lord"* (James 5:14).

I am not a Greek scholar. I use a concordance to do my studying. But P. C. Nelson, who founded the Southwestern Bible Institute, was a Greek scholar. And he brings out the fact that the Greek word translated "sick" here in James 5:14 means *sick*, yet it carries with it the thought that a person is so ill that he can't do anything for himself.

In other words, this verse does *not* mean that if a person has a headache he should send for the elders of the church to pray for him. There are some who want to send for the pastor or for someone else to come and pray for them for every little thing that happens to them or for every minor symptom that tries to come against them.

That is not what James 5:14 means when it says, "*. . . let him call for the elders of the church . . .*" (James 5:14). Interpreting this scripture incorrectly, many times a person with a minor ailment who needs prayer will want to run to the pastor for prayer. That isn't what these verses mean. A church congregation could actually wear the pastor out by not fully understanding and obeying this scripture.

Actually, "Let the elders pray" carries the thought that the person is so ill he's become helpless and can't motivate himself to use his own faith. James tells the sick one what to do when this is the case.

JAMES 5:14,15
14 . . . let him call for the elders of the church; and let them pray over him, anointing him with oil in the name of the Lord:
15 And the prayer of faith shall save the sick, and the Lord shall raise him up; and if he have committed sins, they shall be forgiven him.

Also, James isn't saying that everyone who is ill is suffering with sickness because he's committed sins. But he is saying the reason *some* people are sick is that they have sinned. So he said, "*. . . if he have committed sins . . .*" (James 5:15). He didn't say just one sin; he said *sins*. Then he said, "*. . . they* [those sins] *shall be forgiven him*" (James 5:15). Thank God, there is forgiveness and healing for the people of God.

Many have thought, *I have missed God, so I'll have to go on being sick. I'm going to have to pay for my sin.* Then they will go to church and sing, "Jesus Paid It All" while they continue to suffer with something Jesus paid the penalty for! But James 5:15 does not say, "If he has committed sins, he is going to have to go on being sick in order to pay for it." No, the Bible says, "*. . . they shall be FORGIVEN him*" (James 5:15).

JAMES 5:16
16 Confess your faults one to another, and pray one for another, that ye may be healed. . . .

We dare not take verse 16 out of its setting and context and put it somewhere else. Many people think verse 16 is referring to public confession of sins. But you don't go to church to have a confession meeting; that is unscriptural.

No, what James is talking about is this: If a sick person sends for the elders of the church to come and pray for him, if he has sinned, he will have to confess it to the Lord.

The sick person can't just obey the first part of this scripture — calling for the church elders. He must also obey the next part — confessing his sin to God. If a person has unconfessed sin in his life, he is not going to get healed just because the elders of the church anoint him with oil and pray for him.

So although James said in James 5:14 that if you are sick, you are to call for elders in order to receive prayer, he also said in verse 16, "*Confess your faults one to another, and pray one for another, that ye may be healed. . . .*" Actually, you are not going to get healed with unconfessed sin in your life — no matter *who* prays for you.

It would be good sometimes for us to examine our lives. And if we have any sin in our lives, we need to confess it to God. That doesn't mean we are to condemn ourselves. (There is a difference between examining yourself and condemning yourself.)

But the Bible says we *are* to cleanse ourselves of any sin that defiles us (2 Cor. 7:1). We do that through confession and repentance before God. The Bible says, "*If we confess our sins, he is faithful and just to forgive us our sins, and to cleanse us from all unrighteousness*" (1 John 1:9).

Something else to understand about this passage of Scripture is that the phrase "elders of the church" is referring to those in the church who are called to the fivefold ministry.

We must remember that when James wrote his epistle, the New Testament Church was a baby church. In other words, the Early Church was in its infancy. Disciples would go into a place where there was no church, win people to the Lord, and establish a work. They would pioneer churches.

But these new churches were in their infancy and didn't necessarily have ministry gifts functioning in the local body. Not having a pastor, they would appoint the oldest person in the congregation to be in charge. Or in some places, those who had matured more spiritually would be appointed because someone had to watch over and shepherd that local flock.

So in the infancy stage of the Early Church, "elders" were simply the most mature believers in the flock who were chosen to oversee the work that the apostles had begun: *". . . let him call for the ELDERS of the church . . ."* (James 5:14).

Then in the process of time, the church developed and grew. As believers matured, it became obvious as to whom God had set in the Church as ministry gifts. Those then became the true elders. God gave some *". . . apostles; and some, prophets; and some, evangelists; and some, pastors and teachers"* (Eph. 4:11).

Thus, in the process of time, there were those who knew that they were called and separated unto the fivefold ministry, and they became the true elders of the Church.

I never read in the Bible where Paul stayed less than six months at a given place where he made converts. In one place it says he stayed there three years (Gal. 1:18). You can understand that Paul stayed in those areas in order to establish a local church. When Paul would prepare to leave, as the Holy Ghost directed him, Paul would appoint elders to carry on the work and to look after the flock, the people of God.

In some places where Paul just stayed a short time, the members of a local body were all just baby Christians. That's why Paul appointed the oldest people to oversee the flock.

The Effectual Fervent Prayer of the Righteous

James concludes verse 16 by saying, *". . . The effectual fervent prayer of a righteous man availeth much"* (James 5:16). Then in verse 17 James gives an example of a righteous man. At first when I read those scriptures I didn't understand what James was saying. But it finally dawned on me what he is saying here.

James was saying that Elijah was a human being just as we are. In other words, Elijah didn't receive answers to his prayers because he was a prophet. James said, *"Elias [Elijah] was a MAN . . ."* (James 5:17).

JAMES 5:17,18
17 Elias was a man subject to like passions as we are, and he prayed earnestly that it might not rain: and it rained not on the earth by the space of three years and six months.
18 And he prayed again, and the heaven gave rain, and the earth brought forth her fruit.

Someone said, "Yes, but that was Elijah praying. He was a prophet. He was a great man of God. Certainly, *he* was righteous." But James said he was a *man*, "subject to like passions" just like we are. James *didn't* say, "Elijah was a *prophet* who prayed." He said, "Elijah was a *man* who prayed." God won't hear a prophet pray any more quickly than He will hear any other believer pray.

It's not the one praying who gets the job done anyway. The Bible says, *". . . The effectual fervent prayer of a righteous man availeth much"* (James 5:16). *The Amplified Bible* says, *". . . The earnest (heartfelt, continued) prayer of a righteous man makes tremendous power available — dynamic in its working"* (James 5:16). The effectual fervent *prayer* of a righteous man is what gets the job done.

Someone said, "Well, if I was righteous I could pray that way and get results." But if you are saved, you *are* the righteousness of God in Christ (2 Cor. 5:21). God *made* you righteous. You can't make yourself righteous. That was one of the most difficult aspects of the Bible for me to understand in studying the subjects of faith and healing.

I pastored nearly twelve years. During those twelve years, I saw people in my congregation who didn't live nearly as consecrated as others did, and yet, they could do twice as much praying and get twice as many answers as the others did. They would get the job done, so to speak.

But they weren't the ones who were getting the job done. It was the Lord who was getting the job done in response to their prayers and their faith. Some of these people could pray the prayer of faith for themselves and for their families more quickly than those who seemingly lived more holy lives.

"Lord, why is that?" I would ask. Of course, the Lord finally showed me through His Word that you do not get your prayers answered on the basis of how good you have been. You get answers to prayer based on faith in God's Word and on who you are in Christ. You are *made* righteous in Christ Jesus. Righteousness for the Christian is a present-tense reality today.

2 CORINTHIANS 5:21
21 For he hath made him to be sin for us, who knew no sin; that we might be made the righteousness of God in him.

One definition of "righteousness" is *rightstanding with God*. You see, Jesus became sin for us that we might become the righteousness of God in Him. Jesus is our righteousness. We have the same righteousness, or rightstanding with God, that Jesus has. And every single one of us who is born again has this rightstanding with God. We are invited to come boldly to the throne of grace by the blood of Jesus (Heb. 4:16).

So in James chapter 5 it says, "Elijah was a man." Although Elijah operated in the ministry of a prophet, he was just a human being like you and me. It says, *"Elias [Elijah] was a man subject to like passions AS WE ARE . . ."* (James 5:17). In other words, Elijah was subject to the same faults, the same shortcomings, the same mistakes, and the same failures as every other human being is subject to. Yet his prayer worked; and so will yours.

What Peter Said About Prayer

Let's look now at what Peter said about the subject of prayer.

1 PETER 3:7
7 Likewise, ye husbands, dwell with them according to knowledge, giving honour unto the wife, as unto the weaker vessel, and as being heirs together of the grace of life; THAT YOUR PRAYERS BE NOT HINDERED.

Of course, Peter is talking here about a husband and wife who are both saved because he said, *". . . being HEIRS together of the grace of life. . . ."* This verse applies to a married couple who are both born again. This verse is telling us that a husband or wife can hinder their own prayers.

Don't Allow Your Prayers To Be Hindered

I believe we all know that a saved husband and wife can either help or hinder one another spiritually. They can pull together or they can pull apart. So Peter gives husbands and wives some instructions.

He starts off in First Peter 3:1 by saying, *"Likewise, ye wives, be in subjection to your own husbands; that, if any obey not the word, they also may without the word be won by the conversation of the wives."*

The word, "conversation" here in this verse means *manner of life or conduct.* Peter suggests that one's godly conduct or behavior is a way of winning folks to the Lord without necessarily preaching. That is an amazing thought, isn't it?

1 PETER 3:2-7
2 While they behold your chaste conversation coupled with fear.
3 Whose adorning let it not be that outward adorning of plaiting the hair, and of wearing of gold, or of putting on of apparel;
4 But let it be the hidden man of the heart, in that which is not corruptible, even the ornament of a meek and quiet spirit, which is in the sight of God of great price.
5 For after this manner in the old time the holy women also, who trusted in God, adorned themselves, being in subjection unto their own husbands:
6 Even as Sara obeyed Abraham, calling him lord: whose daughters ye are, as long as ye do well, and are not afraid with any amazement.
7 Likewise, ye husbands, dwell with them according to knowledge, giving honour unto the wife, as unto the weaker vessel, and as being heirs together of the grace of life; THAT YOUR PRAYERS BE NOT HINDERED.

This passage of Scripture is talking about prayer. Prayer works. God has given us His Word to teach us how to pray and to teach us how to receive answers to our prayers. If our prayers are not working, we need to examine these areas about which the Scriptures instruct us.

Peter said something else in verse 12 of this same chapter: *"For the eyes of the Lord are over the righteous, and his ears are open unto their prayers: but the face of the Lord is against them that do evil"* (1 Peter 3:12). The eyes of the Lord are over the righteous. We are the righteous ones whom Peter is talking about here. We are in Christ, and He is righteous. As a Church, we are the Body of Christ; therefore, we are the righteousness of God in Christ (2 Cor. 5:21).

Do you think the Body of Christ is unrighteous? Certainly not. Since the Head of the Church, the Lord Jesus Christ, is righteous, then we — the Body — are righteous, too. If we are in Him, we are new creatures in Christ (2 Cor. 5:17). Do you think God made any unrighteous new creatures? Certainly not.

And the Bible says about the righteous, *". . . the eyes of the Lord are over the righteous, and his ears are open unto their prayers . . ."* (1 Peter 3:12). I'm glad God has eyes and ears, aren't you? He sees us, and He hears us.

But the rest of that scripture says, *". . . but the face of the Lord is against them that do evil"* (1 Peter 3:12). Thank God, God is not against us. We are God's children, and we are the righteousness of God in Christ (2 Cor. 5:21). His ears are open to our prayers.

But Peter is telling us in verse 7 that we can hinder our prayers. God doesn't hinder our prayers. He doesn't refuse to hear us. But we hinder our own prayers by not obeying the Scriptures. Let's see to it that we don't hinder our prayers so that we can confidently know that God's ears are open unto our prayers.

Be Diligent in Prayer

1 PETER 4:7
7 But the end of all things is at hand: be ye therefore sober, and watch unto prayer.

Peter wrote this epistle under the inspiration of the Spirit of God. Peter wrote this letter to believers, and it included some general instructions for believers living in that day and for us too. Then by the Spirit of God, Peter is seeing into the future and begins to talk about the day in which we live. He said, "... *the end of all things is at hand: be ye therefore sober, and watch unto prayer*" (1 Peter 4:7).

In the Book of Mark, Jesus made the statement, *"Take ye heed, watch and pray: for ye know not when the time is"* (Mark 13:33). Jesus was talking about the Last Days. We are to be diligent in prayer as we see the Last Days approaching.

What John Said About Prayer

Now let's look at the First Epistle of John. John gave us some important principles about prayer too. Many times we dwell on the things Jesus said about prayer and the things Paul said about prayer. But we may have missed some other good nuggets of truth in the Bible that would help us in our praying.

Asking According to God's Will

1 JOHN 5:14-16
14 And this is the confidence that we have in him, that, if we ASK any thing ACCORDING TO HIS WILL, he heareth us:
15 And if we know that he hear us, whatsoever we ASK, we know that we have the petitions that we desired of him.
16 If any man see his brother sin a sin which is not unto death, he shall ask, and he shall give him life for them that sin not unto death. There is a sin unto death: I do not say that he shall pray for it.

The word "pray" is not used in these verses, but the words "ask" and "petitions" are. *"And this is the confidence that we have in him . . ."* (1 John 5:14). What is this confidence that we have in Him? This is the confidence: *". . . that, if we ask any thing according to his will, he heareth us"* (1 John 5:14).

Remember this, if whatever you ask is according to God's *Word*, it is according to God's *will*. Some people think that verse says, "Well, you pray for it, and if it is God's will, He'll give it to you. And if it isn't, He won't." That isn't what John said.

John said, *". . . if we ASK any thing ACCORDING TO HIS WILL, he heareth us: And if we know that he hear us, whatsoever we ask, we know that we have the petitions that we desired of him"* (1 John 5:14,15). Remember, God's Word is His will.

JOHN 15:7
7 If ye abide in me, and my words abide in you, ye shall ask what ye will, and it shall be done unto you.

Notice how this scripture agrees with those verses in First John chapter 5.

1 JOHN 5:14,15
14 And this is the confidence that we have in him, that, if we ASK any thing according to his will, he heareth us:
15 And if we know that he hear us, WHATSOEVER WE ASK, we know that we have the petitions that we desired of him.

In other words, if we know God heard our petition, we know we have the petition we desired.

The Sin That Is Not Unto Death

First John 5:16 goes right along with verses 14 and 15.

1 JOHN 5:16
16 If any man see his brother sin a sin which is not unto death, he shall ASK, and he shall give him life for them that sin not unto death. . . .

Therefore, First John 5:14-16 are all talking about asking.

For example, if you ask God to forgive someone according to First John 5:16, then that request is according to God's *Word*. Therefore, it is also according to God's *will*. And God will answer that request.

First John 5:16 poses an area of prayer that we preachers have generally stayed away from in our teaching. That's because these scriptures in First John 5 didn't always fit our theology or our church teaching. But the truth is there in the Word just as plain as the nose on your face!

In 1944 I drove through my hometown on my way home from a meeting. I stopped by to see my mother, who said to me, "Go by and see your grandmother, for she hasn't been feeling well." My wife and I went by to see my grandmother, and to this day, I am sorry I didn't have a word of prayer with her right then.

Granny liked me to kiss her on her cheek, so I kissed her before I left. She called me her boy because I had lived with her when I was nine years old. My wife and I greeted her and then went on to begin another meeting. We were running behind schedule and we were in a hurry to get to our next meeting.

My relatives phoned me two or three nights later and said that Granny had just lapsed into a coma; she was unconscious there in her home. The doctor came, and he said she would never come out of it. I went down to see her after my evening service (it was only about 40 miles away). I would sit up with her from about eleven o'clock in the evening through the night. That would give other members of the family a chance to rest, and they could be with her in the daytime.

I would take my Bible and books along to study while I sat by her bedside because she was just lying there unconscious. Someone had to be there in case she died. About the third night I was sitting up with her, I prayed. I said, "Dear Lord, I'm so sorry I didn't pray with Granny the other day when I was here."

I knew she was a Christian and loved the Lord, but there are sins of omission as well as sins of commission. Granny wouldn't have told a lie for anything in the world. She wouldn't have stolen anything; she would rather have her head cut off than to steal anything. But I could see areas where she had missed it. (We can each see areas where other people miss it better sometimes than we can see where we have missed it ourselves.)

I said to the Lord, "Lord, I wish I had prayed with her. I just wish You would bring her out of this. In fact, I am going to ask You to bring her out of this. Just let her revive so I can have a word of prayer with her." (I knew she was elderly, and I knew in my spirit that she was going to go home to be with the Lord.)

I said, "Let me just make sure there isn't any unconfessed sin in her life."

When I prayed that way, I heard someone say, "Why don't you ask Me to forgive her?"

It was so real to me, and it so startled me, that I jumped out of the rocking chair where I had been sitting. My Bible was lying on my lap, and I had a book in my hand. That Bible and book went shooting across the floor. I must have jumped three feet off that chair! That Voice was so real to me that I thought someone was standing right behind me and had heard me praying. I didn't say it out loud; I only said it in a whisper.

When I jumped like that my Bible slid across the floor and under the bed. I had to reach under the bed to get it. I got the Bible and the book, and laid them down.

Then I said, "Who said that?"

It was so real to me, I thought someone was standing right behind that rocking chair. I thought someone had come into the room and had heard me praying and that he was just teasing me.

I looked around and didn't see anyone. I opened the door and looked outside Granny's room, but I didn't see anyone there either. I sat down again to read my book. I read and studied for a while, and, finally, I closed the book. It seemed as if I couldn't concentrate like I wanted to, so I began praying again.

I said, "Lord, why don't You just bring her out of this coma and let me have a word of prayer with her to see that she doesn't die with any unconfessed sin in her life."

Again that Voice said, "Why don't you ask Me to forgive her?" I jumped up again, and my book went sliding across the floor again.

I said, "There is someone in here playing tricks on me."

I got down again and looked under the bed to make sure no one was under the bed. I looked behind the dresser, and there wasn't anyone behind the dresser. I went into the living room and looked around. I turned the light on and looked behind the couch to be sure no one was there.

There was another open door in the corner, and I looked behind that door to make sure no one was there. The kitchen was near the bedroom, so I went into the kitchen. I looked under the table. I went out the door at the back of the house, and I listened. I knew no one else was in the house except Grandpa and Mama, and I could tell by the way they were breathing that they were both sound asleep. So I went back to the bedroom and said to myself, *Well, my imagination is playing tricks on me.*

I sat down and started studying my book again, looking up scriptures in my Bible. It seemed as if I just couldn't get away from what that Voice had said, so I shut my books again. I started praying the same prayer, and when I did, the third time the Voice said, "Why don't you ask Me to forgive her?"

This time I had presence of mind to remember that when Samuel was a boy and was staying with Eli, Eli had told him to answer when God called. You see, Samuel had thought Eli was calling him (1 Sam. 3:3-8). When Samuel responded to God, then God talked to him.

It was the Lord talking to me. This time when He asked, "Why don't you ask Me to forgive her?" I answered Him back.

I said, "*Me* ask *You*?"

He said, "Yes, *you* ask *Me*."

God knows I am a *stickler* for the Word. And He always leads us in line with the Word, I asked him for Scripture to back up His statement.

So He said, "Don't you know that My Word says in First John 5:16 that *'If any man see his brother* [that means sister too] *sin a sin which is not unto death, he shall ask, and he shall give him life for them . . .'?"*

I read that and said, "That's right. That's exactly what it says. All right, Lord, I ask You to just forgive Granny. Forgive her for any sins of omission in her life and for anything else she didn't see or that I don't see. You forgive her."

The Lord said, "All right, I do."

So I thanked Him for it. To me that settled it. Can't you see that First John 5:16 is according to God's will just as much as First John 5:14 and 15 are? And when you ask God to forgive someone according to First John 5:16, you are asking according to His will.

Of course, my praying this way was not so much for Granny's benefit as it was for my own peace of mind. Granny was a Christian and was going to Heaven when she died, but my being able to pray for her according to First John 5:16 put my mind at ease concerning her readiness to go.

When *Not* To Pray

The last part of First John 5:16 says, "*. . . There is a sin unto death: I do not say that he shall pray for it.*" Someone said, "What is this sin unto death?" Well, the Book of Hebrews tells us.

This sin unto death isn't a sin that a sinner can commit, but it is a sin that a Christian can commit.

Notice First John 5:16 says, "*If any man see his BROTHER sin a sin which is not unto death. . . .*" Also, John was not talking about physical death. He was talking about spiritual death or eternal separation from God. This is the sin of denying Christ. Only a mature Christian can commit that sin.

Actually, according to Hebrews chapter 6, there are five qualifications a believer would have to meet before he or she could be guilty of committing the unpardonable sin.

HEBREWS 6:4-6
4 For it is impossible for those who were once ENLIGHTENED, and have TASTED OF THE HEAVENLY GIFT, and were MADE PARTAKERS OF THE HOLY GHOST,
5 And have TASTED THE GOOD WORD OF GOD, and THE POWERS OF THE WORLD TO COME,
6 IF THEY SHALL FALL AWAY, to renew them again unto repentance; seeing they crucify to themselves the Son of God afresh, and put him to an open shame.

Before Christians could be guilty of committing the sin unto death, all five conditions mentioned in this Scripture would have to apply to them. These conditions are listed below:

1. They are enlightened and see their lost condition and need for a Savior.

2. They have tasted of Jesus Christ, the Heavenly Gift; that is, they have been born again.

3. They are filled with the Holy Ghost.

4. They have grown spiritually enough so they are not just a baby on the "milk" of God's Word or a child in the things of God. In other words, they have tasted the good, solid meat of God's Word.

5. They have had the gifts of the Spirit, or "the powers of the world to come" operating in their lives and ministries.

You can readily see that very few believers could even qualify for committing the unpardonable sin, or the sin unto death. Let's look at another passage of Scripture in Hebrews which also talks about the sin unto death.

HEBREWS 10:26-29
26 For if we sin wilfully after that we have received the knowledge of the truth, there remaineth no more sacrifice for sins,
27 But a certain fearful looking for of judgment and fiery indignation, which shall devour the adversaries.
28 He that despised Moses' law died without mercy under two or three witnesses:
29 Of how much sorer punishment, suppose ye, shall he be thought worthy, who hath trodden under foot the Son of God, and hath counted the blood of the covenant, wherewith he was sanctified, an unholy thing, and hath done despite unto the Spirit of grace?

This is the sin unto death that John was talking about in First John 5:16. It is not the sin of lying, or cheating, or anything like that. God will forgive you of those sins if you are genuinely sorry for your sin and you confess it to Him.

But the writer of Hebrews explains that a person sins the sin unto death who "*. . . hath trodden under foot the Son of God, and hath counted the blood of the covenant, wherewith he was sanctified, an unholy thing, and hath done despite unto the Spirit of grace?*" (Heb. 10:29).

If you are familiar with church history, you know that the Hebrew Christians were under great persecution, and they were tempted to go back to Judaism. When a Jew accepted Christ, he was cut off from his kinfolks, and, as a result, the Christian Jew had it hard financially and every other way.

But Paul was warning the Jewish Christians, saying, "If you are going to go back to Judaism then you are going to have to deny Christ to do it; you are going to have to deny that He is the Messiah and the Son of God. And to deny Christ is the same as saying that the blood of the covenant, the blood of Christ, is an unholy thing."

In other words, to go back to Judaism after becoming a Christian was the same as saying the blood of Jesus was common blood like any other man's. Our blood is unholy and common, but Jesus' blood isn't. And the writer of Hebrews was saying in essence, "If you deny Christianity and go back to Judaism, you are going to tread underfoot the Son of God."

The thing that made you a Christian was accepting Christ as your Lord and confessing Him as your Savior. In Christ we have eternal life. But James said it is possible for a brother, a Christian, to commit a sin unto *death*; that is, spiritual death.

You could see a believer do something that is wrong, and you could pray for him as John suggests here in First John 5:16. And if he has not sinned the sin unto death, God will forgive him. But there is a sin unto death. And John said we are *not* to pray for the believer who has committed the sin unto death.

There have only been two people for whom the Lord told me not to pray because they had sinned the sin unto death. One of them was a Pentecostal preacher's wife who had backslidden as a mature Christian and had denied Christ. She met all five conditions which are listed in Hebrews 6:4-6 in order to be guilty of committing the unpardonable sin.

Jesus said to me, "Don't pray for her."

I asked, "Why not?"

He said, "Because she has sinned the sin unto death."

I didn't know then what I know now, so I asked, "What is the sin unto death?" And the Lord gave me these scriptures (Heb. 6:1-6; 10:26-31).

I asked, "What will happen to her?"

God said, "She will spend eternity in the lake of fire which burns with fire and brimstone" (Rev. 21:8).

That is what the sin unto death is — it is the unforgiveable or unpardonable sin. One who commits this sin will spend eternity in the lake of fire which burns with fire and brimstone. As I said, the sin unto death isn't talking about *physical* death. It is talking about *spiritual* death — eternal separation from God. Of course, physical death is a result of spiritual death. But I'm talking about spiritual death.

I would encourage you to pray for those whom you see sin, as the Bible instructs. The Bible says you pray for folks who have sinned and God will give them life. Only if God shows you *not* to pray for them because they have sinned the sin unto death will you know not to pray. The Bible says, "... *There*

is a sin unto death: I do not say that he shall pray for it" (1 John 5:16).

Once a person has sinned the sin unto death, you can't change that. There is absolutely nothing you can do. The Bible says, "*For it is impossible . . . to renew them again unto repentance . . .*" (Heb. 6:4,6).

There was another person for whom the Lord said to me, "Don't pray for him."

Again I asked, "Why not?"

That person had been saved and was a child of God. There is no doubt in my mind that he had the call of God on his life to preach because he told me God had called him to the ministry. But he never listened to it, and he never obeyed the call. He even fell away from the Lord. I prayed for him for many years.

I was holding a meeting out in west Texas in 1945, and I became greatly burdened to pray for the man. I went to the church between two and three o'clock in the morning and began praying at the altar.

Finally, the Lord spoke to me and said, "Don't ever pray another prayer for him. Don't pray anymore for him."

I asked, "Why not?"

Jesus said, "Because he has sinned the sin unto death. Don't ever pray for him anymore. He will never be saved. He has gone away from Me, rejected Me, and he will never repent."

This man also had denied Christ as a mature Christian; he knew fully what he was doing when he rejected Jesus.

So, you see, as long as a person stays in Christ, he is eternally secure. But the Bible also says there *is* a sin unto death, and we don't want to forget that. The Bible simply says, "... *There is a sin unto death: I do not say that he shall pray for it*" (1 John 5:16). So you wouldn't know if someone actually sinned the sin unto death unless God told you or gave you a revelation of it or showed you.

God Wants Us To Prosper

First John 5:16 is something God told us *not* to pray about. Now let's look at what John tells us we *are* to pray for.

3 JOHN 2
2 Beloved, I wish above all things that thou mayest prosper and be in health, even as thy soul prospereth.

According to *Strong's Exhaustive Concordance of the Bible*, in the Greek the word "wish" actually implies *to pray*. So we could read that verse,

"Beloved, I *pray* above all things that you may prosper" (3 John 2).

If John was motivated by the Holy Spirit to pray for those he was addressing to prosper, then that would be the desire of the Spirit of God for every person, for God is no respecter of persons (Acts 10:34). So, you see, it would be scriptural to pray that believers would prosper and be in health even as their souls prosper.

Did you notice that John said he prayed this above all things? So John was saying he prayed for prosperity and good health above all things. Of course, this means financial and material prosperity too. And he said, *". . . thou mayest prosper and be in health . . ."* (3 John 2). That's physical prosperity, isn't it? So God wants us healthy physically.

But the verse also means more than that, because John says, *". . . even as thy SOUL prospereth"* (3 John 2). God wants us to prosper in our souls too — our mind, will, and emotions. So we can see from this verse that God wants us to have prosperity in every area — mentally, emotionally, physically, materially, and financially. Therefore, we know we can pray for prosperity in every area of our lives.

What Jude Said About Prayer

Then Jude said something about prayer that is enlightening and helpful.

JUDE 20
20 But ye, beloved, BUILDING UP YOURSELVES on your most holy faith, praying in the Holy Ghost.

Praying in the Holy Ghost is praying in the Holy Spirit (the Holy Ghost and the Holy Spirit are the same). It is praying in the Spirit.

What Jude said here agrees with what Paul said to the Church at Corinth. Paul said in First Corinthians 14:4, *"He that speaketh in an unknown tongue EDIFIETH himself. . . ."* Speaking or praying in an unknown tongue edifies you. The word "edify" means *to build up.* Therefore, praying in tongues edifies or builds the believer up.

And here in Jude 20 it says, *"But ye, beloved, BUILDING UP yourselves on your most holy faith, praying in the Holy Ghost."*

Praying in the Holy Ghost is a means of spiritual edification and spiritual *building up.* Therefore, praying in tongues is *". . . building up yourselves on your most holy faith, praying in the Holy Ghost"* (Jude 20).

No, praying in the Holy Ghost will not *give* you faith. Faith only comes by hearing the Word of God (Rom. 10:17). Praying in the Holy Ghost helps you *build up* the faith you already have.

I think we are very foolish sometimes to take a text out of its setting and try to prove something with it. For example, some people will use Jude 20 to try to prove that praying in tongues *gives* us faith. But praying in the Holy Ghost will not *give* you faith. Faith only comes by hearing the Word of God (Rom. 10:17). Praying in the Holy Ghost helps you *build up* the faith you already have.

Spiritual edification or building yourself up on your most holy faith is just one scriptural purpose for praying in other tongues. (For a further discussion on the scriptural purposes of tongues, *see* Rev. Kenneth E. Hagin's study course, *The Holy Spirit and His Gifts.*)

Interpret Scripture in Light of Other Scripture

We can't take a Scripture text out of its setting and make it say something that contradicts what the rest of the Bible says. For example, people try to prove that praying in tongues gives us faith, using Jude 20.

We must interpret Scripture in the light of Scripture. Put all the verses of Scripture together and they will amplify and clarify one another. They will fit together. So interpret one scripture in the light of the other.

One particular evangelist held a meeting for me. He was preaching along certain lines, and he lifted a verse in the Book of Revelation out of its setting and out of its context. If you just took that verse of Scripture away from other verses on the same subject, you would think it said what he thought it said and what he was teaching.

In talking with him, I said, "I can't agree with you on that subject. That isn't true because the Word of God says something else entirely in other places in the Bible."

"Yes," he said, "but it says such-and-such right here in Revelation. It has to be true."

I said, "Well, if what you're saying is true, then other parts of the Bible are a lie." But the entire Bible is true from Genesis to Revelation. This evangelist just didn't understand the law of Bible interpretation, which says that Scripture is to be interpreted in the light of other Scripture. When you put two scriptures together on the same subject, one will throw light on the other, and vice versa. Then you can clearly see the entire picture of what God's saying.

This evangelist insisted, "No, no, it says this right here, and I am going to stand by that."

I said, "Well, what are you going to do with the other verses in the Bible that contradict what you're saying?"

He answered, "I'm not going to do anything about that, but I am going to stick with this one."

I knew how to get him to see the truth, so I said to him, "Well, Jesus said, *'And these signs shall follow them that believe. . . . They shall take up serpents . . .'* [Mark 16:17,18]. I know people who handle snakes to try to prove their faith. Following your same logic, then why don't you handle snakes?"

He said, "I have better sense than that. I know what the Bible says in Acts 28 where it says Paul took authority over the effects of a snakebite because he was *accidentally* bitten by a snake."

I said, "That is the very thing I am trying to say to you! You see, you were interpreting that verse in Mark 16:17 and 18 about signs that follow the believing one by what the Bible says on the same subject in the Book of Acts.

"You didn't read that the apostles handled snakes to prove anything over in Acts, did you? No, you read that Paul was *accidentally* bitten [Acts 28:3-6]; and since it was something that happened accidentally, Paul had a right to claim the promise in Mark 16:17 and 18. The apostles, or anyone else for that matter, didn't have any right to handle serpents just to prove something because it says in another place that we are not to tempt or test the Lord our God" (Matt. 4:7).

When I said that he began to laugh, and he said, "Oh, Brother Hagin, you've got me pegged. Yes, I've been doing the same thing. You're right, I'll have to interpret what I've been teaching and preaching in the light of these other scriptures on the same subject."

It is true that many times we can become lopsided in our thinking by just taking a verse out of its setting and context and trying to build a doctrine on it.

I was once discussing the Scriptures with a certain fellow. This man told me about the time he was discussing the Scriptures with another minister, particularly the scripture where Paul makes the statement that all of Israel will be saved (Rom. 11:26). My friend said that this other minister said, "There is no use praying for the Jews; they are all going to be saved anyhow."

But this minister lifted that statement in the Bible out of its setting. You have to read the context to see what the Scripture is saying. My friend told me, "In a brotherly way, that minister and I discussed that for hours and hours. But he just stayed with what he believed — that all Israel shall be saved. He never went to another scripture to prove what he believed. He just stuck with that one scripture."

Paul made the statement, but that didn't mean all Israel was going to be saved whether or not they received Jesus Christ. We know that because Paul stated also in the same letter to the Romans, writing to the Church at Rome, *"Brethren, my heart's desire and prayer to God for Israel is, that they might be saved"* (Rom. 10:1).

In other words, if Israel were all going to be saved anyway, why in the world would Paul need to pray for them? That would be a contradiction. Do you know how important it is to interpret Scripture in light of other Scripture?

I am using these examples as illustrations. As I said, the scripture we looked at, Jude 20, does not say that praying in the Spirit will *give* you faith because in another place in the Bible it says, *". . . faith cometh by hearing, and hearing by the word of God"* (Rom. 10:17).

Jude 20 actually says, *"But ye, beloved, building up yourselves ON YOUR MOST HOLY FAITH. . . ."* That means by praying in other tongues, you can be built up spiritually on the faith you already have. How can you do that? The rest of that verse says it's by *". . . praying in the Holy Ghost"* (Jude 20).

We've looked at what four different New Testament authors — James, Peter, John, and Jude — said about prayer. And each one of the principles of prayer which they discussed are vital to the success of our prayer life.

One of the principles we looked at was found in James 5:16, where James talked about the prayer of a righteous man. Remember, if you are born again, then you *are* the righteousness of God in Christ (2 Cor. 5:21). Therefore, James 5:16 is talking about *you*. As *you* practice these biblical principles of prayer, *your* earnest, heartfelt, and continued prayer will make tremendous power available, dynamic in its working!

Questions for Study

1. How do we know that the words "afflicted" and "sick" in James 5:13 and 14 don't mean the same thing?

   _____

   _____

2. In James 5:13 and 14, what advice did James give to the afflicted, the merry, and the sick?

   _____

   _____

3. Why should you do your own praying when you're afflicted?

   _____

   _____

4. In James 5:14, who does the phrase "elders of the church" refer to?

   _____

   _____

5. In 1 Peter 3:1, what does the word "conversation" mean?

   _____

   _____

6. Complete this sentence: God's _____ is His _____?

7. Who cannot commit the sin unto death? Who can commit it?

   _____

   _____

8. What five qualifications would a believer have to meet before he or she could be guilty of committing the sin unto death?

   _____

   _____

9. Praying in the Holy Ghost will not _give_ you faith. What does praying in the Holy Ghost do?

   _____

   _____

10. What is the law of Bible interpretation?

    _____

    _____

Chapter 23

The Will of God in Prayer — Part 1

And this is the confidence that we have in him, that, if we ask any thing according to his will, he heareth us:

And if we know that he hear us, whatsoever we ask, we know that we have the petitions that we desired of him.

— 1 John 5:14,15

In these next few chapters, I want to discuss further the subject of the will of God in prayer. We know that it is God's will that we receive answers to prayer and that we bear much prayer fruit as we pray according to the Word of God (John 15:7,8). God wants us to have *confidence* in His Presence when we pray.

Another translation of First John 5:14 says, "And this is the *boldness* we have toward Him, that if we ask anything according to His will, He hears us." Immediately, our natural minds want to fasten upon this phrase, *". . . according to his will. . . ."* Therefore, many times folks pray, "Lord, do this or that, *if* it be Thy will."

God's Word *Is* His Will

Other times we pray for things about which we already have God's Word, so we know His will concerning those things. Therefore, it is incorrect to insert the expression, "If it be Thy will," into our prayer when God's Word already plainly states that it is His will.

To say, "If it be Thy will," when you already know what the Word says, is confessing that you doubt His Word — that you don't believe it. That kind of praying will not work. Remember, God's Word is God's will. God's Word *is* the revealed will of God. Therefore, if you know what the Word says, you know what the will of God is.

Some have supposed that you can find out the will of God by praying, "If it be Thy will." I'll share an example of this with you.

Many years ago when I pastored, there was a woman in my congregation who was ill. She was one of my Sunday school teachers, and her husband called me in the night to come and anoint her with oil and pray for her. He was acting according to the Word to call me to come and pray for his wife. As we discussed in a previous lesson, the Bible instructs the sick to call for the church elders to come and pray.

JAMES 5:14,15

14 Is any sick among you? let him call for the elders of the church; and let them pray over him, anointing him with oil in the name of the Lord:

15 And the prayer of faith shall save the sick, and the Lord shall raise him up; and if he have committed sins, they shall be forgiven him.

So I went to the home of the Sunday school teacher. I knew that you can locate people by what they say. That is, you can know the level of someone's faith by the words of their mouth. The Bible says that faith must be expressed in *words*, in the form of a confession: *"For with the HEART man believeth unto righteousness; and with the MOUTH confession is made unto . . ."* (Rom. 10:10).

I wanted to find out what this woman believed and get a confession of faith from her. Just because she was a member of my congregation and a Sunday school teacher, and her husband was a deacon in my church, didn't mean she had developed her faith or that she was a doer of the Word. Faith is of the heart. This woman didn't necessarily have faith just because she was my Sunday school teacher.

As I stood by the bedside ready to anoint her with oil, I asked her, "Sister, will you be healed as I anoint you with oil and lay hands upon you in Jesus' Name?"

She said, "Well, I will if it's God's will."

I said, "How are you going to find out whether or not it is God's will to heal you?"

"Well," she said, "I thought you would pray and if I'm healed, then I'd know it's God's will. If I'm not healed, then I'd know it isn't God's will to heal me."

It is amazing to me how some people — especially those who should be a little more knowledgeable of the Bible than others — can sit in services week after week and hear faith taught and yet not grasp it.

Don't Just *Hear* the Word — *Give Heed* to the Word

As a pastor, I taught my congregation on other subjects besides faith, of course. But I also taught my congregation a great deal on the subject of faith. Still there were some who didn't comprehend what the Word of God says about faith.

Much of the time, the Bible just runs off some people like water off a duck's back. Those people will sit in church and say, "Oh, I enjoy good preaching and Bible teaching. No one enjoys it any more than I do. I sure love to go to church."

But if you should ask, "What did the preacher teach on?" they give you a blank look and say, "I don't know, but it certainly was good!"

That makes about as much sense as someone saying, "I'll tell you, I had the best meal yesterday at such-and-such restaurant. They have the best pie in town," but then he can't even remember what kind of pie it was he ate!

"Well, what kind of pie was it?" someone would ask him. "I don't know," he'd say. If you heard someone say that, you would have reason to doubt whether he had even eaten at that particular restaurant.

I have told the story many times about a deacon in the last church I pastored. This deacon in my church attended a youth rally. I usually attended the rallies too. In fact, I suppose that was about the only time I missed a rally during a three-year period. But pastors can't always attend every activity because they also have many other responsibilities in the church.

Anyway, the following day after the rally, this deacon came to the parsonage and said, "Oh, Pastor Hagin, you missed it! You missed it. You should have been at the rally last night."

I said, "Well, I would have liked to, but I got tied up and just couldn't make it. Was it a good service?"

"Oh, yes," the deacon replied, "So-and-so preached and it was an outstanding service. He preached the best sermon I have ever heard in my life."

I asked, "What did he preach on?"

This deacon looked at me blankly and said, "I don't remember."

A fifty-year-old man shouldn't have a problem with his memory! So I asked him, "Well, what did he use for a text? What was the subject of the sermon? Did he preach about John the Baptist? Did he take his text from the Old Testament or the New Testament?"

This deacon answered, "I just don't know. I can't remember."

I suggested a number of different Bible characters and a number of different subjects, thinking I might help him refresh his memory, but he couldn't recall what the preacher had said.

His wife was sitting in the car, so he said, "Wait a minute, let me ask my wife."

So we walked out to the car, and he said, "Honey, do you remember what Brother So-and-so preached on last night?"

She replied, "No, but it was the best sermon I ever heard in my life."

I said, "I don't understand that. You can't remember one word he said. You don't remember the text; and you don't remember one verse of Scripture he quoted. You don't remember one person in the Bible that he mentioned.

"Yet," I said, "both of you say it was the best sermon you ever heard in your life! I don't understand that. How could it be the best sermon you ever heard when you don't know a thing he said?"

They both spoke up at once and said, "Oh, I'll tell you, that preacher just ran up and down the aisles and jumped and shouted and ran all over the building."

I said, "That's not preaching! That wasn't the best sermon you ever heard; that was the best *run* you ever saw!"

You see there is a difference. This couple got inspired and blessed by the preacher's inspiration and enthusiasm, and that is all right in its place. But if that's all you ever get out of a sermon, it will wear off after a little while. This deacon and his wife didn't really get anything spiritual of any lasting good.

If we don't know what the Word of God says for ourselves, and if we just go to church and pay very little attention to the Word, we really miss the main blessing — the Word of God.

I didn't say we didn't get blessed. And I didn't say it's wrong to go to church. I said we miss the main blessing if we just go to church and don't ever get into the Word *for ourselves*. We can become confused if we don't give heed to the Word of God — in the church or outside the church.

Praying, 'If It Be Thy Will' Negates Faith

So I had asked this Sunday school teacher if she would be healed the minute we anointed her with oil and prayed. She said, "I will be if it's God's will."

This Sunday school teacher had never missed any of the services, and she enjoyed coming to church. Many times she would testify that she was blessed by the services.

But if the *Word* had really meant much to the woman, I couldn't tell it by her words. If the Word had been abiding in her heart, she would surely have known better than to say, "God will heal me if it's His will."

I had asked her, "How are you going to find out if it is the will of God to heal you or not?"

"Well," she said, "I thought you would anoint me with oil and pray, and if it's God's will, He'll heal me; and if it is not His will, then He won't."

Of course, I knew under those circumstances that the woman was not going to be healed. I knew it would actually do no good to anoint her with oil, or lay hands on her either for that matter.

I don't mean to be sacrilegious about it, but it would do about as much good for me to twiddle my thumbs over her and say, "Twinkle, twinkle, little star, how I wonder what you are." That would do just about as much good because her unbelief would stop the flow of God's healing power. She was in pain and misery, but I knew I couldn't pray for her under those conditions. Her lack of knowing God's will would have negated my faith. She needed to know for herself what the Word said.

Sometimes folks are in pain and suffering, but you can't just stop and preach them a quick sermon. Many times they need to be schooled in faith before they are ever in a position to receive from God.

I intended to talk to this Sunday school teacher a little longer and bring her attention to what the Word of God says about healing, but she said, "Go ahead, I am in so much pain and misery. Go ahead and anoint me." So I anointed her and prayed, knowing that she wouldn't receive anything because she wasn't believing in line with the Word. I stumbled through a prayer, and I had hardly gotten out the word "amen" when she said to her husband, "Go call the doctor."

I couldn't understand that! She had just finished saying that if it was God's will that she be well, He would heal her, and if He didn't heal her, then that meant it wasn't God's will that she be healed. She didn't get her healing; therefore, by her own admission, it wasn't God's will for her to be healed. Yet she was calling the doctor so the doctor would treat her and get her out of the will of God!

Can you see how ridiculous that sounds! It doesn't make sense. If I believed as she did — that if it is God's will, He'll heal me, and if it is not God's will, He won't heal me — then if I didn't receive my healing, I would have to conclude that it isn't God's will that I be well. Then I would be wrong in even wanting to get well if it is not God's will. I would be wrong in trying to get out of the will of God. It would be wrong then for me to go to the doctor or to take medicine. But that is wrong thinking.

If people really believe like that Sunday school teacher believed, they wouldn't be spending money, enlisting professional medical help to get out of the will of God! Many times we have taken a superficial view of some of these verses and have not dug into them to see what God is saying to us.

Many times in similar situations, where people are endeavoring to receive something from God, they will come to the wrong conclusions. They try to find the will of God by saying, "If it's God's will, He'll answer me, and if it is not His will, He won't." People say that all the time.

For instance, when it comes to trying to help people receive the baptism of the Holy Ghost, I run into the same thing. I say to people before I pray with them to be filled with the Holy Ghost (because I want to learn where their faith is), "Will you be filled with the Holy Ghost now as I lay hands on you and pray?"

I have heard many people say, "I will if it is God's will."

I am thinking of one woman in particular who wanted to receive the Holy Spirit.

When I asked her, "Will you receive when I lay hands on you?" she just looked at me rather startled.

She said, "Why, I thought that you would pray, and if it was God's will, He would fill me; and if it wasn't, He wouldn't."

I said to her, "No, I can't pray under those circumstances because you wouldn't be filled with the Spirit. You're not in a position to receive because you're not in faith. Then you would leave and say, 'Well, it's not God's will for me to receive the Holy Spirit because Brother Hagin laid hands on me and prayed for me and God didn't fill me.'"

Faith begins where the will of God is known. And we know that God's Word is God's will. This woman didn't know God's Word or God's will on the subject so she couldn't be in faith.

Then I asked her, "If the Word of God says that this promise of the Holy Ghost belongs to you, does it belong to you?"

She said, "Yes."

I said, "Then, let's read the Bible. Let's read the will of God. Let's find out what His Word says."

I reached for my Bible, opened it to Acts 2:39, handed it to her and said, "Read that out loud."

She read, *"For the promise is unto you, and to your children, and to all that are afar off, even as many as the Lord our God shall call."*

I said, "What promise is that?"

She hesitated a moment and I said, "Read the last part of verse 38 and it will tell you what the promise is."

She read, "*. . . and ye shall receive the gift of the Holy Ghost*" (Acts 2:38).

She simply closed my Bible, handed it back to me and said, "Yes, the promise of the Holy Spirit is for me. Just lay your hands on me and pray, and I'll be filled right now."

You see, just a moment before she was questioning the will of God, and she thought, *Now the preacher will pray and if what we are asking here is God's will for me, then God will do it.* But that is wrong thinking because it's unscriptural. We already know what the Word says about receiving the Holy Spirit. Therefore, we can be in faith and receive what rightfully already belongs to us.

Many people don't know the will of God in prayer because they don't know His Word. But in the case of this woman who received the Holy Spirit, as soon as she saw what the Word says, then faith came, for faith comes by hearing and hearing by the Word of God (Rom. 10:17).

I laid hands on her head and had barely touched her when she lifted both hands and instantly began speaking in tongues. I didn't even get to pray for her! She received the Holy Ghost because she was in faith. She knew it was God's will that she receive. The thing that convinced her was the Word.

Praying According to God's Will

There shouldn't be any problem praying in line with the Word of God because if God's Word says it — if God's Word promises us something — we know it is God's will for us to have and to possess and to enjoy all that He has promised and made provision for in His Word.

Before I pray for anything, I find the answer for what I want or need in the Word. And if I don't know what God's will is, I find out what the Word says because God's Word is God's will. I don't just pray to be praying. I would be wasting my time trying to pray in faith if I didn't know what the Word says. I couldn't pray in faith. I would be praying in doubt and unbelief and it wouldn't work. It would be just words.

Now it's true the believer won't find specific direction for every decision he must make in life. But the Bible promises that the Spirit of Truth who dwells within us will guide us into all truth (John 16:13). And the believer who is walking in fellowship with the Father and obeying His Word can rest assured that the Holy Spirit will lead and guide him in all the affairs of life.

The believer walking in fellowship with the Lord through His Word won't ask for anything outside of the will of God. If a believer is not walking in fellowship with the Lord through His Word, he is not going to have a successful prayer life and get answers anyway. Jesus said in John 15:7, "*If ye abide in me, and my words abide in you, ye shall ask what ye will, and it shall be done unto you.*"

John wrote the Gospel of John and the three epistles of John. In First John 5:14 it says, "*And this is the confidence* [boldness] *that we have in him, that, if we ask any thing according to his will, he heareth us.*"

Then in John's Gospel, quoting Jesus, John writes, "*If ye abide in me, and my words abide in you, ye shall ask what ye will, and it shall be done unto you*" (John 15:7). John was saying, "You shall ask what you will, and it shall be done unto you."

In First John 5:14, John says, "*. . . if we ask any thing according to HIS WILL, he heareth us.*" In John 15:7 he says, "*If ye abide in me, and my words abide in you, ye shall ask what YE WILL, and it shall be done unto you.*"

John 15:7 says you will have whatsoever you will, but under what circumstances? *If you abide in Jesus and His Word abides in you.* When God's Word abides in you, then you know God's will. His Word is His will, and when you ask for something according to the Word, you are asking according to God's will. Then you don't have to pray, "If it be Thy will," because you know what His will is.

For instance, we know that it is God's will that the lost be saved. How do we know that? We know that because the Word of God tells us it's so. We know that because the golden text of the Bible, John 3:16 says, "*For God so loved the world, that he gave his only begotten Son, that whosoever believeth in him should not perish, but have everlasting life.*"

We also know that the Word of God says, "*The Lord is . . . not willing that any should perish, but that all should come to repentance*" (2 Peter 3:9). There are a host of other scriptures that say the same thing. I am just citing one or two.

Therefore, you do not have to pray, "Lord, if it's Your will, save my son." Or you don't have to pray, "Lord, if it's Your will, save my daughter," or whoever your unsaved loved one is. You know God's will for saving the lost, don't you? Why do you know God's will? Because you have His Word.

1 JOHN 5:14
14 And this is the confidence that we have in him, that, if we ask any thing according to his will, he heareth us.

Did you let that soak in? It says, "This is the *confidence* that we have in Him, that if we ask anything according to His will, He hears us!"

Then did God hear you when you prayed for that unsaved loved one? Certainly, He did. Is it His will for that loved one to come into the knowledge of the truth and be saved? Certainly, it is. Didn't you ask on behalf of that unsaved loved one according to God's will? If you did, then you can have this confidence, that if you ask anything according to His will, He hears you.

1 JOHN 5:15
15 And if we know that he hear us, whatsoever we ask, we know that we have the petitions that we desired of him.

Don't Take Sides Against the Word

Did God hear you when you prayed according to the Word for your unsaved loved one?

"Well, yes," someone might say, "but my loved one is not saved yet, Brother Hagin."

But First John 5:15 says, "*. . . if we know that he hear us, whatsoever we ask, we know that we have the petitions that we desired of him.*" If you pray according to the Word, the Bible says you *have* the petitions you desired of Him. But your prayers won't work for you if you take sides against the Word.

You see, when we say to the Lord, "If it be Thy will," when we already know what God's Word is, we are unconsciously making God out to be a liar. We don't mean to, but by our actions and our words, we are many times unconsciously taking sides against the Word and saying it isn't true. We are really saying, "No, it isn't so; the Word doesn't work."

But what if you were in need of a little extra money, so you borrowed money from your bank. Then suppose you wanted to borrow more money, so you said to your banker, "I want to borrow $100 for ninety days."

Your banker says, "All right."

You say, "But I don't want it today. I just want to get it arranged because a financial need is coming up, and I may need this loan."

Your banker says, "All right, when you need it, just come and get it. You may borrow the money."

Now you have your banker's word for it that your loan is approved. But then suppose you say to your wife, I'm afraid the banker isn't going to loan me the money after all!

You are going to have to act on what your banker said and believe what he said in order to get the money. You can't take sides against what he said.

No, you have to go down to the bank and go through the business transaction and sign the bank note in order to receive your money.

By the same token, if you are going to take sides against the Word and say, "No, that's not going to work. The Word doesn't work. I prayed but it didn't work," then you are saying that what God said isn't so. You are taking sides against the Word, and the Word is not going to work for you.

But the Bible says, "*And this is the confidence [boldness] that we have in Him, that, if we ask any thing according to his will, he heareth us*" (1 John 5:14). Thank God, we can be bold and have confidence before God in our praying.

Praying for Unsaved Loved Ones

Another area where we can have confidence in prayer is praying for our unsaved loved ones. After I learned about the authority I have in Christ, I never prayed anymore for the salvation of my family members — those in my own household who were under my authority. You see, I had authority in that realm — for those living in my household. We see this principle in the Scriptures (Acts 16:15,34).

So I prayed for my other relatives. I prayed that laborers would be sent across their path (Matt. 9:38). But for those in my household (of course, my wife was already saved), I just claimed their salvation in the Name of Jesus. I never let the thought even enter my mind that those in my household would not be saved. My two children were saved and have always served the Lord. One of my nieces came to live with us for a time, and she was also saved.

You see, you do have some authority for those of your immediate family who are not living in your home under your jurisdiction. But, of course, you have greater authority for those of your own household. For family members not living in your household, you can rebuke Satan and tell him to take his hands off of them, and you can claim their salvation in the Name of Jesus.

Also, you can pray according to Matthew 9:38, that God would send laborers across their paths. I knew I was praying according to God's Word, so I had boldness and confidence before God. When the thought would come to me that they might never be saved, I would just laugh out loud if I was by myself.

It is just like the devil to try to harass you once you've claimed the promises of God's Word. The devil would wake me up in the night with thoughts that my family members would never be saved, and I would just start laughing.

You see, I had confidence — I had boldness — because I had prayed according to God's will (1 John 5:14). And I knew it is God's will that my family members be saved. God is not willing that any should be lost.

That is the confidence I have in God, that if I ask anything according to His will, He hears me. So I knew God heard me because I had prayed according to His Word or His will. And if I knew that God had heard me, then I knew I had the petitions I desired of Him. I *knew* I had them!

God and His Word Are One

How do I know I have the petitions that I desired of Him? Because I know He heard me. How do I know He heard me? Because I prayed according to His will. How do I know I prayed according to His will? Because God's *Word* is God's *will*, and I prayed according to God's Word. Therefore, I prayed according to His will. If God doesn't keep His Word, then He is a liar. If God's Word is no good, then He is no good. But God is not a liar. God's Word is good and *He* is good! God and His Word are one.

You know that you and your word are one. If your word is no good, then you are no good. We are known by whether or not we keep our word. We know that God's Word is the expression of His will — of what He is eager to do for us. And we know that God cannot lie (Num. 23:19). God keeps His Word because He is faithful who promised (Heb. 10:23).

This is an interesting truth to look at in the natural. If a person's word is of no value, then when you quote that person, people will just laugh at you. Accordingly, if God's Word is no good, when we quote His Word, we should just laugh at God because there is nothing to Him. But, thank God, God's Word is good! He keeps His Word.

Healing the Sick Is God's Will

We know that it is God's will that the lost be saved. We also know that healing the sick is God's will, too, don't we? How do we know that? We know that because God's Word says so, and, remember, God's Word is God's will.

The Bible says, Christ bore our infirmities or sicknesses and carried our diseases (Isa. 53:4; Matt. 8:17; 1 Peter 2:24). We need to get the Word settled in our hearts, not just in our heads. In Full Gospel circles particularly, we hold divine healing as one of our fundamental beliefs because the Bible is the truth, and the Bible proclaims that healing is God's will. We should act on what we believe.

I have read most of the statements of fundamental truths that Full Gospel churches believe and supposedly preach, and most of these statements include tenets of divine healing and give Scripture to back them up. One such verse of Scripture is Isaiah 53:4 and 5.

ISAIAH 53:4,5
4 Surely he hath borne our griefs [sicknesses], and carried our sorrows [diseases]: yet we did esteem him stricken, smitten of God, and afflicted.
5 But he was wounded for our transgressions, he was bruised for our iniquities: the chastisement of our peace was upon him; and with his stripes we are healed.

MATTHEW 8:17
17 . . . Himself took our infirmities, and bare our sicknesses.

1 PETER 2:24
24 Who his own self bare our sins in his own body on the tree, that we, being dead to sins, should live unto righteousness: by whose stripes ye were healed.

Then I found out that folks will state that they believe one thing, while they practice something else.

For example, I received light on divine healing on the bed of sickness. I was a denominational boy reading Grandma's Bible, and I received my healing. I then began to fellowship with Full Gospel people because they believed in divine healing. And when I found out that they also believed in the baptism of the Holy Ghost, I was filled with the Holy Ghost and spoke in other tongues.

Then I began preaching in Full Gospel circles, and I would hold healing services to minister to the sick. And someone would invariably come forward for healing after the service was over.

Once a young woman came forward with a baby in her arms. The baby was sick, and the woman wanted me and the pastor to pray for the healing of this child. Actually, the woman came to the pastor, and he said, "Brother Hagin, pray with me for this child."

The pastor and I laid hands on the baby. I began to pray in faith, believing the Word, that Jesus Christ Himself took that child's infirmities and bare that child's sicknesses and diseases, so that baby would not have to bear them.

I was appropriating that promise, but I heard this pastor say, "Lord, heal this child if it is Your will." How I wished at that time for the boldness of Smith Wigglesworth!

Wigglesworth was quite bold and in similar cases would yell right out loud, "Stop him! Stop him! Oh, God, stop him right now! He is charging the atmosphere with unbelief!" And at times that needs to be done.

A pastor who knew Wigglesworth personally said they went out to eat together and Wigglesworth asked this pastor to pray. So this pastor quietly bowed his head and prayed softly. He said Wigglesworth just shouted right out loud so that everyone in the restaurant could hear him, "My God, young man, if you are going to pray, *pray*! Don't sit there and mumble over your food."

Wigglesworth then jumped to his feet and lifted both of his hands and started praying at the top of his voice right there in the restaurant. He believed if you are going to do something, do it with all your might. And if you are not going to do it that way, then don't do it at all. I don't know but what Wigglesworth was right about that!

Wigglesworth tells about one such incident in his book, *Ever Increasing Faith*. (If you don't have a copy, I encourage you to get one.) I have worn out four or five copies of this book, reading it extensively. I just keep reading it over and over again because it feeds my spirit.

After all, in the natural I keep going back to the table and eating at mealtime. For instance, I have had eggs for breakfast many times over the years. But I am not going to quit eating eggs for breakfast just because I already have had eggs for breakfast before. Are you going to quit eating bacon because you've eaten bacon before? No, many times over the years I have eaten bacon for breakfast, and I still eat it. I like it.

Do you see what I am talking about? So don't just read these books, such as *Ever Increasing Faith* and lay them down and forget them. If you do, they won't do you much good.

If you stopped eating food just because you've eaten food before in the past, you'd starve to death. If you just ate a big meal last week and said, "Well, I ate last week and there is no use in eating anymore. I am going to wait until next year before I eat again," you would be dead before next year gets here. In the same sense, keep feeding along these lines spiritually, so that your faith is constantly being built up.

Wigglesworth talked about going to pray for a certain sick person. Two other ministers were also going to accompany Wigglesworth. Wigglesworth had gotten a little light on healing and although he knew these other two ministers didn't really believe in healing, he let them go with him anyway.

Wigglesworth asked one of these ministers to pray, and when the minister started praying, he prayed "all around the world" (that is the way Wigglesworth put it). This minister prayed for all the missionaries. He prayed for all the orphans. He prayed for all the widows. But that was not why they were in that sick person's room. They were there to pray for the woman who was on the sickbed.

That is why we are not effective in our praying many times — because we pray "all around the world" and never even get to the thing about which we should be praying. Doubt and unbelief takes the long way around, wandering in prayer, but faith always gets to the point — to the heart of the matter. Of course, it is right to pray for the missionaries, and it is right to pray for the orphans, and it is right to pray for the widows, but there is a time for that.

The sick woman for whom Wigglesworth was praying was the wife of one of these unbelieving preachers. The doctor had said she would never regain consciousness and that she would die. So, finally, this preacher who was praying "all around the world" said, "Now, Lord, here is our fellow minister. His wife is going to die (He just accepted as final what the doctor had said). Now I pray that You would comfort him in this hour of bereavement and give him grace for this dark hour ahead of him," and he closed his prayer.

Then the preacher asked the sick woman's husband to pray. He was a minister, too, and he started praying, "Oh, yes, Lord, answer our brother's prayer. Help me. My wife is going to die. Help me in this hour."

Wigglesworth said, "I just shouted right out loud, 'Stop him! Stop him! Lord, stop him! He's charging the atmosphere with unbelief.'"

Well, he *was* charging the atmosphere with unbelief. By the words of their own mouths, the two men had this woman dead already. If you listen to some preachers and to some people, you will never get anything from God. They will have you dead before you actually die! They would just pile words of fear, doubt, unbelief, despair, and distress on top of you and bury you alive if you let them.

Wigglesworth said that up until this time he had never anointed anyone with oil for healing. But he knew the Bible said to do it, so he took out a bottle of oil that he had put in his hip pocket. He didn't know how to anoint her, so he just took the cork out of the bottle and poured the entire bottle of oil on her, bedclothes and all. It wasn't the oil that healed the woman; it was Wigglesworth's faith and belief in God's Word.

Wigglesworth simply said, "Oh, Lord, heal her now."

Wigglesworth related, "When I said those words, Jesus appeared at the foot of the bed. I saw him but the other two preachers didn't."

(No wonder they didn't see Him; they were too far down in the well of unbelief to see anything. They couldn't even look up and see the light. All they could do was see the darkness of unbelief.) The woman who was unconscious awoke, and she saw Jesus too. She said, "There's Jesus! There's Jesus!"

Then Jesus disappeared and she rose up well. She was a denominational minister's wife. It certainly wasn't her husband's faith that healed her because he was saying, "Dear Lord, help me. She is going to die. Help me in this hour." It wasn't the other preacher's faith because he said, "Lord, this pastor's wife is going to die. Help him in this hour."

Don't misunderstand me, friends, there is another side of this subject. Folks do die, and the time to die does come to everyone because the Word of God tells us that death hasn't been put underfoot yet. It will be put underfoot, but it hasn't yet. Death is the last enemy to be put underfoot (1 Cor. 15:26).

Even in the event of death, thank God, God does comfort us. But let's wait until a loved one dies before we get the comfort. There is hope as long as there is life. Surely that is the truth.

Therefore, we know that it is God's will to heal the sick because His Word says so. So when this young woman came forward after the service with her sick baby for prayer and the pastor prayed a prayer filled with unbelief, I thought to myself, *I hope she didn't listen to this pastor's prayer.* He had prayed in unbelief because he prayed, "Lord, heal this baby if it's Your will."

I didn't have the boldness to call him down and correct him, and yet I suppose I should have. However, one would have to do something like that in an attitude of love because if it weren't done in love, it could do more harm than good.

I said to myself, *I trust she didn't listen to his prayer, because if she did, he injected his doubt into her mind.* That pastor was telling her that it might not be God's will to heal her child because he said, "Lord, heal this child, if it be Your will."

Praying like that when the Word clearly says what the will of God is, won't produce any results. That pastor might as well have said, "Twinkle, twinkle little star, how I wonder what you are."

We Must Accept Our Responsibility in Prayer

Many folks want to relieve themselves from all responsibility in these areas of prayer. They want to put all the responsibility on God. Then if they fail to receive an answer they can say, "Well that must not have been God's will, because I prayed, 'If it be Thy will,' and God didn't do it. Therefore, it must not be His will."

In other words, it's human nature to try to put all the responsibility on God. But we can't get away from *our* responsibility in prayer even if we want to. Most of us do not want to accept any responsibility in prayer. We would rather put it on God. That way we would never have to say, "*I* failed. *I* missed it somewhere." That's the truth.

But God has given us His Word. And the more we submit ourselves to the Word and conform our thoughts to the Word, the more successful and effective we will become in prayer.

People often come to me and say, "Brother Hagin, why won't the Lord heal me?" Then sometimes they will give me all of their qualifications for receiving healing. People don't get healed based on their qualifications. In other words, you don't earn healing. Healing and every other benefit has already been paid for by the Lord Jesus Christ, and healing is God's gift to us in our redemption.

Once a certain woman came to a meeting I was holding in Texas. She was a denominational woman who had never been to a Pentecostal or Full Gospel service in her life. She and her husband had heard me teaching on the radio on the subject of divine healing, so he brought her to the meeting. She had been given up to die by the doctors, with only a few months to live at best. But she was gloriously healed in my meeting.

The following Sunday night these folks came back and brought the husband's mother. Because of high blood pressure, this older woman had had a couple of strokes and was confined to a wheelchair. The son and his wife had been there on Friday night, so this was the second time they had attended a Full Gospel service. But it was the first time this man's mother had been in a Full Gospel church. When we laid hands on the mother and prayed, she got up out of her wheelchair, healed. They folded the wheelchair up, carried it out, and she walked out to the car.

As soon as the service was over, a woman who was a member of this particular church made a beeline to me. She had tears in her eyes as she spoke to me. I am not making fun of her, God knows that. I felt sorry for her.

With tears streaming down her cheeks she said, "Brother Hagin, I wish you would tell me something if you can."

"I will if I can," I replied. "I don't know whether I can or not, but if I can, I will tell you."

She asked, "How come God healed those denominational women, and I am Full Gospel and He won't heal me."

You can see how people can be wrong in their thinking to begin with. God loves one person just as much as He loves another person. The denomination a person belongs to has nothing to do with it. That is the reason some folks don't get an answer from God. They are too self-centered, selfish, and ignorant because they think God is obligated to do something for them just because they are Full Gospel.

God is not obligated to you just because you are any particular denomination, but He will meet your need if you will come on the right grounds — because of *Jesus.*

This woman said, "Why, those two women don't even have the baptism of the Holy Ghost!"

But the baptism of the Holy Ghost is not a prerequisite for healing. A person can be healed before he is baptized in the Holy Ghost. I was raised up from the deathbed and healed of a terminal heart condition and almost total paralysis. I had been bedfast for sixteen months when I was healed. I hadn't yet spoken with tongues.

Not only that, but I got other people healed when I began preaching that Jesus heals. As a denominational minister, I laid hands on people and even saw some of my Sunday school teachers who were slated for major surgery just rise up off of their sickbeds instantly healed.

I still wasn't filled with the Holy Spirit at this time. The baptism of the Holy Ghost isn't the prerequisite for healing. Believing God's Word and having faith in His Word is the prerequisite for receiving anything from God. It is taking God at His Word that counts.

This woman continued, "Those denominational women don't even have the baptism of the Holy Ghost, and I have the Holy Ghost. I am a member of

this church." I didn't tell her, but I thought in my own mind, *Sometimes being a member of certain churches is a detriment instead of a benefit.*

I don't mean to be disrespectful, but to tell you the truth about it, some of these Full Gospel churches teach more doubt and unbelief than you could imagine.

For example, I was holding a meeting in this particular Full Gospel Church, and the pastor himself talked doubt and unbelief to me all day long. I know he was bound to be preaching doubt and unbelief to the congregation too. Therefore, in this particular case, this woman's membership in this church could have been a detriment to her instead of a benefit.

Five years later I preached a meeting for several weeks in this same church for the same pastor, and he said to me, "Brother Hagin, I don't know whether you are improving in your preaching or whether I am growing spiritually, but I am beginning to grasp what you are saying about faith and prayer. I didn't get it five years ago, although I heard you every single day for several weeks."

I said, "Well, it's both, Brother. I am growing spiritually and am able to take the same subject and handle it a little more adequately. But then you are growing enough spiritually that you can get ahold of what I am saying."

"I am beginning to see that," he said.

All of us — preachers included — are at various stages of spiritual growth. In fact, just because someone is a minister doesn't make him a full-grown Christian. He could still be a baby, spiritually speaking. The calling of God on a man's life doesn't mature him spiritually and make him a full-grown Christian instantly. We need more patience with one another, don't we?

This woman who was crying because God had healed the denominational women asked, "How come God healed these women and He won't heal me? I'm Full Gospel, and I've got the baptism of the Holy Spirit, and they don't. How come they could get healed without the baptism in the Holy Spirit, and I can't get healed *with* the baptism in the Holy Spirit?"

In asking this she was confessing, "God won't heal me. I don't know why He won't, but He won't."

Sometimes we have to bring people to their spiritual senses, so to speak, just as we have to bring people to their senses in the natural. For example, if someone's house was on fire, you would endeavor to alert those inside the house and awaken them any way you could, even if you had to slap their faces or grab them and pull them out of bed.

I didn't physically shake this woman, but I sort of startled her when I said to her, "Sister, God has done all He is ever going to do about your healing."

She looked at me, startled, and said, "You mean that He isn't going to heal me?"

I said, "I didn't say that. I said He has done all He is ever going to do about your healing. He laid your sicknesses and diseases on Jesus. For it is written in Matthew 8:17, '. . . *Himself* [Jesus] *took our infirmities, and bare our sicknesses.*' He has already done something about your healing. First Peter 2:24 says, '. . . *by whose* [Jesus'] *stripes ye were healed.*'"

But, you see, the Word didn't mean a thing in the world to this woman. She said, "Well, I am going to keep on praying. I tell you what I believe about it," and she proceeded to tell me what *she* believed. That was the thing that had her defeated. She was going by what *she* believed the Bible said, instead of by what the Bible actually said. "I am going to keep on praying and seeking God, and sometime, somewhere, in His own way — if it is His will — He'll heal me." That's what she believed.

I don't have to tell you that when I went back to that church five years later this woman was still sick. Why? Because she was not believing the Bible. She was not trying to find God's will by studying and appropriating His Word.

I had told this woman that God had already made provision for her healing in Christ. But she didn't believe what I told her. She had not discovered God's will for herself regarding healing. Therefore, she could not pray in faith and receive her healing.

God Has Blessed Us With *All* Spiritual Blessings

EPHESIANS 1:3
3 Blessed be the God and Father of our Lord Jesus Christ, who hath blessed us with all spiritual blessings in heavenly places in Christ.

God has blessed us with *what*? He has blessed us with *all* spiritual blessings. That scripture doesn't say, "Who is going to bless us?" No, it says, ". . . *who HATH blessed us with all spiritual blessings . . .*" (Eph. 1:3).

Another translation says, "with *every* spiritual blessing." That means every blessing there is to be had. How has God blessed us? He has blessed us ". . . *in heavenly places in Christ*" (Eph. 1:3). That means we are blessed by God's great plan of salvation that God planned and sent Christ to consummate.

In Christ there is all that we will ever need. All that we will ever need has already been provided for us. Every need that you will ever have from the time you are born again until the time you step out of this world into eternity has already been provided for you.

When we know this fact, we can appropriate God's promises, God's blessings, for our own lives. We also know that it is God's will that every need be met because the Scripture says we are blessed ". . . *with ALL spiritual blessings . . .*" (Eph. 1:3). That would include being blessed with every blessing the believer would ever need.

How do we appropriate all the scriptural blessings we have in Christ? We appropriate the blessings and the promises of God through faith and through prayer. Believers everywhere should learn how to pray effectively — in line with God's Word — and bear much fruit in prayer.

Questions for Study

1. When you already know what God's Word says, and you pray "If it be Thy will," what are you really doing?

   _____

   _____

2. What can stop the flow of God's healing power?

   _____

   _____

3. Why shouldn't there be any problem praying in line with the Word of God?

   _____

   _____

4. When can a believer be assured that the Holy Spirit will lead and guide him in all the affairs of life?

   _____

   _____

5. How do we know that it is God's will that the lost be saved?

   _____

   _____

6. How should you pray for unsaved family members not living in your household?

   _____

   _____

7. Why does God keep His Word?

   _____

   _____

8. Why do Full Gospel circles hold divine healing as one of their fundamental beliefs?

   _____

   _____

9. Why do many people want to relieve themselves from all responsibility in the area of prayer?

   _____

   _____

10. Ephesians 1:3 says that God "... *hath blessed us with all spiritual blessings in heavenly places in Christ.*" What does that mean?

    _____

    _____

Chapter 24

The Will of God in Prayer — Part 2

And this is the confidence that we have in him, that, if we ask any thing according to his will, he heareth us:

And if we know that he hear us, whatsoever we ask, we know that we have the petitions that we desired of him.

— 1 John 5:14,15

We looked at this text in First John chapter 5 in the last lesson. In this lesson, let's discuss a little further what the Holy Spirit through John is saying in this passage. First of all, let's focus our attention on two words in verse 14: "confidence" and "heareth."

Under what conditions do we have confidence, or as another translation reads, "boldness," that God hears us? Under this condition: *that we ask according to His will.*

There is another thought that goes along with this, and it is found in verse 15: *"And if we know that he hear us, whatsoever we ask, we know that we have the petitions that we desired of him."* If God heard us when we prayed, we know we *have* the petitions we desired of Him. But First John 5:14 and 15 imply that there are prayers that God *doesn't* hear.

For example, God doesn't hear prayers that are prayed in doubt and unbelief. God responds to *faith.* Now He will put up with a little doubt and unbelief if the person is a baby Christian but is earnest and sincere. But He expects more out of mature believers. However, if we pray in faith according to His will, then we can be confident, *knowing* that we have the petition we have desired of Him.

Also, it is important to note that without the confidence or boldness John talks about in verse 14, our prayers will be ineffective. If we don't fulfill our part in prayer, our prayers will not work. God hears us when we pray according to His Word.

Knowing the Will of God in Prayer

What is it that gives us confidence, boldness, and faith to stand before God in prayer? It is the Word of God. The Psalmist of old said, *"The entrance of thy words giveth light . . ."* (Ps. 119:130). Again, the Psalmist said, *"Thy word is a lamp unto my feet, and a light unto my path"* (Ps. 119:105). When we walk in the light of the Word, we are not walking in darkness, and we can be effective in prayer.

Many times when we pray, we pray in darkness because we are not basing our prayers on the Word of God. I'm not talking about natural darkness as in nighttime. I'm talking about darkness spiritually, or blindness concerning a subject or situation. Many times in prayer we don't know what God's will is when we should know the will of God. We are praying in the dark, spiritually speaking.

Certainly, there are situations that arise about which we do not know how to pray as we ought (Rom. 8:26). But the Bible gives us light as to what to do in those cases too. That is when we are going to have to trust the Greater One on the inside of us, not only to assist us in prayer, but to lead and guide us in all the affairs of life (John 16:13).

When we don't know the will of God on a certain subject, we can't come before Him with confidence or faith. We can't come with boldness. We come trembling and somewhat fearful, hoping God will do something for us. God is a merciful God, and many times when we come to Him that way He *will* still help us. But He desires to show us from the Word how to pray so that we *can* have faith and confidence before Him.

God's best is that we know His Word, His will, and that we pray accordingly. We can go to the Word and find out that God's will is already expressed about practically everything we may want or need.

God's Will Is That *All* Be Saved

For instance, we saw in the previous chapter that saving the lost is God's will, for it is to this end that Jesus Christ died and rose again — so that all of mankind could be saved. I know of no one who would pray for a loved one who was lost and say to the Lord, "Lord, if it is Your will, save So-and-so." That sounds ridiculous because God's Word says that it is God's will that *none* should perish, but that all would be saved (2 Peter 3:9; 1 Tim. 2:4).

Much of our praying for our loved ones or for the lost is not effective because we question the will of God in it, and also because we do not come with confidence and boldness. When one has confidence and boldness, and he prays according to God's will, then he can *know* that he has the petitions he desired of God. Once a person has prayed this way, he should settle it once and for all that he has the victory, and he should settle that in his heart forever.

Then again, much of our praying in this area of loved ones who are lost is very often done in the natural instead of in the Spirit. In other words, it is entirely mental or emotional, and it is based on what we see in the physical realm.

For instance, we pray fervently, "God save our loved one," and then we wait to see if God has answered our prayer. And if that loved one gets saved, we believe God heard us. If that person doesn't get saved shortly thereafter, or if we see no change in that person's thinking or way of life, we think, "Well, I guess God didn't hear me."

Praying like this is walking by sight and not by faith, and it brings confusion. We say, "Well, I have prayed and prayed, and it just seems like my praying doesn't work." But if you will come right back to the Word, God's Word will enlighten you. God's Word will instruct you as to why your prayer was not effective.

Let's read our text again: "*. . . this is the CONFIDENCE that we have in him, that, if we ask any thing ACCORDING TO HIS WILL . . .*" (1 John 5:14). But walking by sight and not by faith is what is hindering your prayers. Doubt and unbelief will rob you of God's greater blessings and render your praying ineffective.

There is no question that it is God's will to save the lost. Therefore, to pray for lost loved ones to be saved is to pray *according to God's will*. When we know God's will, we should have *confidence* before God when we pray.

1 TIMOTHY 2:4
4   Who [God] will have all men to be saved, and to come unto the knowledge of the truth.

2 PETER 3:9
9   The Lord is not slack concerning his promise, as some men count slackness; but is longsuffering to us-ward, not willing that any should perish, but that all should come to repentance.

JOHN 3:16
16   For God so loved the world, that he gave his only begotten Son, that whosoever believeth in him should not perish, but have everlasting life.

Knowing what the Word says, you can see with what confidence we can come to God in prayer. If our praying is according to His will, or His Word, He hears us, for His Word is His will.

JOHN 15:7
7   If ye abide in me, and my words abide in you, ye shall ask what ye will, and it shall be done unto you.

Under what conditions did Jesus say, "*. . . ye shall ask what ye will . . .*" (John 15:7)? He said, "*IF YE ABIDE IN ME, and MY WORDS ABIDE IN YOU,* [then] *ye shall ask what ye will, and it shall be done unto you*" (John 15:7). If you are born again, then you are abiding *in Him*. But then He also said, "*. . . and my words abide in you. . . .*"

I remember a denominational minister in my home county — just a country preacher — who never had an opportunity to pastor a very large church. Most of his churches were small community churches. His limited high school education prevented any promotion by his denomination that he might otherwise have had.

However, this preacher was in constant demand for revival meetings because of his success in soulwinning. He would go to a church where no one was being saved, where no one had been saved for years, and would have a landslide meeting and many people would be brought into the Kingdom of God. You can understand why he was in demand.

I talked to him when he was in his early sixties, and he was still having phenomenal success in revival meetings winning the lost. In his own churches he had altar services as we used to have in Pentecostal circles. He would get the people in his church on their knees, praying.

He said, "People are always asking me my secret. It is a very simple thing. I just apply faith in the area of soulwinning like I apply faith in the areas of healing or whatever I am believing God for. It never enters my mind to doubt that people will come to be saved. If the doubt does try to come, I resist it in the Name of Jesus. It is just that simple."

He said, "I don't do a great deal of praying, any more than others do, but I do pray. I do seek God. However, I attribute my success to that one point — I just have confidence that people will come to be saved. By the eye of faith, I see the people coming to my services; I see the altar filling up with those who want to be saved.

"If the meetings aren't going like I think they should and people aren't coming forward like at other times, I don't necessarily increase my praying or seeking God about it; I just exercise more faith. When I begin to give the invitation, I can just see the people coming, and they come."

What this minister said and did was an expression of his confidence and his faith in God. He had prayed, all right, but not excessively. Many times in our praying, we keep looking at the wrong things.

We keep looking at the circumstances, and we keep looking at what is *not* happening.

Someone might say, "Well, hardly anyone came to the meeting last night, and people probably won't come tonight either."

Or in the area of finances, someone might say, "Well, the finances haven't manifested yet. When I get the money, then I'll believe I have it."

Or if it is in the area of praying for the lost, someone might say, "Well, when I see my family and friends saved, or when I see a change in them, then I'll believe God has heard my prayer and is dealing with them."

You see, that kind of attitude doesn't demonstrate any confidence in God's Word. That kind of attitude isn't letting the Word of God dwell in you at all. That attitude or way of thinking is nothing more than having faith in what you see.

Oftentimes people undo all of their prayers by doing that very thing — by walking by sight when they should be walking by faith in God's Word. But instead of looking at the circumstances when they pray and looking at what is *not* happening, they should be seeing with the eye of faith what God's doing on their behalf in answer to their prayers.

Negative Speaking Can Nullify Prayers

Many people have prayed and prayed and have solicited the help of others in praying. But then these same people undo their prayers and even nullify the faith of other people who are praying by speaking negatively. Their prayers didn't work and their faith was ineffectual because of their negative words. In other words, they didn't have any corresponding actions to their faith. People can also hinder the effects of other people's prayers for them by being negative and by speaking negatively.

For example, I held a meeting for a minister who would pray for his children and would ask others to pray for them too. But when I stayed in his home while holding a meeting for him, I observed something. At the same time he was praying and requesting prayer for his children, I heard him keep telling his boy, "You'll never amount to anything. I don't know what in the world I am going to do with you! I have done everything I can do. I have prayed and prayed, and it looks as though my prayers haven't had any effect on you. I have asked others to pray and it hasn't done any good."

But what good is it going to do to pray if you are going to keep talking the way this man did? That is the same as confessing that your prayers and the prayers of others are not working. You are confessing that God isn't working on your behalf, that God isn't helping you in any way, and that the situation is getting worse.

The fact that this minister was criticizing his son, telling him that he'd never amount to anything, showed the minister's lack of faith. Actually, with his words, the minister was building doubt and insecurity into his own son. And his negative, critical words nullified all of his own prayers for his son, as well as the prayers of others. I talked to this minister about it, and I was able to help him to a certain extent, and the boy turned out quite well after all.

It is important to make sure that you don't take away from your prayers by talking doubt and unbelief and criticism, but rather that you add to your prayers by talking faith. If you are praying for your children in your home, you must not do anything that would nullify the effects of your prayers. You have to build confidence and security into children, instead of doubt and insecurity.

All of the praying that you may do simply isn't going to work for you if you are speaking words of doubt and unbelief. Words of doubt and unbelief will negate your faith and nullify the effects of your prayers. That is where so many people have lost their children spiritually. They have just nullified the effects of their own prayers with their negative speaking.

My own son, Ken, told me when he was in high school that the most difficult problems at his school were with preachers' or missionaries' children.

He said, "It didn't take me too long to find out the main problem with these young people. I would mention participating in some activity and they would say, 'Do you mean your Dad would let you do that?'"

For instance, my son had his driver's license. His friends would ask, "You mean your Dad lets you drive the car?"

Ken would reply, "Why, yes. I drove the car all the way from Texas to Oregon." (He had driven his mother out to Oregon once when I was holding a meeting there.) One of Ken's friends said to him, "Why, man, if I even *insinuated* I wanted to get behind the wheel of our car, my Dad would knock me in the head." (This boy was a preacher's son!)

All the praying in the world a parent could do for his child would be nullified if that parent spoke negatively to his child or mistreated him. I stayed in a pastor's home one time and witnessed his mistreatment of his son. I really felt sorry for this pastor's son.

Years later as a grown man, at forty years old, this son broke the heart of his parents. Although he grew up in a pastor's home, he never amounted to much. He had been married several times and had never provided a living for his family.

As a young boy preacher myself before I was married, I stayed in these folks' home. They constantly told this boy that he would never amount to anything, so he didn't. They would pray for him, but then they would say, "I don't know what I am going to do, Kenneth. I wish you would pray for him."

If the son didn't do things just right, that pastor would knock that twelve-year-old boy in the head — nearly halfway across the house — and then kick him while he was down, so to speak. They lost their tempers with him, you see. How could they expect him to amount to anything when he grew up!

As a young fellow before I was ever married, I saw many ministers' children who were neglected or mistreated. Their mothers, who were pastors' wives, worked in the church and were so busy that their children were left alone to do as they pleased — to run with whomever they wanted. I could see these ministers losing their own families through negligence.

What am I saying? I haven't digressed from the subject of prayer. I'm saying that these ministers prayed and prayed and even asked the church to pray, and they probably shed many tears and did a lot of fasting, but really they had nullified the effects of everyone's prayers through their actions.

Hindering Prayers by Wrong Actions

Let me share an example of how a person can hinder his own prayers by acting contrary to God's Word. There was a woman in one of the churches I pastored who was a marvelous Christian and Sunday school teacher. She was one of the best Sunday School teachers and, actually, the most able Bible teacher in our entire church. I thought so then and I still think she was one of the best teachers I've seen after all these years.

In the process of time in about 1943 (during World War II), she had two or three boys who went into the service. With tears, this woman would stand up in church and request prayer for her boys, and we would include them in our prayers. She was a great woman of prayer too. Certainly, it is correct to pray for our servicemen and to pray for our children.

After a certain length of time, one of the boys was going to be shipped overseas. Before he left, he had a thirty-day furlough, and he came home to be with

his mother. During those thirty days, this Sunday school teacher never did come to church. She didn't even teach her Sunday School class; the assistant teacher had to teach the class. She didn't even come to church on Sunday because she and her son were out visiting kinfolks on Sunday.

Then on the very last Sunday that her son was home on furlough, they had a family reunion. This woman and her husband had eight children of their own, and some of the older ones had been married for a number of years, so there were many grandchildren at the reunion too. It was a big affair. She, of course, didn't come on that Sunday either. Her son was home for thirty days, and then he left.

The very first Wednesday night this woman came back to church, she got up out of her seat and with tears, asked us to pray for her boy. "Pray for my son," she said. "He is being shipped out and is on his way overseas right now. He's not a Christian. Pray for him that he'll be saved."

Right from the pulpit I said, "Now, Sister, we're not going to do it."

That startled the whole crowd. Some of them were sitting there half asleep and they instantly became wide awake when I said that.

I said, "I'm not going to do it because you have been turning in prayer requests for your son for months now. Almost every time we have prayed, you have turned prayer requests in. We have believed God for your son and we've prayed. I know this boy of yours. I have talked to him in times past. I know him well enough to know that if you had asked him to come to church just one time while he was home on furlough, he would have come."

I knew that her sons greatly appreciated their mother, more than they did their father, because she had been a Christian before the father became a Christian, and she had carried the load in the family, spiritually speaking. And she was a very stalwart Christian. They had great respect for her and great respect for her Christian experience.

I said to this woman, "We have prayed and prayed, but people don't get saved just by people praying. They get saved by hearing and believing the gospel and by calling on the Name of the Lord Jesus Christ for themselves. Many people get saved in church or in a church service."

I said to the woman, "Your son was home for thirty days. I know him well enough to know that if you had asked him to come to church he would have come. Then the last Sunday you had a great family reunion. Everyone got together to talk from the natural standpoint, but you neglected your Sunday school class and didn't come to church for a whole month; you missed four Sundays.

"Even if you had said to your son, 'Well now, son, this is the last Sunday you'll be home. Come and go to church with Mama, at least on Sunday night,' I know he would have come."

That seemed to come as a surprise to that dear soul. She had been standing up in church to turn in her prayer requests, and when I said this time we were not going to pray, she just stood there and looked stunned. But then a bright look came on her face. She realized what she had done wrong. But she acted as though she hadn't even thought of taking her son to church. She acted as if it came as a surprise that she could even ask her son to come to church.

She said, "Well, that's right. That's true, he would have come," with the expression on her face that seemed to say, "Why didn't I think of that?"

You would think any Christian would know better than to do what this woman had done. It seems like the obvious thing to do in this woman's situation would be to ask her son to come with her to church. That doesn't mean that a person should nag people to get them to go to church.

She could have said to her son, "I have a Sunday school class to teach, and I must go to church. You can go with me. I'd like you to go with me."

If her son had refused her invitation at first, then on the last Sunday he was home she could have said, "This is your last day home, Son, and I would appreciate it if you would come to church with me."

I knew him well enough to know that he would have come out of respect for his mother. I know of plenty of other people who came to church under similar circumstances, and while they were under the influence of the Word of God and the Holy Ghost, they were convicted of their need for the Savior and were saved.

"Do you see what I mean?" I said to this woman. "You see, instead of helping our prayers, you did everything, whether consciously or unconsciously, to hinder our prayers."

There was another woman in our church one time, and every time we took prayer requests (which we did in about every service in those days), she would ask us to pray for her husband. He would come to church with her once in a while, or maybe he would slip into the service after she had already gotten there.

I'm sure it was a little embarrassing to him when his wife got up in the service and requested prayer for him. Right in the middle of a revival meeting, she would stand up and request prayer for him, calling his name, with him sitting right there in the service. She wanted us to pray that he would get saved.

Once in a Wednesday night service, when only the church members were present, she came and requested prayer again. I didn't want to embarrass her. I simply wanted to make an object lesson of her request because I wanted to illustrate something to the crowd.

I said, "Sister, we're not going to do it. You have turned in prayer requests here for your husband time and time again. We have prayed and prayed. I have talked to your husband. I have visited him in your home and have talked to him for two or three hours at a time.

"There is no reason for us to go on praying for him because you are nullifying all of the effects of our praying. You go home and tell him everyone's faults in the church, and gossip to him about everyone." (There were some things which, unless she had told him, he just couldn't have known. I know no one else would have told him.)

Then I explained, "You air all of the pastor's mistakes and all of the Sunday school superintendent's mistakes and all of the mistakes of everyone else in the church. You just constantly talk badly about others. I dare say that at every meal, that is all you talk about, until he almost asks the question, 'Why do you even go down there to church? You don't believe anyone down there is worth anything, anyway.'

"Until you learn to keep your tongue from speaking negatively, you are going to nullify the effects of all of our praying and believing for him. Your husband still comes to church occasionally, but you have just about talked him out of the idea of coming altogether. He has more of a chance of getting saved here than he does anywhere else. Yet you have just about talked him out of coming to church."

That was like giving that dear soul a spanking. She resented it at first, but she finally straightened up and became one of the staunchest supporters we had in the church. Up until then she had never even paid her tithes, although she had money of her own — more than her husband did. She was a businesswoman and made much more money than he did. She began to support the church and to keep her mouth shut.

I told her publicly, "Your main trouble is you just talk too much. You ought to learn to keep your mouth shut." When she learned to stop criticizing everyone, her husband began coming more and more to church and was eventually saved.

What am I talking about? I am talking about praying for things which are the will of God, but nullifying the effects of our own prayers through our negative words and actions. So, let's not work *against* God; let's work *with* God.

God's Will To Supply Our Financial Needs

I am going to give you another example of God's will in prayer. Philippians 4:19 says, *"But my God shall supply all your need according to his riches in glory by Christ Jesus."*

Since this scripture is true, then we know that it is God's will for us to have the finances to meet our obligations. We can have faith to claim that as our right and privilege in Christ because it's in the Word. Therefore, it's God's will that all of our needs be supplied. Actually, when Paul said, *". . . my God shall supply all your need. . . ,"* he was specifically talking about material and financial needs.

But I believe that Paul meant that God was talking about meeting *all* of our needs, whatever they are. "All" means all. Or we could say that God will meet "every need" of yours, and "every need" means *every need*, whether it is a spiritual, physical, material, or a financial need. "All" means *every one of your needs*. I believe that. And you need to believe that, too, if you want to appropriate the promise and receive the benefit.

Lest someone think that it is not true that God is concerned about our financial needs, or that Paul is not talking about finances here, read the entire context or passage in Philippians chapter 4. You will find out that the people of the Philippian church had collected an offering of money and goods to send to other Christians. Paul was saying to them, "Because you have given to others and have helped them, my God shall supply all of *your* need." Paul was talking about material and financial matters.

Hindering Our Prayers By Not Cooperating With God

We believe that God shall supply all our needs, but there is another side to this coin of believing God for finances. In other words, we have *our* part to play by cooperating with God and obeying the Word in order to see our needs met.

Once I was holding a meeting in another state, and the pastor talked to me about a man who had been in the services. This man the pastor was talking about was an example of someone who was *not* cooperating with God, and therefore he was hindering people's prayers for him and his family concerning his finances.

The pastor said, "Brother Hagin, if you would, please talk to that fellow. He has taken a special liking to you."

I asked, "What is the problem?"

The pastor answered, "I'll put it this way: He has a wife and five children, and they are Christians, all right, although they are not members of our church. They have been coming here for about a year. I don't know where they came from, for they didn't live here in this city until about eighteen months ago. After about six months, they started coming to our church and have come to this church ever since. His wife is a precious Christian and some of these children are the most precious children you have ever seen, and they love the Lord.

"The father is a well, able-bodied fellow, about thirty-eight years old, but he just won't work. Some of the other men in the church have tried to help him. They have made arrangements for him to go for an interview at the place where they work, for he can do that kind of work. The men have talked to the foreman on the job, and the foreman said, 'Tell him to come in; I'll hire him.' But he wouldn't go."

The pastor continued, "Folks here in the church have helped that family. We have taken up 'poundings' — food offerings — for them. We have gotten groceries for them and clothes for the children. They have gotten some things from the local welfare department.

"Some of the women in the church have helped this man's wife in every way they can by giving her work to earn a little bit of money. She is a good worker and would ask some of the folks if they had anything she could do. They would provide ironing for her to do and other small jobs just to give her some money.

"The husband has taken a special liking to you, Brother Hagin. Maybe you could help him. When I try to talk to him he says, 'Well, the Lord said He would meet all of our needs.'"

I did go and talk to the man. This man actually told me, "Some folks tell me to get out and look for a job, but I am just waiting for the right one to come to me. The Lord will do it. He said in His Word, '. . . *my God shall supply all your need according to his riches in glory by Christ Jesus'* (Phil. 4:19). We are getting along quite well, although we may not be living in just the best style in the world."

Someone else was paying his house rent. In fact, the church was paying about half of it to keep him going. That fellow was really hindering their prayers for him by his own actions.

A person can't just sit down and wait for something to come to him; that's not faith. The only thing that will come to him is a pile of bills to pay! A person can believe that God will help him and bless him financially and materially, but then he needs to move in that direction and do whatever his hand finds to do. The Lord said He would bless all that we set our hands to (Deut. 16:15; 24:19). If the job he gets isn't just right, at least it will help him right at the moment, and then he can pray about working some place else. God can open another door for him and give him another job.

This man hadn't done any type of work in that town for eighteen months that the church people knew of. He was an able-bodied man, and by his own admission there was nothing wrong with him physically. But he was just hanging around, lying around, doing nothing, waiting for God to bring him something. He should have been embarrassed that his wife had to work as much as she did with five children to care for.

Some of the men of the church actually could have provided jobs for him — maybe not the biggest and the best jobs in the world — but something that could have been a stepping-stone to something better. He wouldn't even go see about those jobs. He was waiting for God to send something to him.

But God is not going to put a job in an envelope and mail it to you in the mail! You have to get out and let people know that you are available to work.

I know of preachers who believed that way about getting meetings. They wouldn't cooperate with God by making themselves known to other ministers who might invite them to preach. It is the strangest thing to me that a preacher wouldn't have more sense than that.

When I first went out on the field in ministry, I had to learn how to do my part and cooperate with God so He could meet my needs. I went out in field ministry in 1944 during World War II. The church where I pastored had reelected me, and I could have stayed if I had wanted to. I was a little hesitant to let my name go up for reelection, for I was pondering in my mind whether I should stay or go. I was trying to find God's will concerning my ministry. But it was time for an election, so I said to the board, "Well, I'll just leave it up to you."

I would have been thrilled if they hadn't reelected me and had just sent me on my way. That way I wouldn't have had to make the choice myself. I could have said, "Well, bless God, I have to go out in the field ministry now." But they did reelect me, and they wanted me to stay. But about a month afterwards, I just couldn't become reconciled to staying at that church.

I sensed in my spirit that it was time to go. I went out in field ministry with just one revival meeting slated. When I finished that meeting I didn't have any more meetings scheduled. When a man has already been out preaching for a while, folks know about it and invitations for more meetings come in. But if he has never spent very much time out in the field, having mainly pastored, then there won't be many who know that he is available for meetings.

After we finished this meeting, we went back to my wife's parents' house for a few days. I said to her, "I am going down to the ministers' fellowship meeting next Thursday."

I mentioned a certain man and said, "I have no proof of it — he hasn't said anything to me — but in my spirit I have the feeling, the impression, that he has been trying to contact me to hold a meeting. I'll go down there, and if he doesn't ask me to hold a meeting, someone else will. Then when I start my meeting, I'll come back and get you and the children."

So I drove down to this fellowship meeting. I knew they started about ten o'clock in the morning, but I got in at about eleven o'clock, in time to hear the speaker. The custom was that they would introduce all of the visitors, and I felt they would introduce me and let it be known that I was an evangelist. At any rate, I slipped in and sat down.

There were several preachers sitting in a pew right in front of me. The very fellow I was talking about was sitting right on the end, and he just reached back, took my hand, and said, "I've been trying to reach you. I want you to hold me a meeting."

I said, "I know it."

He said, "When can you start?"

I said, "Tonight."

He said, "Well, we can't start tonight with no advertisement or anything, but come home with me after the meeting tonight. Tomorrow we have our Friday night service in our church. You can preach tomorrow night, then we'll get our advertisement out Saturday, and we'll start your meeting on Sunday."

So I did, and he did, and the Lord gave us one of the best meetings they said they'd ever had in the history of their church.

By this time, another fellow who was in the meeting had contacted me and I went to his church to hold a meeting. Going to fellowship meetings to let folks know you are available for meetings is a necessary part of the work of the ministry. Otherwise, how are others going to know you're available? Are you just going to sit home and ask God to send someone by? That may happen occasionally, but that is the exception, not the rule.

I had a preacher friend at that time who refused to go to these fellowship meetings. I said to him, "Come and go with me to the fellowship meeting." He was living in that area, and, really, he needed to go. He had gotten a little bitter because he wasn't being asked to preach, although he had never made himself available to preach. (I never asked anyone for a meeting in my life, but I did get into circulation to let people know I was available for meetings.)

This man had resigned his church, moved to this place, and had just sat down, so to speak, and quit circulating. He had given up even trying to get meetings. He rarely went to anyone's church, not even on Sunday. He just sat around the house and did nothing.

Just because folks didn't come by and say, "Well, come hold me a meeting," he had gotten bitter. He sat there for several months and no one said a word to him. I guess they thought he was trying to withdraw from society and that he didn't *want* anyone to say anything to him.

I said, "Come on and go," and at first he said he would go.

Then when I went by for him, he said, "No, I'm not going."

I said, "Man, you can't just sit here and expect someone to call you for a meeting. They don't even know you are available! Many of the folks in this area think you are still the pastor of this church over here. It hasn't gotten around yet that you are itinerating. They don't know that you are looking for meetings and are available."

I continued, "You know yourself that if you went to this meeting, they would probably ask you to preach in the meeting. I don't know of another minister that's available. Besides that, they introduce all of the visiting ministers and evangelists so that people will know who is available."

"No, I'm not going," he said.

I said, "Well, that's the way I did it."

He said, "Well, I'm not stupid like you are."

I said, "Well, bless God, I'm not sitting around doing without like *you* are. If you want to sit here and do nothing, then just sit here and do nothing." He just sat there, getting more and more bitter, and he never did anything more about preaching. Later he moved to another city.

Several years later, I was holding a meeting in his city, and I talked to him again. I said, "Brother, I'll help you get meetings." I contacted pastors where I had been and I already had him lined up for six months of solid meetings that year. I knew he was a good enough preacher that if he went that long, he could keep going, getting more meetings through making contacts on his own. These fellows all contacted him, and he accepted the invitations. But then at the last minute, he backed out and wouldn't go.

What I am talking about is this: You can hinder your prayers by not cooperating with God. You can hinder your prayers by not entering into the doors that God opens for you. You must learn to yield to the gentle leadings of the Holy Spirit.

God's will is that you as a believer know and understand God's will for your life. We walk by faith and not by sight. And we have the Greater One, the Holy Spirit, living on the inside of us to lead us in all the affairs of life.

It is also God's will that we understand how to pray according to His will. In this chapter we've looked at a few subjects for which the Bible specifically states God's will.

We saw that it is God's will that all would be saved and come to a knowledge of the truth; therefore, we should pray for the lost. We also know that it is God's will that we are healed. And God's will is that His children prosper in every realm of their lives, including in the financial realm. So we can claim His provision for our every need and have confidence that we are praying according to God's will.

As you pray for these things, learn to cooperate with God in your words and actions. Determine never to speak negatively or act in a way that will hinder your prayers being answered. In all that you say or do regarding what you have prayed for, be sure you magnify God and His Word, not the problem or circumstances. Then you will receive the answers to your prayers according to God's will.

Questions for Study

1. What is it that gives us confidence, boldness, and faith to stand before God in prayer?
_____
_____

2. What is the reason that many times when we pray, we pray in darkness?
_____
_____

3. Name three reasons why much of our praying for our loved ones or for the lost is not effective.
_____
_____

4. When we pray, what should we be seeing with the eye of faith?
_____
_____

5. How do people hinder the effects of other people's prayers for them?
_____
_____

6. If parents are praying for their children in their home, what do the parents have to build into their children?
_____
_____

7. What are three ways a person can nullify or hinder his own prayers?
_____
_____

8. According to Philippians 4:19, which of our needs will God supply?
_____
_____

9. What part do we play in believing God for finances?
_____
_____

10. In all that you say or do regarding what you have prayed for, what should you be sure to do?
_____
_____

Chapter 25

The Will of God in Prayer — Part 3

And this is the confidence that we have in him, that, if we ask any thing according to his will, he heareth us:

And if we know that he hear us, whatsoever we ask, we know that we have the petitions that we desired of him.

— 1 John 5:14,15

Let's continue our discussion of the will of God in prayer. I mentioned in previous chapters that God's will concerning almost anything we could want or need in life is expressed in His written Word. God's Word is His will.

Certainly, there are situations about which we do not know how to pray as we ought, but even in those cases, we have the Holy Ghost to help us pray (Rom. 8:26). And we have the Holy Ghost to lead us into all the truth (John 16:13).

As I've already said, God's will is that you as a believer know and understand God's specific will for your life.

Follow Your Spirit, Not Circumstances

The Bible says the primary way God leads His children is through the inward witness (Rom. 8:14). We need to listen to our spirits, rather than look to circumstances to determine God's will in any situation.

Too many times believers try to ascertain the will of God by circumstances. Sometimes circumstances do have something to do with understanding the will of God for us, but not always. But nowhere in the Bible do you find that believers are to be led by circumstances.

ROMAN 8:14
14 For as many as are led by the Spirit of God, they are the sons of God.

For example, in Chapter 24, we talked about the minister who had become bitter because no one had asked him to preach. This minister had taken the attitude, "Oh, well, I guess it isn't God's will for me to preach anymore. No meetings have opened, no one has asked me to preach, so I'll just quit the ministry."

But, now, wait a minute. The calling of God and the gift of God is without repentance. The Bible says so (Rom. 11:29). If God called a man to preach, then

that man is not going to be able to get rid of his calling that quickly.

I am simply making the observation that too many times we try to find the will of God by the circumstances we *see* without taking anything else into consideration. That can be dangerous because we are not to be led by circumstances; we are to be led by our spirits by the Holy Spirit in our spirits. We need to take God's Word into consideration first. Second, we need to take into consideration what God has said to us and how He has dealt with our own spirits. And *then*, third, we are to take the circumstances into consideration.

Again, there have been pastors who have told me that they were going to leave their church. I knew in my spirit that they were missing God. Once a pastor told me, "Well, I'm going to leave my church." I knew by revelation in my spirit that he should not leave. I didn't tell him, but I did everything else *but* tell him.

I didn't come right out and say, "Boy, you are a fool. You are missing God if you leave your church."

But I did tell him, "Now you had better be careful; you might miss God." If that was not telling him, what was it? I was not knocking him in the head, so to speak, but I was telling him to be careful.

He replied, "No, no. I'm not missing God. I put a fleece out before God. They were having a church election, and I decided that I was going to have them vote on me, on whether or not I should continue as the pastor." (He had been previously voted in indefinitely. In other words, he didn't *have* to have them vote on him, but he had said, "I don't want to stay at a church if they don't want me to stay." So he had an election.)

Here was his fleece. He said, "Lord, if I get one hundred percent of the vote, then I will accept that as Your will to stay here. If I don't, I am going to leave."

According to the rules of this particular church, if he had gotten two thirds of the votes he was to remain. But there were two people out of about one hundred people voting who said "no." And just because there were two negative votes, he decided to leave. (You can hardly ever get one hundred sheep together without a couple of old goats in the bunch!)

Too many times folks try to ascertain what God's will is by what they call "putting out a fleece." That can sometimes be similar to walking by circumstances or walking by sight instead of by faith, and it can cause much confusion.

I tried to tell this pastor that that was not the way to find the will of God. For instance, a pastor might not get every vote to be reelected because everyone in the church might not be in the best fellowship with God, where they could listen to the Spirit of God. You can understand that.

People are just as human and as natural as a pastor is, and something might have been said just a few days before that made them take a little offense. Right at that time they might have written "no" on their ballots, when at any other time they would have written "yes."

Can you see how the same thing can be true in the life of any believer? Many times a believer will sense something in his own spirit, independent of the circumstances. In other words, he will have the leading and the witness that he ought to do something.

Yet instead of following that witness he is supposed to follow — the leading of the Holy Spirit — he puts out a fleece and says, "Now, God, if You want me to do this, then You open this door. If You don't, You shut that door." Or, "Lord, if you want me to do this, then You have this person to do that."

But a person gets over into the sense realm and the mental realm that way, and he loses the inward witness, or it becomes indistinct and dim because he is operating in another realm — the natural realm. Can you understand that?

As God's children, we are to be led by the Holy Spirit, not by fleeces! We need to find out what the Word of God says about any given situation. Then we need to learn how to talk to God long enough in prayer that we come to know His will *in our spirit*, rather than depending on outward circumstances to help us determine what to do. The more we do that, the easier it will be to determine God's will in prayer and in our lives.

Our Confidence in Approaching God

Let's look at our text once more. First John 5:14 says, "*. . . this is the confidence that we have in him, that, if we ask any thing according to his will, he heareth us*" (1 John 5:14). Another translation reads, "This is the *boldness* that we have toward Him . . ." (1 John 5:14). Confidence and boldness are similar in meaning because if we are confident, we are bold, aren't we? And if we don't have confidence, then

there is a lack of boldness, and there is an insecurity about us.

Many times when we read scriptures such as these in First John chapter 5, we don't completely comprehend the meaning. I once read a book in which the author said that oftentimes folks have found a few jewels and gems on top of the ground without doing much digging. But he said if a person really wants to get down where the valuable veins of gold and precious jewels are, he will have to dig for them.

That is also true of the Word, isn't it? If we just go along reading on the surface, we may pick up a little diamond occasionally. But if we will dig down a little deeper, we will find veins of gold, so to speak, and larger spiritual gems and jewels.

Reading these verses in First John 5 in only a casual manner, we can come to the wrong conclusions entirely concerning what John said here. As I said previously, many have thought John was saying, "If it is God's will, He will hear me, and if it isn't, He won't."

Therefore, people conclude, "If I get my answer, it is God's will. If I don't get my answer, then it isn't God's will."

But that isn't what John was saying. He said, "This is the *boldness* we have in Him, that if we ask anything according to His will, He hears us" (1 John 5:14).

We have added our own thinking to that and have said, "Well, now, we'll pray, and if it is God's will, He will hear us and answer us. And if we don't receive the answer, then that means it was not His will."

But that is not correct. We're still missing it, for the simple reason that if we have God's Word for anything we need, we don't have to say, "If it is God's will we'll receive the answer." We will know His will because His Word is His will. Then we can pray and *know* we have the answers by faith. Do you see the difference? If we have God's *Word* for it, we have God's *will* for it.

That is the reason I encourage folks to find scriptures that cover the situation about which they are praying. Find scriptures that promise you whatever it is you are praying about.

Sometimes people ask me to pray with them about a certain need, and I ask them, "What scripture are you standing on?"

Many of them say to me, "Well, not any in particular."

I always say, "Then that is what you will get — nothing in particular!"

If we pray according to God's Word, then we know our petition is based solidly on God's will. It has to be God's will for Him to promise it in His Word. And it is God's will that we appropriate and possess everything that He has provided for us in His Word.

If we know what we desire is according to God's will, or His Word, we know that He hears us when we pray. *Then* we can have confidence that we have received our petition from God.

That would agree with what Jesus Himself said in John 15:7.

JOHN 15:7
7   If ye abide in me, and my words abide in you, ye shall ask what ye will, and IT SHALL BE DONE UNTO YOU.

So then *". . . this is the confidence that we have in him, that, if we ask any thing according to his will, he heareth us"* (1 John 5:14). How do we know He hears us? Because we ask according to His will or His Word. *"And if we know that he hear us, whatsoever we ask, we know that we have the petitions that we desired of him"* (1 John 5:15).

We know we have the petitions we desired of God before they ever materialize, before those things ever come to pass. Why? Because we know we prayed according to God's will — according to His Word. We know God hears us. Therefore, we know we have our answer. I didn't say it: The *Word* says it.

You can see with what confidence and what assurance we can come to God. As I said before, the believer who is walking in fellowship with the Word, won't ask for anything outside of God's will. If the believer knows the Word, then he knows what is promised to him. He knows the will of God.

When we know the Word of God, we don't have to be concerned about whether we're going to ask for something that is not God's will. And we don't have to be concerned whether or not we'll receive answers to our prayers. When we ask according to God's Word, we can *know* that we have the petitions we desired of Him.

However, if a believer is not walking in the light of the Word and in fellowship with the Word, his prayers aren't going to be answered. His prayer life isn't going to be effective anyway, because Jesus plainly stated, *"If YE ABIDE IN ME, and MY WORDS ABIDE IN YOU, ye shall ask what ye will, and it shall be done unto you"* (John 15:7).

When God's Word *abides* in you, in your heart, *then* the Bible says you can ask what you will and receive answers to prayer.

Praying in Line With God's Word

Many people stumble in prayer and do not pray effectually because they don't know God's will. When you abide in God's Word, you will know His will.

As we have stated before, we know that saving the lost is God's will. We know that because We know the Word. It was to that end that Jesus died.

JOHN 3:16
16   For God so loved the world, that he gave his only begotten Son, that whosoever believeth in him should not perish, but have everlasting life.

2 PETER 3:9
9   The Lord is not . . . willing that any should perish, but that all should come to repentance.

Therefore, we don't have to pray, "Now, Lord, if it is Your will, save this one." Or "Lord, save that one." We know it is His will to save the lost. The lost person for whom we are praying may not be willing to be saved, but we know that God is willing to save every soul. In fact, God has already purchased their redemption and the forgiveness of sins for them through Christ's redemptive work on the Cross.

All the sinner must do is accept what God has done and receive Jesus as Savior and Lord. We know that this is God's will. And we know that if we pray according to God's Word for someone who is lost, God will begin to deal with the unsaved one for whom we are praying. And as we ask in faith, God will send laborers across his path to help lead that unsaved loved one into the Kingdom of God.

We know we can pray for unsaved friends and loved ones. But we can also pray for the lost in our own country as well as in other lands. We know that it is God's will that none perish, but that all would come to repentance and be saved (2 Peter 3:9; 1 Tim. 2:4).

As we discussed before, we also know that healing the sick is God's will. Many people have the mistaken idea that sometimes it is God's will to heal some, and sometimes it is not His will to heal others. But the Bible says that Christ bore our infirmities and carried our sicknesses.

ISAIAH 53:4
4   Surely he hath borne our griefs, and carried our sorrows: yet we did esteem him stricken, smitten of God, and afflicted.

MATTHEW 8:17
17   That it might be fulfilled which was spoken by Esaias the prophet, saying, Himself took our infirmities, and bare our sicknesses.

Therefore, God's will concerning healing is plainly stated in His Word. It is not the will of God for believers to be sick. Don't misunderstand me. I know that we are all going to have to die sometime. God didn't promise us that we are going to live down here on this earth forever. But it is God's will that folks live out their lives on the earth in health and not die prematurely.

Also, God has told us that physical death will eventually be put underfoot. Death is the last enemy that will be put underfoot (1 Cor. 15:26). But that time has not yet come. But if we are ill, we certainly have the right to believe God for healing because the Word of God says explicitly that it is God's will to heal.

1 PETER 2:24
24 Who his own self bare our sins in his own body on the tree, that we, being dead to sins, should live unto righteousness: by whose stripes ye were healed.

So healing has to be the will of God. We don't have to put an "if" in our prayers for healing, saying, "If it is Your will, Lord, heal me," or "If it is Your will, heal this other person." We know His will because His Word is His will.

I will grant you this, there are those people who are not in God's will — they are living outside of the will of God. There are some who, before they can receive their healing, will have to get back into the will of God. But you still don't have to pray for those people, "Lord, if it is Your will, heal them," because it is always God's will to heal, just as much as it is always God's will that all people be saved.

However, people have a free will and they have a choice. People can choose whether or not to believe God's Word. And many choose wrongly. They choose not to believe it. That is why many are facing some of the troubles and circumstances they are facing, because they have refused to believe God's Word.

Also, we saw in previous lessons that receiving your needs met is God's will too.

PHILIPPIANS 4:19
19 But my God shall supply all your need according to his riches in glory by Christ Jesus.

The margin of my Bible says, *"every need of yours according to His riches in glory by Christ Jesus."* All of your needs, *every* need, means just what it says — *all* of your needs.

Practically everything you could want or need is covered in these areas of salvation, healing, and prosperity that we have discussed.

We can also pray for ministers, that they will speak forth the Word of God in the power of the Holy Spirit. For example, Paul said to the Church at Corinth, *". . . a great door and effectual is opened unto me, and there are many adversaries"* (1 Cor. 16:9). Then later Paul said, "Pray for me."

Paul was asking believers to pray that he would be able to speak in the power of the Spirit.

The Word Is a Light Unto Our Path

If a person would just study the Word, instead of saying, "If it be Thy will, Lord," he would be able to boldly and confidently say regarding his request to God, "Let it be done, Lord, *according to Your Word.*" Then he would have his prayer in the right focus — in *faith*, not in doubt and unbelief.

I have found in my own experience that I can find in God's Word a promise for every situation of life. Then I can know just how to pray, and I can have the assurance of God's will before I pray.

Many times the reason prayer isn't working for people is that they are trying to get God to help them or do something for them apart from the Word. Actually, they are praying in darkness. The Psalmist said, *"The entrance of thy words giveth light . . ."* (Ps. 119:130). The Psalmist also said, *"Thy word is a lamp unto my feet, and a light unto my path"* (Ps. 119:105). God's Word is a lamp unto our feet.

We are to walk in the light of the Word. No one can build a successful prayer life if he doesn't know the Word. A successful prayer life is built and based upon the written Word of God. When you pray according to the Word, the Word is a lamp unto your feet and a light unto your path. You know which way you are walking. You are not praying in the dark.

Too much of the time, because of a failure to know the Word and to see what God's Word has to say about a subject, we are simply praying in darkness, and we don't know where we are going. Prayer becomes a matter of begging God in desperation to do something for us.

But when you know what the Word says, then you can come to God in prayer with confidence and boldness. That is what our text says, *"And this is the confidence that we have in him, that, if we ask any thing according to his will [His Word], he heareth us"* (1 John 5:14).

Many times, folks wouldn't even have to pray about some situations if they were simply walking by the light of the Word. For instance, I've told you the story of the woman who came at the close of the service and shook hands with me as I was still standing on the platform.

She held onto my hand and said, "Brother Hagin, I want you to pray for me."

I said, "All right. What for?"

I believe that startled her because she asked, "Well, do I have to tell you?"

So I smiled and said, "I'm not going to pray unless you do. After all, if you want me to pray for you, you are expecting me to have faith for something, and I can't have faith for something if I don't know what that something is. If you want me to agree with you, I have to know what I am agreeing about."

I am not making fun of the woman because I sympathized with her then, and I still do. My heart went out to her. However, sympathy won't deliver people or answer their prayers for them.

When I said this to her, she began to cry, and a look of desperation came over her countenance. She said, "Brother Hagin, the cares of life, the anxieties and the worries of life, are just so great."

She began to cry a little harder and said, "I just can't carry them. I wanted you to pray that God would do one of two things for me. Either He would give me grace to bear them, or else He would take about half of the cares away. I can carry half of them. I just can't carry all of them."

We know that sounds a little peculiar, and we may laugh about it, but really it isn't a laughing matter. It was a very serious thing to that dear soul. My heart goes out to anyone who is a Christian and is Spirit filled and yet is walking in darkness because he is not walking in the light of the Word.

I simply said, "Well, Sister, I can't pray either prayer. Both of your requests are unscriptural."

You see, we are enlightened by God's Word. We are enlightened by God's Word if we know what His Word is. And if we know God's *Word*, we know what His *will* is.

It wasn't God's will to give this woman grace to bear these worries, anxieties, and cares. And it wasn't His will to take only half of them away and let her carry the other half.

How do I know that? Because I know what God's Word says. God's Word says, *"Casting ALL your care upon him; for he careth for you"* (1 Peter 5:7).

This verse doesn't say, "Casting *half* of your cares upon Him." And it doesn't say, "God will give you grace to carry your cares, but you will have to carry them yourself." It says, *"Casting ALL your care upon him; for he careth for you"* (1 Peter 5:7).

I said to this woman, "Sister, isn't it wonderful that we already have the answer for your prayer right here in the Word? The Bible already has the answer to your prayer!" I got my Bible and read it to her, *"Casting all your care upon him. . . ."*

The *Amplified* version is more explicit than the *King James* translation.

1 PETER 5:7 *(Amplified)*

7 Casting the whole of your care — all your anxieties, all your worries, all your concerns, once and for all — on Him; for He cares for you affectionately, and cares about you watchfully.

This translation of First Peter 5:7 defines "the whole of your care" as anxieties, worries, and concerns. What are we to do with our cares? We are to cast them upon the Lord. How many of them? *All* of them. We are to cast *all* of our cares and concerns upon the Lord. Why? Because God cares for us affectionately and cares about us watchfully.

I believe God does care about us, don't you? I believe the last part of that verse is as true as the first part of that verse. God cares for us affectionately and cares about us watchfully.

And if I believe that, then I am going to have to believe the first part of that verse, too, and I am going to have to act upon it. I am going to have to cast all of my cares upon the Lord. That includes all of my concerns and all of my anxieties. And the reason I can do that is God does care for me affectionately, and He cares about me watchfully. God is watching over me. He loves me.

I explained all this to that woman and she said she just couldn't do it. She said "I can't cast *all* of my cares upon the Lord. I know I can't."

I said, "Well, God said you can. God is not going to tell you in His Word to do something you cannot do. That would be foolish and unjust."

This woman said to me, "Oh, you are just being hard. You are just hard."

I replied, "Sister, I am not being hard. I'm just telling you what the Bible says. It wasn't I who said, 'Casting all your care upon him. . . .' God said that; I didn't."

She said, "Yes, but you don't understand what I have to worry about."

I said, "Well, I'm sure I don't, but I am not the one who wrote the Bible. It is *God*'s Word, not mine."

This poor dear woman just walked away muttering to herself. She couldn't seem to take God at His Word. How sad!

God is our Heavenly *Father*. He is our God, but He is also our Father. He is not going to tell us to do something we can't do. Believers should understand the character and nature of their Father enough to know this about Him.

I remember when I found out about casting my cares on the Lord, I was never more glad in my life. I found out I didn't have to worry anymore, and I was just tickled pink!

I don't understand some people. From the time I got saved, I always read the Bible from the standpoint of finding all the deliverance and help I could. It seems to me that some people read the Bible to find out everything they can to condemn and hurt themselves and to heap more guilt upon themselves.

But believers should read the Bible as God's personal letter to each of them to bless, help, and encourage them. There is help for those of us who want help.

We as believers should settle upon the integrity of God's Word. What boldness we can have to approach God when we know the Word!

The Bible declares that fact: "This is the *boldness* that we have in Him, that if we ask anything according to His will, He hears us" (1 John 5:14).

What is the result of this boldness? Verse 15 says, *"And if we know that he hear us, whatsoever we ask, we KNOW that we have the petitions that we desired of him."*

Sometimes it takes a little while for many of us to shake ourselves loose from traditional thinking and to really settle upon the Word in our hearts, and begin to appropriate all the blessings and benefits that really belong to us in Christ. Some of those benefits are peace, joy, safety, and deliverance. We have a Savior who will not only carry our anxieties and burdens, He will work things out for us!

But many Christians are so bound up with religious thoughts and what they have been taught in the past that they fail to appropriate all that really belongs to them in Christ. Many times, they have been taught what someone *thought* the Scripture says, not what the Scripture actually says. Therefore, what they were taught didn't produce any fruit.

God wants us to pray effectively and to bear much fruit in prayer. This is the will of God for us as Christians.

JOHN 15:8,16
8   Herein is my Father glorified, that ye BEAR MUCH FRUIT; so shall ye be my disciples. . . .

16   Ye have not chosen me, but I have chosen you, and ordained you, that ye should go and bring forth fruit, and that your fruit should remain: that whatsoever ye shall ask of the Father in my name, he may give it you.

As we said, it is God's will to save the lost. Praying effectively for the lost to be saved is certainly scriptural and will produce prayer fruit.

Particularly, on this subject of praying for the lost, every believer has authority in his own household (Acts 16:15,31). You have more authority in your own household than you do anywhere else.

Believers, in praying for those in their own household, have struggled and struggled and have begged God to save their loved ones. Sometimes their loved ones got saved and sometimes they didn't. One reason folks fail to get their unsaved loved ones saved is that they pray for them in the dark, scripturally speaking.

When I first read First John 5:14 and 15, I took this portion of Scripture and I thought of it like this: "This is the confidence I have in Him, that if I ask any thing according to His will, He hears me. What I am asking is according to His will. Therefore, I know I have my petition."

It is that simple. *"And if we know that he hear us, whatsoever we ask, WE KNOW that we have the petitions that we desired of him"* (1 John 5:15).

When I read that scripture I said to myself, *Well, why should I keep on asking for the same thing over and over again? According to these scriptures I have that petition. It's mine now.*

Then I just stopped asking God and started thanking Him for the answer. I put my faith into action by thanking God. It is amazing how faith works.

Certainly, if you pray for salvation for your unsaved loved ones, that doesn't mean your entire family will come into the Kingdom of God overnight. But as you stand in faith, thanking God for the answer, they will come in.

You see, if you kept on asking and begging God for their salvation, that would be a confession that you don't believe you have the petition you desired of Him. If you believe you have your petition, you would be thanking God for your answer, wouldn't you? You would be thanking Him already for the answer because you believed He heard you. It's that simple.

Sometimes we go through the right motions of faith, all right. But without right believing, right speaking, and having the right corresponding actions, you can go through all the motions and nothing will be accomplished.

In other words, you can't go through all the motions of faith just because someone told you to do it. You must be responding to the Word. The Word has to be abiding in you personally in order for prayer to work (John 15:7).

For example, we could pray about something in agreement, and after we had prayed, I could say, "Now let's lift our hands and praise God for the answer."

Praising God signifies that we believe we have the petition we desired of God. We believe that what we have asked is according to God's will, and if we ask according to His will, then we know He hears us. Therefore, we believe we have our petition.

But you could also be lifting your hands and praising God just because I told you to do it. In other words, if your heart is not in it, it won't work because no faith is involved. And if you are not responding to the *Word*, it won't work either, because it is faith in the *Word* that bears fruit.

Faith is what moves God. Just the form or act itself of praising the Lord doesn't bring results by itself. But when your praises really come from your heart and are a result of your faith, then you'll receive the answers to your prayers. Then you are praising God because you believe God and you are acting on His Word. That is walking in the light of the Word, and that's when results to your prayers will come.

In this study course, we have discussed many insights from the Word of God regarding prayer. I have shared what I have learned about prayer from the Word and from my own experience. But it is up to you to appropriate the promises in the Bible for yourself, and to practice the principles of prayer in your own prayer life.

Remember, all prayer is not the same. Just as different rules govern different kinds of sports, there are different rules or principles which govern the various kinds of prayer.

As you put these principles of prayer into practice in your life, you will surely grow in your fellowship with the Heavenly Father. And as you learn to allow the Word to abide in you so that you can pray according to God's will, you *will* receive the answers to your prayers. Then Jesus' words in John 16:24 will be fulfilled in your life: Your joy will become full!

Questions for Study

1. What does the Bible say is the primary way God leads His children?

   _____

   _____

2. Many times we try to find the will of God by the circumstances we _see_ without taking anything else into consideration. What two things should we consider _before_ we consider the circumstances?

   _____

   _____

3. There are some who, before they can receive their healing, will have to get back into the will of God. So why don't you have to pray, "If it be Thy will" for those people to receive healing?

   _____

   _____

4. What can a person do to have his prayer in the right focus?

   _____

   _____

5. What is a successful prayer life built and based upon?

   _____

   _____

6. When a failure to know the Word and to see what God's Word has to say about a subject causes us to pray in darkness and we don't know where we are going, what does prayer become?

   _____

   _____

7. Complete the following sentence: Believers should read the Bible as God's _____ _____ to each of them to bless, help, and encourage them.

8. Why don't the things many Christians were taught produce any fruit in their lives?

   _____

   _____

9. If you believe you have your petition, what should you be doing?

   _____

   _____

10. Without right believing, right speaking, and having the right corresponding actions, what will you accomplish by going through the motions of faith?

   _____

   _____

About the Author

The ministry of Kenneth E. Hagin has spanned more than 60 years since God miraculously healed him of a deformed heart and incurable blood disease at the age of 17. Today the scope of Kenneth Hagin Ministries is worldwide. The ministry's radio program, "Faith Seminar of the Air," is heard coast to coast in the U.S., and reaches more than 100 nations. Other outreaches include: *The Word of Faith*, a free monthly magazine; crusades, conducted nationwide; RHEMA Correspondence Bible School; RHEMA Bible Training Center; RHEMA Alumni Association and RHEMA Ministerial Association International; and a prison outreach.

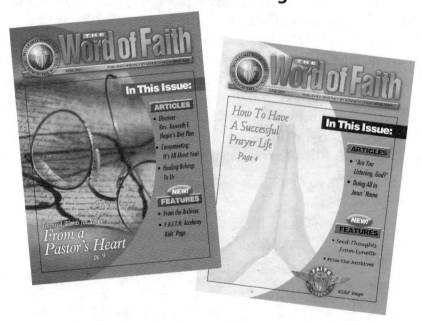

RHEMA

Correspondence Bible School

• Flexible •

Enroll anytime: choose your topic of study;
study at your own pace!

• Affordable •

Pay as you go — only $25 per lesson!
(Price subject to change without notice.)

• Profitable •

**"Words cannot adequately describe the tremendous impact RCBS has
had on my life. I have learned so much, and I am always sharing my
newfound knowledge with everyone I can. I feel like a blind person
who has just had his eyes opened!"**

Louisiana

**"RCBS has been a stepping-stone in my growing faith to serve God
with the authority that He has given the Church over all the power of
the enemy!"**

New York

The RHEMA Correspondence Bible School is a home Bible study
course that can help you in your everyday life!

This course of study has been designed with the layman in mind, with
practical teaching on prayer, faith, healing, Spirit-led living, and
much more to help you live a victorious Christian life!

For enrollment information and course listing call today!
1-888-28-FAITH — Offer #862
(1-888-283-2484)

www.rhema.org